Catwoods

*Stories and Studies of Our
Feline Companions*

Volume 1

Leah T. Alford

Portions of this work have appeared on my website, Catwoods Porch Party, and on the website Itchmo Forums for Cats and Dogs, both under the screen name "catwoods."

A portion of the proceeds of this book will go to our resident cats and to feed ferals.

This book is best read in the company of a cat or cats.

Borgo Publishing Edition

Front cover: Design by Leah Alford, formatted by William Alford.
Cover photos: "Glorious Minx" by William Alford
Background by Leah Alford
Back cover photo: "Leah and Orange Cat" by Hope Hamilton
Spine: "Bud the Editing Cat" by Leah Alford

ISBN 978-1-7339165-2-3

Internet sources change rapidly. While writing over time a few sources vanished so I tracked new urls or alternate sources. A few of those may gone by the time the book is published.

Printed in the United States of America

To my beloved husband, William Edward Alford,
companion of my heart

and

to my beloved mother, Hope Haynes Hamilton,
August 7, 1924–October 6, 2011

and

to the memory of William Douglas Newby,
a longtime friend of the household.
He worked for social justice and freedom.
He worked for peace.
He loved his partner-in-life, his cats, and his dogs.
He never forgot his old friends; he came back to talk to us;
He always talked to our cats, too.
January 31, 1949–December 16, 2008

Acknowledgements

A special "thank you" goes out to all friends, those living in my long-time Alabama community, those who lived here and moved elsewhere, and those who always lived elsewhere. Their friendship, encouragement, and support not only sustains me, but has helped me to actually think I can write this book.

I also thank all marvelous online friends, local, nationwide, and global, for their support and camaraderie.

Thanks to my late Mom who, who always said "You do that so nicely," when she saw me typing the book.

Thanks to husband William Alford for all encouragement and support.

I must also thank my feline Muse for all ages, the late Minx, and the feline editors: the late Minou; the late Bud the Editing Cat; and my late editor of the past year, Ultraviolet.

Major thanks go to my editor, Sandra K. Barnidge, who helped to untangle, refine, and organize this narration. She has really made it flow!

Major thanks go to Easty Lambert-Brown of Borgo Publishing for her expert, long term guidance and assistance in the publishing process.

Contents

Prelude

Sitting by the highway, taking shape out of the forest, trotting along the city streets, they appear. We find them, and they find us. Black, orange, brown-striped, patched black-and-orange, white, spotted and all combinations of the above: the felines come meowing, bounding to the door and pressing against the glass, leaping across our paths and into our lives. Or, on the edge of the road or the clearing, they wait serenely until we take notice. They've been abandoned, walked away from, shoved out of cars into the woods, turned out of doors, ignored on city streets and left to reproduce profusely, with kittens they scrounge to feed, and they don't know the why for any of it.

They expect help from us; they come with searching looks, voicing their concerns. They're mewing and purring like doves, or screeching like banshees. Out of the scenery they lock gazes with us; in traditional wordless feline dialect, the stories begin. Their personalities are wide-ranging and complex. They're sunny and affectionate and moody and complicated; old-school mannerly and scent-pile brash; they're pranksters and prima donnas. A few are as territorial as wildcats, strong meowing types who walk alone. And some of these 'lone tiger' individuals will have to live together! We adopt many; for the others, we find good homes.

That's been our decades-long feline-centric life. By November 2004, when I began this book, I had lost some of my cats to the ailments of old age. I've been ill for many years and we have found no way out of the blasted disease affecting me, which sometimes blanks out part of my memory while intact islands of sharp recall stay accurate. I figured it was high time I started writing down the stories of my cats. I thought they should be celebrated, not simply forgotten. All were such quirky characters; I knew they would pop off the page.

Starting a cat book is daunting when you glance at a room full of sleepy muzzles tilted skyward and figure, *it's just me and these cats lounging around*. But when using precision watchfulness and rapt attention, the actions and musings come direct from an onsite living laboratory of natural history. I hope I've woven something engrossing and astonishing out of ordinary moments. I hope I've captured the ways cats enlighten us with their presence, as well as some facets of the "why" of living with pets, in all its glory. I hope readers who don't already have pets will want the joy of adopting and cherishing animals when they put the book down — a big hope maybe, but hope all the same.

1

This book is primarily about communication between animals and humans. My husband and I are 1960s-vintage, offbeat Southerners. At our home in the deep woods of Alabama, domestic cat rescue is now a major part of our lives. We must learn to translate the constant, wordless cat-to-human dialogues and diatribes of feline individualists who open with *meow*, and then take center porch to get their druthers across to us. When we settled into our forest home, every cat living out in the leaves turned up at the door, locked gazes with us, and then darted right inside. Each cat who comes to claim us schools us in feline language; each has a story to disclose. I revel in the feline repertoire of expressions, posturings, and vocalizations used to make contact with their fellow cats — and to maintain their loving bonds with us. Strict behavioral interpretation will translate these actions; a dash of light anthropomorphism and some southern conversational idioms and ways of speaking will help to get the stories told and the meanings across. Always with an eye on the science, I compare my local impressions of cat intelligence and behavior to those of premier feline experts. This book is equal parts story and study. It's also a celebration of humans and animals together. Here, biographies of humans and cats intertwine and examinations of natural history, zoology, poetry, and music illuminate the stories. All paths lead eventually towards a deeper sense of harmony and belonging.

(I have quirky notions about language and will employ language structures that are regional, variant, colloquial, slang, and/or irregular.)

I may post vintage photos of the cats whose stories are told in this book on my website at catwoodsporchparty.wordpress.com.

"For in his morning orisons he loves the sun and the sun loves him."

—Christopher Smart, "On Jeoffrey, My Cat,"
from *Jubilate Agno* 1756–1763.

Chapter 1

The Naming of The Minx

Glittering iridescence broke the profound gloom and drew my eyes to the subterranean nacreous rocks and minerals. The underground air felt moist and cool. On July 3, 1988, we were walking through the Crystal Palace in the Raccoon Mountain Caverns, the last stop of our vacation. I went wide-eyed with visual excitement but was glad when we emerged from the caves, squinting at the sunlight and the reassuring Tennessee surface. I was tired, fretful, and really antsy for the drive home in our little peach-toned Ford Fairmont. The sizzling summer day was partly sunny, the cerulean blue sky streaked with an expansive, wavering skein of cobweb cloudiness blunting the July glare. A few country roads away from the caverns, we neared the Interstate. Anticipating the long stretch of road ahead, I set my tourist's scrutiny on low. I leaned back in my seat, slid down, and half-gazed at the asphalt edge and the weed fuzz alongside the road as we picked up speed on the access ramp. At the periphery of my vision, a dark oil slick ahead seemed familiar, going in my lax attention from smudge to sharp silhouette and then fuzz again against the blanched shimmer of pavement as we reached and passed it.

"Was that a cat?!" I burst out, sitting upright, turning to look. Bill was already slowing the car. Yes, he thought it was.

Far past the spot, we stopped and Bill got out and walked back. He returned carrying a four-week-old kitten. "I called 'Kitty, kitty,' and it came right up to me," he said. The little cat squirmed and writhed and pranced and purred, ecstatic, doing a jubilant dance in his hands for fifteen minutes before it finally sat still and he was able to hand it to me. I placed a road map in my lap and set the kitten on it. "Sweetums, you've been found by the right people," I reassured the kitten as I petted and scratched around the little furry ears. We scanned the area beside the road, just a brushy field and some woods beyond. Nothing stirred; there were no signs of any other kittens or cats. It was as though this lone animal had been waiting for us. To this day, the image of the small dark cat in sitting position, facing the road and watching, remains etched within my recollection of that first instant's blurry glimpse. We took the next exit off the highway and went back down a side road to ask at the only house near the area where we'd found the cat. No one, they responded, had lost a kitty.

The kitten was female and black, with the most beguiling little cat face I'd ever seen. On her throat was a short, curved white streak. I slowly extended my fingers towards her muzzle, one of the first things I do with any feline stranger. Her little nose worked as she sniffed her new friend's immensity of un-cat scent. She angled her head up and with a barely discernable, infinitesimal upward eyeball rotation, her gray-blue kitten eyes met mine. Those eyes sparkled with a wry and knowing look. She knew we were non-feline, but she didn't mind. We drove on to a fast-food restaurant. I waited in the car with the animal while Bill went in and bought a plain hamburger. He asked if anyone knew who had lost the kitten. No one did. Did anyone want the kitten? He added. Nowadays we would ask all kinds of questions when selecting owners for our giveaway animals, but in those very different times we went by an instinct for detecting hearts of gold. One of the employees did want it, but she was hours away from the end of her shift. She asked the manager if she could keep the animal on the premises until she got off work, and he said no. As Bill relayed all this to me, the ravenous kitten gobbled down chunk after chunk of the hamburger as I hand-fed them to her, poor hungry little thing that she was. Bill drove us back to the highway, and she fell asleep on my lap, tilting her head back, nose skyward, showing off her white-tufted throat, looking smug and content. With all four feet stretched out, her posture was one of total trust and affection towards us. We had joined her travels and now would keep her from all danger. Her coat was burr-encrusted so I carefully pulled the stickers out and rubbed her little head between the large ears. I took her photo as we zipped along the road, sliding down through the mountains, through the corner of Georgia into Alabama where the lower lands, hilly and slanting, were still the Appalachian edges with a roll to the terrain, just not so sharply high. I snapped photos out the closed car window, carefully moving my arms so as not to disturb the snoozing little feline.

My fretful mood had been replaced by serenity — and curiosity. The brambles sticking in her fur, along with her scruffy, dull coat, indicated she must have ranged around in the brush for some time before she approached the highway ramp that day. Many events and twists had put us at that very spot, at that very time.

From the urban jungle to a wilderness of my own

I have lived in the Deep South since my college days, having met and married a native. At the time, Bill and I had two cats: the half-Siamese with a dark slate gray color on his mask, ears, feet and tail we called Cat and the big fluffy guy of frosted orange over a white undercoat we called Orange Cat.

Both were toms, and both had become round, purring creatures difficult to pry off laps. These two seemed enough for our somewhat small dwelling, and we weren't really looking for another kitty.

We obviously hadn't put a lot of thought into our cats' names. Maybe it was due to our very demanding mom-and-pop T-shirt printing business. We had started it about sixteen years earlier, and the phone sometimes rang not only all day but all evening and, at times, all hours of the night. That was the downside of modern cottage industry: The deadlines were always tight, and the work days were always long. We didn't have a lot of energy left at the end of the day, and as Mr. T.S. Eliot so correctly noted in "The Naming of Cats," matching names with cats takes effort.[1]

Work had also kept us from taking vacations, and by the late 1980s I hadn't been out of the South in many years, although I come from the D.C. area and my relatives all lived in Virginia on northward. A fear of flying hadn't helped, either. I do not like being off the ground, where my feet belong. I have flown when I've had to, but separating myself from the earth's surface seems fundamentally wrong, and I don't like being in anything I can't just hop out of, if need be.

But to get to a family reunion in New England I had to fly; our work schedule that week didn't allow me the time I'd need to go by bus or train, and Bill couldn't get off work until the week after the event. We both had a lot of apprehension about me flying. Me, actually taking a plane!

The family reunion was for a part of my family that I'd never really known, so I had all kinds of other jitters, too. I'm progressive-minded, I have demonstrated for peace and social justice, and I have an inclusive view towards all humanity; I'm one of many like-minded people living in the South. But would the people "Up North" expect otherwise? Would they immediately apply narrow stereotypes? We were offbeat counter-culture persons and Southerners. Some of our word-ways and accents were distinct to our region. Friends who traveled out of the South had at times experienced the frustration of feeling pigeonholed as less cosmopolitan and literate. I found those attitudes tedious and antiquated, though I knew they were also widespread. I'd been hanging out in the back leaves of Appalachian Paradise, and although it was exciting to go explore unknown civilizations, it felt unfamiliar, too.

I decided to carry grits with me. The moment I tucked the box into my suitcase, I felt more confident.

A highway rescue and a terrible fire: Spirit Bird's dramatic adoption

In summer 1988, I stroked the dark fur of a friend's litter of black kittens shortly before the trip to the reunion Up North. I wanted to keep one, but we just weren't looking to adopt. The night before I left, Bill had a dream. He saw the plane I was on against the sky; a blackbird appeared nearby. There was a spot on its throat that glowed, emitting a light. The bird flew alongside the plane until it made a safe landing. The blackbird then turned into a black cat that came to live with us. This was a most agreeable dream, the kind you wanted to believe in even though you didn't, really. I kept it in my thoughts as I weathered the plane ride alone, and a hawk, not a blackbird, flew alongside like an escort as we landed.

Reunion activities began and thoughts of Bill's dream took a backseat. My fears had mostly been of no substance, and I had a wonderful time! A week later, leaving Cat and Orange Cat in the care of a neighbor, Bill drove up to meet me in Virginia, where we saw more of my relatives. Then we went on to D.C. to wander, bedazzled and spellbound, through the Smithsonian and the National Gallery. On July 2 it was time to leave, to cross over the blue mountains and drive back down the western side towards Alabama.

I hadn't counted on the July Fourth traffic starting already, but around Knoxville, near the Dollywood and Gatlinburg vacation spots, the highway was jammed. We drove and drove, alongside other overtired drivers, before we could find a motel room. It was midnight or 1:00 a.m. when we stopped. So we slept later than we would have on the morning of July 3. We made it to Chattanooga and spun around Lookout Mountain, the immensity of rising earth on one side and the Tennessee River on the other; and then Bill wanted to go to Raccoon Mountain Caverns.

I know I must have groaned and grumbled inwardly. I was ready to be home. And I wasn't too crazy about placing myself under the earth's surface, either, but after all, I was a tourist that week. Having recently survived being way too far up, maybe I could also survive being way too far down. So we both went into the caverns, which, along with all the events that tweaked our travel time that day, put us on the highway access ramp at the exact instant the kitten was hovering there.

That, along with my yearning for black kittens and Bill's dream, might cause some folks to say these were definite episodes of precognition. Our found kitten even had the white throat patch, or "locket" in the official lingo of cat enthusiasts, like the blackbird who had helped guide the plane in Bill's dream. But I'm not one of those folks. I can't affirm or deny the existence of wishes mysteriously fulfilled and dreams of portent. I'm only reporting the facts. Readers are welcome to make happy sense out of it, and to view this meeting as "fate," while I, a bit of a skeptic, reserve comment or commitment. I am a solidly practical person, albeit one who keeps running into events that carry traces of the fantastic.

For her part, the kitten seemed to know exactly where to sit to be noticed and hitch a ride with us: on the very edge of the ramp, where she would not be run over under normal driving circumstances. How long had she waited for someone with the sharp eyes to notice her, along with the inclination to stop for her? She was friendly and no doubt used to people, and she may have understood first, that humans had given her food and pats in the past, and second, that cars, although moving at speeds which must have amazed her, contained humans. Therefore, she would have concluded, she would wait by the cars. At least some of the time, as the tell-tale briars in her fur indicated she'd roamed around in the roadside thicket of tall grasses. Either she had made her way to the highway from a point across the field where she had been lost or deserted, or she was abandoned beside the highway. She had ventured into the field and found it devoid of help and humans, and had returned to the highway.

All this may seem like a lot of abstract thinking for a kitten, but fifty years of association with cats has convinced me that they have astonishing "smarts." Cat literature, indeed, often describes their ability to observe things carefully and to make use of the information. Then there are those who believe that cats are borderline psychic, as when the one scheduled to go to the vet knows to hide, and that this explains our kitten's presence beside our path. I can't settle these questions, of course. But I favor the view that cats work with the precision observation they employ in survival tasks, like hunting, and shape that skill to serve other scenarios.

Beyond cat cognition questions, there's always the mystery with a found animal, of how did it become a stray? Had she wandered away from an out-of-sight house somewhere? Or had someone actually put this sweet, friendly thing out on the road? The access ramp was a perfect spot for the clueless to slow down and shove an animal out of a car. Or could she have crawled under a car hood at her home, and then jumped out after the car was taken on the road? This does happen and would remove the suspicion of heartlessness by an unknown perpetrator.

One thing I can say for certain is most stray animals have no such chances to be rescued as our kitten did, either by plain accident or fate or spooky sense. No one should put animals out on the road or in the woods thinking someone will take them in, because it usually doesn't happen. Cats used to being cared for in a home often don't do well on their own, even with the skills they've retained from the wild. Not only are they vulnerable to the haz-

ards of starvation, cars, disease, and larger predators, they're domesticated
animals (up to a point) and in my opinion they do need people. I share the
view that feral cat colonies can be trapped, neutered, and returned (TNRed)
and left in place because they are as capable of survival as other wild animals, having changed little from their wild ancestors. However, I feel it's still
hazardous for the cats to be in this situation without a caregiver and a neighborhood that agrees to their presence. Cats that "go feral" may be seen by
various communities as undesirable. They may be rounded up and taken to
shelters. If they have become unfriendly towards humans, chances are shelters will not give them an opportunity to be adopted, and they will be euthanized immediately. So no one should release a cat to the wild thinking
they can always survive out there.

When we left the Chattanooga area with the sleepy kitten, we had about
three hours left to reach our house. The road stretched ahead, looking like a
tunnel through green gauze between the cities. As we drove on, closer to
home, there was a cloudburst thunderstorm with frequent lightning going
pop-pop-pop, one of the fiercest lightning storms we had ever driven
through. After the rain stopped, we came upon a young woman with a bro-
ken-down car on the side of the highway and gave her a ride to call for help.
We offered her the kitten; she said she would think about it.

We finally turned off onto a dirt road, just outside of the medium sized
college town of Tuscaloosa, Alabama. Here the terrain had some ups and
downs — the Appalachians' last gasp before the land flattened out on its way
down to the Gulf of Mexico. We drove down a hill, through profusions of
summertime emerald standing roadside like an immense rooted salad, droop-
ing and sopping from the rain. On sunny days it would have been seasoned
with noisy, buzzing bits. The kitten was still somnolent on my lap, having
slept all that way from Tennessee, as we passed the old hunting lodge on the
land next to our seventeen acres. This building was unlike any other. Built
completely of pine from the surrounding woods, with a fireplace and patio
built of stones from a nearby creek, the creatively rustic furnishings inside
included a huge table supported by the trunk of the tree it was carved from,
in natural form. The Lodge was used for guests and parties by the neighbor
family, whose relatives had owned a big tract of the adjacent land. We had
purchased our small portion from that large estate and placed our home in the
woods that surrounded the Lodge. Another dirt road off this dirt road led to
our modest dwelling, which had been slid into the forest with a minimum of
tree removal. By about 6 p.m. that evening, we were home.

We smuggled the kitten in past Gray Cat and Orange Cat, to the back
where the bedroom was located. I fed her again and got her a water bowl,

stroked her awhile, and took a better look. This kitten had a really expressive little face: sweet and earnest, with a slyness about it. There was a bare spot right below her lower lip, which somehow set off the moods that flickered on her fuzzy dark muzzle like a spotlight. I had a lot to do so I went about getting unpacked. With the kitten asleep again in the back, we settled in the living room to rest after the trip, giving the two toms a lot of pats to try to make up for being gone and then bringing back a kitten, adding insult to the injury of having dared to leave them with pet-sitters for a week. We felt smug and satisfied; we'd actually had a rare vacation. We were saturated with Virginia farm country, Northwest Native American masks, the French painter Rousseau, Jackson Pollock — so many experiences — and we just wanted to sit, occasionally puttering around the house a little.

There is in our life a strange convergence of momentous and exigent events. The result is the stuff of clichés; "everything happens at once," "when it rains it pours," "the doo-doo hits the fan," "everything goes haywire," as my Mom used to say. These are phrases that were no doubt created and uttered repeatedly for and about us. We're always going crazy dealing with five urgent things at any given time.

About 9 p.m., we heard fireworks being popped somewhere. "They're starting early for Fourth of July," Bill said. When he stepped out into the yard for a moment, I expected him to come back in shortly; instead I heard him slamming the car door and tearing off down the driveway, fast. Fifteen minutes later he rushed back in and shouted, "The Lodge is on fire!" As soon as he'd gone outside he'd seen the flames from our yard, shooting above the trees.

The popping sound we mistook for fireworks had come from kitchen items like canned goods bursting in the heat. I needed to be ready to leave if we had to, if the woods caught fire. The old hunting lodge was only about 200 yards from us as the crow flies. Bill called the fire department and then the neighbors and headed back to the fire. I got the cat carriers and placed Orange Cat and Gray Cat together in one and the kitten in the other. If the woods were to ignite, we'd have to pile all cats in the car and floor it past the burning building to get to the highway. There was only the one way to drive out.

I walked down the road to the scene of the fire. It was a sight to see. The flames went up 200 feet into the black night sky. Sparks were spraying, bursting, all through the treetops, raining fire to the ground. You couldn't get within fifty feet of the structure because of the intense heat. Two cars that had been parked beside it would later be found partially melted. There was a cabin not far from the Lodge, but the occupants weren't home. Bill and the other neighbors were using their garden hoses to wet down their propane tank and their roof, since the sky was raining drops of glaring orange flames all around.

I watched for a moment and then a cat walked up to me, a small gray six-month-old kitten belonging to the neighbors living in the cabin. I thought about the fire trucks about to come barreling in and looked at the flames waving amongst the tall trees. To keep him safe I picked up the kitten and took him to my house, letting him walk around in the front room where my cats sat in the carriers. This was the second strange kitten I had brought in that night, but my catboys were surprisingly unruffled. It was as if they knew there was something far more important going on than this dual affront to their territorial dignity. I heard the sirens moving off the highway and towards us on neighborhood roads. I waited, ready to shove the gray kitten into the carriers with the others and drive everyone on out.

For all woods dwellers, forest fire is a permanent strand of dread in the mind. Bill came back after awhile to get the camera and to call some of the many people who had partied at the Lodge over the years. Then we both walked back down the road to the scene. We saw that the flames were not as tall as before, and there was no longer a storm of sparks in the trees. The fire personnel were just letting the structure burn; it had been far beyond saving when they arrived.

Word had spread. People were coming to watch, and several would keep a vigil all night long as the house burned to the ground. When the flames went down still further and all sparks stopped flying, Bill felt that there was no more danger of forest fire, so I went back to our house to reconfigure the four cats. I returned the gray kitten to his home grounds near the now glowering fire; it was again safe for him. I went home for the night while Bill stayed awhile longer to watch.

When we turned in, our two toms got the run of the front rooms while the black kitten went into the back bedroom with us. I awoke the next morning and felt something touching my head. Out of my peripheral vision I saw her little furry face resting against me, with one of her small little forepaws raised, curving upright along my head, and gripping my hair as if to reach up and encompass the entirety of her new friend. Leaning against my hair may have reminded her of her momcat's fur. Kitten-in-my-hair suited me just fine. She must have been thinking, *I like her! She's enormous, five times the size of my first mom and I don't even think she's a cat, but she feeds me and she snuggles right up, and she's big enough to scare away predators. I'm keeping her.* In this way, cat and un-cat fuse purpose, over and over again.

I know I walked down to see all that remained of the Lodge, mainly the stone patio and fireplace. But I have absolutely no recollection of what, if anything, we did to celebrate the Fourth of July that year.

Bill always suspected that lightning was the cause of the fire. The fierce thunderstorm had occurred about 45 minutes before we had arrived back in the woods. If a lightning strike was indeed the cause, the fire had already begun and was smoldering as we drove past on the way in. There will be those who can't resist pointing out, half-jesting, that as soon as we brought a black cat into the neighborhood, bad luck happened: the Lodge fire. Close attention to the facts reveals that first, the forest was frequented by black cats anyway: wandering toms, some from homes and some from a colony of strays just down the road, along with other strays that were abandoned by irresponsible persons because it was a wooded area. In reality, there were natural circumstances, combined with a little good luck, in the unfolding of these events. The Lodge had been built in the 1930s of logs, cedar, and highly flammable heart pine. Some parts deep within pinewood are so resinous they are used to help start fires in woodstoves and fireplaces; it's known as "fat lighter" or "fat litard" in south Alabama. The ferocious electrical storms we have in this region look from the heights on wooden buildings and see only tinderboxes ready to ignite.

Heavy rain had drenched the woods before the fire; had that not happened, the blaze would have spread to the forest and taken out our house and every other dwelling on our road, and maybe 100 acres of the surrounding woodlands. Because the visitors staying at the Lodge had been gone at the time of the fire, there was no human injury or loss of life. I can only hope that no critters, wild or domesticated, were inside the structure during the fire. The timing of our return from vacation meant that Bill was there to discover the blaze and protect the cabin next door to it; otherwise, the flames may have spread. Since no one was living in the Lodge at the time, no one lost an actual home. Seen in this way, at least four aspects of the timing of the fire were fortunate, and in this light, the coming of the black kitten becomes good luck, if luck is actually involved in any way.

Going further back into the day's sequencing, the kitten was likely good luck for the young woman we helped on the highway, as time taken in tending to the kitty may well have placed us at the right place at the right time to assist her, too. In England, according to sources I've read, black cats are considered good luck. This is seemingly contradicted, though, in a number of posts on the Internet by British cat advocates who say their shelters are full of black cats that no one wants due to myths about bad luck — just typing that makes me so sad!

However, black cats are considered good fortune in several other parts of the world. Cats were believed to be good luck for ships, and the luckiest color for a ship's cat was black.[2] If a ship lost its cat, sailors regarded that as a very bad sign. In Scotland, a black cat on the porch is a sign of wealth and good fortune. I've heard that in places in the Appalachians and the Ozarks, black cats are considered good luck, capable of frightening "evil spirits." I'll take the advantage to black cats, but with mixed feelings since it's still based in superstition.

I've come to mostly believe that luck beliefs should not be mentioned with regard to animals because they are completely unscientific and irrational. But I've also slowly realized how deeply ingrained in the human psyche these notions are, whether from being taught in childhood by cherished family or because it's just human nature to want some kind of control over life events and fortune. So I cite the beliefs about black cats and good luck in case that may help cats of any color in the estimations of those who do have these beliefs regarding luck. It may at least show that such beliefs are culturally relative and therefore should cause a questioning of the negative stereotypes, too.

Building a bond with our new black cat

The urgent frenzy of the fire and then the sad loss of the Lodge kept us stunned for awhile. It contained our friends' historic photos, family artifacts, and paintings — a significant loss to our neighbors and the community as well. Built with a huge ballroom, it had served as a party house going back to our college days and beyond, into the past before we arrived. Our entire network of friends and acquaintances had gathered there at one time or another. There had been weddings and pig roasts attracting hundreds. The pig roasts were huge affairs; 500 kegs of beer might be consumed, two pigs, and, as I recall, large quantities of crawdads. Set in this wilderness, the Lodge had afforded our community an opportunity to experience the natural world as we socialized. I was especially saddened by the loss of one friend's beautiful paintings, including people in New Orleans, abstracts inspired by landscapes, and a self-portrait with a cat. The twisted metal soundboard of the old piano that had once stood on a balcony overlooking the ballroom was one of the few remaining artifacts. During the blaze it had fallen and come to rest on the stone mantelpiece below.

Normally a new cat was a momentous event, but the Lodge fire momentarily eclipsed the arrival of the found kitten in our household, who was staying. On July 4, 1988, we both knew we would not give away this sweet and exuberant animal. She was round-headed with somewhat shorter legs than the other cats we'd had and with a plump belly that would persist into adult-hood. She had an exquisite face of tapering slopes, her cheekbones arcing fluidly down from her eyes to her whisker-pads curving roundly above her upper lip. In our sunny front room, light glinted silver on her dark, expressive lower lip. Her ears were large and vigilant. Her coat would soon turn from scruffy soot to shimmering raven.

Black cats are the most beautiful, to me, and this one's mid-length fur was deep and plush with compound shades of night. Her whiskers and paws were black. Besides the white on her throat she had a few feathery tufts of white between her front legs and a larger patch on her back underbelly. Her eyes, kitten-gray when we found her, would later become a luminous gold. After many years, I had a black cat again. I don't recall who was the first to mention Bill's dream. Even though neither one of us was willing to say it was precognitive, the dream made enough of an impression on Bill for him to name the kitten Spirit Bird, reiterating that the white spot on her throat matched the glowing light on the throat of the dream bird. Crows and black-birds out in nature in our neck of the woods, by the way, do not have white spotting on their necks.

Really? I responded inwardly. I was now ready to put more thought into her name and to me, a cat's name should be no longer than two syllables, succinct, and with a twist. I can't say exactly why Spirit Bird bothered me; a bit too conceptual, New Agey, and direct, maybe. But it was about Bill's re-markable special dream, so I let it stand. At the vet's office we shortened it to Bird to avoid a certain kind of raised eyebrow — we enjoyed the amusement on the receptionist's face, the exact response we'd hoped for. Our others be-ing named variations of the "cat" concept, we'd jumped to another species this time.

On July 5, she went to the vet for a health check-up. As he pulled a plant briar that I had missed from the black fur, he said, "It's not very old. It will live a long time, if nothing happens to it." That last part may sound odd now, but it was probably cautionary; those were still the days of indoor/outdoor cats, when so many were hit by cars or met other disasters outside.

Introduced into the front of the house (the living and kitchen area) the Bird kitten found a soft spot on the couch and stretched herself long on her back with her face, stomach, and paws up, confidently. She was at home and knew it. She began to tidy up the litterbox after the sloppy tomcats; she was either very fastidious or she was trying to cover their odors so she could at-tain more dominance. At the time, I didn't know that cats in the wild hide their feces near where they eat and den to conceal their presence from preda-tors, rather than to be "neat." Conversely, at the perimeters and out-skirts of their territories, they may leave scats uncovered to announce their ownership. The toms may have been raising a mild objection to the newcomer by leaving their droppings uncovered. Regardless of the actual intent, the kitten's actions were certainly good feline housekeeping. She was saying, *"Noooo, y'all toms are smelling up the place, giving away our whereabouts."*

Once when the cat tray had been neglected awhile, she raised up on her hind legs and peered into the opening at the top of a nearby bag of new litter, as if to say, *"Can we get some of this fresh in the box here, please?"* When she ate, she'd purr by herself with no one close nearby. Cats who have been hungry strays often exhibit lifelong, overzealous delight at regular chow.

She began to single me out. When I was seated, she'd suddenly direct a lively and gleaming look at me and come running at me, all the while emitting a rapid trill in bumpy staccato. If she heard me laugh, she'd *meowl*, jump up excitedly and run across the room to me. She'd bound into my lap, gallop up my torso and chest, and pat my cheek or my lips with a soft kitten paw-pad. In this manner, via the route up to my face, she'd seek me out for sleeping and/or an intense round of purring.

She often wanted me to walk with her to the kitchen; I was frequently going that way. She'd dash ahead and look around at me to make sure I was coming. It was not that she needed me to get her the food, as we had food out all the time in those days for 24-hour nibbling; she just wanted to walk with me. I knew each cat's voice from the others'; hers was sonorous but with an undercurrent of skirling bagpipes, a pleasing sound to me, with my bit of Scottish ancestry. If I left a room, Bird would *me-yowl* at the door until I came back.

"This one is your cat, Leah," Bill said one day. And she was mine, or maybe I was hers, or both. We flat-out had an instant affinity for each other. In her presence I had a transcendent feeling of camaraderie and belonging. She had selected me for all manner of catly affections. She would later come running to me if I was crying at times of sorrow and share in all my times of contentment. At first I thought of her as a "strange character" because of the way she responded to my voice. Other cats hadn't been quite so demonstrative. There was something unfathomable about the attachment that was forming. In later years, Bill would say he had never seen a closer relationship between a person and an animal. It was a mysterious and sublime bond, an unpronounceable rapport. It was almost enough to make you believe in spooky destiny dreams.

She was fearless and adventurous. In play, she would hurl herself high up and airborne with small paws outstretched like a flying squirrel, gliding directly at, and I mean sailing right into, a topside landing on the respective noggins of our solid old toms. With imperceptible movements, the big cat heads with eyes amazed would twist out from under her, shaking her off indignantly. They would both tangle with her in mock battle, but Gray Cat would fuss if Orange Cat got too rigorous with the kitten. Often, neutered toms are even more likely than altered females to adopt and mentor kittens.

"Hey, that's my little kitten!" Bill spoke for both toms on occasion. Nonetheless, Gray, who had been on the warpath when she first came, was still seen to growl and spit at her when he was trying to sleep and she was relentlessly pouncing on him and slapping at him. I expect Cat was a serious student of the full enjoyment of pleasure — his own pleasure that is — and she had disturbed his concentration. She was always into everything and at times would not leave the boys alone. Orange Cat would hiss on occasion, too. Sometimes, between the heat and the kitten, the older Gray Boy would look sulky. That year, we were still allowing the cats out during the daylight hours, the kitten only with supervision since she was just the right size for a fox or raccoon meal. One day she dashed up a dogwood tree and then out onto a branch too thin to support her. She fell, but fortunately Bill was right underneath; he caught her.

As annoying as she was to our tomcats, they were mentors of sorts, and they would both allow her to cozy right up to them and sleep at times. She was intense and complicated, a sunny and passionate creature about her likes, sounding the loud whirring trill to greet or summon me, but ferocious with growls about her dislikes. Like many intense personalities, she had frequent dreams, some of them nightmares, shaking in her sleep and sometimes growling, eyes rolling. She was as sweet a cat as I'd ever known with the two humans of our house, but at the age of about two she began to be an absolute hellcat-monster-beast at the vet. No behavior at home had prepared us for these atrocious displays of temper. From then on, she required warnings to personnel upon each vet visit, at times a muzzle, and attendance by Bill or myself. When she became even older, she pitched rolling, screaming fits at the clinic that were a sight to behold, no doubt legendary among cat fits.

I used to say this cat "pitched a hissy," or pitched hissy fits. This mainly southern expression has become more mainstream over the years. I think of it as a particularly feline description, as the first thing that comes to my mind is the hissing display that cats make when they're angry or making a warning posture to someone or something. But in 2006, when I applied my admittedly questionable computer research skills to the problem, I came across a variety of opinions and some fireworks. Some experts agreed with my hissing cat thesis, or at least with the word *hiss* as a possible origin. *The Random House Maven's Word of the Day* also notes this was first recorded in a linguistics journal in the 1930s.[3] But the majority of opinions think the word derives from *hysterical.* That opened up a can of worms because hysterical is derived from the Greek word for uterus, *hustera,* and therefore "hissy fit" becomes a sexist term. Many who have lived in the South argue that both men and women are described as pitching hissy fits. After forty-plus years of southern living, that's what I've observed too; regardless of derivation, any gender can pitch this light, somewhat childish fit.

By far the most colorful explanation for the word comes from a brief article by Lady Siobhan Breoghan of the Society for Creative Anachronism. In "Adventures in Etymology" she writes that hissy fit is based on an ancient and angry Finnish god named Hiisi, who possessed people and made them enraged for no reason.[4] That certainly makes sense, but I'd like to know, how did this expression come to the southern United States? Had it been located in areas of Europe at the time of European immigration to the American South?

Adding to the complexity of the picture is the inclusion of "hissy fit" in a list of expressions common to New Zealand. Cats, by the way, are not native to New Zealand. So there very well could be a very old origin that would be difficult to trace, from which the phrase was transferred by Europeans both to New Zealand and the southern United States. The original term may very well have been "hissing fit," of the cat. This might be considered the simplest answer, which is often the best solution, and I like it best, too. Usually it is done as a display by the cat, so it's indeed *hiss*-trionics. The Bird Cat certainly pitched a few, but come to think of it, what she did at the vet was most likely the more fearsomely angry "conniption fit." The hissy fit is a generally light sort of fit; like the hissing fit of the cat, it's the warning display, the precursor to the more serious fit action with the teeth and claws. Cat hisses are often compared to the hissing of a snake and inspire more fear in an adversary due to that similarity, thus serving as a protective mechanism.

Bird was the naughtiest kitten I'd ever seen. She ascended the tall bookcase like a cougar scaling a precipice, sending art objects, knickknacks, and colorful rocks and minerals down to the floor. She would go into the trash can and pull out anything of interest to her, so much so that we had to take steps to secure it. Paper towels had to be stored in really high places, as she would wrap her front paws around a roll and kick with her hind legs, shredding them rapidly and rather effectively. Many times she foiled our paper towel security when our backs were turned, grabbing a roll and starting to work as we swiveled at the unmistakable sounds — brisk, soft, and scuffling — of claws ripping paper into scraps, jumping to salvage what we could of the towels. We came home from work one day to find the living room floor a sea of whitecap confetti, wall to wall, almost an entire roll. In contrast, the kitten sat in the center, shimmering black, looking sly and pleased with herself. She'd pulled off the supreme paper towel caper! This was yet another of many photo ops since the Bird's arrival. The guy in the photo-developing shop ringing up that batch of pictures asked us, "Who made the mess in the house, you or the cat?"

She would not let us alone when we were eating. Given an opening, she would go for anything on your plate; quick plate-stepping paws through the juices got her furry kitten self right up in your face. "Do I bother *you* when *you're* eating?" I'd try to reason with her. One night, Bill set his dinner down on the floor while he adjusted the TV. Our blackBird, liking her chances, started to swoop in. "Get away from my food, you little vixen!" he responded.

Something popped in my head. "Vixen" was not it; the word has, rather recently, taken on sexy connotations; besides, we had a real vixen in the original fox sense coming regularly to the yard. The right word was *minx* — it had evolved to mean "naughty girl" in a playful, pert way, a cattish way. "She's such a minx," I said, and it felt comfortable. "And that's what I'm going to call her." It came naturally to both of us. It was the right name. Spirit Bird became The Minx, and although no longer a bird, she was still in the catbird's seat.

As near as I can recall my earliest encounter with the word *minx* was in Shakespeare. It may still have meant "prostitute" in his times; the dictionary lists that as the archaic meaning. But I took the modern, more appealing connotation of a bold female speaking her mind to be the name of my cat. And now seventeen years later, with the new tool of the computer, I attempted to look up more history of the word. The definitions often use the word "pert," but after that, *Webster's Thesaurus* lists a string of unpleasant synonyms. Origin is uncertain according to some, but I've come across information that is both pleasing and intriguing. There's a lot of the "wanton woman" discussion, but also a lot of references to a word of origin in Middle Dutch, *minnekyn*, meaning darling, from an obsolete word, *mynx*, that meant, of all things, a small, playful dog and was derived from another obsolete Dutch word, *minneken*, or darling, a diminutive of *minne*, love. According to *Encyclopedia Britannica minikin* meant beloved; *Merriam Webster* says it's an archaic word for "a very small delicate creature."[5] Other sources suggest the word comes from German.

I'm satisfied to have the imagery of small, beloved creatures attached to our cat's name, even if one of them might have been a dog. I hope for accuracy because although the Internet is becoming a mainstay of information for me, with its uniformity of typeface and flickering, evanescent quality, its statements still have a hazy and insubstantial feel to me, like the ads in neon signs of old film noir, difficult to trace and fully trust. At least, that used to be my impression during my early days of computer researching. I've had some squirrelly computers and a frequent feeling of being in a human versus machine argument, like the protagonist in *2001: A Space Odyssey* had with HAL.[6] My opinion on the Internet has since improved greatly, but that was the way I felt in the earlier days. I now view the computer as a sort of Ouija board; both work via a series of letters which yield answers when manipulated and applied. As a non-techie, I regard both information retrieval methods as equally puzzling.

Anyway, to me there's still nothing like holding a book in my hand, comfortably seated, cats and papers spread around me, cats sorting notes and papers with their paws, or cats slung across them in stretched repose, holding them down. Stacks of books on the couch beside me, stuffed with papers in strategic places, reading the brush of whiskers against my arm and commingling that sensation with the alertness and concentration of my mental engagement. The dry tickle of a tail across my face as a cat walks up onto me trying to reach the book and park on it. One hand's fingers are keeping places in the book, so with the other I nudge the cat tail out of my mouth and then scribble a note hurriedly so I can remove at least a pinky from the book before fifteen pounds of cat plops down upon it, fingers and all. Now *that's* research. There's no human endeavor that can't be improved by the company of a cat!

With our long-time friend Charlotte, both the names Spirit Bird and Minx met with some resistance. "Don't name her that," she sputtered, "It's way out. Name her a normal name like 'Spot' or 'Socks.'" Although these two names have graced many pets well, I needed something a bit more uncommon and exotic. We were, after all, trying to live down Cat and Orange Cat, names that were working beautifully so far as the cats were concerned, but also left us open for the occasional snide comment. I answered that I didn't want the same names that everyone else named their cats.

Many years later, Charlotte would name her tortoiseshell after the opera *Cosi Fan Tutti* because, she said, she didn't want her cat to have the same name as everyone else's!

The Minx as Muse: creativity in a cat-run household

As I handwrite this on Halloween 2004, Minx is on the bed, sixteen years old, purring, wearing a sheen on her blackness. She skirls to me, placing a paw on the rim of her dish (placed on the bed) to indicate she wants more of her carefully doled-out chow. Still a Minx.

As a kitten, The Minx was clever and resourceful about having fun in every nook and cranny, every cubic foot of space she could access. She was such a disruptive explorer, upsetting piles of art supplies in the bedroom, that I tried blocking her way by closing the door. Nevertheless, I kept finding her there. I kept airlifting her out, and one day I went back to the bedroom, sat, and waited. She soon emerged from the unfinished ductwork around the water pipes. She had entered it through the kitchen, on some kind of intuition or hunch that it led to her destination.

She discovered trails for slinking up on the stove or counter or sink so fast and unnoticed that discovery was delayed long enough for her to investigate new odors. She'd run pell-mell through the house and scramble up the rocky bluff of the bookcase, sit on the summit a moment, jump down, pounce the couch, and launch off the back of it, landing three or four feet away. She might then, with a vivid look my way, trill-chirp to me, come bounding over, land on my lap, run up my chest, flop down, start purring, and do the exuberant face tap with her paw, claws carefully sheathed so as not to stick me. As the naming incident portended, she was on her way to becoming a skilled plate raider.

She was a real adventurer, going everywhere and getting into everything. A roll of pliable screen for a household project that Bill left on the couch was, to Minx, a tunnel, and she was photographed emerging from it with a big grin on her face and a paw upraised in greeting. For awhile she carried a small ballpoint pen around, and even fetched it six times one day, but she eventually tired of that game and discontinued it. She chewed a cord in two that I used to hold my glasses on. But I really didn't mind.

She came bounding into the bathroom after me one day and while bouncing around, achieved a splashdown in the toilet bowl faster than my eye could follow. Fortunately, I was there to fish her out and clean her off instantly. We took heed of this valuable lesson in kitten safety and kept the lid down on the commode afterwards, until she grew much larger.

Old videos reveal her fearless and feisty self with a raccoon visible through the glass door. Orange Cat lolls around nonchalantly while Minx hisses and smacks at the raccoon, hitting the glass.

Often when I attempted to work at my desk, she would place herself in the middle of it, pert and aglow with the desire for all my attention and concentration, which as a cat, she believed rightfully belonged to her. She would place a paw against my hand as if to hold it still or leap onto the cover around the typewriter keyboard. She would even reach a paw into the old electronic typewriter, the one I called the snapdragon or the snapping turtle since it was about that size, as if she was trying to figure out the moving part that carried the typeface wheel across the page so she could stop it. Like as not I would melt and accept furry intrusion, scratching and scritching around the silky black ears, head, and neck. I'd then carefully airlift her to floor level and resume work — until she bounded back up to the desk.

When I sat down at the drawing table, Minx would sit in my lap. Cats are adept at noticing the focal points of your attention and placing themselves there, like when they smack your newspaper or come sit on your book that you are, or were, reading. I had to adjust my drawing motions to cause the least disturbance to the settled kitten. All the cats saw the importance of the drawing table, so it became a favored place for feline sleeping. They'd nudge aside the pesky jars of pencils and the bottles of ink and sashay into place, and not just singly. Minx, usually the first one up there, would be joined by Cat and Orange Cat, who were not about to be outdone in claiming their nap turf in this important area of focus. From their viewpoint, they made the space sizzle; they made it trendy, like bohemians converging upon a coffee shop or eatery. Par-tay!

Later when other cats came into our house, they would also join Minx at this popular hangout. A photo of three cats lounging on the drawing table exists. In those days, I called the camera the chimera partly because the sound and similarity of the words fit and partly because of the way it fused two entities, reality and light.

To actually begin using the table, I'd have to gently remove each cat. I coined a word for removing felines from an area: defelinate. The idea came from the word defenestrate, which I'd discovered one day while dictionary surfing, flipping through an actual large book, that is, before we gained Internet capability. Derived from French, *defenestrate* means to remove something from a room by throwing it out the window. But whereas defenestration is a rather violent, unapologetic act, defelination is a delicate motion, requiring careful sliding of hands under furry bodies and lavish gestures of diplomacy; cats do not like to be removed from the positions and spaces they have chosen for themselves. To defelinate with flair and finesse is an art. You have to not only remain unscathed, you need to see the cat you displace settled contentedly onto the new surface.

Of course, defelinating one area means you refelinate another space or spaces.

Although I've produced comparatively little art with felines as the actual subject, all of my art, with the exception of works left from childhood and college courses, was produced in the company of cats on the drawing table, on my lap, or across the room. Feline proximity might be both tight and loose. Sometimes, with a table filled edge to edge with felines, I just had to get a stiff cardboard to support my paper over my lap. So I'd reach up through the furry boulders of hunkered up snoozing cats and hope that I was allowed to grasp for a pencil or pen without suffering a swat. "May I have this, Your Grace?"

I occasionally sang around the house during the day, when I was alone. My mother had done it, and there are tales of my grandmother, who came from a musical family, singing so beautifully at parties that men were moved to tears. For my part, I have an immense love of music, but no singing ability. That matters to humans, but not to Minx. One day when we had taken Minx to the vet and were driving home, we stopped for Bill to run briefly into the grocery store. Minx and I waited in the car, and suddenly I just sang the old song, "Me and My Shadow."[7] Minx responded with excitement in the carrier, coiling trills and flexing paws, an intense look on her face.

I began singing to her often. She would *mrow* and come running from across the room, or stir and stretch and snug herself on my lap if she was already there. Sometimes she would reach up and press a paw on my face. She was especially fond of songs with the word "blue" in them, like "Me and My Shadow," "Am I Blue,"[8] and "Lady Sings the Blues."[9] We were all about the blues and jazz and Billie Holiday, especially "Mood Indigo"[10] and "Summertime."[11] Later I expanded my repertoire and added "My Funny Valentine,"[12] a few lines from a Cher song, along with "The Wild Mountain Thyme,"[13] adapted to invite 'kitty' for a walk near the heather — anything I could wrap my rather weak and uneven voice around for at least a passable, presentable rendition.

"Them There Eyes"[14] was a Minx favorite and described her glances perfectly. Through around-the-house singing, I discovered that cat was a musicologist! Usually alone, I freely indulged my foolishness of fine-tuning the words and titles: The Temptations' "My Girl"[15] became "My Cats" or "My Minx." As I fed them canned food I sang "I Get A Kick Out of You,"[16] tweaking the words as they paced around meowing fretfully their own catty song, "Want Food NOW" in response to what, to them, was my un-cat-like impossible slowness. The song's animated meter helped me get a rhythm going as I dished up the chow. I sang the last line as I set the dishes down, and the cats ceased listening.

If I felt especially ambitious, I'd try to belt out Aretha Franklin's "I Never Loved a Man the Way I Love You,"[17] and I'd no doubt mangle it, but since Minx hadn't heard the original, she didn't care. Another Minx favorite a few years down the road would start, "It Had to be You,"[18] and end up "It

Had to be Mew," invaded by catwords, a process that later became popular on the Internet and known as "kittification." You can now use online tools that will transform your entire text, resulting in *purrfects*, *furriends*, and many other cat puns in every sentence! (An interesting side note is that Aretha Franklin recorded "I Never Loved a Man the Way I Love You" in Muscle Shoals, Alabama, and subsequently used some of the same musicians from rural Alabama on some of her recordings.[19])

For the cats I chose to sing the haunting, the playful, the nostalgic, the soulful, the deep blues, the rural authentic, the rockin', the old crooner classics, the Celtic. The cats, they like a wide repertoire, near as I can tell. Despite a lack of dancing ability, I used to dance around the house, too. Again, the cats had no interest in or comment on my lack of finesse. They probably thought we humans were the clumsiest critters ever, anyway.

The two catboys had been freely roaming the back of the house before Minx came. They had not been much trouble there, although when Gray Cat galloped down the hall, his normally soft paws pounded like a herd of elephants. But Minx would explore, pulling things off shelves and out of closets, generally plundering and tearing up our "pea patch" in a cat-swift instant. Then, arising at daylight, she would wake us with frenzied pounces all over the landscape, including our faces, if that struck her fancy. So at the side of the kitchen where the hall led to the back, Bill put up a louvered folding door.

But this otherwise-pleasing solution had about two inches between the lower door edge and the floor. That was enough for Minx to learn quickly that she could hook a paw under the fold of the door and pull it convexly toward her, thus opening the door and gaining access. Others would then follow and it would be Cat City back there in no time.

She could also go through the closed door from hallway to kitchen if she raked her paw with claws extended against the louvers long enough to slowly edge the door open. Bill then crafted a metal cat-lock device to hold the door shut at the top, which we could just slide down when we wanted to open the door, walk through, and then slide the lock back up from the other side to secure it. This was for the most part very effective, and Minx raked her claws, meowing, across the door for awhile every night, trying to get to me in the back. The cat lock loosened up with use, and our naughty girl found that if she shook the door long enough with her scratching and pulling the lock would fall to open position, she'd pull the door at the center, and *voilà*, she was in. Usually, I would evict her and tighten the lock. Sometimes I tried to let her sleep alongside me, but early in the morning, she'd rattle the door until she either got my attention and I let her out, or the lock fell and she let herself out. So, sadly, with our demanding work routine, the best solution was to keep all cats out of the back at night — if we could. But if the door was breached, we'd soon be covered in cats.

Many years later, Minx continued to shake the door, and I recall one night when she made the lock drop, then came trotting in, voicing a bumpy *tremolo*, and jumped in bed beside me. I chose to let her stay. She purred all night! She did a rumbling, loud purr, reassuring me throughout the night. Of course with the dawn, she got up and rattled to be let back out front. Dawn is the hunting time for cats, who are crepuscular hunters. That's why they are wired to arise at times that are outrageous for humans.

Most of the time when I sat, Minx would come and sit on me. Before arising, I'd have to carefully extricate her, sometimes while she growled her objections. When I returned to my seat on the couch, she'd come up and claim my lap again. I often had a cup of tea in my hand, and Minx would be on me before I was settled. I had to learn to squirm carefully, holding the tea steady and not over the cat, to reach a position in which we were both comfortable. While she was a sweet cat to Bill too, responding to his pats and rubs as well as mine, she had clearly chosen me to seek out, to call for when I left the room, rub and twirl against, shadow, and snuggle with for hours on end. I'd never thought of it before, but in the past, if our cats had shown a strong preference for one of us, it had usually been for Bill. Indeed, Gray Cat showed a strong partiality for sitting on Bill, although Gray was a sweetheart of a cat to me, also. And Orange Cat was everyone's pal.

But Minx seemed to claim me for her own and to communicate with me on a deeper level than with the rest of the house and the world. She'd look up at me with eyes bemused and intense. I'd look back and it was like we connected and understood each other at heights no two beings had ever reached before. Having been drawn to animals since early childhood, I appreciated having their favorable opinions. In our household, cats are revered, so to be chosen and favored by one felt like an honor. She had the more flamboyant personality; mine is more low-key, but she still loved me. It's hard to describe, but my days and nights resonated with Minx and me, even when I was away from the house. I might be out and about in the world, but I was returning home to my Minx. Was it mixed up with destiny and fate as the dream might suggest? I don't know. All I know is that I was plain crazy-wild about her, and in her cat way, she was crazy-wild about me, too. It did not diminish my love for the other cats, but Minx had picked me to be close and cozy and uncanny with. She would suddenly see me across the room, and with a trilling, chirping *ruhruhruhruh*, come trotting up to love on me. There was no stopping her. The old southern phrase 'love on,' meaning gestures of friendly affection like hugs and words, also suits head bonks from cats.

When winter came, Minx was about six months old and stunning, with those subtle lines of her cheekbones tapering roundly down to her muzzle, her sparkling golden eyes, and her face full of kitten mirth. The front living area had a large picture window to the south and lots of sunlight. It made her black fur lustrous with bluish and reddish highlights; it made her lower lip glisten shiny black against the matte depths of her whisker pads. I took two photo portraits of her in a sitting up stance that reminded me of old paintings of enormous scale; Minx was sitting on Bill's heirloom homemade quilts, with a background of a darkened bookcase topped with an antique oil night-light lamp that I had scrounged to purchase in Maryland back when I was a student. Our home was modest in income and furnishings, but she was an individual of regal bearing, her visage glowing with immensity of spirit.

Minx was radiant and she made everything around her radiant, too. She was like a traveler in landscapes painted by Van Gogh and Gauguin. In November of that year, there was a sunset of layered pastels, green, red, violet, and blue, reminding me of Neapolitan ice cream. Was that Minx's doing? Well I know it wasn't but it seemed part of her mystique at the time. I would look out the glass front door towards the sunlight and if I saw her sleeping beside the threshold there, I would go *ahhh* at the soothing sight of her like nightfall and its secrets.

As a young cat Minx was clearly "my cat," although I was equally if not more so "her person," but she had an adventurous and warm heart. She would go to Bill's lap sometimes, and my mother's and Bill's mother's, where she was photographed stretching out easily in 1988. When she was about two months, I even saw her run up a friend's chest to his face like she did so often with me, but this only happened once. Afterwards she must have decided that running softpaw quickbop to the face, not even excluding my mouth, was for Minx and me only. She would sleep high up upon me, and we would rub faces. We both loved the way the other one smells.

In January, at about seven months of age, Minx went into heat. We had to keep Orange Cat, who was still an intact tom, away from her. Beautiful as she was, she would have had gorgeous kittens, especially so with Orange Cat. But there was only one course of action, and that was to spay her. It was the late 1980s and I was now 40-something, and I was aware that there were not enough homes to handle the overflowing population of cats and dogs that had resulted from too many animals being allowed to breed freely.

Spaying and neutering had not caught on with everyone in our immediate area at that time. I remember seeing newspaper ads for "free kittens to good homes" with catchy phrases like: "ugly black kittens with sweet person-alities," "good bug eaters now, good mouse eaters later, " and "light mouse-work." Friends whose cats were having litters said they had lots of calls in response to newspaper ads and had no trouble giving kittens away to good homes, even black kittens. But opinions were in transition in these years; now many in our region are active advocates of spaying and neutering com-panion animals.

Much of the literature indicates that in the northern hemisphere, domestic cats have heat cycles from roughly February to September under the natural lighting conditions outside. Day length is the major factor in triggering es-trus; it takes 12 to 14 hours of daylight, a condition that occurs slowly as the days lengthen after the winter solstice and spring approaches. This is nature's way of insuring that the young will be born in the warm months. But indoor cats will cycle all year long due to the long periods of artificial light in the home, which might explain the January estrus onset in Minx. There are al-ways exceptions, such as outdoor cats that have kittens in midwinter, and there may be other factors. At least one source mentions temperature as a factor, but this doesn't seem to be a common opinion at this time.

Reflecting on a cat-free childhood

When Minx came we'd had cats in our home going back a long time. I've been drawn to animals and natural places from an early age. Maybe it was heredity, as my mother and grandmother loved animals, too. At age 16 my grandmother had yelled "Stop" out the window of the family's home in Boston at a man beating the horse who was pulling his cart.

"How am I supposed to get this cart up the hill?" the man yelled back.

"Get out and push," called my grandmother. And he did!

As a young woman, she nursed injured birds until they were well enough to fly away. But in those days of incomplete understandings of benevolence towards animals, my grandmother wore those fur pieces with two fox heads wrapped around her neck. As a child I was naïve enough to believe her ex-planation that the foxes had died of natural causes. Maybe she even half be-lieved this herself.

Whatever the source of my animal affinities, they surfaced in my earliest childhood. I was especially taken with toads and frogs in those days, and that fondness would continue lifelong. Mom was very much a homebody and a tidy indoor person, but she saw who I was and nurtured my inclinations to-ward the wild. I'd been born in Washington, D.C., and on weekly trips by bus to the National Zoo, I always wanted to see the cats first: the lions and tigers in one building, the leopards, black leopards we called panthers, and jaguars in another. At the edge of the zoo was a forested, hilly area of Rock Creek Park. I called it the "beautiful mountain forest." We often went there on foot as it was within walking distance, and Mom and I walked by the edge of the creek. She watched as I picked out interesting pebbles to look at, "with a child's eye" as she later told it.

For awhile we had a dog named Snippy, but after my parents divorced, I lived with my mother in an apartment in Maryland with no suitable space for a dog or cat. We did have a parakeet for a time and an aquarium specially adapted for four toads who had been given to us. And in the evenings Mom and I would cross Connecticut Avenue to a wooded area beside a little neighborhood where there was a small stream and sit creekside, digging up worms to feed the toads. On sunny days we'd take them outside and let them hop around in the bug-rich vines growing on the steep bank beside the apartment building, foraging on their own while we watched them. In feeding them worms we accepted the realities of feeding captive toads. This is the way pet frogs and toads are fed according to recent information sources.

(Today I would not keep a pet that had to be fed live prey, not even insects. Some of nature's ways are unfathomable to me, and it's sometimes hard to be a natural history buff when the facts of predators and prey trouble you philosophically. I am also troubled by the fact that we kept small animals in the house confined during my childhood. We did not know better at the time, as our awareness was only beginning to grow. I am conflicted about zoos because the confinement there means less than ideal lives for the animals. Zoos, however, do save endangered animals whose habitats are quickly shrinking.)

While Mom and I were taking our toads for supervised outings, hundreds of miles away my future spouse was watching his yard begin to hop with many toads from twilight into the dark of each night. Yards of bare earth with no lawns were common in his locale at the time, due to the presence of chickens kept around the homes. He began to make "toad houses" in his dirt yard. He would dig a hole about toad sized and cover it with a brick or a board, leaving a space for entrance. Overnight, a toad would take up residence. Sometimes, two would come to live in one toad house. A toad who had lost one leg but could still get around stayed for an extended period of time.

As a child in Maryland, I studied trees and birds and rocks and minerals. I collected leaves and wildflowers, and rocks of many shapes and colors. I would stay outside for as long as I could until dark fell, in any kind of weather, just to be outside, not inside where the surroundings of furniture didn't interest me. I spent lots of time in the Smithsonian, the National History Museum, and the National Gallery. Mom helped to nurture the wilderness-seeking person I was through our walks in the park and the trips to the zoo, and I became an environmentalist by the age of eight.

I was drawn to the neighbors' cats and to the strays. One had a litter in a dry drainage ditch behind the apartment buildings, near a lone catalpa tree. I tried to catch and pet the kittens, but they were wild and fast. Someone may have been feeding them, but in those days, people generally didn't do much to help ferals. I tried to track and catch untamed barnyard kittens when we visited in the country, with the same results. Those dark torties with hints of gold in their fur, as well as the black kitties, they were always several steps ahead of me! In my experience of those times, farm and barn cats that were so necessary to rodent control around the house and outbuildings were not cosseted, tamed, or treated as pets beyond being given a few table scraps to keep them around. The kittens were left to grow up feral. At a riding stable we frequented, we were warned not to pet the resident cats, lest they become too tame and walk off with people. They were needed there, to catch mice in the hayloft. Without human contact from an early age, cats are wary of people and live like wild things. In contrast, in suburban areas cats often were kept as pets, usually indoor/outdoor pets. It's indeed amazing that when humans and cats make friends, the cats take over your entire house and run it for you, molding it to their needs.

When I was nine, a neighbor in the apartment complex we lived in saw me stroke her cat one day. When the cat had kittens, I was invited in to watch the birth, in the space carefully prepared by the owner. I was offered a kitten when they were older, but as per our home limitations, I still couldn't have one. Additionally, whenever I stayed overnight with my cousin, I played with her kitten, Powder Puff, by twitching a string in front of her. The kitten pounced and pounced, got tired, and snoozed. Fascination was taking hold of me. The neighbors' cats, which I could pet, and the elusive ferals, which I couldn't, increasingly occupied my imagination. I daydreamed of one day having a house full of animals, including cats.

Mom was a suburban person but despite her slim resources and not actually being employed at the time, she took a chance and purchased some land in Virginia farm country with an old house on it. We spent a lot of time there. Mom did eventually get work, as she had always firmly believed she would. The land was part of her response to my wish to live in what I thought was the closest thing to wilderness: a farm. I was too young to really understand the differences. We were never financially able to fix up the house to live there full-time, but on long walks on the hilly land with the Blue Ridge on one side and a small range of mountains on the other, I became more deeply enmeshed in fascination with the natural world and a quest to experience the personality of nature. Although I was a suburban kid, I learned much from the farming community that was so different from what I knew, about the hardships, as well as the rewards, of living remote and trying to farm the land.

Mom was a very sturdy person, and once when alone down at the farm, she faced down a pack of wild dogs with her withering green eyes. She somehow knew instinctively not to turn and run. It was unusual in those days for urban and suburban persons like us to have so much contact with farm country. In later years, Mom would get a kick out of it every time she had to sign some farm paperwork as "farmer."

My grandfather, who married my Boston grandmother, had come from the South, and it was only a twist of fate that kept me from being born in Atlanta, Georgia, or Chattanooga, Tennessee, two cities where the family lived before coming to Washington, D.C. When college time came I took my stack of rock, improvisational jazz, and authentic blues records to the University of Alabama to study art and literature. My South Carolina grandfather had gone to college at Bama, and in 1966, even with out-of-state tuition, it was less expensive than anywhere else. To get there from the D.C. area, you cross the Blue Ridge and keep heading south until you reach a pleasant mix of hilly and level land with occasional steeps. Beyond that, the land flattens on its way to the Gulf. I stood out down there, with my mid-Atlantic accent tinged with my grandmother's Boston, along with my long, flat dark hair, little black dress, and purple wrap-around skirt. Beehive hairstyles were over "Up North" by that time, but they had just arrived in the South. I had no real idea what to expect.

Partly due to economics, I had felt like an outsider in the D.C. suburbs, where prosperity had flowered for most of the residents. I had experienced some harassment by bullies because I had neither money nor glamour, and that locale is certainly not devoid of individuals biased in all ways. One bigoted remark from a schoolmate had always been enough to make me drift apart from any friendship with that person. I didn't come away from those suburbs thinking they were universally enlightened, although D.C., a large northern city and its surroundings, is a place where that quality is generally assumed to reside. That's not to say there weren't people inclined towards compassion and inclusiveness there; I did, with regret, leave many fine friends with kind hearts. I just never found the widespread grace and enlightenment that some proponents of the region imply. And, I was one of its citizens but I could not afford to be educated there.

My mother had first set her sights on Hollins College or Sweetbriar for me, but they were financially out of the question. Some of the student population of the South were young progressives. Many came from regular working people so for me there was economic parity and solidarity. Unlike parts of the D.C. suburbs, I encountered camaraderie and rapport among people who didn't judge you by what you had. I connected with a few other progressive-minded persons and found it a welcoming land. But as I had in Maryland, I experienced rejection from those persons who were more conformist and elitist. We won't say too much about who they were, though.

I heard that besides myself, in 1966 there were only about six other out-of-state students at the entire university. Because it was hearsay from long ago, I can't be sure that's true. With a head full of social reform and countercultural ideas in the making, I was at odds with a lot of the culture then, but so were a number of the students, and our little small cluster of "outsiders" survived. This group, contrary to what some in northern and western areas of the United States appear to believe, consisted of many native to Alabama and other southern states. It's my opinion these Southerners have always been here, but weren't visible to the outside world through the negative clouds that shrouded the region at that time. Progressives didn't make it into the news. In our "other" solidarity, I don't recall any division of North and South, and I was always surprised when I encountered such notions. Our opinions clashed with anything rigid, entrenched, or usual, and crackled and flashed in the sodden Alabama air. Our music was John Coltrane, Ornette Coleman, Bob Dylan. I fondly remember the snack bar in the Art Department building, where the art students and assorted other free spirits gathered. It was known campus-wide as "The Little Bo," Bo being short for *bohemia*, the 19th-century French term applied to groups of artists living unconventional lives. At The Little Bo, they served coffee, fountain cokes, chili, beans and franks, hamburgers, and snacks of all sorts, including crackers and MoonPies. Pleasant waitresses, who always had smiles for their long-haired clientele, did the cooking and serving; some were from the country. There was a sitting room with tables inside for the patrons; outside there were picnic tables.

One of my more daring friends climbed up and stood on one of those tables on a cloudy afternoon. A passing English instructor called out, "Hail to thee, blithe spirit," from Shelley's "To a Skylark." Everyone collapsed with laughter. Later at a Zippy Mart in another part of town, the girl running the cash register would ask me if I remembered "The Addams Family" TV show and tell me warmly in a rural accent, as a compliment, that I reminded her of Morticia. "You favor her." That meant I looked like, or resembled Morticia, as in "Y'all favor."

Everyone thought the South was completely insular, but I attended many cultural events in the 1960s at UA, acts that came from around the nation and the world, including a Dionne Warwick concert and a screening of an Andy Warhol film for which Warhol and two of his close associates made an actual appearance onstage. I remember meeting him and standing right next to him at a gathering of Art Department people after the event.

I took part in peaceful, nonviolent demonstrations for peace and social justice starting in 1966, though few outside the region seem to know to this day that we were there during this time. At first there were ten or fifteen of us, thirty at the most. But by 1970, after the tragedy at Kent State, there were a thousand people at our candlelight vigil, including Bill. And after the evening when the police arrested everyone out on the green, including those en route to and from the library and those taking the warm May air on the lawns of the fraternity houses, peace signs were draped from the balconies of every sorority and fraternity house!

The grassroots progressives in Tuscaloosa during that time frame are just now beginning to be recognized and written about. It's high time someone told the story of these progressive people from the Deep South — and their cats.

In Alabama, the real work for the rights of all humanity, which drove significant social change, had been done by those in the marches and sit-ins and voter registration drives of the earlier 1960s, when I was still in high school in Maryland. The courage of these activists changed this nation and brightly lit the way for nonviolent protest. Their efforts for civil rights and human rights benefitted all humanity and should forever be recognized and celebrated worldwide. These were the events that resulted in great social shifts. I would like to see greater recognition for them; the stories of so many advocates have not been fully told.

Less well known, there were also people working behind the scenes to aid this movement, people who were secretive because of the atmosphere of intimidation during that era. By the time I arrived at UA, the major changes had been accomplished by the civil rights marchers and advocates, but there was still everyday living to do, and changes in that living needed to occur. The civil rights advocates never ceased working towards this harmony. And I feel we all tried to begin to live differently, inclusively, around that time, though perhaps this was only within the small circles where I existed. I had been taught by my mother to be gracious to everyone I came in contact with, so I said "thanks" and smiled at all dormitory cafeteria workers as they handed me food and all store clerks as they sacked my purchases, regardless of skin tones. At first I got some looks in the dorm for doing that, but I didn't care. Years later, I exchanged warm greetings at the mall with one of the ladies who had worked in the dorm, and I have always tried to extend courtesy, friendship, and cordiality to everyone. I know it wasn't much compared to the efforts of the marchers, but I hope this helps somehow to shift the norms. We try to mentor the next generation, the children of friends, in ways that differ from those of our parents. These are small, quiet things that don't make the papers, but we still mean what we lived in the '60s. We had been awed by the beauties of the commitment to nonviolence for social change and political expression, and by the power of grassroots efforts. We grew a thriving countercultural community in the Deep South.

Later, some of us would go on to work for progressive political candidates. One friend who did so, who came from rural Alabama, suddenly felt himself to be in danger in a small town one night and fled with his fellow campaign worker in the late hours. I did also go through some experiences of meanness, sometimes frightening, and I have witnessed much that is heartbreaking and wrong.

I may have had to fight harder for my identity as a progressive here than in D.C., but when I was younger I didn't mind a good fight against mainstream ways. I want no credit for living the way we thought was right in the days even when it went against the prevailing grain, or for being part of the countercultural changes. I just don't want to be stereotyped in unpleasant ways that aren't me and aren't us. I just want our existence, our progressive nature as part of the South, known. Not all Southern people are like the negative representations that appear in other regions of the United States. I've seen Northern people I love really miss the mark in their characterizations, with no thought as to whether they might be stereotypes or unfair. We do not downplay, dismiss, or forget the terrible past, but we are not in the past. We are moving on, living now, and addressing the problems, the strengths and the weaknesses of today. Whatever remains of the old ugliness, we don't take it lightly, and we still feel driven to work, breathing fire, against any remnants we come across.

All over the nation, something changed in our generation, and we all knew it. It wasn't just youthful bravado; it was a real divergence in thinking, and we were vastly different from our parents. This too added to the great social shifts. Whatever can be said, pro and con, about the hippie era, some of the lasting effects on us were a lifelong commitment to peace and a love for all humanity — and a preservation of the natural world and its creatures, along with a dedication to a life of scholarship and creative endeavors.

Later, many college friends from our circle went on to thrive creatively in the South, although again we aren't so well known, and we still didn't make the papers often. Those in large cultural centers probably consider the place the Outer Bog, but I daresay our rousing countercultural exchange and sparkling innovations in arts rivaled that of large cities. Eventually, many things changed here and at times I've mostly felt as comfortable in the South as in any other region I've known. In truth, this is not the case for all of my progressive friends, who chafe at being surrounded by lingering conservatism and newer strains that seem to have increased in recent years compared to the 1970s, 1980s, and 1990s. Of course I get bugged by some things I cross paths with, but as noted, when I was growing up, I saw enough bias in Northern areas to know that bigotry is a nationwide problem.

Those of us who went through the 1960s, and the great many of us who came after, just aren't the same as the society we still remember from before those times. Back in the 1970s, more and more of the progressive minded people began to stay in Alabama. That was a reversal of previous trends, when native, reform-minded Southerners felt stifled and often quickly left the region once they came of age. But gradually, more of the artists and others who had gone to the big cities for economic opportunity and a more open cultural life — or who had left out of revulsion during the ugly old days of social injustice — came back down home. I arrived in 1966, and by 1970, there were many more persons from all over the nation who had come to attend UA and ended up staying. After a few more years, persons from many other nations began making their homes here, too.

The South is not the same demographically as it used to be. It's now sparkling with currents from all over the United States, the world, and some of its own. I sense a completely different feel to being here, another ambiance and a more inclusive way of talking and relating, than there was back in the "old times" of the 1960s. I see it not only in the old 1960s protesters themselves but in the ways people around town with definite rural accents relate to each other, sweet moments to witness.

I have tended to live in the present, so when I read Civil Rights Movement histories and re-experience the appalling and horrific events of past years, it's painful and chilling. Whenever news crops up that seems like a rotten remnant of the bad times, it's wrenching and disheartening to me. A few friends are again beginning to talk of fleeing the region, but Bill and I are in the "stay and fight" camp. We and others remain, hoping we are living the difference, being the change. We are here to oppose and denounce any old, sick ways, hoping the differences between past and present that we perceive are really there, and solid.

Will living for now and the future ever be enough to atone for the horrors of the past and to foster a better future? These are the questions that still trouble me in 2018.

Alabama has its charms, there's still a lot of wild land here. You don't have to go far to "get back to nature;" in fact, in these towns full of trees, you are never really out of it. In my college days it only took about five minutes to drive out of town and into the wilds. Picnickers and dating couples went "creekbanking." At the public lakes that were minutes away, I once saw a profusion of young frogs hopping around the banks of a remnant stream below a dam that had created, and then held, a huge lake from that stream. Travel to the edge of town and you were soon riding through forests and fields. A popular restaurant was located "in the sticks." We went out into the woods often, visiting old abandoned houses, old coal tunnels, hidden vistas, and an old cabin for rent at the end of a walk by Hurricane Creek, a deep forest space that someone had once lived in. We thought of renting it, but it just felt too remote, despite the beauty of clear water flowing through large boulder formations nearby. Precipitation is an experience here; hot gentle breezes sound the Aeolean heart and make a storm of rain, blown broken branches, melodies, rhythms, even discordant howling notes that lead the imagination onward.

The South is also a great place for language enthusiasts. While remaining a strong adherent of standard English for ease of business and formal communications and for the preservation of a common and understood national way of speaking, I recognize that every region innovates phrases and has its clever and colorful colloquialisms and speechways. These variants grow the living language. Southern accents are like the cushy velvet on the underside of a leaf. Some voices are like honey, and some expressions from the backwoods sound like poetry, as in "it don't make no nevermind to me," or from Bill's rural and small-town Wiregrass Region of the state, " dark as a bushel of blackbirds at midnight."

Other sayings are particularly effective, like (so and so) "doesn't have walking around sense," or, (so-and-so) "can't walk and chew gum at the same time," "lower than a snake's belly," and (ouch, poor baby), "nervous as a long-tailed cat in a roomful of rockers." Anything I never heard when I lived "Up North" in Maryland I assume is southern in origin. Adding "spice and color," Bill's repertoire of expressions from his LA (Lower Alabama) origin includes "raining like a cow pissing on a flat rock" and "shit fire," the latter of which is widespread in the Southeast, but some local wit in Bill's town has playfully added "and save matches." Correct language isn't a constant, it's a flux of the way people are speaking. American English, with its truncated mishmash of phrases and diced words and shape-shifted idioms, is the amalgamation of many nations and regions, frankenspeak.

Lewis Thomas, whose *The Lives of a Cell* made me gasp, wrote about language as well as science. He thought that language was never finished but was an unending continuum, constructed daily (although without awareness) by all humans.[20] I've become a "Power to the People" linguist, my ownself. Some accents are treated as "wrong," but actually, everyone has an accent. Rightness or wrongness is a matter of arbitrary opinion. I adore regional accents of all types and I think it will be a tragedy if the flow of discourse, including people with attitudes, cause any to disappear. There are, by the way, many varying accents in the South, not just one. They have similarities but also distinct differences.

Thomas Hardy noted in *Tess of the D'Urbervilles* that Tess spoke her home variant at home and the "standard" English of the day at school, as pointed out in "The Story of English."[21] In my opinion, everyone potentially speaks two languages, the one learned at home and in the neighborhood and the "standard" or "broadcast" language taught at school.

But where I live, when people gather and the stories begin to flow, everyone's a raconteur and all the world's a porch. If someone asked me now what's the best way to learn to write, I might seriously say come to the American Southeast and just stand around, listening to people talking. I'll be lucky if I've absorbed a tenth of the storytelling abilities I've seen in the folks down here.

Chapter 2

Black and Beauty

It was 1969 when I met and married Bill. Before then, I'd never actually had a pet cat. He had grown up in the Wiregrass Country of South Alabama in a small town; it was mostly a farm-based community. He'd had a dog named Bubba as a child, but in rural areas in those days, cats were yard animals that were fed table scraps and served well as rodent control. Bill's father, Eddie Alford, described this function in his historical work, *The Smoke Eater of Geneva County*: "Animals are necessary to have on a farm, especially mules, dogs and cats ... The cats controlled the rat population to keep them from eating your corn and peanuts in the cribs."[1]

Bill's mother did feed the neighborhood cats that came to the yard, so all the cats in town tended to cluster there. But they were outdoor animals, not pets. Bill recalls one old yard cat named Stinker who would kill wharf rats as big as she was. He saw her dragging many a large, dead rat underneath her, walking straddle-legged around it. He also recalls cats named Scooter and Littl'en, as well as others without names. Another cat knew how to pull the screen door open with her claws and enter the kitchen; and how to get back out by knocking the door back open with her paws. One momcat in particular had so many kittens that his folks felt they could no longer handle her fecund presence. They drove her out in the country to give her to a farmer, where she would join his barn cats. Farmers were always in need of good barn cats. The farm was several miles away and across the Pea River, a good-sized waterway. Like so many cats who get somehow stranded far from a place they have settled, several years later that cat came running back into the Alford yard, bellowing her happiness to be home.

The older farming community sometimes did look benignly upon the area strays, as passed down by Bill's mother, who quoted something her father once said: "Anything hungry comes along, you should feed it." These were people who had known some really lean times, but were nevertheless very generous.

One of Bill's aunts had kept alligators in a pen in her dirt front yard. They dug holes to live in and would come to be fed when she thumped on the ground. We don't know where they had come from; it was close to Florida, where alligators usually reside, but gators weren't common in the waterways of the community Bill grew up in.

So Bill never actually had a cat as a pet before we got married, either. During a particularly humid summer we were staying on the coast of Florida, near the water I called the *Gulp!* of Mexico when I saw it for the first time. We decided we wanted a cat. I'd yearned for one for a long time. As a high school student I had daydreamed of having horses and collie dogs, but somehow in college the daydreams became about cats. And it had to be a black cat, because I'd always thought they were the most beautiful. I had been raised to regard superstitions about luck as ridiculous, and I was of a mind to question traditional notions that did not seem logical or reasonable. Supernatural tales can make for good cinema but when taken seriously, they make me yawn. We had no hesitation in deciding to adopt one of these most gorgeous natural beings, the black cat. In those countercultural days, I admit there was an aspect of going against traditional nonsensical grains, of just being "contrary." All of this added up to plain awe of black cats and the ways they fascinate.

We obtained this sweet creature by reading an ad in the paper for "free black kittens to good homes." The lady said she could tell we would be good for the kitten, because we had bothered to come to get one. No one really screened potential adopters in those days, but in this case she was certainly right. The kittens were part Siamese, she told us. "All black cats are," she added. I didn't question this at the time, but I now believe it's just a myth. Black cats as a mutation developed from the original tabby-coated wildcats. Her statement may reflect some factors of feline genetics additional to the tabby line of black cats, to be discussed later. Regardless, we took home a fuzzy little female. Thus began my lifelong romance with all things cat. This was also the first and last kitten ad we ever answered.

Bad magic: The history and harm of black-cat lore

Much has been written about the shameful persecution of black cats, and all other cats, too, during the Middle Ages and other times when animals were not regarded as worthy of compassion. I prefer not to write or even think about this in detail. The descriptions in the literature sicken the heart of any decent person. For the most part in modern life, all that remains of the belief-driven acts of cruelty (from many types of belief) are superstitions about luck of one sort or another, and the association of black cats with Halloween.

Sadly, present-day atrocities against cats and other animals still exist, the acts of mentally disturbed and/or evil individuals. These brutalities are increasingly being treated as criminal acts, and the well-established link between violent behavior towards animals and violent behavior towards humans is being taken more seriously. The fact is, almost all serial killers have been documented as having abused animals in childhood. Historically these atrocities were treated as misdemeanors, if not ignored outright by callous or misguided parents and civil authorities. Such indifference to the suffering of other beings is yet another shocking reminder of how slowly humanity has progressed towards any kind of intelligent, compassionate, and enlightened behavior. For my part, all animals are astonishing and marvelous, and I cannot fathom how anyone could not be captivated by all of the world's fauna. Neither can I understand why humans don't always act with kindness towards animals and other humans.

Cats of all colors are now venerated as beloved household pets. Nevertheless, I have during my lifetime witnessed, to my astonishment, persons who wished to avoid black cats, and one who actually stated that "all cats represent evil." This was a most disturbing bit of ignorance, and it illustrates the need to make sensible attitudes towards animals a part of basic education. I wish I'd retorted that if cats hadn't saved our ancestors from famine and disease many times, a lot of us wouldn't be here today. This human-serving argument would probably have been more effective than speaking the plain facts, that animals are simply the earth's creatures, and it's absurd to put evil off on them. Indeed, some scholars believe that the only thing that saved the cat from extinction during the Middle Ages is the eventual realization that they were useful to humans in controlling the plague-spreading rats. Well, duh. Without modern means of rodent control, it was a suicidal society indeed that turned against its cats. In *Classical Cats, The Rise and Fall of the Sacred Cat*, Donald Engels details how the combined effects of poor sanitation and the low population of cats, reduced through persecution, contributed to the rapid spread of the plague through Europe.[2]

Unfortunately, the association of cats with "magic" or "spells" persisted in ways that continued to be detrimental to cats. A remark by an older acquaintance of my mother, "You need a bag full of cat paws to trick 'em with," while clearly just an expression used wryly by that speaker, likely refers to what was once an actual cruel practice.

Cats are natural animals, part of the world's fauna, like any other species. They are intriguing and stimulating to live with, as they go about their day casting glances your way that are a challenge to interpret. It's flat out ludicrous to put anything "evil" or "sinister" on them. They are just wild creatures, but unique among small wild things, in that when they have been socialized with humans, they not only readily become part of our households with a small amount of acclimation, but in many cases appear to seek our homes out.

The holiday that black cats are so often identified with, Halloween, was in my early experiences always good spooky fun. It actually still is, despite some disturbing cultural trends that obscure the happy popular holiday time it was when I was young. I may not always go for spooky sense, but I do like benign spooky fun. I recall fondly from my early years in D.C., the yearly Halloween parade on 14th Street and the pastel confetti of all colors thrown on the sidewalks. We bought it in little waxy paper bags from the dime store. Everyone dressed up, some in commercial costumes, others, like myself, in clothes from the oldest corners of Mom's closet. So for me, the association of black cats with this time of golden harvest moons, cider, apples, leaves turning colors, chilly fall nights, and the changing of the seasons made such cats desirable. It was all about wholesome "spookies" to me.

I've been greatly saddened over the years by the evil persons who have used this time of year to commit violent acts towards people and animals, and I wish I knew what the most effective prevention would be. I can only suggest more humane education in schools as a foundation for learning how to treat one's fellow beings, animal and human. Formerly convinced that kindness was intrinsic to the human psyche, I now feel that what should be our innate ability to envision compassion and act accordingly might need to be coaxed out and learned. "Empathy 101" and "Basic Compassion," need to be taught in schools, beginning in kindergarten or pre-school. Many adults need a remedial course, as well. Whereas obviously everyone doesn't need this instruction, crimes against both humans and animals suggest that many do. Factors that produce anti-social behavior also need to be addressed. These are my gut responses to the question of whether we can do anything to change these behaviors and produce more compassionate people. Perhaps a shift is also needed in the public's perception of Halloween, to get back to the coming of autumn and the playful, festive feeling I had from childhood in 1969, the year when I first sought out as a pet: a black kitten.

In modern times Halloween has culturally morphed into something more sinister, a concept way beyond what it was in the 1940s and 50s. I did encounter the mean side of it myself in Maryland during my early teens; boys from the wealthier neighborhood next to our lower middle-income street attacked me, throwing eggs on me and my makeshift outfit of Mom's old black taffeta and velvet. The witch image as an archetype used to be attractive because it was one way women who felt powerless in actual life could imagine themselves with some independence, ability, and strength. It's of interest in classic literature, studies of folk belief, and in horror movies. But any serious ideas of "witchcraft" with bad purposes and ill will spoils that image entirely and ruins all the fun.

The name "Halloween" is derived from All Hallow's Eve, the day before All Saint's Day. The October 31 date coincided with ancient harvest festivals (which weren't always benign) and essentially absorbed the old celebrations. The coming of autumn does inspire thoughts about the cycles of life and growth and our place within them. These can be beneficial and natural, if we allow kindness and compassion to rule our thoughts. Hopefully, benign celebrations, a "dress-up" theater of concepts and a welcome to rhythms of nature can reclaim this holiday to one of purposeful fun. At least, it will for some people; there will always be a few who have negative intentions.

Perspective gained from passing years means a scramble of ideas for protection of our cats — and our black cats — from people who just don't get it. I have growing concerns about any depiction of black cats, or any cats, in a (so-called) supernatural context. I don't mind the association with benign mystery — unknowns of nature, the darkness of natural night and mist and the moon. I feel cautious towards images suggesting serious associations of black cats with the supernatural.

I know some will say "lighten up," and I've seen that response on the Internet when others bring up these same points. I'm all for any religion that's based on compassion and kindness and love. Some of the old religions involved cruel animal sacrifices, too, even the religion of the Egyptians, who sacrificed young cats in the temples. Among the cat mummies found there are young cats as well as kittens, who did not die of natural causes.[3] So my approach is always, convince me you are part of the good-hearted side of belief. I know it's out there.

I rejoice whenever a black cat has a good, loving home. This joy of course extends to any cat or other pet. The following is my own opinion and not meant as criticism of anyone else's cat-naming patterns, but I myself won't name any black cats anything with heavily unpleasant supernatural connotations, even though it's usually done just to mock those negative associations. They're meant to be ironic, but irony doesn't come across unless you can provide contextual tones of voice. It must be addressed to individuals who have irony receptors, and sometimes, similar backgrounds of cultural reference, which can change from generation to generation even within one neighborhood.

Irony also doesn't work universally on the Internet, not even with every outright joke typed there; it does not always float true and maintain its shape when you let snark loose without knowing where it might end up. No matter how benign, supernatural references involving cats are, in my opinion, too much fodder for those same old and surprisingly persistent beliefs about black cats being bad luck. I once enjoyed playing with concepts and was a horror movie fan, but times have changed, and somehow, concepts are being taken much more seriously than they were in the decades I came of age in. Shelters report that black cats are still not adopted in the same proportions as other colors of cats. (The same is true of black dogs.) Some articles say this actually occurs because black cats are more prevalent within the feline population, but even so, I feel this trend is at least partly due to superstitions about luck, fate, and darkness.

I may be mystified by the way events often unfold, but I don't truly believe in luck as an influence on occurrences. Even so, ideas that black cats are good luck I will endorse, because it works to ensure kind treatment of cats. Midnight, Shadow, Ebony, Silhouette, Eclipse, Inky, Crow, and Raven: facts of nature and description are always good names. I can go humorous and literary, too: Morticia, Merlin, Boo, Spooky, Poe, Edgar. Magic, Hocus, and Pocus are all light enough in weight since they refer to the art of illusion. I'm even okay with Nightshade; not all parts of the plant are "deadly;" we eat potatoes, tomatoes, and eggplant all the time, and I'm drawn to the word in the literal sense, the "shade of night." Snowball has perhaps enough blatant irony to carry well, even out of context, "enough to make a cat laugh." This is just me; I don't presume to tell people how to name their pets, but I'd like to raise questions about the portrayal of black cats and cats in general, and how it might influence attitudes and actions towards the cats. Names for cats tilted towards the seriously unpleasant and supernatural give me pause. But I will still click "like" or "love" for all cats regardless of name on the Internet, in celebration of another cat in a good home — and its loving humans.

A phenomenon that does not help black cats at all: those persons who adopt black cats in October to use as decorations for Halloween parties and then take them back to the shelters or abandon them when Halloween is over. Conversely, the proliferation of websites and pages devoted to black cats and their photos, their beauties and affections as pets, is a marvelous, positive trend.

While I know it's hard to shake ingrained beliefs you've been taught, most people grow to realize the foolishness of animal luck notions. As for those who don't and remain unpleasantly biased, perhaps the presence of a black cat or cats will keep such persons away from my door: *This house protected by small black cats; don't cross them!* We who are advocates for cats need to "tell it" when it comes to our positive experiences with black cats. I live to see beautiful black cats crossing my path!

The science (and theory) of the color black

I'm going to tell my experience of the romance of the world's coloration, so completely entwined with dark and light. Although it's from painter's eye, I feel anyone can relate. Light plays upon items in the world; fur that displays as black on cats is just one permutation of an endless differentiation, a fact in the physics of light and color and the reflection and absorption of rays that help determine color variations. The array of cat coat colors encompasses individuals reflecting light in their myriad, differing ways.

According to the *American Heritage Encyclopedic Dictionary*, the perception of black is a response to "zero stimulation of the retina," due to little or no reflection of light by the object. This "color" is described as without hue, or achromatic in the dictionary.[4] My reading and experience, however, suggest more complexity.

Colors throughout history have acquired the baggage of traditional symbolism; usually, as Walter Sargent points out in *The Enjoyment and Use of Color*, carrying both good and bad aspects. Blue can be seen as peaceful but also represents sadness, as in "the blues"; green suggests growth but can also mean jealousy; and black is known for meaning darkness and all our ancestors' fears of it, but it also embodies a basic quality and stillness, as opposed to the animation of radiant light.[5] Color symbolism is a fascinating study in itself, and meanings of color may derive more from history or emotions than from fact. For instance, white light may be described as "pure," but it's actually bursting to spill its rainbow of color upon objects as it bounces around.

Tradition or not, black was never sinister to me as I glanced about the visual world. It meant mystery, and nights when crickets sang, flower fragrances were more intense, and the stars and moon came out. And, I have since the day of the first kitten, lived with and known many achromatic cats, who have all made some of the finest, most affectionate pets and companion animals as any I've seen.

When I adopted the first black cat, I was a painter, a color wrangler who was always making on-the-spot studies of the ways the spectrum can be divided. I was especially drawn to blacks and dark hues, because always there in the natural world, in concert with other colors, they were part of many beauties present in nature. The best colorists understand how to use both tints and shades of color to achieve their effects, and painters work the entire spectrum. The part of electromagnetic radiation from the sun that humans can see is composed of all colors. Painters take the blacks and the darker hues, the whites and the brighter hues, the ranges of gray between shadow and light, and fuse them with the visible spectrum. Painters work that rainbow and all its degrees. We play up and down the gray scale and sound a flourish at either end! All permutations are counterpoint to each other, weaving contrasts together.

This isn't just the painter's eye view and this isn't just true of the world of visual art: it's true of the way humans see brightness, shadows, hues, and forms out there in the physical world. Sunlight just behaves this way. Color in nature is compound, and our vision and perception are both attuned to respond to its intricacies. All shades, tints, and colors are needed in living and painting. All colors work together to make daily experience; combinations of dark, light, and color reveal the landscape out there in full. If we humans were to startle every time murky color or shadow crossed into our view, we'd be one jumpy bunch of folks! (We'd be like long-tailed cats in rooms full of rockers.) Animals of all colors stroll through this landscape of contrasts, living, moving accents who rouse and delight our attention and senses.

Professor Walter Sargent's aforementioned book is one of the best treatments I've ever read on the subject of color theory. Written mainly as a textbook for artists, it is also for anyone who could benefit from greater understanding of color in the world. Through its description of the physics and optics of color perception, Sargent has much to say on the integral role of black coloration in nature. White light of the sun is composed of many wavelengths, including the spectrum of colors human eyes are structured to detect.[6] We can see this display of colors when the light is refracted, as through a prism, so that the rays are bent, and the colors are seen at their individual wavelengths. Objects upon which the white light falls may reflect only one wavelength and absorb the rest; thus, we see the color that vibrates at the one reflected wavelength.

Actual perception of color occurs because the structure of our eyes discerns the different wave speeds and wavelengths as different colors. White objects appear white because they reflect all the light, and black objects appear black because they absorb all of it, which is the practical model of understanding the different "values" of black and white and the gray scale in between. But, says Professor Sargent, not only can we not achieve full reflection and absorption (i.e. absolute white and black) in paints and papers, but nature rarely does, either. Natural white is rarely absolute due to slight differences of absorption that result in a few hues reflecting enough to show up as slight degrees of coloration.[7] Similarly, there is also no total black seen in nature, either. We will see glints and/or iridescence in black fur and feathers.[8]

Scrutinize things in nature — a twilight landscape with darkened tree trunks, a black cat on your couch across a sunlit room — and you'll see these concepts in practice. Watch the blackbirds, called Common Grackles, and you'll see auroras produced by sunlight twisting through their feathers, as though dark itself has a spectrum. Sargent indicates that white does not completely contain the colors within it, and black does not fully absorb all hues. Instead, black displays traces of color, and both black and white will show the influence of surrounding reflected colors.[9] He says elsewhere that although in theory black is absence of color via absorption, black surfaces usually do reflect light and color.[10] Various surfaces and textures, from shiny to plush and deep, change the ways in which the small quantity of reflected light in blacks appears. Sargent also points out that the color of night tends to actually be dark blue or violet-blue and therefore cannot be depicted in paintings correctly by grays and blacks. Also, the entire gray scale in nature tends to have tinges of colors, and colors in nature are never flat and even, but include gradations of texture and intensity and value. Lastly, the hue reflected usually includes some rays of the hues adjacent in the spectrum to the dominant color. Not many surfaces reflect light of one wavelength.[11]

To me this means there is no case of a smooth, unbroken hue in nature. You will find the expanse of color is a side-by-side stippling of one shade's parodies of itself, lying beside samplings of other hues. Painters and colorists work from this understanding of using hue plus adjacent to accentuate reality; for fun, they might throw in a few colors from around the spectrum, sometimes willy-nilly, sometimes with precision intent.

When the spectrum of colors found in white light is placed in a circle, each color has an opposite hue on the wheel, known as its complementary color. Complementary pairs are especially harmonious combinations. If you look at an area of color for about twenty or thirty seconds and then shift your gaze to an area that is white or grayish, you will briefly see an after-image of the color complementary to the one you just viewed. Painters make frequent use of this fact to maximize color impact. Crafters of rattlesnake quilts, such as those handed down to Bill from the women of his family, work instinctively to stitch pleasing color arrangements.

Thus, any colors observed long enough set up complementary resonance in the eye. Complements themselves, mixed together pigmentally or visually, produce gray and silver tones. Seeing a painting of seemingly limited colors is really like seeing an alphabet of hues in the eye if one looks long enough. Paintings with complementary pairs enhance this process, getting the jump on the eye's own tricks, forming a parade behind this traveling harlequin patch-garbed entity of paint and light who bursts color itself and scatters the shrapnel of confetti in syncopated display, just as soon as the retina can slice and shred it. "Our eyes work prismatically upon the white light, till *spectra riot*," was a musing I wrote long ago, not quite accurate science-wise, but to me, it works. The human eye can distinguish about ten million of these colors.

No color is an island. Every color shines with spectral adjacents. People who work in advertising and even department-store displays understand this very well. They often show an item of clothing with all the colors it comes in, grouped together in various ways, and we are drawn to the articles by the myriad hues working in concert. When we take an item to the dressing room or back to the home after purchase, we may find that it doesn't look as vibrant by itself as it did in the store display.

Sargent also discusses light upon complex surface textures, which transmit light back and forth through and between (for example, fibers) before it emerges, enriching a color by showing a range between the silvery qualities of light almost completely reflected, and the deep darks where absorption is near total.[12] And concerning grays in combination with other colors, Sargent says that black, white, and the gray scale in between serve to enhance the intensity of the colors next to them. When our eyes look at color, it is at its most intense appearance for less than a second; then the intensity decreases to about two-thirds or one-half. If we glance at a neutral area next to it and then back to the hue, the intense color sensation is revived for another part of a second.[13] In this way, natural scenes and artwork with neutral areas between the color areas will keep the color sensations at the peak as the eye travels over the expanse and takes "rest breaks" (all those rays!) on the neutrals.

So, black cats enhance the colors around them just by being present. They really do "go with everything" and "match any decor," as we now see in lists of reasons to adopt them, stated with a little wry humor. Another point in their favor is that black cats are always "dressed" for a formal evening. This is quite true: Cats named Midnight or Eclipse or Shadow are always dressed for a program of music. They are ready, instantly elegant, and waiting while I reach for my little black dress.

Dark and light and the continuum between them also gives us the contrasts which define form. This is a way we experience our visual world, the way our eyes are built to perceive. It's part and parcel of our world. These facts of light and color reveal that color, or lack of it, is not fixed or constant, but a matter of complexity that makes natural things lively and more beautiful to look at. To fully appreciate and comprehend the effect takes study and careful looking. Black and white are part of the larger continuum of light acting on objects in the world, seen by our eyes, which are structured to see different wavelengths as a display of separate colors and to enjoy the enhancements provided by the neutrals. Black is an integral part of the phenomenon of light and even serves the function of intensifying the colors contained within that light. Darkening and lightening, differences in oscillation length and speed, all have roles in the actions of light shining on the world. Colors and light levels must interweave to create our experience of them, in the ways our human eyes are designed to receive them. A little physics reveals a description that should fit anyone's philosophy or religion, despite whatever strong cultural bias against the color black may, or may not, have persisted.

Although it was first published in 1923, I didn't have Sargent's book and its scientific background to support my feeling for the color black in 1969. I just knew that I liked black and black cats with their beautiful fur. In the late '60s and early '70s, there was plenty of color around the house for a black cat to enhance. We even cooked food coloring into our staple plain white rice, rotating different hues over several evenings. It made the meals more visually interesting, and we had not yet become aware of the health disadvantages of food additives. (In present times, I have learned about an ancient variety of beautifully multi-color corn called "Glass Gem Corn" It isn't edible except as popcorn but if it was, I'd want grits made from that![14])

From Sargent's book and other sources, I've also gained an understanding of the highlights on the fur of black cats in sunlight. Silvery areas are reflecting large amounts of the white light, which does not penetrate the fur very far before being reflected back out. Black cats with short, dense fur most often have these highlights, but it also depends on the angle at which the rays illuminate them. A bluish, reddish, or coppery shine occurs when the light penetrates the surface of the fur more deeply and is refracted into a color (or colors) before being reflected back out — to the extent it is reflected at all, since the black fur will of course absorb most of the light. Medium- or long-length black fur would be more likely to have such hints of color. As Sargent says, this effect is at its most intense on blackbirds that are essentially black, but they'll shine with a rainbow of hues in some lighting situations.[15]

Shadows are often recognized by painters as having color. Natural dark has its own shades and intensities. Black kitties named Shadow contain many degrees of shadow! When painting towards a natural effect, an artist may mix colors into black paint straight out of the tube or build dark areas with glazes. When using black ink in drawings, I used to layer over it with pencil marks of both neutral and bright color. In a poetic sense, then, a black kitty contains the rainbow. And the sight of a black feline reclining in strong sunlight is astonishing and glorious.

Sargent tells us that black has an affinity for the long wavelength colors of red and orange, because they are closer to the end of visible light in the spectrum.[16] These are warm hues, and indeed, black is warm also. Black objects absorb the most heat, and radiate the most heat when warmer than their surroundings.[17]

So, black is associated with warmth and the hearth just as cats often are; and the warm-toned black cat perhaps most of all.

When light encounters any object, all photons are transferred to other energies; objects of each color emit new photons of that same color's wavelength in the original light. If white is seen, all colors of visible light have been converted to new photons, same frequencies. So, a black kitty's coat has absorbed most of the visual rainbow, converting it to heat and leaving black as the hue we see. Kitty blinks at you and purrs. Pet and scritch your black, fuzzy feline, feel the vibrant warmth; in strong sun, you'll see light glittering on the lush fur surface. Dusky black kitties are not only snugglebugs; they're an intrinsic fact of nature, like nightfall and daybreak. (Oops, went back to poetry again. Cats have a way of doing that to ya!)

When I originally condensed these reflections for my website, Bill (who has two degrees in electrical engineering) read it and caused me to come to a full stop. "Physics all wrong" was what he said. When he answers science questions I call him Dr. Photon, an apt and buoyant moniker originated by our friend Tim. Dr. Photon told me that absorption and reflection are much more complex concepts in physics than what I have described here, and that when light illuminates things, there is an interaction of electromagnetic radiation and matter. Now, all color theory books I have ever read have used the terms "absorption" and "reflection" without qualification, so I had not been aware of this. These books were written for artists of course, not for scientific purposes. Though I felt if matter was involved it was "matter of semantics," Dr. Photon told me you cannot join poetry and physics; science must have precise terms. This makes me say, "Hold my beer," or in the Lower Alabama parlance I learned from him, "Just hide and watch." So, many thanks to Dr. Photon for his contribution; any science errors in this chapter are my own; and yes, I will eventually read the 2-inch-thick textbook-looking thing he recommended.

Cats as scientific muse, or maybe not: The myth of Newton's cat flap

In my country during summer, daytime dark resides in tree trunks, shaded leafy alcoves and creek depths, Black-Winged Damselflies with teal bodies, and iridescent blackbirds gathering on fields. Nighttime dark carries fragrance, katydid clacking, frog chirps, *whip-poor-will* calls. The black cats, along with all cats, are seen reclining in the house's sunny spots year-round, but now and then they'll seek partial shade. In other regions and seasons, dark also has its own splendors, there for anyone to find who looks. Nearing the earth's poles, dark enhances the auroras.

Many sources on the Internet describe how to take professional-grade photos of black or darker animals. I have come to call my own amateur experiences "black cat noir." For some ideas on how anyone can make photos of black cats that aren't technically perfect but still engaging, see "Black Cats in Sun and Shade, A Painter's Eye View" on my website, Catwoods Porch Party. Of course I am not suggesting we amateurs can match the finesse of truly accomplished photographers, but we can work within our limitations.

Strong sun plus ambient room light makes for silvery highlights on fur, and sunlight roars at this latitude. We're pretty close to the sun in the southeastern United States. I have good illumination for photos, even indoors.

I've never really needed any science or philosophy to love animals of any color. I mention the science and Sargent's book both because color remains a passion of mine, and because it might benefit someone finding themselves in the position of defending black cats. That's less common nowadays, but I still encounter a few people who could use a little education on the subject. As painters or persons who move through a sunlit world composed of every color, we may arrange hues differently, choose favorites, assign meanings and symbolism, but every spot of color is part of the spectrum and only radiates for us beside its adjacents and spiced up by its opposites. It's part of the greater whole that is light and dark, daybreak and nightfall. Every increment is simply a matter of light meeting surface.

The physics of light reveals a harmony in nature that can easily be meaningful. As for me, I'm a lifelong wilderness advocate, having first read about conservation at roughly the age of eight. I was probably among the very few in elementary school to whom "The Happy Wanderer" really spoke. I have gone to the wild to sift for art images, to gain solace and refreshment. I'm more comfortable, fascinated, and at home sitting by a creek than I am in a room of fine furniture. Yet it's dicey looking to extract philosophy and meaning from every element of nature. The mechanisms of predators and prey, when scrutinized seriously, trouble and sadden me. I can't find a meaning there that's consistent with my worldview in which compassion towards all beings plays the main role. I do know that predators, top-of-the-food-chain characters, keep the ecosystems in balance. But this way is still a mystery and paradox with no solution: I can't explain or assign purpose to the eating of animals by other animals. It's at odds with all ethical systems I go by. Indeed, the actions of some parasitic insects have been the basis for works of horror fiction. These are things I keep suspended at the back of my consciousness lest they intrude on everyday thought and horrify me.

Nevertheless, I also know that in the world as we know it, there are many times and places when human groups could not have survived if the rodent population had gone unchecked by cats and other carnivores. And animals do not have the same choices we humans do about their eating habits; in most cases they cannot conceptualize compassion and observation of true altruistic behavior in animals is rare, though not unknown (exceptionally good care of their young is an instinctive survival technique), and they should never be blamed for being precisely what nature makes them. I respect and accept carnivores as natural and magnificent beings, and I understand that cats, for instance, are obligate carnivores who must be fed meat. Case closed. I keep these little predators and I feed them according to what they need, canned and kibbled carnage, while trying to minimize any chances they have to prey on ambient wildlife. I'm crazy about my little carnivores, but in contrast to the beauty of the wilderness and the beauty and grace of the cat itself, I find no philosophy or relief in cats' rather gruesome natural feeding habits. This drastic and mysterious contrast with regard to cats leaves me puzzled, but comes as no surprise. Cats are innately mysterious and contradictory.

The facts about light and color, however, do evoke meanings for me. They suggest that everything under the sun is intrinsic to the whole and every component is interdependent upon the other, mosaic and connected, a natural harmony. Nature's palette is totally inclusive; all are important, everything joins, everything works together, and that's how beauty is made. So I have now laid all my color chips on the table. No permutation along the continuum of light and dark and color is "wrong." All are components of our world and universe. Everything on earth is a part of the visual feast that nature provides.

In 1666, Sir Isaac Newton was the first to say that all colors are found in white light and not added by the prism, as was generally believed. (An old term for the prism was "fool's Paradise," according to Phillip Ball in *Bright Earth*.[18]) Newton separated the white light through the glass prism into its spectrum of colors and back again to white using a lens and a second prism.[19] He designed the first color circle by joining the two ends of the spectrum. The color circle became the basis for most of the color theories to follow, along with the systems for placing colors together in the most harmonizing and pleasing way. Newton is also well-known for inventing calculus, describing gravity, and the laws of motion.

It's widely reported that Newton also invented the cat flap, though usually without citing any primary sources for this information. Dr. Photon first told me this forty-eight years ago, meaning it's likely a common anecdote in the scientific world. It had to have come out of Bill's experience studying science at UA and not from cat enthusiasts, since there were none around him at that time. The cat flap would be a stellar accomplishment, if true. On the Internet, many different versions of the story have turned up: Newton's light experiments were conducted in the attic where there was only one window, and he needed a blacked-out room to control the ambient light while he directed the beam of light through the prism. His cat wanted to enter the room and kept nudging the door open, letting the light in and therefore ruining the experiments. To allow the cat free passage in and out, Newton cut a hole in the doorway and secured a piece of felt to the top. Problem solved.[20] The cat was evidently named Spitface, according to *Cat World UK*,[21] although recently around the web you see Spithead.[22] Those are two aptly descriptive but a little prosaic and unflattering names for a lady cat!

While some old European houses had holes to allow cats access, Newton was the first to use a flap. When the cat had kittens, he cut smaller holes with small flaps for them. He had many cats and enjoyed watching them play, according to some now-vanished Internet sources. Nothing is written about what happened when Spitface, as any cat might, took a swat at the prism or decided that the single beam of sunlight was the place to settle for a snooze! I might speculate that Newton's cat, or cats, not only wanted Newton's company, but also recognized important work and immediately gravitated to it, just like mine have always done. (There's a cat on the papers I'm typing this first draft from right now!) This great scientist not only enlightened us on the nature of light and color, but benefited many cats and their people by designing the cat flap. This story shows us that there is no problem with animals that cannot be solved by applying a little thought and benign effort.

Or so the story went, until I encountered the Newton Project. This group at the Imperial College London is engaged in the enormous task of placing all of Newton's writings on the Internet, as well as many biographical writings about him by his contemporaries. John Young was kind enough to respond to my email about the story, and it turns out he had never even heard it. Worse, he'd never encountered it in any of the pertinent sources, and in his opinion it's fiction.[23] These are the folks in the position to know, though I'm a little sad to say it. I hate to be the one to break it to the world of cat enthusiasts, and it's a bit like telling physicists that Newton didn't discover gravity or laws of motions or make a better telescope. But the cat flap invention does seem unlikely without a solid, written source somewhere. I like to see history written truthfully, even if it's more charming otherwise. I haven't been able to run down any information on how this story got started, but it is fairly widespread. When I've searched "Issac Newton cat flap" over the years, there's a multitude of entries. These include an abundance of cat websites on both sides of the pond, trivia websites, as well as websites of a few science museums. In *Catlore*, Desmond Morris notes Newton as being the inventor of the cat flap, and in *Secrets of the Cat*, Barbara Holland lists him among famous cat lovers in history.

However, one might hold out a glimmer of hope with such an elaborate anecdote, and say, "where there's smoke, there's fire." In "The Chronology of Ancient Kingdoms Amended," Newton writes that "he condemns all oppression, and every kind of cruelty, even to brute beasts,"[24] which is certainly a worthy sentiment and advanced for those times in which animals were so tragically mistreated. I also encountered a story that states Newton had a dog named Diamond, who turned a lighted candle over on a table and burned up some of his papers. But at least one biography casts doubt on the veracity of this story, too, and to further undermine popular historical anecdotes, some sources are expressing doubt regarding the story that the theory of gravity was inspired by an apple falling from a tree. So I must reluctantly give up this perfect cat flap anecdote as probable fiction, and marvel at the way stories and myths come into being and are widely believed over the years. It makes a great story, which is the likely reason it has became so widespread. A charming legend wins over plain facts every time. The anecdote fit my book perfectly, and yet I'm doubting it in the interest of accuracy. As I've often said, truth is mangier than fiction.

Two biographies of Newton indicate he did not keep cats or dogs at all. However, an 1827 memoir by someone who knew Newton at Trinity, J.M.F. Wright, reported the story of the invention of the cat flap: "Whether this account be true or false, indisputably true is that there are in the door to this day two plugged holes of the proper dimensions for the respective egresses of cat and kitten."[25]

Holes in buildings for cats to enter grain storage spaces have been used for a long time in rural areas and still persist in a few of those places in Europe today. There is even a mention of this in the 14th Century, in Geoffrey Chaucer's *Canterbury Tales*. "The Miller's Tale" describes someone looking into a house through a hole made for cat use.[26] The wildest cat flap account I have found is from Victoria Finlay's *The Natural History of the Palette*. It's about the English artist JMW Turner, who made a flap for his seven Manx cats by tearing a painting.[27] Many sources mention Turner's Manx cats, and several indicate that the first written reference to Manx cats in history, in 1810, was about Turner's cats.[28]

Color through the cat eye

Light shines, full of oscillating colors ready to be absorbed and reflected, falling on the cats of the world, enhancing them for human viewing. Derived from the basic tabby variations of their ancestors, the randomly breeding domestic cats' coats now come in a luscious proliferation of colors, always beautifully reshuffled and varied by differing patterns.

Light serves cats, too. Their vision differs from human vision. Cats can distinguish only a limited number of colors, but their eyes make much more efficient use of light than ours do. Our eyes don't absorb all the light that enters. Cats have a layer at the back of their eyes called the tapetum lucidum that reflects all light taken in back to the retina, maximizing use of the total light that enters their eyes. This helps them see in low light situations, hunting at twilight and at night. Paul E. Miller, DVM, details several ways the cat's eye fine-tunes its vision in "Vision in Animals, What Do Cats and Dogs See?" The tapetum can change the wavelengths of the blue rays, increasing their effect upon rhodopsin, a light-sensitive component of the eyes, therefore causing evening and night skies to appear brighter to the cat and making the objects stand out more. Due to respective positioning, the tapetum lucidum can lighten the ground view, and the tapetum nigrum can lessen the glare when the sky is bright.[29]

In *A Cat is Watching*, Roger Caras states that cats can also see ultraviolet light and possibly other parts of the spectrum that we cannot.[30] But they cannot see in complete darkness, as is often believed; they just make better use of available light than humans can.[31] They need one-sixth of the light we do to equal our daylight vision, according to Jeffrey Masson in *The Nine Emotional Lives of Cats*.[32] With other advantages, such as better peripheral vision than ours,[33] cats don't need to see color well, and they do not require color vision to hunt at night.[34]

For a long time it was believed that cats only saw grays,[35,36] but according to Morris and Caras, it has been proven that they can perceive the following color differences: red from green, red from blue, red from gray, green from blue, green from gray, blue from gray, yellow from blue, and yellow from gray; questions still remain as to whether they can tell red from yellow.[37,38]

However, experts don't always agree. According to Stephen Budiansky, studies show that cats have only two kinds of cone cells. Those cells respond most to green and blue. According to this theory, cats only have two-color vision and will see everything as green or blue.[39] Budiansky goes on to note that for nocturnal animals, seeing well in low light is more important; more retina space is devoted to these kind of receptors, the rod cells, rather than to the cone cells sensitive to color. Rod cells register light and detect differences in black, gray, and white, but not color. Rod cells mean greater visual acuity in low light situations. Cats have lost color receptivity in favor of seeing well at dawn, dusk, and night. Cats also see less color than other mammals with two-color vision, including dogs.[40]

Budiansky also notes that European wildcats have more cones,[41] which is of interest to me since I'm always one to try to sort out what separates domestic cats from their close wild relatives. Humans, some primates, and birds have three-color vision, which is important to animals that eat fruits and need to see hidden predators. Birds, reptiles, and fish often have three-color vision; some fish and birds have four-color; they can see into the infrared. Early mammals co-existing with dinosaurs had to adapt to nocturnal activity and likely evolved away from three-color vision at that time.[42]

Jeffrey Moussaieff Masson also notes that green and blue are the colors cats see, and some species of cats that hunt in bright daylight have more cones in their eyes than domestic cats and therefore have full-color vision.[43] Masson also states that newborn domestic cats have a potential for a wider range of color vision. This unneeded ability does not develop, but he notes there is some data suggesting feral cats (domestic cats that are born or become unsocialized to humans and lead largely outdoor lives) see more colors than their domestic-living counterparts.[44]

Most of the literature appears to favor the view that cats cannot see colors in the red range and that these colors appear to them as grays or greens. A project by Nickolay Lamm, in consultation with Kerry L. Retring, DVM, DACVO, of the All Animal Eye Clinic; Dr. D.J. Haeussler of The Animal Eye Institute; and the Opthamology Group at Penn Vet, developed photos supposedly color-adjusted to the way cats would see the scenes.[45]

All these sources support the idea that cats cannot see red, and that is the view I believed to be correct. *BUT, wait a minute, hold it!* One day we were at a friend's house playing with her cats, and later I had an idle thought: What about that red dot laser, anyway? A host of cats respond to it, so much so it's the subject of Internet humor. How do cats see and chase that red dot if they can't see red?

My own first thought was that cats respond to the movement; their eyes are better at seeing movement than ours are. More review of the literature suggests that their exquisite dim-light vision means they can better distinguish varying shades of grays than we can anyway; therefore, it's likely they can see the dot even if it appears to be another shade of gray to them. Or, it seems likely they can detect differences in luminosity, independent of color. That plus the fact they hunt because they see small animal movement explains cat ability to see and chase the red dot. That's my opinion but it isn't fixed; I just wanted to introduce this provocative question. There is always puzzlement and mystery about cats, and that's fitting.

As I write this, I sit with Bud the Editing Cat here in the forest, looking out the window on a blue-green day. Bud stays indoors now as all our cats do, but he daydreams. "I can see out well there today, it's all very sharp," I imagine he says. "It'd be a good day to hunt."

"Too bright," I answer. "Better day to snooze."

Color is a visual feast for us, but cats just need to keep the chow coming while they decorate the landscape for our aesthetic sense. Cats' eyes, admitting six times as much light as human eyes, are sun-sensitive and will narrow to thin slits to control the amount of incoming rays in bright sunlight. We see much better in bright sunlight than cats. Their eyes are perfect for prowling the night, the dawn, the dusk. A sunny patch is a place for a cat to sit things out and doze happily. In fact, according to Wendy Christensen in *Outwitting Cats, Tips, Tricks, and Techniques for Persuading the Felines in Your Life That What You Want is Also What They Want*, warm sunlight has such a definite calming effect on cats that a sunny room can reduce inter-cat tensions.[46] Cats seem to seek naps in sunshine, maybe for the very reason that they can't hunt well in that kind of light, so to them it means time to rest and renew energy for pounces when the rays are softer.

In later years I began to question whether the use of flash photography was harmful to cats' eyes or at the least annoying; after all, it certainly can be to humans! House feline eyes take in six times the light ours do, so it seems reasonable to think that the same jolt we feel from a camera flash might be more intense for them. But since their eyes have the tapetum lucidum mechanism for scattering light around within the eyeball to derive maximum illumination from the light, does that diffuse or intensify the impact of the bright flash? One of my cats in the 2000s would always turn away from the camera, and that started me thinking. I've changed entirely to available-light photography when it comes to cats. Ferocious regional sunlight is enough, but other techniques can enhance indoor light. For soft illumination without flash, lights can be set up and the beams bounced off reflective surfaces. A handheld, discretely directed flash can also be employed.

The tapetum lucidum also makes cats' eyes glow in the dark. According to Barbara Holland in *Secrets of the Cat*, for this reason the Egyptians believed their eyes held the light of the sun, preserving it so that it would return the next day.[47] Though not scientific, it's a poetic expression of the cat as an integral part of the earth's cycles, guarding the bounty of the sun. Holland states that *mau*, an early Egyptian word for cat, also means seeing or light.[48]

As for the exact origin of the application of this word to cats by the ancient Egyptians, I think Holland makes a good case for the simplest explanation when she describes a small animal coming to the door of a home saying *mau, mau, mau.*[49] Many of us cat people have experienced that routine ourselves repeatedly.

Ligeia, our first and most mysterious black cat

To indulge in a flight of fancy for a moment: a cat, with its eye for detail and exquisite focus, built for precision prey capture, would make a great cinematographer. The only problem would be that the scenes would be underlit for human viewers. You can't expect a crepuscular hunter with eyes that make six times the use of light that ours do to know how to light a scene for human vision. You would really need a dog in charge of lighting. The one exception to this might be noir lighting. Cats might well ace the black-and-whites and general dark atmosphere of noir. On a similar note, cats would be bad Fauvist or Impressionist painters, but they'd finesse the Ashcan School with darker palettes, especially if they are alley cats who are already hanging out at some of the best *plein air* locations for Ashcan.

The world of color as used and understood in the arts goes to the core functioning of light in this world and reveals why the rainbow has always been such a powerful symbol in so many ways: of hope, of environmental healing, of inclusiveness. So I have learned from my later studies of color theory that our first black kitten was not as hueless as we believed way back then. I like the creepy stories of Edgar Allan Poe and Bill is a fan of "Frankenstein" and "Dracula" movies, so I named this little thing Ligeia, after a woman in the Poe story of the same name.

The first wife of the protagonist, Ligeia had hair "blacker than the raven wings of midnight,"[50] which seemingly described our kitten. She was knowledgeable and intense, which were cat-like qualities. But Cat Ligeia was not Storybook Ligeia, who was determined to come back from her premature grave to her love-obsessed husband, even if she had to snatch the second wife's body to do it. It's macabre stuff, and the kitten was not named for that but rather for her dark hair and eyelashes. Cat Ligeia was a cuddlepuss who required snuggling and nurturing of her bright, playful kitten spirit.

Storybook Ligeia assisted her husband in his metaphysical and transcendental studies, and it could be said that cats, inadvertently and guilelessly, in and of themselves, do propel us to contemplation of mysteries. William Blake thought so, writing in "The Tyger:" "Tyger, tyger, burning bright, In the forests of the night, What immortal hand or eye, Shaped thy fearful symmetry?" Blake uses the tiger as the inspiration for ultimate questions. In that sense, Ligeia's name fit.

Over the long run, time has made recollections of our earlier cats murkier than those of our cats who came later, just as the events have been partly forgotten by the protagonist in Poe's story. But as in the story, these obscurities do not detract from the intensity of the affection we hold for these long-departed animals. The memories have to be contemplated up and duct-taped together, but they come straight from the heart. Cat Ligeia was all sweetness and all natural. In those days I just liked going against the grain, and I had a literary interest in the use of supernatural concepts in fiction. The kitten whose name came from a book was prancing a display of the cat's natural ways throughout the house, and my lifelong study of natural history was rekindled.

I probably identified with black cats, too, as well as with fictional "raven-haired" women, because of my own dark hair, complete with extremely pale skin and green eyes, inherited from my half-Irish great-grandmother, who had similar coloration, just blacker and greener. I cannot recall what color Cat Ligeia's eyes were, but I think they were green. Years later, I looked up the origin of the name Ligeia and found it to be from Greek, derived from *ligys*, meaning "clear-voiced, shrill, and whistling," and also the name of one of the legendary Sirens.[51] I do not know if Poe took the name from this source, but I haven't seen it anywhere else. Ligeia certainly had the vocal and singing abilities that all cats do.

The joys of living with cats began to unfurl like tight fiddleheads unrolling into fern fronds of spring, all over us and our home. Kitten Ligeia was photographed playing in a bag in my lap, being cradled in Bill's hands, and nuzzling the face of a visiting friend. She must have quickly learned our faces, because once when Bill walked out of the bathroom with shaving cream on his face, she got spooked at this radical new look and ran from him as if she didn't know him. We kept a bottle of bubble blower on the table and sometimes when we blew bubbles, Ligeia would chase the nacreous-gleaming spheres. When she caught one and it popped, she would jump back, arched and with her fur pouffed out, at the little splatter it made. We never observed any harmful effects from this, but now, years later, I know so much more about cats and their extreme sensitivity to so many chemicals and substances, so I would never again present soap bubbles for kitties to chase and contact. She'd chase those fluffy seedballs made by dandelions, too, and pounce them into frilly airborne swirls.

Ligeia had come to us in 1969 in the Florida Panhandle, part of the self-named "Redneck Riviera." Hurricane Camille headed straight for us but veered elsewhere at the last minute; we had wind and raging surf but escaped the worst impact. Those were the days when air conditioning in rental houses was rare, when we would go out to the beach every afternoon and then to a local bookstore every evening, partly for the purpose of cooling off. The summer had been built around sugary sand, seabirds and sea animals, waves, a near-disastrous encounter with an undertow, that weirdly cosmopolitan little bookstore, inexpensive abalone jewelry, the moon landing, heat, and our beautiful black kitten.

That year was eventful for me. I had surgery for the first time, dropped out of the University of Alabama, saw the moon landing at a friend's house since we had no television of our own, foolishly walked out on a pier swaying from the boiling waves of Camille's lesser edge, saw a moon rock and the Pacific Ocean and the Berkeley campus and was in the second People's Park march singing the chorus of "Hey Jude" in the streets during a trip to California, flew in an airplane for the first time, got married outside on a warm evening in December in the magical southeastern twilight, saw Janis Joplin in concert at UA, re-enrolled at the university, and got Ligeia, my first-ever cat. (On the plane ride back to Alabama, science fiction plus a preoccupation with what might be "out there" in space helped me to think outside the box and win 2nd prize — a pack of cards with the National Airlines insignia — in a contest to calculate the plane's arrival time using math factors like wind speed, etc. Second prize was awarded to the answer that was the farthest from correct. I had answered "19 o'zorans.")

Back at college in Alabama, we still had no air conditioning, and Ligeia grew to be an elegant animal. She had a beautifully squared-off muzzle, and she was sleek, shiny, lithe, and on the petite side. She moved lightly around the house, in the cat way. I was tall and thin, and one day as I stood in the bathroom in front of the mirror, almost before I knew it, a willowy six-month-old Ligeia swiftly climbed me like I was a tree until she reached my shoulders, where she stood and posed, pleased with herself.

We listened to Bob Dylan, Jethro Tull, Beatles and Stones, John Coltrane, and also Mozart, Stravinsky, Goose Creek Symphony, and harpsichord pieces. Ligeia would glide through the house when we had visitors. "She's moving to the music," Larry declared as the Grateful Dead played.

We picked pecans off the ground from the surrounding trees, and I sat and cracked them with Ligeia on my lap. Old Victorian houses in town were all split up into apartments in those days, along with smaller homes behind the larger houses that we surmised may have been servants' dwellings in previous times. We lived in just such a place in an alley, with a one-half after the street number, and Ligeia had free run of the apartment and the neighborhood outdoors. She was a true alley cat! This was a town of trees and a foliage barrage of shrubs, so it was at least a bit of a jungle for the cat to enjoy.

In present times, we've learned to keep cats inside for their safety, but this was the early '70s, and we were young. We balked at the idea of restricting the cat's freedom to enjoy the outside. We were in an alley between minor streets, which reduced the chance of Ligeia encountering fast traffic. Ideas have now changed, but other friends thought the same way, and most pet cats were indoor/outdoor at the time. I recall a neighbor across from us who rejoiced when he noticed his cat eliminating outside, therefore reducing his litterbox work. Nobody would think of confining a cat to the indoors in those days. It was rather like present-day Britain where for the most part, with lesser traffic in neighborhoods organized differently than those in the United States, cats are thought to be entitled to indoor/outdoor access.

But time flows seamlessly onward as ripples flatten out and we forget the very different texture of how things used to be. For a long time, Ligeia did well going in and out. It was in this apartment that we encountered a repairman who would not come inside to work on the house until we had removed the black cat from the room. For me it was a shock; before then I had not realized anyone actually believed such nonsense. At an estate sale, we were shocked, to read a Sunday supplement booklet from the *Birmingham News* dated October 31, 1954, with a black cat on the front cover and a line of text stating that "he is not bad luck." Inside the booklet there was a note that the cat had a white spot, which "exempted" him from the bad-luck label. The booklet went on to say the cat's name was Jet, and his owner thought he was good luck. They were trying to fight superstition, yet they felt they had to use the white patch of fur to soften the message enough to avoid offending the part of their audience that believed the old bologna.

Our policy regarding kittens was different in 1969. We didn't feel right about neutering animals and interfering with their natural lives. So we didn't get Ligeia spayed, which I deeply regret now. But again, times were different and there wasn't as much public awareness about the terrible overpopulation of cats and dogs or about the horrible truth of so few animals in shelters being adopted. Few people were really aware that the animals who weren't adopted were actually killed. Few people spayed and neutered back then. Giving away kittens and puppies successfully was so routine it was hard to conceive of anyone actually needing to take animals to shelters.

It was the Stone Age of cat-keeping compared with present-day advances. Cat care in urban and suburban households was much like farm-cat care in that cats came in and went out as they pleased. In the non-farm model where cats were pets, we humans were the doorkeepers. Our policies on all of this are totally reversed in the present day, and I am a strong advocate of indoor cat homes and spaying/neutering. When viewed from today's perspective, it's important to realize that ways and thinking really were different in earlier eras. Changing the course of ingrained cultures can take monumental jumps and efforts. My story is in several senses a cautionary tale. One caution is to get some perspective, instead of being "judgy" on reflex. Another caution is to come along for this history ride, but "do as we say, not as we did" in those earlier, less-enlightened times.

We placed ads in the newspaper and always gave away Ligeia's kittens to pleasant people, usually young couples, students, or close friends we knew well, those we felt would give them good homes. Everyone who had cats in those days reported success in giving away kittens, and we trusted the people who came to adopt them. In those times we perceived far less meanness and irresponsibility and much more essential goodness than we see today. This may well have been our slant and maybe we just didn't know enough about people. It was certainly true that our immediate friends and countercultural community had good hearts. We didn't have much contact outside of our small circle, but when we did, we had developed a knack for detecting the kind people who would always do right by an animal. We never took any animals to the pound; we were always willing to work to find the right people, the salt of the earth, the hearts of gold, for our giveaway kittens. The problem with that old way of doing things is that, of course, no matter who it was, absolutely no one spayed and neutered in those days. And people who did take animals to the pound had a mistaken notion that their really cute animals would always be adopted.

In later years for awhile when I learned of stray black kittens and saw ads for kittens in the local newspaper, I felt guilty, and I fancifully wondered if we were responsible for every proliferation of black cats around town. That's not realistic, but it pained me to think that I contributed in any miniscule way to cat-population problems. But that was the way things were in the old days, even among responsible pet owners, and there were economic reasons, too. Spay or neuter surgery costs were about equal to the cost of a month's groceries back then, way out of our budget. We were skipping routine dental care because the funds just weren't there. There were no low-cost spay/neuter programs.

There are always those who are inclined to say that these now-antiquated ways existed only in the "unenlightened" South. But in that era, early '70s-ish, I saw people give away kittens on the campus of the University of California at Berkeley, a place generally regarded as glowing and enlightened, with far less scrutiny towards potential adopters than we practiced. I assume they subscribed to a belief and knowledge of their community somewhat similar to ours, that the students and young countercultural persons gathered there were all good people, and the kittens were therefore all guaranteed good homes with those taking them. (After staying briefly in California, when I came back to Alabama, the southern accents were strangely refreshing and gave me an odd feeling of relief. I wasn't sure then if I wanted to always stay in the South, with its numerous flaws. Yet there was something about the place, and some people who come to the South from other areas — think best spooky voice, with drawl if you like — never get back out. Do I hear a *muhahahaha?* Actually, you can usually find people like us living happily and quietly on some pleasant road.)

Ligeia's first suitor was a convivial and splendid fellow, a black neighborhood tomcat named Freaky, and her first litter was all black. There were five beauties, and I began handling the kittens very early to begin socializing them, at two or three days. When I first began, their eyes weren't open but they sensed the approach of my hand, and they all made soft hissing sounds, kitten sized. That miniature *hiss-hiss-hiss* was by far the cutest thing I have ever seen and heard in my life! When I got that response I would quickly withdraw so as not to spook the little things. After awhile I'd try again.

It was only after the hissing stopped that I actually tried light finger pettings on tiny kitten noggins. Soon they were enjoying being stroked, and they all became people-friendly kittens. However, I probably moved in too early and too boldly in front of Ligeia, although she never objected. I have since heard of mother cats attacking people over kitten issues, usually feral cats but sometimes snuggly lap cats have done it too. At the very least, the moms may relocate the nest if the humans lionize the kittens. Although she did move them around, Ligeia was amazingly tolerant of our attentions to her kittens and must have had great trust in us.

I have observed and heard tell of momcats moving kittens after a few weeks even with complete privacy. In the wild, it's a stratagem that throws predators off the track. I also think that when the kittens are a few weeks old and near crawling stage, momcats become somewhat anxious and become more "paws-on" as this new life era begins. If one of the fuzzy little toddling kittens strayed too far and felt lost, they would cry out in fear. Ligeia became particularly attentive whenever this happened. She was clearly in kitten-defense mode. A human needed to be careful not to hover too close to the marooned kitten and become associated, in the queen's mind, with the kitten's *I'm lost and scared* mews. This is an important time to handle kittens to socialize them, but use caution.

I must admit, it was a delight to experience Ligeia's kittens. Of course I would, years later, come to absolutely believe that cats should be spayed and neutered. I regret denying cats their normal courtship lives, but population problems are just too overwhelming. Desmond Morris, in his 1987 book *Catlore*, advocates cutting or tying the females' fallopian tubes and doing vasectomies on the males as an alternative to traditional surgeries.[52] Fallopian tube/vasectomy methods for cat birth-control are finally being introduced in the United States and are being suggested as a better method of population control, at least for feral cats. This has caused a storm of controversy, as there are advocates who believe this does nothing to eliminate the fighting behavior between tomcats that can result in wounds and other problems associated with aggression amongst outdoor cat groups.

When Ligeia's kittens were about three weeks of age and starting to crawl around, one kitty's hind legs weren't supporting him properly; they were splayed out flat behind him, and he couldn't move much. We took him to the vet, who was perplexed as to what to do, and we discussed building a sling to support his little undergirth for short times each day, in hopes this would encourage the legs to grow and develop properly. Bill began plans to make the sling to go under the little belly, but within a few days the problem had worked itself out, and the kitten was standing. His gait was a little different, but he began walking and playing, and tusseling with his siblings, and he was equally active. If this kitty had never been able to walk, though, he would have always had a home with us. In recent times I have become aware of other kittens with this condition, called "swimmer's legs" in early kittenhood. In the reports I have seen, it does generally improve with time, like our kitty's did.

Ligeia and kittens were well-supplied with kibble when the kittens started eating solid food, but being well-fed does not stop cats from hunting and teaching hunting skills to their young. Ligeia went to work bringing an assortment of mangled wildlife to the kittens. It's always shocking and disturbing when your kitty acts on instinct and kills wildlife, but this comes with the territory of life with cats allowed outside. (It's yet another good reason to keep cats inside, and we would later come around to that viewpoint.) Ligeia proved to be creative and stealthy, returning from one of her summer forays with her chops gripping a steak (grilled rare) that she'd snatched from someone's plate of freshly cooked barbeque. At that point, with catmouth all over it and with the rightful owners nebulous and likely enraged, there was nothing to do but let the cats have it. The captured quarry was almost as big as Ligeia was, and she and the kittens chowed down big time in the warm silver light of an evening perfect for grilling out.

After seven or eight weeks, Ligeia's sweetness and devotion to the kittens changed; she began to slap at them and growl at them too. "What in the world?" we asked the vet, mystified. It wasn't unusual, he said, for the mom-cat to become hostile to the kittens after the seventh or eighth week, but even that didn't prepare us for what happened next. One morning I saw her calling to the kittens to follow her, which wasn't unusual; she'd done it every time she'd come home with something for the kittens to eat, and we went on to class.

A few hours later when we returned, Ligeia was there, but no kittens. We began a frantic search of the neighborhood. Ligeia, we now realized, had meowed to them to follow her so she could lose them! We found them all within the block, fortunately. Two were found together in the access hallway of a duplex, another two at a different location, and one lonesome kitten had been left by himself a few back yards down the block. The message was clear from the cat: time for these kids to go off to college. We quickly contacted the friends who had said they wanted kittens, and in the end we kept one, a longhaired boy who had become Bill's lap-fungus kitty. Bill named him Yeti, the Tibetan name for the Abominable Snowman, a.k.a. Sasquatch or Bigfoot. Yeti would sit in Bill's lap while he studied at the kitchen table.

I regret to say Ligeia had more litters after that. We always found homes for the kittens. Taking them to the pound was not something we would have done, ever. She became the Earth Mother of black cats in town. Someone living nearby owned a big black-and-white tom named Luther. He was a real terror when he encountered other toms, screaming out horrendous sounds I didn't know cats could make, causing us to run out the door to try to intervene. Ligeia's second litter was all black and white, little "tuxedo" cats with the white gloves and vests. They all went to good homes with friends.

Hippie kitties in "Little Haight-Ashbury"

California was the golden and shimmering counterpoint in the counter-cultural imagination, the solution to the alienation, ennui, and angst of living in U. S. mainstream cultures, especially for Southern hippies. We graduated from UA in 1971, I with a BA in English, and Bill with a BS in Electrical Engineering. The plan was to go to California to live, driving ourselves in Bill's old, black Ford car. We didn't have cat carriers and the car wasn't air-conditioned, so for the journey Bill installed screen from a discarded door over the car windows so they could be rolled down, but the cats could not jump out.

Before heading out West, we drove to Atlanta for a vacation, leaving the cats in the care of a neighbor. On the Atlanta streets, the screened car windows raised some eyebrows, and at least one favorable comment was yelled after us as we drove along. When we came back to Tuscaloosa to stop in, pack, and complete other details before we went on our way, we just never left for California. Suddenly it seemed like a long way off and full of strangers. We were somewhat eccentric and quirky, nerds who actually read books for pleasure, but we had found a group of like-minded people in Tuscaloosa. The counterculture was thriving in this Deep South locale. The section of town we lived in was known as "Little Haight-Ashbury." There was a vegetarian food co-op within these blocks in an old house; you could buy healthy foods in bulk, and their granola mix, sold in jars, had labels that said "Good Shit." Our friend Kay originated both the mix of grains and the name.

There was a bar downtown we all frequented that welcomed anyone who was non-mainstream, though a few mainstreamers went in, too. There were paintings by local artists all over the walls, and the place hosted art shows; some of my own art hung there briefly. Robert Register wrote "Eat cornbread, raise hell" on the wall, a statement that might could be taken as the motto for all the bar's times. (Robert indicates that this is not to be confused with another slogan, "Raise hell. Eat cornbread," that has appeared in some of what he calls "country music/tractor rap videos."[53]) Outside in the courtyard behind the bar was a brick wall destined to be painted purple. We even had a coffee house of sorts, a nightspot in a trailer where local musicians played and local poets read their work. On a memorable evening when an English-instructor friend had been reading and taking requests, I asked for Shelley's "Ode to the West Wind," my all-time favorite poetic work.

We'd made our apartment walls purple; others had old mantelpieces painted lime green. Then there was that five-minutes-to-the-wilderness thing. Those were the days of California Dreamin'[54] and I had spent some time out there. But aside from the lovely ambiance of musicians playing live in the streets in that Western state, the main difference between the two scenes, to me, was that out there you had to ride for an hour or two to get away from the city and into the wilds. We had a variety of entertainment come through Alabama, too. Dionne Warwick had graciously autographed an album for me when she had given a concert here; Bob Dylan, Jimi Hendrix, Janis Joplin, the Czech Philharmonic, Jethro Tull, Sun Ra — they all played here or within driving distance. I remain astonished at having met Andy Warhol in Tuscaloosa, though I've heard since that he visited Birmingham twice in later years, the steel town connected to his city of origin, Pittsburgh, Pennsylvania.

It was hot as blazes the day we'd planned to leave; as we stood in the yard looking at the car, sun glaring down on us, our resolve just melted. We just never reached "escape velocity," as they say around here of those who attempt, and fail, to leave the area. Now when I muse about what might have been and "roads not taken," I wonder how different life would have been. It was 1971, on the cusp of the computer revolution, and Bill had an electrical-engineering degree. Would we have been Silicon Valley dotcom millionaires if we'd have gone on to California?

Certainly we would have had access to a culture with a higher head-count of like-minded individuals. We would have been spared a certain amount of provincialism and bad old attitudes still lingering in those years. But by staying and being who we were, by living differently, we helped to shape the culture of where we are today, as every individual does. Staying also meant we experienced and became participants in the Raudelunas Art Collective. The earliest phase, a musical group of friends called "The Blue Denim Deals Without The Arms" expanded into vocal improvisations with Bill and I in our apartment, in the presence of Ligeia and Yeti. Raudelunas was the basis of an adventurous non-mainstream art scene and is now the subject of a film; and is also being studied for a book by an art historian. Around this same time more and more of the liberal and progressive people were deciding to stay. What we may have lacked in numbers, we made up for in commitment and intensity. We'd given up our apartment in anticipation of the cross-country move, so a friend agreed to take care of Ligeia and Yeti for us while we went to stay on another friend's houseboat until we could find a new place to live.

That summer we stayed partly at the houseboat on a slough off the river and partly with the friend taking care of the cats. Across the slough was a forested "island," a glorified sandbar, if you will, between us and the actual river. Having just learned to swim, I used to jump into the slough and swim out a short way before coming back. When I caught sight of a line of moving ruffles in the water, Bill said, "Snakes!" Another snake surfaced in the short channel right under the plank that led from the ground out to the boat. That meant instant disenchantment for me with both river swimming and house-boat living. Soon we spent most of our time back in town. I do have to hand it to the UA swimming instructors, though. They had turned me from a per-son fearful of water into someone who would jump into a river full of snakes.

In late summer we moved into an apartment that was in a big house on the main thoroughfare of town, set far enough back from the street so that we continued to let the cats out. Ligeia had at least one litter here. A friend brought over an orphan kitten she had found, and we tried to slip it in amongst our momcat's own to get it fed. This worked briefly until Ligeia stirred, smelled and saw the intruder, and began to hiss.

There were many students and people about our age living in this neighborhood. A friend a few houses away who had a tame opossum used to bring it outside so it could hang by its tail from a branch, and we used to go out and admire it. How he came to have raised this possum we cannot recall, even if we once knew. It's likely the possum was an orphan. Whereas nowadays I would advocate taking all orphaned and/or injured wildlife over to the state wildlife rehabilitation center, back in those days we had no such service.

One evening we played some of my John Coltrane records for some of our musician friends. They had never heard "The Father, The Son, and The Holy Ghost," from the *Meditations* album. Roger Hagerty said the musicians were actually talking to each other. Everyone was taken with the music. They were already moving in the direction of improvisation and hearing this master work was mind boggling.

Sadly, Yeti became ill. The vets could not figure out why, and when they X-rayed him, they could not see his intestines. Slowly he was wasting away, with greatly reduced activity at times, but still going strong at others. We did not want to give up on him, since he appeared only subdued and not in distress; he was still eating, cheerful, and affectionate. We had him neutered so he would no longer roam off looking for tomcat fights. Bill tended and nurtured him, and he lived another three years. I have wondered recently if he had FIP, feline infectious peritonitis, before it was well known, but if so, Ligeia never caught it from him.

When we moved into the neighborhood we had seen no black cats, but while we lived there, we began to notice a bloom of the achromatic felines. Only half-joking, we began to say we were responsible for that. The same thing happened in the next neighborhood we lived in, and even years later, if we drove through the old neighborhoods and saw black cats, we felt pangs of largely imagined responsibility for increasing the cat population. Ligeia seemed sadly mythic, the mother of all black cats in our town. The truth since learned is that the feline population boom was more extensive than we realized back in those days. Many of our friends, as well as other young graduates from the university, favored black cats as pets. Black is also one of the most common colors of cats in general.

In the spring of 1973 we moved again. This time we rented a whole house, and a friend roomed with us. It was a classic, older southern house with a big front porch. The street was full of student apartments in mixed antebellum and Victorian houses, ours being the latter. Although the road was well-traveled, the traffic wasn't especially fast so we felt it was safe for the cats to go outside. For a while Yeti kept going back to the old neighbor-hood, a distance of about eight blocks. Bill would go back and always find him. Yeti did settle in and remained at our new home after a time.

In our hearts for all time

Bill had entered graduate school and was trying to start a business pro-ducing sound reinforcement for live musical concerts. I was working as a secretary at first, and then as a teacher's assistant. At night, using needle-nosed pliers, I'd help build electronic circuit boards for the sound business equipment. It was a difficult pace. We were scrambling to make a scanty liv-ing; good jobs were in short supply when I graduated. When I had free time I kept up my drawing and painting. Circuit-board construction involved a screen-printed phase in those days, and when it got around town that Bill could screen print, we began to get requests to print T-shirts. We began a cottage industry that would later turn into a full-scale business. One of our bathrooms became a darkroom. There was no money to buy the equipment, so Bill built it himself from scratch in the yard. When I came home from work, I'd go to work unpacking blank shirts and stacking printed ones.

Ligeia enchanted us with more kittens. One was such a sweet little thing, with gray and orange markings, and we became especially fond of her. But we had enough cats for our circumstances at the time (now called "being at catpacity"), so we gave the tortie and all her littermates away. In those days, there seemed to be no shortage of people who wanted to adopt them, mostly young couples who came and petted the little furries gently, making *oohhing* and *aahhing* noises at the cuteness, and impressed us favorably. It was a dif-ferent world back then, and we trusted people. Bill also has a considerable instinct into character. Ligeia was nicknamed "Mama Kitty" now.

We ended up with another cat anyway. The house next door was divided into student apartments. It was three stories and the top apartment had a screened-in porch at the back. Outdoor steps led up to it. Every spring the students would all move away, to be replaced by others later when the term began again. We were so busy we were barely aware of it when a girl in the top apartment left. One day there was a kitten crying non-stop from the top porch all day, and we realized the girl had gone for good and was not coming back for the kitten. Bill went up the outdoor stairs and managed to open the porch door, which was latched from the inside. He came back carrying a black kitten, a boy, whom we immediately fed and watered, and then kept.

This animal had been left locked on the porch without food or water by the departing student. Since then we have encountered other cats abandoned by students who move off. Such end-of-school-year animal abandonment is now a big problem in college towns, but the pets are usually left outside. This one had not even been released where it might have been able to catch a bug, but instead locked in to starve. Because I can't imagine such a thing, I want to tell myself that she had arranged for someone to pick up the kitten, some-one who failed to show up. Or that having seen our cats, she thought that we would notice the kit in time to save it — which we did, fortunately — but she had only to ask us to care for him, rather than leave him to yowl his plight, no doubt terrified at being alone and without sustenance. This rocked my world as far as ever trusting persons unknown to us with animals again.

Having been caught unprepared for the arduous work of naming a cat, Bill took to calling this kitten Quelan, an old bit of South Alabama rural slang that was a fond term for "goofy country boy," sort of like the modern "doofus." I had no alternative name in mind, so this not-so-flattering name stuck. It was ironic as it was the opposite of what we thought about cats. Some of them might indeed be country boys, but they were canny country boys, whose intellects were most urbane. I had always thought the spelling was "Cullen" myself, so when I began this narrative, I looked up some of its meanings. Most sources described it as derived from an old Gaelic word, perhaps from a word for holly, or a town in Scotland, or the Irish Gaelic word for handsome or, best of all, handsome young animal.[55] That's the one I like best, and that describes our Quelan. He grew into a fine tomcat. He was affectionate and a joy to have around.

But tragedy struck. A wandering tom had shown up in the neighborhood, who came around from time to time and jumped on everyone's cats. He was a really wild outlaw of a cat, unapproachable. Contrary to what we would do now to sustain and neuter a feral, back then no one knew what to do about a cat you could not handle. He would have been welcome to eat alongside our cats if he would have stayed long enough and walked up peacefully. His tail was bent up as though it had once been broken, and our friend Cliff, who roomed with us, called him Crookshank. This wildcat had burst into our world, coming and going erratically, before we had a chance to think. *Does he or doesn't he have a home? Should we feed him? Should we try to tame him?* We were cat novices compared to our present-day knowledge and did not know then what we know now about the territorial forays of cats, and that separate feeding stations may (or may not) have dampened the aggression towards our cats. Back then, we just thought he was a mean cat.

One day Quelan was sitting on our porch when Crookshank jumped him. We heard the sound of them tangling up and Bill ran out there, with me fol-lowing. But already, instantaneously, Crookshank was chasing Quelan across the yard and then into the street — and into the path of a car. We saw Quelan get hit right in front of us. Crookshank had veered off in time to avoid the car. We both ran out to Quelan, who had been knocked to the sidewalk. I could tell he was still alive, and I was afraid to touch him for fear of worsening the injuries, but Bill knew he was gone. Bill stroked him as he died. The driver stopped to say she was sorry. It really had not been her fault. The two cats had run out with lightning-flash rapidity. There had been no time to stop. Neither could I blame Crookshank. Fighting with another cat in what he perceived as "his territory" was a natural feline behavior.

Stunned and devastated, I ran into the house and cried. We'd had Quelan for a very short while. I'd stopped taking photos during that time frame; I was exceedingly busy, and money was so tight that funds were hard to come by for film and processing. So we don't have a single picture of Quelan. I thought I would have time later for pictures. There had been no other such disasters of pet loss on that low-traffic road, and I never thought for an instant that his life would be so brief. I recall him trotting into the house so many times, rubbing on my hand while I stroked his smooth form, saying "Quelan."

Bill buried him in a quiet place, at the base of a giant pine tree.

Not long after, Yeti died of whatever it was the vets could never find. Bill buried him in the same place as Quelan. Yeti had been his special, floofer buddy of a cat.

And, one day, Ligeia never came back. Bill's grandmother had died; when he left for the funeral Ligeia tried to get in the car with him and had to be gently held off. She had never done that before. That was the last time we ever saw her. We searched and searched the neighborhood, but we never found her. I remember that for a considerable time after that, I would make Bill stop the car, so I could walk up to a black cat that had caught my eye to see if it was my black beauty, but it was never Ligeia. We came to think she may have been picked up by someone — she was an exquisite cat. If so, I hope they gave her a good home and cherished her as much as we did.

It was all too much heartbreak. Every moment with our cats had been precious but cut off far too soon. We felt we never wanted another pet. Meanwhile, there again seemed to be more black cats in the surrounding blocks than when we arrived. There was still something haunting about them; my imagination was longing for some semblance of our sweet girl, Ligeia, and our fine boys, Yeti and Quelan. Sometimes even now, passing cats of raven color have a familiar nuance about them.

Chapter 3

Neighborhood Cat Scan

We lived in that older dwelling until the summer of 1976, when our screen-printing business began to outgrow the space. We found a large house for rent in a commercial zone, with room for the business downstairs and living space upstairs. Our roommate friend moved with us, too. The neighborhood, like many in town, was a mix of rentals full of students and young working people, old mansions, a few persons who were well-off, and an empty apartment building. In the parking lot across the street from our house, which led to a small shopping plaza, we encountered some men singing a Hank Williams song one Labor Day and doing a fine job of it, too.

If I had any extra time, it was still spent drawing and writing. One day I went out and sat in the evening in the thick, gray light. Someone was playing a flute down the street. The trees looked animalistic, as though they might move of their own power. I went out and sketched some wisteria, which in repose had an oddly male look at the time. That darned wisteria with its maddening scent, making me think such things! When dusk came, the shadows cried out in their sleep, broke, and bled into the air; leaves seemed as if splattered with silver. We reach into the earth for our metaphors — at least in this town, where nature smacks us in the face every day; that's what we do to furnish the mind.

In this oddly stitched work spanning several decades, the reader will see my language changing over the years, as it did in real life. Old notes I used to scribble down have preserved some of the more lavish wording I slowly began to develop as the '80s approached.

Things were hectic in those days, frantic. Printed T-shirts began to boom. People called us day and night about shirts and also knocked on the door at all hours. We would grow to ship all over the United States, to museums, art galleries, libraries, and universities that demanded products made with the individual, hands-on care and attention to quality that we maintained. The sound production business had not succeeded and just faded away. We were so busy, and so grieving, that we gave no thought to getting another cat. Ligeia, Yeti, and Quelan had been my first cats and the first times I'd experienced cat losses; the searing pain caused emotional paralysis. Even in the whirl of work, it was daily aching and flagging spirits.

We hired good friends to work for us at first, and later some of the employees we hadn't known became good friends. In those early years, we were all a bunch of creative people "stuck" in the work-a-day world. Like myself, a few of us had given up trying to become part of mainstream artistic circles and were essentially renegade artists. Those were my days of feeling majorly alienated from ordinary life. Our eccentricity and artistic focus were sourced from and tangled with the surrounding land and people, but face-to-face it was sometimes a snarl and a snag, partly because art seemed an extravagance to many who had grown up in an economically challenged land.

Roughly speaking, I would say that new economic growth was just beginning in the late 1970s and early '80s in this university town surrounded by a countryside of agriculture, coal mining, and pulp wooding. The economy before this time may have been solid, but I wouldn't have called it versatile, or a place where artists could make a good living. When I photocopied some art at a copy place, a friendly lady told me that her daughter was an artist, too, but couldn't make a living at it.

In our workplace of outré artists, conversations were about art, music, and philosophy. Our friend Tim, a natural actor, humorist, singer, and songwriter, was never in a serious mood. If you interacted with him, you never knew who would show up — he would do Humphrey Bogart, James Cagney, Elvis, and several characters of his own invention. One day in the shop when I was tired and frustrated, I said, "If it weren't for words and images, we wouldn't have to do this bullshit." He went on to say that we should print T-shirts that just said, "Words and Images." This free-wheeling discussion went on to, roughly, the contents of our minds and the ways in which other people thought, and on to whether we'd ever seen or heard things that weren't there, and how well we could remember odors, or rather "picture" them in our minds like we can colors. I might even have said that, with the coming of the first cool night in a long time, I'd had a high incidence of seeing those "eye corner things," all those personable tall grasses that move about, all those moving air tricks that may be blamed on "wind spirits."

A cat by any other name ...

The house had a big backyard and beyond that was another small dwelling, rented by friends. In good weather, we left the back door open where the kitchen was located. In those days, it seemed quite safe. Around 1977, we began to hear a clattering noise from time to time coming from the kitchen. This turned out to be a bold cat exploring whatever was left on our frequently undone dishes. At first she'd bolt whenever discovered, but she soon became friendly — a cat with a delicately tawny, ochre-ground color and a few, faint tabby markings. So we put out food, and she came and went as she pleased, still investigating the dishes, as cats will, even when furnished with food of her very own, designed for her species.

Then, in the landlord's woodpile next door, a kitten suddenly appeared. He was mostly a soft gray, with darker ears, paws, and tail, and powder-blue eyes. He looked just like what is known as a blue-point Siamese (which looks gray-point to me), except for a few faint, darker gray tabby stripes down his hind legs. Bill began to lure and tame this little wild guy slowly with food, and he came over to live with us. Busy as we were, we couldn't dwell on the major enterprise of cat naming, and he became Cat. At some point, Bill decided this was okay because in the distant past, in some unre-membered source, he had read that the only reason to name something was if you had more than one — but with one animal, species identity seemed fine for designation. The tabby kitchen phantom was still ephemeral enough at that point to not quite seem to be ours.

We would subsequently say that Cat was short for Cat-aleptic, in honor of Poe's "Fall of the House of Usher," and in keeping with the style the writ-er had employed in naming one of his own cats: Caterina. We also tried Cat-atonic and Cat-astrophe, but none of those really suited, since sleeping cats are often very responsive to stimuli, not actually cataleptic or catatonic, and Cat was delightful, not catastrophic. In later years, he would be called The Old Boy. The French writer Colette had a cat named La Chatte, which is French for "the cat," so perhaps we were not as derelict in our naming duties as I used to think.

Many years later, friends would have a cat named Gata, Spanish for fe-male cat; our naming technique, when done in a language spoken elsewhere, could have an exotic effect. Gata had been a stray that the neighborhood children had been calling Pumpkin, and during the transitional period, one of Gata's persons announced to the children, "You can call her 'Pumpkin Gata,' or you can call her 'G. Pumpkin.' But please don't call her 'Gata P.'" Later the vet discovered that Gata should really have been named Gato, but it was too late to change it.

Cat was allowed to roam during the day, but we called him in at night. Later that year, I quit my job to work full-time in our screen-printing busi-ness. So both of us were at home all day to watch, and if he strayed around to the front of the house toward the road, we went out and brought him back to the safe territory of the backyard. This house was set really far back from the road, much safer for kitties. Sometimes I was able to use a herding technique, letting him know I wanted him to walk to the back. But most times, he would veer away from the direction I wanted him to go, and I had to lift and carry him to the back. One of Bill's South Alabama expressions is to say something is as "difficult as herding cats." That's an expression with a solid basis, I found out. (This saying, in fact, now seems to be used nationwide and was recently the basis for a famous commercial. I do not know if it's southern in origin or not. It could well be, since I never heard it "Up North" while growing up, but the Internet spreads innovative language like wildfire these days — "y'all" is distinctly and definitely southern but is now also being used nationwide, and I've even seen it used by Canadians.)

The gray kitty, who started out extremely shy and appeared to have grown up wild, eventually became a really sociable cat. While still a kitten, he liked to ride on Bill's shoulders, and if I stood with my shoulders close to Bill's, Cat would step off Bill's shoulders and over to mine and stand, and then step back and forth between the two of us. The literature sometimes reports that Siamese like to ride on shoulders. Cat used ours as an elevated highway of sorts.

His meow of greeting was an incredibly long, drawn-out affair. In his early days of kittenish nocturnal hijinks, he had been confined to the downstairs at night. In the mornings when Bill opened the door to the kitchen, Cat would tear up the stairs emitting a sound with a long drawled out single note, a *meeeeeeeeeeeeee-ow* that seemed endless. This was his share of the famous Siamese blarney. If we were out and came back home, Cat would meet us at the door, again with one of these long playing intonations. Bill always wanted to record this but never got around to it. I quite often sang along with Cat; his sounds always suggested accompanying vocal parts to me. I tried to describe Cat's riffing during this era: *eeeow, ooooohhh, whoop! eeraheeow, oopp* were his resounding, clear feline phrases. This is the first time I recall noting the musical connection of cat voices and human voices. The one thing I don't think they sing very well is opera, but I do think music could be based on cat vocalizations. As for Cat's reaction to our own spontaneous goofing around with words in the shop, that was a different story. Cat listened to all this, and looked at us, but did not meow an opinion! In these early day of my understanding of how cats communicate with us, I did not realize he was expressing his views with his eyes.

Cat's vocalizations led me to think of natural sounds as akin to human-made music. I went on to believe that a flutist or a piccolo player could accompany a mockingbird quite well. There is indeed a symphony with bird sounds interspersed, and I have found references to birds and symphonic music. Vivaldi wrote a flute concerto called "The Goldfinch"; Handel wrote an organ concerto called "The Cuckoo and the Nightengale," and Beethoven's Pastoral Symphony is mentioned in connection with bird song inspiration.

Cat's mom had her own rare way of making a little half-cough barking sound, described by Bill as *werf, erf, erf.* She continued to be a come-and-go cat, and we strongly suspected she had another home. Because of this intuition we had restrained ourselves from stepping into the realm of naming her and allowing our lives to become fully entwined with the kitty. The heartbreak of our recent losses had predisposed us to an atypically realistic guardedness. The subsurface contract in these gray-area cases was different. *We will feed you my sweet, but you are not truly ours; your first owner might one day move and whisk you away.* We had been feeding her whenever we saw her for about a year, when one day Bill decided to follow her to see where she went when she left us. On the other side of the landlord's house next door, there was a small rental house. As Bill approached and watched the cat gliding towards the dwelling, a guy came out and asked him what he was doing in his driveway. Bill said, "I'm following my cat." "That's my cat, too," was the reply. So we learned some history of Cat and his mother.

From good intentions to a neighborhood tragedy

Cat's momcat, as well as Cat's dadcat, were each half-Siamese; both had been owned by this two-doors-down neighbor. So Cat was half-Siamese, inheriting a quarter from each parent, which explained his coloring, which most friends would always take for a full-blooded Siamese. There had been sibling kittens, somewhat wild, since the momcat kept them in the woodpile behind the house in-between the owner's location and ours; the neighbor had been able to catch the rest of the kittens, but not Cat, who was the wildest of them. His litter mates had been bathed, dried with a hair dryer, fitted with decorative bows at their necks, taken in a box to the mall, and given away, but the owner hadn't known what had become of Cat. He came over to see what a fine feline fellow Cat, who was about eight months old, had become. He agreed Cat was a fine beast, but fortunately, he did not want him back. With sad hearts, we ceded ownership of the momcat to him, thinking that was what he wanted. It seemed the most tactful and neighborly thing to do at the time, since he had been the original owner. He was a nice fellow and the kitty's home had every appearance of being solid.

All in all, we thought things had turned out rather well. But we found out about six months later that this guy had taken the mother cat to the pound because she wouldn't stay home. This was a crushing heartbreaker for us. It was too late to go to the pound and retrieve her. He hadn't said a word about no longer wanting the cat. Had he asked us, we would have taken her care over completely. Had he told us at the time that he was taking her to the pound, we would have gone to get her out. I wish we had been warier, but in those naïve days it was unthinkable to us that anyone would part with a pet in this way. Apparently it was some kind of affront to him for the cat to work two households.

I'm not assigning fault, because I do understand that not everyone knows cat behavior like we do. To us, it was an amusing, intelligent stratagem for getting more chow; a story to tell, a study of cat traits — opportunistic, clever creatures who will turn the charm on wherever they roam. Cats, though thoroughly tamed, are still animals whose behaviors can often be explained by biological imperatives; in this case the cat was developing every possible food source in the area, a completely natural survival strategy. Pets can't be expected to fit into a predetermined mold or image, especially not one based on human value systems. Animals must be taken as they come, with the behaviors of their species, as well as the individual quirks that they reveal.

I have since read in cat literature about cats that maintain two or more homes, and I've personally known of one who got herself fed at two houses with greater acceptance by the co-owners and happier results for the enterprising animal. In hindsight, it's tempting to think that the pale-hued tabby may have intuited that she hadn't really met minds with her owner and she was not on solid ground, and she may have been shopping for a more stable home with us. After all, she had chosen the woodpile of the home that was next door to hers to either have her kittens or hide them later, rather than keeping them at the dwelling of her owner. I would come to know another case in which I felt the cat was home-shopping because he had reason to be dissatisfied with his present home.

However, some cats do just try to get themselves fed all over the neighborhood or investigate other houses out of curiosity; at times, if the houses have cats, it's just to see how another cat group lives, from plain curiosity. After Bill had sat with Cat and fed him for long times in order to tame him, Cat had decided to throw in his lot with us, the adoring humans with the interior accommodations, rather than the woodpile where he had spent his kitten days or the iffy house his momcat had come from before being deported to the pound. I missed that little tabby kitchen phantom. To this day my heart breaks when I think of her.

An Officer and a Gentlecat

Our rented house was laid out in a way that did not permit us to confine Cat to the living quarters, so he roamed the business area of the house at will. He frequently stretched out luxuriously on piles of T-shirts, and he was a gorgeous sight. Customers commented on what a beautiful cat he was, and Cat glowed with satisfaction at the praise. Not only was he a fine pet; he was also a business asset. On a weekend trip to New Orleans once, we had seen a sumptuous black cat in the window of a jewelry store in the French Quarter, sacked out amidst the displays. I wasn't into jewelry but if I had been, I would have definitely patronized that establishment over all the other stores that had no cat.

Not every cat is a lap cat, but Gray Cat went from wild kitten to constant lap warmer, a real sweetheart. Again I basked in the joy of thinking, *Sleep peacefully, sweet cat.* He was also a polite cat, and Bill thought he was the most civilized cat we'd ever known. He had an interest in pizza (a frequent food for busy people) but would wait till everyone had eaten to sniff and paw at the crust, so we didn't have to snatch it away from him. An actual bite would have been too spicy for him, and onions are deadly toxic to cats, so we would not have allowed him to try it.

In his first year, Cat developed some respiratory troubles that the vets couldn't diagnose. Like most toms, when he became a full-grown boy, he started slipping off beyond the parameters we had previously maintained for him, in search of ladies. Looking for him, we had to scour several blocks one day, and we found him in a romantic tryst. A passing student gave us a shocked look as we approached the honeymoon couple for the purpose of scooping up our boy to take him home. Because of his health and for his safety, we felt it best to have him neutered, though we still felt sad about denying him a natural life. Overall though, neutering does work out for the best. Intact tomcats fight other tomcats and come home with bite wounds that can get infected. And they celebrate, repeatedly, their complete ownership of your house by spraying effusions of urine scent to inform other toms. They also make more kittens.

During Cat's neuter surgery, his respiratory problems came on and he stopped breathing. The vet picked him up and shook him to restart his breathing. A big plug of mucous came up from his throat, and at this point Cat started breathing again. After that, his respiratory problem went away, and he became perfectly healthy.

Bill often praised Cat's civility. He never tried to get our people food. He never jumped on counters or kitchen tables. He was the most tranquil and well-mannered cat we ever had, a real gentleman. Bill enjoyed Cat's clean scent and said he smelled like the inside of a glove. I thought of him as the "cat of silk" as he glided off the couch and landed quietly, drawing my attention to the fact that our Cat was serenely guarding and gracing the room. He liked my typing table for sleeping but would get off when I started to work, leaving me a writing space uncluttered with the major distraction of grand and actual feline presence. As the living furry one padded off to another site, the lithe word dreams and the metaphors would creep in, full-hearted and cat-like. Our house was notable for good cat behavior when Cat took up residence with us. (Of course, all that would change when we became the House of Minx.)

Considerate though he could be, he also treated any objects that he sensed we valued as his rightful province, as all cats do. One day I spread a group of small paintings out on a bed so I could look them over. In an instant Cat was playing hopscotch on them, making sure he stepped on each and every one. I held my breath, knowing that to try to lift him up and away would only result in extended, grasping claws scraping at the paint surfaces. But he had his walkabout without doing any harm; it was only his due, after all.

Cat was a foot drinker, which means that rather than lapping up water, he would cup his paw, dip it in his water bowl, lick the water off the paw, and repeat. He'd have to do this many times to get a good drink. I don't know why some cats paw drink, but I have read that those who do lack good visual depth perception, and perhaps rather than sticking their muzzles in the wet to an uncertain depth, they prefer to use the foot. I've also read that cats don't like to place their very sensitive whiskers into water, and some use foot drinking to keep their whiskers dry. I always try to keep cat water bowls full, so they can lap the surface with less chance of dunking their vibrissae.

Cat loved a dust bath, and when I was sweeping, he'd roll in the swept-up dust whenever I set down the broom to get the dustpan. I found this amusing, and many times I had to fluff his fur to get the dirt off and whisk it all back up as soon as I could. I wasn't always fast enough before he oozed himself back down, rolling and scattering debris again.

He could be boisterous outside as a young cat. He would scramble up a tree about twenty feet in a fit of high spirits, but he had not yet learned how to get down. Finding himself stranded, he would howl and caterwaul his head off. Bill would get a ladder and a pillowcase and go up after him. He'd carefully work the kitty into the pillowcase while the frightened Cat clung to the tree with his claws. Once he had him, Bill would carefully place the sacked cat over his shoulder and climb down the ladder, with the feline howling and writhing inside the pillowcase. Once down and released, all was well. Cat's tree-climbing passion led him skyward over and over again, but his knowledge of getting down was slow in coming. Bill went up the ladder to get him time after time. We should have named him Catalpa, which is a tree, just not the type he climbed.

One evening I was sitting on the couch with Cat sleeping about a foot and a half away from me. With a jerk he awoke suddenly, went wide-eyed, and meowed loudly with a questioning inflection. He ran frantically over to my lap. I responded with pats and words of comfort. It was clear that Cat had experienced a nightmare and also that he was capable of asking me a question. *What was that?*

Cat was usually a cool customer, but he did break his composure when he first came upon — of all affronts — a canine in his very house. Friends usually entered through our always-open back door and came up the stairs from the kitchen to the living area. One evening such a group began the ascent with their friendly old shepherd mix following them. Bill started down the stairs and Cat raced down ahead of him, confronting the dog with an arched back, hisses, and yowls. The dog, who lived with a Siamese cat, wagged her tail as if to say *Ho hum*, and tried to follow her people on up the stairs. This was too much for Cat, who aimed a slasher strike at the poor dog's nose, raking it open with his claws along the entire length of her muzzle. Everyone went back to the kitchen to put compresses on the bleeding pooch's nose. After this initial incident, when people brought pooches for visits, Cat was reticent and padding around, crouched carefully and with faintly twitching nose, but he kept his spitting to a minimum and he eventually ignored the dogs as though they were beneath his notice. One major, foaming-up statement of his opinion on the dog matter had been enough. This was either his gentility or the heights of his catly arrogance and composure, or both.

Gray Cat also loved to gaze at the actions of a water closet. When he heard the flush he would come running, put his front paws up on the lid, and watch the water swirl.

With Cat, we sat one March in the season of high winds and fresh dreams, in the languid iconic evenings when there was much afoot at night. Cat knew that himself and swiveled his fine ears anxiously while we patted him and fretted about the possibility of severe weather. If the wind hit the house just right, there would be a metallic, near-vocal moaning from the hardware in the front door casing. The wood was worn away just enough to permit the air to "play" the house, a fact we were most fortunate to realize, in preference to thinking we were being peculiarly haunted.

Cat's curious ways also helped innovate human language. Our friend Tim watched him sniff carefully around the house and the yard and began to call him a "smell head." Soon Tim was calling all felines "smell heads." So if that ever catches on outside of Alabama, you'll know where it started.

Chapter 4

Aves versus Felis Sylvestris Catus

Like most cats, Cat became a skilled hunter even with his food bowl spilling over every day. Cats, like humans, continue to hunt even when well-fed. Cats, though, have the better excuse of acting on instinct bereft of the advanced degree of choice-making abilities that humans have. He got mostly small, ring-necked garden snakes, which was sad enough, since we're champions of harmless snakes. One summer day I took a cicada away from him and placed it on a tree, where it began crawling upwards to sing with the others — this particular evening, a blues song and a cautionary tale about the huge, furry-whiskery, gray shimmer of a beast that had been lifted off of him that day.

Cat also got a sparrow once, and later, an old, bedraggled mockingbird that had been hanging around and who we looked upon fondly as a familiar wildling. We fed the birds and spent a lot of time watching them, just as I had watched and studied the different species as a child. We seeded the ground heavily, and word, or rather tweet, got around. One spring it remained brisk into May, and we enjoyed the electric, flashing-iridescent blues of the flocks of Indigo Buntings that lingered in our area a few weeks because of the coolness. Their brightness made me feel that their species name should really be Indigo Bonfire. Woodpeckers came to the ground for the seed and sat back on their rears in a comical manner, since they are built to hang on trees; they even came to the window sills sometimes. There were always flurries of birds in our yard, even with Cat and other owned kitties prowling the outdoors.

In many older dwellings, fireplaces had once been the heat source, and the house we lived in had a now-unused chimney. On the second floor, the old fireplace had been closed in and plastered over. On the first floor, Bill duct taped a piece of Styrofoam over the hearth opening so our heat would not go straight up the chimney in the winter. Duct tape is the universal panacea for fixing anything here in Alabama. All the humorous lists of things you will never hear in the South include the statement "Duct tape won't fix that." (I've been unable to find the identity of the original author of that very true witticism.) Bill then pushed his drawing table, where he worked on artwork for T-shirts, against the fireplace.

After a while, we had a mystery to solve: the mystery of the murmuring chimney. I saw Cat fixing his gaze on it, going alert with nose quivering, and generally acting as if something was in there, especially at night. Whether sparked by his instinct and suspicions or ours, one evening at twilight we went outside and saw a horde of gray birds looking black in the failing light against the dusky sky. The birds were circling the chimney and diving into it one by one; the old chimney was full of roosting Chimney Swifts. On many subsequent evenings we enjoyed watching the whirling vortex of birds, and friends even came over to watch with us. Not being morning people, though, we never did arise at dawn to see the birds come back out.

That wasn't all, though. At night, about every half-hour in that upstairs living room, I'd hear a whooshing sound around the old fireplace. The only clue was the birds in the chimney and I knew there had to be a connection. Bill solved it one night when he was working late at the drawing table, hearing a breathing sound pulsing in and out and squeaking sounds. He looked under the desk and the Styrofoam was breathing — it was actually moving outward towards the room and then flattening back towards the fireplace opening it covered. He put his ear to it and heard the rustling of thousands of wings. Bill's take on this is that in order to ventilate the shaft so that the birds at the bottom could breathe, they all rustled their feathers in unison every so often. This would pull the air into the chimney from the top and fan it down towards the floor so that all the birds would have fresh air.

On the Internet I found that birds roosting in chimneys is well known, but I have yet to find any descriptions of their ventilation actions. We are convinced that this is an instance of coordinated, cooperative flock behavior, and it's one of Bill's unique discoveries about the natural world. Friends also came and crouched near our old fireplaces, listening to the wing-powered suspirations. Cat continued to occasionally stand before both fireplaces and their murmurings, ears forward and eyes glaring with excitement. It was entertainment for all.

A Chimney Swift actually got into the house one day and was quickly evacuated to the outdoors before Cat noticed. Similarly, one night there was a flying squirrel in the downstairs bathroom and it, too, was hastily deported. Exactly how these two got into the house remains a mystery.

Singing against the choir: The case against cat impact on songbird populations

It's always a peculiar shock when your cat kills a bird. Coming face to face with the predatory prowess of these snuggly animals is unsettling. Nevertheless, cats are predators, and you have to accept this if you live with them. People blame cats for preying on songbirds, but in reality, many other species also kill birds. To the extent that the avian population is actually being ravaged, there are multiple factors. As much as the predator and prey facts put me off my feed, it's the way the natural world works. In town we would see the occasional raccoon, and they eat birds' eggs and nestlings. In *Complete Guide to Game Animals*, Leonard Lee Rue III states that opossums eat ground-nesting birds.[1] Some birds, like Blue Jays, Crows and Common Grackles, also eat the eggs and nestlings of other species. An occasional owl or even a hawk shows up in town, and they, too, prey on smaller birds.

Habitat reduction has probably had the most drastic effect on songbird numbers. *The Birder's Handbook, A Field Guide to the Natural History of North American Birds,* by Paul R. Ehrlich, David S. Dobkin, and Darryl Wheye, discusses destruction of forest breeding habitat, as well as destruction of tropical forests where many species overwinter, as major causes of the decline of Eastern songbird numbers.[2] They also cite forest fragmentation, which creates more bird borderland with open country, where cowbirds thrive. Cowbirds are nest parasites who reduce the breeding capacities of their songbird hosts. In suburban areas, predators include jays, crows, gray squirrels, dogs, rats, raccoons, and cats.

Raptors, ravens, crows, red foxes, and raccoons are also important predators of shorebirds. Ground-nesting birds are susceptible to rats, ground squirrels, gray foxes, red foxes, and coyotes; even mice raid the nests of shorebirds.[3] There's no mention of snakes, but they, too, climb trees and pillage nests, and some even eat birds. A friend living in the country here once explained that he kept outdoor cats around his house because they ate the mice. And when there were no mice, he continued, the snakes wouldn't come, since the cats had reduced their major food source. So the cat's rat- and mouse-catching abilities can benefit birds.

Sometimes you have to look at a picture larger than just a single bird kill by a cat to see the ways nature makes adjustments; you also have to research widely to catch a glimpse of understanding about mutable, functioning ecosystems. In *Catwatching*, Desmond Morris writes that for cats, mice are the normal prey. A study he describes in the United States found that for a group of feral cats, only four percent of their diet was birds. Their sharp eyes and flying ability make them difficult for cats to catch.[4]

By consuming rodents who prey on birds and eggs and by discouraging snakes, cats occasionally fill a predator niche that actually helps birds. Many other species also prey on both the birds and the eggs. Yet we continue to see studies that blame free-roaming cats for bird population decline and proposed legislation, in at least one state, that would allow hunters to shoot cats on sight because of their supposed effect on the bird numbers. That repulsive idea is not an answer. In the Middle Ages, cats were viciously persecuted for phony reasons, and now again in modern times they are being blamed far out of proportion for the decline of birds, which is mostly the result of human-related habitat loss.

Predators such as raccoons, foxes, and coyotes are primarily nocturnal and therefore less visible to those bird enthusiasts who observe day-roaming cats stalking birds. Rodents don't seem to get much blame for their bird depredations either, perhaps because it's not a subject that often turns up in popular culture. It's common knowledge that cats prey on birds and mice; that they prey on insects and lizards is lesser known. Yet everyone also knows that coyotes eat road runners, at least theoretically.[5]

I understand it is distressing when a cat stakes out your bird feeder and/or actually kills a bird. (I recommend *The Birder's Handbook* for an excellent discussion of the pros and cons of supplemental feeding of birds.[6]) There is certainly plenty of pressure on birds already, and we of course react with sorrow to any bird loss due to cat predation.

At our household, we've come to believe that it's safer for all — birds, small wildlife, and cats — for the cats to live indoors. A great many owners keep their kitties inside now, and rescuing stray cats and placing them in homes helps. Managing and returning or relocating feral cat colonies has become widespread and is a large part of the answer.

But before we switched to keeping our cats indoors only, we were often outside with them. Whenever we caught Cat, or any of our earlier cats, stalking a bird or squirrel or even a lizard, we made a commotion that startled the potential prey into a speedy escape. And I might say to bird lovers who lose occasional birds to neighborhood cats that this is part of the sadder side of life in nature, of which cats as well as the other wildlife predators that hunt birds, are all a part. I don't handle it very well emotionally myself; for example, I don't even like to watch the nature shows that document lions hunting. But at the same time I know we cannot blame the predators for their instinctive acts. Birds are prey species that reproduce at a high rate to allow for the individuals taken by predators. This is nature's way, even though as compassionate humans, we don't like or fully understand it.

As for prey/predator being a given component of the universe, in a more flip mood I might say that I would have designed things differently. That's a joke, a slice of bitter humor regarding an arena beyond our control, of course! That said, I think it would be ill advised for cat advocates to not show understanding toward bird advocates' concerns about actual bird kills by cats. We need to express our sympathy. When the neighborhood dogs gang up, run down, and kill a cat, this too is natural behavior, to which we cat enthusiasts react with revulsion. It's a failure by the dog's humans if they have routinely allowed the animal to roam off-leash and unattended. Cat advocates need to come together with bird advocates in a manner that is receptive on both sides, to work out mutually agreeable solutions. But sadly, I am now witnessing the online debate between these two sides become extremely acrimonious.

There were times when I wanted to be a wildlife scientist myself, and I know they have done some fine work. I know cats do get some birds. However, many studies and estimates blame feral and free-roaming housecats for staggering numbers of bird and small mammal deaths. What they never say is how many of these small mammals are rodents? And, who is actually following the cats around keeping track of each move and each kill? I do have to wonder when I see the words "estimated to kill" usually followed by some huge number of birds and/or wildlife each year. That has to mean some extrapolation has been made from limited observation of actual predatory actions. I know there are sound methods used in some studies, and the fact is, cats do prey on birds and small mammals, but estimates don't impress me. We have also had occasion to be around many doctors and to hear them speaking of well-designed studies, meaning that some studies are better than others and that all studies are not equal. We should keep this in mind every time we hear that studies have shown and proven one thing or another. We should look closely at these studies to get answers about medicines, foods, and other matters.

Tracking down studies in their original publications, as opposed to just reading media coverage about them, isn't always easy, but it's the best thing to do. Some studies have shown that the numbers of birds killed have been exaggerated, and thoughtful scrutiny by Alley Cat Allies has discredited a frequently cited study.[7] Other studies of feral-cat diets vary by location but generally show high percentages of mammals, rodents, insects, or amphibians, and lower numbers of birds.[8] When confronted with the common and seemingly popular assumption that cats are responsible for bird decline according to several frequently cited, flawed studies, we must consider what else these studies do not measure, such as the impact of environmental devastation on birds and what proportion of cats are not effective hunters. (Although it may seem counterintuitive, some of my cats would turn out to be indifferent, or klutzy as hunters.) At the end of the day, humans would benefit birds more if we could stop building and developing in their habitat areas, which is not likely to happen. It isn't fitting to blame cats when the cause is mostly our own activities.

In the town neighborhood where I lived temporarily at the time of this chapter's first writing, there was one free-roaming owned cat (not mine) reported by neighbors to be a good hunter, and at least three strays or ferals that I see periodically but never long enough to try to tame. The owned cat goes on the prowl and hunts in the yard next door every night, and the others hunt there whenever they wander by. Yet the yard is constantly tweeting and fluttering with all manner of birds in great numbers, and rustling and jumping with many squirrels and chipmunks. And out in the forest where we rescued (or found homes for) most of the free-roaming cats and therefore now rarely see a kitty padding around loose, there are far fewer birds.

It's like two comparative living laboratories. Out on the forested land where we moved in 1984, there are wild predators of birds all around and a few free-roaming cats. In town at my Mom's home, with many owned outdoor cats, we see vast numbers of birds including some less common species like the Yellow-Shafted Flicker and the Great Crested Flycatcher. Do birds like lawns and low shrubbery amidst tall trees better than the solid forest's leafy profusions and plentitude of tasty bugs? What seems much more likely is that the lesser number and diversity of birds in the forest is due to the greater efficiency of forest predators that prey on birds, eggs, and nestlings. In town where far more cats roam but only an occasional raccoon or hawk appears, the birds are flourishing. This is anecdotal evidence but it's very carefully observed, long-term anecdotal data. We've lived in this forest for thirty years, and we've noted these differences.

Apex predators like cougars used to keep the smaller forest predators in check, but those big cat guys and gals don't live here any more and that again is the result of human activities. In the 1970s and 1980s I recall seeing articles about grackle and blackbird eradication programs. Their gigantic roosts were viewed as health hazards, and they were regarded as agricultural pests because they ate wheat and corn. I'm partial to those birds, and I was saddened by those mass killings. Now, no surprise, the population of Common Grackles has been greatly reduced. This again is a man-made problem. Large numbers of birds have also been killed at airports, and while I understand the need for airline safety, I'd rather see the use of non-lethal methods, such as noise, to frighten the birds away.

As for the undesirability of rodents, the nature guides spell it out. They carry plague, typhus, and food-poisoning microbes, and they cost millions of dollars every year in damage to goods and crops. Rue III and Whitaker, et al., both cite another source that indicates they have killed more people worldwide by spreading disease than all past wars and revolutions.[9, 10] Their reproductive rates are impressive. House mouse females have several litters of three to sixteen each per year, with gestation being only eight to twenty-one days and mating recurring soon after each litter is born.[11] Norway rat females are capable of twelve or more litters a year, though each usually has only about five litters of seven to eleven due to limitations of food supplies.[12] Black rat girls usually have several litters of two to eight a year.[13]

Most rodents will breed year-long, especially in warmer climates. Mice thrive in every habitat in North America and in many, they are the most abundant of the mammals residing there.[14,15] According to many sources, rats consume and spoil twenty percent of the human food supply each year and spread diseases through their droppings and the fleas, ticks, and lice they may carry. *Hmmm*, is there a species that might help control mice and rats? Could that be … cats? Any estimated study done on cat predation in a given area should include a breakdown of how many of those kills are estimated to be mice and rats. (Some rats, especially the Norway, or brown rat, are ferocious, and some cats are afraid of them, though not all.)

Mice and rats are skilled at getting into houses, where they create sanitary hazards and even fire hazards when they chew on electrical wires. In rural Virginia when I was growing up, I heard that mice and rats can flatten out their skulls and slide under doors into small spaces. I know now that's not true. They supposedly have flexible connective tissue and can flatten their rib cages, but their skull size limits the spaces they can enter. Rats determine whether they can fit into a space by using their whiskers, much like cats do. I did find one source, a British pest control company, that states this skull flattening is true of mice but not rats. What I know for sure, from personal experience, is that keeping rodents out of your rural home is a formidable task.

Let's not forget that songbirds themselves are often predators; it's just that they prey mainly on insects, unsavory little nuisance critters to us humans. Ignoring birds as hunters is an emotional rather than a logical view of what amounts to flat-out predation. While we lived in town, I witnessed birds running cats off, presumably away from their nests, on several occasions. I've seen a single jay dive-bombing a cat and a pair of mockingbirds who were very successful at running the cat off, at a rapid trot. Bill also has witnessed smaller birds ganging up to run crows out of their territory, sometimes three or four birds at a time. I think humans do like to see the predators thwarted.

In the case of feral cats in areas where there are endangered birds and wildlife: in an ideal world I recommend advocates of both cats, birds, and wildlife, work together to trap-neuter-return (TNR) and re-locate the colonies of cats if necessary. I know this chapter opens up a can of worms in many minds, and there's a wide range of opinions on these issues. It's my firm opinion and passionate hope that the problems can and will always be solved in ways that do not involve killing cats, whether owned kitties or poor, cast-off strays and ferals. Humans have created the feral cat populations by abandoning cats. There's a certain unfairness in not solving conflicts in ways that allow the cats to live.

I prefer feral cats to feral rats any day. Sometimes people claim feral cats poop in the yard, but even in neighborhoods with free-roaming cats, I've never found the poop. And I prefer animals whose poop I can never find to those who tunnel into the house and leave poop I definitely, always do find. For those who are troubled by the presence of free-roaming cats, owned or otherwise, there are non-toxic cat-repelling sprays that can be applied to yards, which can be formulated out of citrus components like lemon and oranges. Under no circumstances should strong chemicals like mothballs be used as an animal repellent. The same goes for cayenne. Cats and other animals can suffer greatly from the burning caused by contact with cayenne.

This presentation of rodent facts should not be taken to imply disrespect. Rats bred for the pet trade can be good and affectionate pets. Even wild rats are much more intelligent than people think[16] and work communally, showing altruism by taking care of their ill. And no animals should ever be treated unkindly. But fast-breeding wild rodents are a hazard to agriculture and food supplies, and to public health. Their population growth is cat-mediated — cats are nature's ancient balancing predators that befriend and benefit humans.

The world's cats have always done the work of keeping rodent populations in check and they do it largely unseen and silently during dawn and dusk hunts, their preferred prowling time. Cats need to be shown some respect and gratitude.

Other threats to wildlife — and humans, too

As some readers know, I've been working on this book for a long time. The first draft of this chapter was written from 2004 to 2006. Since then the situation between bird people and cat people seems to have worsened. Not in my immediate experience, where our birding friends appreciate us for having had indoor-only cats since the '80s and for taking and homing so many cats off the streets and out of the forest. But online relationships between cat people and bird people, as well as the science cited by bird people, have deteriorated.

I've been disappointed by the positions of the Smithsonian and some of its researchers, as well as some of the bird groups, that I used to support. They contributed so much to my early development as an animal-focused advocate and environmentalist but I feel they have now lost their way.

Internet debates can be truly vitriolic, and I'm sorry to say that in my experience, the bird advocates have exhibited the most anger. Nasty comments and personal attacks are the marks of those who have no solid arguments. That said, I've seen some heartening instances around the notion of bird groups and cat groups working together. Often, cat enthusiasts and bird enthusiasts are the same people. I'm advocating for everyone to play nice; I too have concerns about bird populations. However, the extrapolations and estimates about cat predation on birds are based on thin science. Direct observations by those who dwell in bird habitats and watch bird populations and numbers of cats over time, have great validity in my view. I've done that in two neighborhoods, a forest and a small city.

Bird advocates also need to acknowledge the importance of cats in the life of humanity. The selective targeting of feral cats as the cause — and the recommendation that they be poisoned or rounded up and killed — again fails to take into account the facts that most bird losses are from other causes. In my experience, one of those causes that doesn't appear to get around the grapevine so much is the airports that kill birds to protect planes from bird strikes. This is necessary since we can't have conditions hazardous to aircraft, but it places causation squarely back on human activity.[17]

Another cause I rarely see cited is the tremendous number of smaller birds and eggs taken by crows, jays, and larger birds of prey, such as hawks, falcons, eagles, and owls. These birds of prey to the best of my knowledge are all, or mostly, protected species. Smaller songbirds are snatched right out of the air by these large predators. Some falcons have a grisly and cruel habit of imprisoning small birds alive to keep them "fresh" until the falcons decide to consume them. Cat detractors may counter that cats cruelly toy with their prey until they are ready to kill it, but that isn't an accurate description of their behavior. Cats smack their prey around to weaken it before going in close for the killing bite to the neck, because active prey could injure their faces. It's one of the sad facts of predator and prey, but it isn't deliberate cruelty. The whole system freaks me out but it's beyond my control. In some bird species, a nestling may kill a fellow nestling. Even mantises have been observed killing hummingbirds. Tropical Storm Cindy blew and washed away substantial numbers of shorebird nests and chicks, another act of the natural world.

Yet another area where I never see any follow-up attention is the massive bird die-offs that are surely due to environmental factors that bird advocates would do well to scrutinize. It would be much more productive to investigate what could have caused these die-offs and keep those issues in front of the public, rather than to keep focusing on cats. Yet another human-made problem that impacts migratory birds: tall, lighted buildings in cities disrupt their migration patterns and cause deaths not only when birds fly into them but also by disrupting the signals they respond to. This may not yet be a well-established theory, but it does further suggest that human-made problems for birds should get a closer look. Lastly, another example: recent research reveals cedar waxwings dying from consumption of berries that are toxic to them, which shows another big-picture ecological instance of bird loss unrelated to cats, and the dangers of some kinds of invasive plants to birds.[18]

Part of the "cats cause bird extinction" rhetoric is to describe cats as a non-native and invasive species, a domesticated animal that is being unnaturally released into the ecosystem. They're talking about cats in North America as though small felines are comparable to Burmese Pythons in the Everglades. While it is true that cats aren't "native," they were brought over on ships and kept by humans here for a compelling reason: rodent control. These services are increasingly needed as human-dwelling expansion drives native predators of rodents, such as snakes and raptors, away. Also, calling cats a domesticated species is true to an extent, but they differ from many other domesticates in that they can still live on their own in a wild or feral situation.

Cats and dogs have a special relationship with humans, and they occupy a unique niche. While all species of animals deserve humane treatment, we owe cats and dogs big-time. There are also biologists who now think the whole "nativist" concept in regard to ecosystems is a flawed theory and that species range changes are part of a healthy, natural process. While I'm not trained enough to speak to this with authority, I'll venture to say that the truth is somewhere in the middle and depends on the characteristics of various translocated species. Some have disastrous effects, but in other cases, the dangers are highly overstated.

Bats are a federally protected species because they eat mosquitoes, which are major pests. I found this out when a local arts center had to move while pest control rigged devices that would enable bats to exit their building if they so chose — you cannot legally harass them into leaving. I'm happy for the bats! And I would like to see feral cats extended the same protections; cats eat rats and mice, pests of enormous magnitude. These rodents are cute, but they can be direct threats to human food supplies and dwellings.

In addition to the issues listed above, West Nile Virus is also killing off many birds. Bill had West Nile in 2013. He almost died, but survived miraculously. West Nile is a growing threat to human health, and birds are known to be the major reservoir host, although mosquitoes are the vectors,[19] but we wouldn't think of calling for the elimination of all free-flying birds.

Similarly, calls for the extermination of all free-roaming cats is pure bias, in my view, though zoonotic diseases are often used as scare tactics by those who want to remove outdoor and feral cats. (Please see Volume 2 of this book for an in-depth discussion of the two diseases usually mentioned: toxoplasmosis and rabies.)

I admit to staying in a state of vexation when I see way too many "cats harm wildlife" articles that are based on poor science continue to inflame sentiments against cats. Perhaps I shouldn't expect the writers of these articles to consider the broad range of causes of bird decline? Perhaps I should allow that not everyone would be researching West Nile Virus? Or are the writers just guilty of sloppy journalism as part of some short-sighted, anti-feline bias?

In 2011, our little town neighborhood with its thriving bird and small mammal populations was deforested instantly by a tornado. Every tall tree went down; we only managed to save one severely battered pecan tree, along with some smaller mimosas and red tips. The bird population plummeted. Owned cats were evacuated from the ruins. The feral cats stayed hidden from the noise of clean-up, and the rodent population soared. But the feral cats slowly came back. And as smaller trees grew, birds also came back slowly and are now co-existing with the feral cats, and thriving.

An article on the decline of whippoorwills, which also mentions a drop in numbers of its relative, the nighthawks, notes that both consume moths.[20] Moth populations have been crashing for a long time. I've watched it here in Alabama. They used to be wall-to-wall, both inside and out. Now we rarely see a moth. Recent research is now addressing the decline of insects and the impact on bird populations.[21]

Finding common ground to solve ecological problems

This chapter was first written in 2006. Some of the ideas I had then, especially about rodents consuming birds' eggs, the role of cats in maintaining the ecosystem, and the impact this makes to the view that cats are detrimental to bird populations' survival, are now showing up regularly on the Internet. I'm happy to see these sensible ideas out there to help raise esteem for the feline in the public view!

New information keeps emerging. For example, recent studies have looked at deer eating birds and nestlings.[22] This is unexpected and appears to be understudied. It's another possible non-feline impact on bird populations, and it fits my own observations about our neighborhoods, that we have had more birds in town than in the country. The usual forest predators I noted are out here, and we've seen or heard reliable reports of smaller numbers of those predators in town. And the one local species that's never, to my knowledge, been sighted in town in recent times is deer.

Even more new information has come from the results of an Australian study.[23] This work indicates that cats venturing outside wearing brightly colored "cat scrunchies" made a dramatic decrease in the amount of wildlife taken. Birds, reptiles, and amphibians were caught less often, but there was no reduction in the numbers of small rodents. The excellent color vision of birds accounts for these results. My response is, great news! Outdoor and indoor/outdoor cats can still catch rodents, while birds would be largely spared. Although the pictured scrunchies stood out around the cats' necks Elizabethan style, I would logically think that bright colors on traditionally styled collars would have the same effect on wildlife. Surfing the Internet, I found those to be readily available as both rainbow style and ornately designed artistic works. This is speculation, but I believe that rainbow style or anything with large blocks of color would best suit this purpose. Floral designs, in my view, might not work because they would come into the birds' view as natural multi-color against outdoor settings, similar to the way predator coat patterns blend into landscapes and provide camouflage. I also can't say this for certain, but I don't think a single bright color collar would work as well either; different colors placed together on a collar is probably the best visual indicator of an intruder who's not part of the scenery. And any time a cat goes outside with a collar, I recommend the breakaway safety collars that are designed to release if the cat gets it caught on a branch or other hindrance. I am indeed now seeing ads for the bright color collars saying they should be used with breakaway collars for cat safety.

One concern about bright colors on cat collars is that hawks, eagles, and other birds of prey also have the sharp color vision possessed by so many bird species. Hawks and eagles will take cats, and so will owls, though owl vision is limited to black and white and grays. Would the additional colors on a kitty's collar make hawks and eagles notice cats outside more, or less? Would it signal an unknown and therefore inedible pattern, or would it disrupt the natural camouflage perks of cat fur coloration? I tend to recommend indoor cat keeping with supervised outings only, or enclosed catios. If your cats do roam on their own, I advise keeping them inside if hawks and eagles are known to be in your area.

Please note that the scrunchies worn by cats in the studies were specially made for felines. Do not attempt to use hair scrunchies made for humans, or other products made for humans, on cats.

Another article details the action of a field biologist in killing an endangered bird species for a specimen. Perhaps there should be a study on the impact of field biologists on bird populations![24]

There's more! I see greater recognition of the value of feral cats as rat deterrents in urban areas. Not only do cats prey on rats, but sometimes feline presence itself keeps rats away.[25]

Final thoughts on misguided feral cat policy

I was majorly discouraged and enraged when the Western Governors' Association decided to list feral cats as an invasive species. Cat advocates are resisting by finding solid articles that document things I've suspected all along, such as this one: "Shot and gassed: Thousands of protected birds killed annually."[26] Studies are finding steep declines in bug populations, which are being linked to declines in bird populations.[27] This information needs to be more widely circulated and recognized.

As I watch the unfolding arguments and trends in thinking, this is what I see: Flawed studies[28] with their wildly inflated numbers of birds taken by cats are cited often. Studies about island populations are erroneously applied to continents, and/or understudied for factors besides cats. A little wrong information goes a long way. Everyone loves songbirds and raptors, but blackbirds, starlings, grackles, pigeons, not so much. Raptors get respect. Raptors and other bird species are major predators of small birds, but because their raids take place aloft or shielded by leaves, largely outside of human view, avian predation gets little mention. If information about this becomes popular, will the public be convinced to eradicate raptors? I'm saying this to demonstrate how extreme the kill-off-the-feral-cats approach really is.

The few zoonotic diseases that roaming cats may carry are often brought up in reckless ways that cause emotional reactions, and lack citation of any solid research into these diseases, let alone a complete survey of the literature. (In Volume 2, I will review and analyze the research into those diseases.) Also missing, any mention that rodents can just about out-vector any other species when it comes to serious diseases. (And no one is suggesting we kill all free-flying birds just because they are major reservoir hosts for the dangerous West Nile Virus.)

Online, many people recognize that humans are the ones causing loss of species, and they are right. I see little study of bird populations that compares specific habitats comprehensively, with data as to what else lives in those habitats and whether or not cats actually live there. I also don't see big-picture depictions; I see habitats described as though only birds and cats populate the world. It appears to me that many bird enthusiasts are taking the easy way out by blaming cats, rather than looking for creative ways to manage outdoor cat colonies or working on the thorny environmental problems that are the real causes of extinctions. Ignoring real causes in favor of killing cats is a tragic blind alley, and serves no species. It also appears that species blaming is entirely arbitrary; bypassing bird-on-bird predation to land on cats and irrationally harping on whatever's getting the most attention at a given moment only fuels the public's emotions. To address this, we need more education and a shift of awareness. I know what we need, though I don't always know how to effect it.

Sadly I am seeing around the Internet, more negativity expressed towards cats, more suggestions to round up all feral cats and destroy them. This would mean the destruction of many pet cats too as there are many indoor/outdoor pet cats as well as quite a few who slip out at times no matter how carefully their people try to keep them inside. All cats who are caught by strangers will behave fearfully; there is no way to distinguish owned from feral upon capture.

Bud, my indoor Editing Cat says of birds, "I hear 'em tweetin' up a storm out there all the time, you don't know 'cause you don't hear worth a toot! Any of those flitter-flappers flits into my air space, I'll flat sure chatter at 'em, I will do it, *RAWR*."

Maybe that's a bit rude to the birds, but it's no use arguing with him. As a feline, Bud's vision is attuned to motion, so that shapes his fauna descriptions.

Or maybe he's just smarting off.

Chapter 5

Crazy About A Fox

Our house was in a neighborhood I wanted to stay in, close to the University and downtown, but also full of trees and older houses. Built in the 1920s, it was a tall, odd design for a southern house, with a steep gable on one end. Down the block and across a street was a house built in the 1820s, an antebellum structure no longer in good repair and sometimes described as haunted. It was huge, made of brick with a small porch on front. Wisteria vines covered the porch, webbing it in, and there were two wisteria bushes on either side of the walkway. When the front door was left open, you could see a chandelier inside. On the second story there was a door to a balcony that had crumbled long ago. Every evening in warm weather, a mysterious elderly lady was visible through that door, sitting and enjoying the twilight and the raspy hum of the cicadas.

Cicadas are a constant on summer evenings. Although some people don't like the sound of them, to me they have the rhythm of an amplified purr, but with the added *scree*. It doesn't compare in appeal with the divine murmur of cat purring of course; the feline purr is a superior natural sound. (The cats were adamant that I included that qualification.) Any afternoon when a large carpenter bee has gotten into your house for hours, that nonstop, grate-on-the-nerves buzzy fellow will prove to you that purrs are not only superior, but also the most soothing continual vibration a human can hear. It's almost like purr was tailor-made to relax and mesmerize a human.

One day back in that old neighborhood, we were under a tree with low-hanging branches at dusk, and it was full of cicadas, almost at eye level. We noted that the sound did not seem to be made by the legs or wings but seemed to originate somewhere in their butts, which were working up and down as the bugs sang. When I looked this up later, I learned that the cicada sound does indeed originate in the abdomen. Only the males do this; it's their mating call. They gather together to advertise for females when the weather is hot. Sometimes you can find the trail of their finely wrought, brittle husks on the ground. They emerge from these and go into the trees.

Now all the old houses in the neighborhood are fixed up and preserved, all polished up, full of office personnel. They did need some preservation. But the vines are gone, and the neighborhood looks manicured and homogenized. I prefer the look of prior days, when the wisteria was growing wild and the oldest houses, built by enslaved people, were full of ghosts, ruin, sad

93

history, and untold stories. Those scenes were the backdrop to my youth but there's more than nostalgia for me; there's also a need to grasp a significance that seems elusive.

And, I don't care much for gentrification.

In winter, we had clear views of sunsets where the sky was often, as I recorded on December 12, 1982, absolutely blue-violet. In this town full of trees, rains would play percussion with concrete and leaf-skin alike. At dusk, the city might turn vibrating pastels, making all strange things seem less strange. The nighthawks that nested on the flat roof of the shopping plaza directly across the street would fly and call over us; making sharp turns, they swooped low enough that I could see the white stripes of their wings and the lines between their feathers.

I saw many birds there and learned much about them, such as the ferocity of mockingbirds. One day I'd seen a large clump of dual mockingbird plumage streaking towards the sidewalk — one bird forcing another down. Flocks of so-called blackbirds, which actually shone like rainbows when they walked on sunlit lawns, stopped by our yard frequently.

"Some things about the town I like," I wrote back in those days. Tuscaloosa sort of grows as haphazardly as the forest; things fall, things are built for no reason, lights appear, odd illuminations splash the streets. The birds sit on flat roofs, the sidewalks sprout stuff, and in the windows, the cats show themselves. Crumbly old houses stay inhabited and get painted sometimes. The odors of grand gardens past haunt us every spring. Even the young and eccentric might live in something old and huge and sporting ionic columns, with tops that look like the tongues of plastic cooties. (We'd heard of one such group living way out in the country, naming their ancient building Toad Hall.)

A scattering of poets might walk the old streets, craving to scare the ghosts. We'd had gatherings in our house and barbecues in the backyard; we'd seen summer evenings there of lively indigo rain clouds, with a playful sun flashing its animal tawniness as it set, the sky changing like a calico cat rolling about. Walking down the streets at dusk, the sky is spattered and seething with leaves, there were so many trees in town. After dark, the shadows and day colors stampede and take refuge in the branches. Lights look out of the windows. Fireflies light up and crickets converse. We take walks at night, it's safe. I want to paint natural and artificial light against darkened colors, sort of like René Magritte's *The Empire of Light*. Mornings, and out on the sidewalk, the hues of gold and smoke might slink by on a passing cat.

After the tumult of the '60s and our formative years, we had come back from the trenches and the dreaming to the everyday life of work, friends, yards, and town; we were seeking home. From the struggles of demonstrations and free expression, we went into the struggle to survive economically, but we brought with us our new ways of perception. Everything glowed; language became ornate, "purple," in response. Through visiting, we walked in and sampled various interiors in town, yet we had never fully arrived at our own.

We had to leave some time. Our genial landlord had other plans for the house. Our business had increased, and we now had a moderate amount of disposable income. It wasn't necessarily enough to buy a house — we just weren't comfortable with that — but we were able, around 1980, to buy some wooded land. Bill then purchased an old trailer, took it to the land, and with the help of friends, proceeded to build an addition onto it, as well as a workshop a short distance away. This house in the woods was intended to be temporary.

Into the woods

Our land is about ten miles from town. Some friends were part of a family that owned about a thousand acres of forested land, and in addition to the huge old hunting lodge on the grounds, there were several smaller houses that our friends lived in. They wanted the land to remain mostly wilderness. So when their elders began to sell off parts of the tract, they arranged for like-minded friends, such as ourselves, to buy lots. We ended up with about seventeen acres that partly bordered a stream that had once fed a manmade lake. The earthen dam that held the lake had broken in a 100-year rain. The creek, or "branch" as we call it here, is gorgeous with its sparkling rapids. It connects this land to all others along its banks. Upstream, its origin is in a lake fed by two other streams that issue from lakes. It empties into another, winding lake, man-made, that narrows back to stream and then flows into a longer and wider creek that eventually reaches a major river.

Parts of this larger waterway, called Hurricane Creek, flow through rock formations so rugged, steep, and majestic that people hike out there to enjoy them. This large creek and its branches, its tributaries, now even has its own advocacy group. It is the last free-flowing stream in the Appalachian chain before the coastal plain meets it, somewhere around Tuscaloosa. All I know is that the University of Alabama is on the coastal plain, but here in the woods, we are technically back in the Appalachians, about ten or twelve miles away from the plain. In all, this water system is the recipient of run-off from three thousand acres of watershed. Meandering through the length of our section of land is a smaller stream that you could cross with one big step, which flows into the main branch. Upstream, on a neighbor's land, it makes a scenic, miniature spray of water as it cascades through small-scale cliffs. Back then, there were no fences in the community that was forming out here, so we were moving into an unfettered forest setting.

I have asked Bill if we can ever flood here, being so close to the stream, and he says no, that we are at too high an elevation. Still, we have to ride downhill to get into our neighborhood, and the cold air sinks down on our lower-lying location. When I ask Bill why we often have such crappy Internet service, he says, "We're in a valley."

It would have been more exciting if we had actually set out to boldly venture "back to nature" to reclaim Paradise. Indeed, we set out with a few rugged aspirations that would not last: we would heat with a wood stove only, we would live without a phone, we would be what is now called, "off-the-grid." But basically, the circumstantial availability of affordable land had brought us to the woods. That said, our home-forest landing has been in keeping with a destiny in both our lives that shines clear when I look back: to shake off civilization and be in the wild. I have always had a passion to blend myself with nature, to jump into shallow rapids if I want to, slide down hills on my tush or walk through rained-upon foliage, where my face might become stained with lichens and mud.

Back then, I had romanticized notions when it came to nature; I identified with animals. If I were to choose an animal persona for myself, I felt more like a wild lynx than a housecat. I would be the lady, or the fox, as the occasion arose. I laugh now thinking of it, those young ideas. But I still hold with some of it. *Boondocks, sticks, hick,* all these terms come from a view that the wild is an outer reach and that an urban area is a center of sophistication and learning. To me, the forest landscape is the center of the world and wisdom, the legitimate landscape. The city and the suburbs are the intruders. In any city, I imagine the forest it used to be and then the buildings look odd and out of place. I get a lost and haunted feeling when I'm "in the bricks."

Bill told several people we were going to be "raising Rottweilers," which of course wasn't true. It also played on people's breed-specific fears, which we probably wouldn't do today, but that was certainly a positive use of said fears. It's not unusual at all for those living in the country to tell some lies on themselves for security reasons. However, the place we have gone is indeed rugged, full of ticks and snakes, and is not easy to find; and those are no lies.

We edged our buildings into the forest with as little disruption as possible to the trees. It was like we just pushed a few pesky branches back and inserted our dwelling in alongside the underbrush. We had no lawn, no cultivated magnolias; the local magnolias are wild, a less well-known variety with two-foot-long leaves and garishly large flowers. Along the highway traveling out here, near the creek on the dirt road in and towards the back of the land: those are all places we find these Broad-Leaf Magnolias. They are known colloquially as cowcumber trees, cowcumber magnolias, or swamp magnolias; I call them big-mouth magnolias.

There isn't a cotton field in sight. It's the deep woods in the Deep South. We are right in with the dense tall pines and scattered hardwoods. I've heard "piney woods" for this at times, but I've also seen that term used as an exclusive designation for woods several states farther west. The place was logged sometime in the 1900s, possibly the early 1960s. Even in Alabama, you won't find much virgin forest. (There's some old-growth primeval forest in the Dismals Canyon of northwest Alabama, "like a tropical rainforest," Bill says.) We placed our driveway and our home along an old logging road. It isn't old growth, but it has been undisturbed a long time, and the trees have grown high, and it is definite woods, not suburbs.

When we look up, we see an irregular aggregate of sticks, thick branches making a latticework of obliques. For yard we left the underbrush of poke-weed, wild flowers, blackberries, fern, and anonymous bushes around some dogwood trees. An elaborate, beautiful thistle sprouted beside the driveway, as though in defiant counter-rhythm to future cultivars; *you think you could plant anything as beautiful as this?* it says with its deep, red-violet strands. I was actually glad to have it, because it looked Scottish. I had tried to establish plants exotic to our area such as English lavender and heather as house-plants, but they had yelped and fallen over dead when summer came. Along the creek, we found fossils of calamites ferns. My environmental essay "Tributary: Becoming Green Warriors of the Red Earth Country" was written about walks along this creek and one of its smaller tributaries and was published by the online literary journal, *Steel Toe Review*. It can be read there or at the Catwoods Porch Party website, where you can also find photos of this sparkling tributary in all seasons.

Sweetgum fruit, little multi-chambered spiky seedpod spheres, litter the ground. Bill planted a cutting from a tree that grew in his grandmother's yard; it blooms pink and magenta every spring. His family always called it a Judas tree, as well as a kind of crabapple. Searching tree guides, we found that it does not match the specifications for either. The Judas tree is actually an Eastern Redbud with a much larger leaf, and our tree is also devoid of crabapples or leaves matching the crabapple. So we have a mystery tree. He also planted a gardenia from a cutting off our friend Cliff's plant, as well as Cliff's rose bushes with the idea he might someday come back for them. Slowly, Bill built a patio, transplanting a patch of ferns from deeper in the woods alongside of it. They were the ferns of home, and they are cat-eye green. We joked that a house built onto the trailer was the building code for the area; several of the neighbors moving there around the same time used this starter-home construction.

Around July 1984 we had moved the print shop downtown, but the house in the country still wasn't ready. Construction always takes longer than planned. We needed to be out of our rented house but had nowhere to go, until friends living at the end of the block generously offered us, and our cat, a section of their place. Attached to their apartment were two attic rooms with a refrigerator and a bathroom. There was no stove, but we could make do. Our section was almost completely shut off from the rest of the old 1820s house. They weren't supposed to sublet, but we were guests of sorts, there for only a few weeks.

Cat adjusted very quickly, especially considering he could no longer go outside — animals were not exactly welcome there, so he couldn't be seen entering and exiting. Bill and I worked long hours at the shop and then he went out every evening to the land to finish up the house. The nights were lonesome. I watched, without Bill, the Scottish actor Nicol Williamson in the lead in *Macbeth* on Public TV[1] and got shivers and chills up my spine. I looked over at Cat, quietly sitting and looking back with cool, blue eyes. He may not have known why, but he knew he was needed to instill calm and dispense comfort by example into my "wuss" moment. Years later, I would consider writing a spoof of *Macbeth* with dogs, called *Macbreath*, or *Macfishbreath*. *Macbreath* might have gagged his victims with his doggie breath. Further ideas on that one didn't develop, but I did write a parody of *Cat Hamlet*:

Cat Hamlet doesn't last nearly as long as the original.

Cat Hamlet wouldn't hesitate to engage his culprit uncle in a yowling and staring contest. They would then tangle up, disengage, and take off running. Cat Hamlet would run Uncle to the docks, where he would vanish into the hold of ship bound for Norway. Legend has it, Uncle clobbered some Norway Rats.

Cat Hamlet would pause to sample the fresh fish scattered about the docks.

Cat Hamlet would then spray the borders and leave scent piles on the main roads around Denmark, to make sure Uncle does not return.

Meanwhile, you know Cat Ophelia's not going anywhere near that water. She's curled up napping in the palace through all this.

Cat Hamlet takes one sniff of Yorick and makes scratching motions on the ground.

When Cat Hamlet returns, he goes to sleep on the throne.

Feeling feisty from his victory, Cat Hamlet wakes, stretches, and grabs Cat Ophelia by the nape of the neck.

The curtain falls.

The audience either hisses en masse, or as a group, rolls around and purrs.

When our popular friends had company, we were welcome any time in their section of our temporary home, and I often went downstairs to enjoy the pleasant conversations that took place there. But of course I still missed Bill.

Weeks became months as work on our house went slowly. On yet another day when I was alone, I heard one of our friends in the hallway, talking to someone I just knew had to be the landlady. The voices were advancing towards the stairs. Whereas normally I would have been absorbed right back into my writing despite the murmur of voices from below, the intonations were different this time, more urgent. It sounded like the landlady wanted to pick up something that was stored in the attic area I was living in!

Quickly I shoved the litterbox and food and water dishes into a large closet. Then I grabbed Cat and entered the closet myself, holding him. I stroked and stroked him and hoped he would not purr too loud or meow. Bless his sweet kitty heart, Cat did not make a sound. I heard footsteps on the stairs. As they came closer, I could hear my friend saying it was going to take them forever to furnish this place, it really wasn't presentable up there, couldn't he just find it himself and bring it to her in a few days? And then, the sound of the footsteps going back down. I mean, he was smooth! I waited a long time before going downstairs to talk to my friend, to be sure the landlady was gone, feeling contrite about our lengthy stay. "Oh it's okay," he said, and we laughed about the close call. I remain grateful to this day. (He had even, on a prior occasion, stopped the insect exterminator from spraying our upstairs area because he knew of our cat's previous lung condition. I had asked to be told if the electronic typewriter disturbed him, and he never complained, although someone else said that it sounded like a freight train from downstairs.) It was now November, and it was clear we needed to move.

And over the next few days we did move as a light autumn rain came down on us, even though the house wasn't actually finished. Cat had another new place to adjust to, at first staying inside until he gained a sense of where he was. Then we let him go out during the day, at first only for short, supervised times. It seemed safe. Coyote sightings or noise were rare back then. We were on a dirt road off a dirt road — it was some distance from the main road that led to our drive, and there was very little traffic, moving at very slow speeds.

We were also a long way from the neighbors and could not even see their lights at night. I had to adjust to the absence of those comforting signals of lighted windows, indicating that you are not alone, that humanity is around. The large picture window in the living room opened us up to a world of forest, but our entire little scene was hidden from mainstream living. Turn off the highway onto our road and the trees hang low over you as you advance; you might not even find the right thinned place in the woods to turn off that dirt road to the one leading to our place. In a summertime aerial photograph, the roads are hard to trace out under the heavy vegetation.

Cat, too, settled in gradually. He found a sandy place up our driveway he liked to roll in. One day he ran down our drive ahead of Bill, to the road out of the neighborhood, and sprinted up a pine tree twenty feet, just like he had at the previous house, only this time he fell. Luckily, Bill got there just in time to catch him. (Contrary to popular belief, cats don't always land on their feet, and they can be injured in a fall. No one should ever throw or drop a cat! And a tumble from a high place can cause injury even when the cat does land on its feet.) Later, Cat climbed a post to the top of the trailer when Bill wasn't home, causing me alarm as to how he was going to get down, although that time, he figured it out on his own.

Space in our home was limited, and unfortunately we had to store one of Cat's favorite snoozing chairs on the second floor of Bill's workshop. The workshop was also unfinished, open to the critters and the elements. Cat made his way there, and we found him sacked out on that chair on several occasions. We also would observe Cat drinking from the muddiest puddle he could find, in preference to his well-tended water bowl inside. I think cats go for the novelty of any pool of water they haven't sampled before; they will drink *eau de mud puddle*, either vintage or freshly rained, at every opportunity! But in *The Cat Whisperer* by Mieshelle Nagelschneider, I read that cats in the wild don't drink water close by where they eat, in case of possible contamination by the prey.[2] That's why they retain the instinct to drink water that's distant from their food bowls. Nagelschneider also notes that they like running water.[3] I expect this preference has a similar basis; stagnant water tends to harbor more microbes than running water.

The few photos we had of Ligeia and Yeti were taken with a camera I'd had since 1955, but sometime in the late '70s it became so outmoded I couldn't find film for it anymore. In the '80s, we got a disc camera, and Cat was photographed looking out through the panes of glass in the door, lounging on Bill and stretching his head up as Bill scratched a place on his neck, or reclining about the house.

We'd also been taken over by The Barbecue Spirit, and cat watched many a cook-out that took place in the yard through those glass panes in the door as well as from a window facing the bricked area among the dogwoods that serves us as a patio. When the twilight deepened, everyone tromped in to eat, plates in hand, and Cat was sure to get a piece or two of meat, pulled from the areas without the spicy sauce, of course.

He had become a major lap cat, especially with Bill, and he was plumping up in those years. From above he looked like a giant hornet, with a small head and a large tush. But he still had that regal look and was referred to as "His Royal Highness" at times.

Exploring our new "neighborhood"

Fall and winter were a wet haze of muted, mottled colors, but spring colors began to brighten up to near-tropical intensities. The forest we lived in was one big chlorophyll fest jammed with critters. It was a living laboratory; we could look out upon a natural history adventure happening moment by moment. There were birds, not so many as we'd seen in town, although sometimes the dry leaves and pine moult were shifty with sparrows. We saw Yellow-Breasted Chats with golden breasts and gray everywhere else and heard their calls — quick laughing *clucks*, *whoops*, *clicks*, and melodic whistles. We saw a Blue-Gray Gnatcatcher and a Downy Woodpecker. There were owls and hawks. Daylight meant an occasional crow would flap down to the ground like a shard of night. We left the doors open back then, and one day a Purple Marten flew in, hesitated, and flew back out. Raccoons came right up on the porches.

Moths, known poetically as candle flies in rural south Alabama parlance, had been all gray and brown back in the city, like flying clumps of dust. But in the woods, the moths were plush. Huge chartreuse Luna Moths, their wings sporting tassels, skittered at the windows in spring, and we saw Imperial Moths with four-inch wingspreads. Smaller moths came in colors too; orange with black patterning like ironwork, or pink and yellow patch shapes, like on a painted pony. Some were brown with pinkish highlights, rust red and purple with a white spot on each wing; besides the traditional triangular and fan shapes, I saw one that was like two ovals joined by the center body, with a black tipped point on each outer wing. They all came in the house, frantic, fervent, for the light bulbs. I wondered what the moths had done at night before we came along, before we humans had made this valley spotty with houselights, out there in the lightless, longingless, houseless, humanless dark of all that forest of blackened greens beyond the porch.

The moths liked to roost on the rims of Cat's water dish, so I wondered if they stayed near water in their natural outside habitat, too. Moths are pollinators along with butterflies, and I've heard talk in the country of flowers that bloom at night, such as gourds, being pollinated by moths. Some Internet sources confirm this about gourds, though others indicate it's done by beetles and bees.

So many insects! The summer forest was a dense infinity of leaves, an immense salad humming with noisy, buzzing tidbits. The variety of insects was staggering; the forest was packed with them. Never had I been buzzed, bumped into, used as a landing strip, crawled upon, followed, stung, poisoned, scissored into, or had my very blood drunk by so many differing individuals. After twilight the forest became a singing soot swirl. At night during the first spring lacewings, glazed with pale transparent iridescence, buzzed around the indoors lights or just in the dark. The bedroom was workin' alive with 'em, keeping me awake.

I'm convinced the insect population in these woods contains species of bugs that are off the charts, unknown to science. The speciation is grandiose. Some are charming, like the dirt dauber wasps, also called mud daubers, which are smaller and lighter than the other wasps; non-aggressive and non-stinging, they build long mud houses in rows on any flat outdoor house surface they can find. They are iridescent, blue, green and gold like grackles, like flying bits of carnival glass. Iridescence is a phenomenon that I don't think can really be translated into words. Huge dragonflies sail around outside, along with the similar but smaller damsel flies with spots of blue on their bodies. June bugs careen about inside. These half-inch beetles seem incapable of any sensible flight plan, randomly tumbling straight into us and then buzzing off drunkenly to crash land somewhere else.

Of course there are pests, too, like regular wasps that pack a wallop, small scorpions that pack the same, fire ants (non-native, arrived by ship from South America through the Port of Mobile), the occasional snake, and a Rednecked Biped who lives by the axiom: "See woods, will shoot." To run these latter off requires aggressive verbal confrontations.

Our first summer in the woods, it was clear the critters wanted our space back; they came in through every nook and cranny of the unfinished architecture to buzz their point. At the windows, assorted unknown beetles hummed raucously at night, frantic to come in to the light. The firefly density was so great that our visitors were drawn to walking our blackened road after dark, even with its rutted, uncertain footing, just to see them. Those meandering lightning-bug legions could twist our imaginations up from somnolence to the forefront of our attention. They turned the night forest into moving tor-toiseshell.

During deep night, up in the trees, katydids made drum cadence. If we took a night walk, we'd often get webbed in the face and hope we'd see the spider running away in our peripheral vision while we slapped silk off our heads. Bill, who has been fascinated with insects since childhood, liked to show me especially unusual and interesting bugs. All bugs, of course, were observed in their natural settings, or were only briefly detained before being released back to their outdoor spaces.

In town, we had studied a praying mantis that lived on a big sunflower we grew in the yard one summer. When Bill looked at it, the mantis would move its head around and look back. It had even jumped on Bill's nose one day! (The praying mantis can articulate its head, unlike most insects.) Out in the woods, bug life included walking sticks and staghorn beetles. The volu-minous number of species inspired contemplation of infinity and poetry. Here we were adrift in this huge green salad topped with leggy bits that were loud with buzz yet not conversational, except for a type of big buzzy that just sat in the air and looked at us while we were walking or sitting in the yard, with its striped behind and seeming but inexpressible message. Known as a good news bee in the South, it's actually a fly, the Yellow Jacket Hover Fly. (All buzzing insects have come to be called "buzzies" at our house.)

In the summer the more green the leaf cascades, the more the birds shone hotly, metallically. Here in the confetti bag of flora and fauna, the bird lan-guages were foreign twittering. I didn't know yet the language of crickets, frogs, and shy things. As with the languages I studied in high school, I only know a few phrases. Evening serenades were like rapid French; I had ink-lings and affinities but mostly I just heard the melody and the passion. Trying to talk to them didn't work. All awaited study and translation. Under-brush and canopy alike invited investigation; it was all unfinished mystery, feinting denouements draped here and there, trailed willy-nilly through the woods, capricious.

Outside critters that came inside the house were safely captured and giv-en an escort back to the door and into the forest. Usually a former fast food soft drink cup was designated as a "bug cup" for this purpose. Lizards were larger and sometimes required Tupperware. Stinging wasps made their way inside and were caught in a wadded up paper towel, held there firmly as we walked to the door and tossed them out in one sweep, paper towel and all; but only if it was a solitary wasp, not a group that would attack us when we disturbed one of their members. This is not something anyone should try at home. When rushed by a group, we just let the invaders buzz on and find their own ways out.

In the mid-1980s when we first moved, after each rain there were puddles everywhere and all manner of frog yelling broke loose right outside the window, *whoops* and *chirps* and whistling *screes*, loud amphibian choral eroticism throughout the steaming jungle. Bill scooped tadpoles out of the pools of water by the windows and transferred them to the creek. Otherwise, they would have died when the heavy sunlight came out and sizzled up the water. Even at dry times, the ground was often hopping with toads and frogs. Really small frogs made crashingly loud noises, keeping us awake at night. Frogs even barked sometimes. Every time the frog voices began snapping and cracking in the trees, I'd get lost in the noise. It was almost as intense as the great clacking din we'd heard when we visited a friend who lived by the river. When our rural route finally became a named road, I tried to get it called Frog Bottom Road. We were, after all, in a sort of valley, so the land could be called "bottom land." For some reason though, that idea just didn't take, and the city went with something else!

There were also lizards, cheery little chameleons (actually called Green Anoles) that changed from chartreuse to sepia, and iridescent blue-colored skinks. Cat caught a big, five-to-six inch lizard and brought it in, and I had to transport it back outside. It looked like a basic alligator, but it had blue speckles on its throat and belly. One weekend when Bill was out of town, Cat came running swiftly in the door from outside and plopped down on the floor, breathing fast and hard. I knew immediately he'd gotten into some kind of poison. I phoned the vet who said most likely, Cat had eaten one of the blue-tailed lizards, which are poisonous to cats! I am a non-driver, but fortunately I was able to get a neighbor to take us to the vet, where Cat got a shot of the antidote. His breathing had already begun to improve, and he bounced back quickly after the shot.

The Audubon Guide to Reptiles and Amphibians confirmed that the Southeastern Five-Lined Skink is toxic to cats,[4] though now in this age of instant information, I find there is controversy over this toxicity. Some websites detail many anecdotal cases of poisoning, and others say there is no real proof. My own gut feeling is that the vet made the correct assessment since Cat recovered fully after receiving the antidote. If real proof can only be obtained by studies in which cats are deliberately exposed to toxins or lizards to see just how much will harm them, then I can say I'm satisfied to remain cautious and evict all blue-tailed lizards from the house, sans any further study. For two contrasting opinions, see the links at this note.[5] I've also read anecdotal statements from locals in Alabama who say that the blue-tailed lizards are toxic when eaten by cats. I lean towards reports by those who live with cats and report the lizard toxicity.

One day I weathered my first snake, the old "snake in the path where you are about to step" routine. I remained calm and called for Bill, who determined that it was not a venomous snake. I was then ready to graduate to the old "snake in the house where you are about to sit" routine!

After some years, the frogs outside the window disappeared and we were no longer seeing toads hopping around. It happened so subtly and we were always so busy that we really didn't notice. It was just when we looked back that we went "wow" and were stunned. Later we only had tree frogs high up in the branches singing; we called them "rain frogs" when they struck up a chorus right before a storm. We saw the occasional individual frogs that came out of a tree at night and onto our glass-front door during a shower. Either a heavy downpour had knocked them out or the rain had made them more active and they jumped onto our door, thinking it was another, peculiar, kind of tree. The frogs could have come down for the bugs, which were clustered by our door, drawn by the house light. Each frog would cling to the glass for awhile with its sticky pads, affording us an opportunity to view its inch-and-a-half, slippery self closely before it hopped back to the trees. I would look to the treetops where the frogs were hanging out unseen and wonder exactly where they were; I think of the canopy as packed full of frogs.

One of the most singular experiences of our early days in the woods was the sight and sound of the Pileated Woodpeckers. They generally avoid populated areas and are not too common, but we were forested enough for their tastes. They are not to be confused with the Ivory-Billed Woodpecker, once thought to be extinct but now reported and/or recorded in a few wild areas of Louisiana, Arkansas, and along the Choctawhatchie River in Florida. (Opinions differ as to whether the Ivory Billed actually are making a comeback.) Standing about fifteen-inches-tall with black-and-white bodies and flaring red topknots, the Pileateds make an undulating *whook–whook–whoop–whoop–whook–whoo* sound out there in the trees, very loud, very long. It has a cackling and resonant quality. Everyone who sees and hears one immediately thinks of Woody Woodpecker. However, now on the Internet we find information that suggests Woody himself was not based on the Pileated,[6] nor was his laugh based on the Pileated calls. Instead, Mel Blanc, the voice of many cartoon characters, developed Woody's laugh and says that it went back to his high school days.[7] Dang Internet! Dispels all the charming stories! Still, inspiration for Woody or not, that sound makes you feel that you have arrived deep in the jungle.

A starry-eyed perspective on country livin'

You can see many more stars in the country than in the city, because city lights brighten the darkness and there's not as much contrast between star-light and sky. So everyone living out our way tended to go out at night, sky-looking. Because we were so remote we didn't even need curtains, we could catch a nocturnal sky scene through the windows. I remember evenings watching the blackness bleed into the green, spreading its way.

One night during those early years, around 1984 or '85, a neighbor phoned and said "Go out and look at the moon." We did, and we were aston-ished. The moon was full, veiled over with light misty clouds. And surround-ing the moon on those clouds was a circular rainbow, from refracted moon-light. I don't recall which color was on the outermost edge, but I have seen photos of moon rainbows both ways — with red on the inside and blue on the outside, and vice versa. The entire spectrum was there: purple, indigo, blue, green, yellow, orange, red bands; each grayed on the clouds but clearly visi-ble. We spent a long time outside. Although we didn't find anyone else who saw the moon that night, and there was no mention of it in the paper, my later research indicates that it's a genuine phenomenon that occurs rarely when conditions are just right.

The moonlight, which is of course reflected sunlight, is refracted by ice crystals in the upper atmosphere when there is a layer of high, cirriform clouds. They're thin enough for the moon to shine through. It's called a moon corona and is not to be confused with the much larger moon halo, which is also caused by cirrus clouds and refracting ice crystals. It's also not to be confused with the corona of the sun, the outer gases that are visible dur-ing a solar eclipse. I don't really know if city light makes a difference in the visibility of moon coronas or not. We've seen many cloudy nights when the full moon casts reddish or golden tones on surrounding clouds, in the city and country alike, but we never saw the rainbow around the moon again.

We probably told Cat that the moon and the sky were amazing that night, but he no doubt kept cool and showed no reaction. Although animals do seem to react to coming earthquakes and disasters, cats are practical and their interest in the sky probably extends to whether it's raining on them or not, and whether they can get under something to keep dry or not. The "smell-head" noted our absence using his feline smell-recognition-sensory-technique to detect our two odors leaving, and then saw us in the yard via his superior ability to see into darkness, so he was probably thinking, *what are they doing out there looking at the sky when they could be feeding me, and when is din-ner, anyway?*

On another night, in 1986, Haley's Comet came around and was visible from Earth, so Bill called a few of our neighbors and they went up to the highest point on the adjacent large hill with binoculars. Conditions weren't optimal for viewing and they only saw a fuzzy glow, not the tail. But in town it wouldn't have been seen at all because of nighttime lights. I don't recall why I missed out on that expedition; I can only imagine that I knew the going would be rough, and I didn't feel up to climbing that evening.

Days could be as suddenly scenic as nights. One afternoon after a storm a partial cloudiness made trees on the other side of the lakebed look on fire, the rounded treescape patched against deeper tones, like a piebald horse. There was a complete, whole arc rainbow, with another rainbow above it.

Despite all this glory, there were things that were difficult to deal with in the country at first. My narrow work room, our slim hallway, the solitude, the boxes of unpacked books. While drawing I tended to envision faces and masks, an impulse to see other humans. It was a beautiful fleshy green out there in the forest, but it felt desolate, too. Country nights could feel neighbor-less, endlessly black and muzzy and smoke gray; it was a black, black walk through the woods after dark until we came upon the one "streetlight." I was sometimes in the doldrums from too much Paradise.

People in the city often want to move to the country, and I think this is a worthy goal. Yet after our experiences I do believe you need to thoroughly investigate what you'll be getting into. There were unanticipated differences for us, and giving up the conveniences of city life can be quite an adjustment. In town, friends had frequently dropped by to "shoot the breeze" for an evening, or we could suddenly run out to stop by friends' houses or to meet them for a movie or concert or art event or to grab a meal, which gave zest and spontaneity to the flow of our days. The wilds were just too far off the beaten paths for this to happen; visits had to be planned, invitations issued, friends called ahead of time. It just didn't feel as much like a freewheeling community, although the visits that did happen, shared out in the wild, often had an extra dimension of camaraderie to them. Nevertheless, these walks weren't without added concerns, too. Laws vary throughout the country on when and if hunters can come on your land. If you like to walk in the woods, you will need to add Day-Glo orange to your fall and winter wardrobe, or perhaps forego those wanderings entirely during hunting season when you might be shot for a deer.

Finding a friend in the woods: Hopalong the fox

The forest always displays, presents, and improvises. Bill made a bird feeder and placed it about fifteen feet from the living room window, on a tall, slick metal pole that Cat couldn't climb and with no branch hanging close so he could not jump onto the feeder, either. That way, Cat had no chance of stalking or catching the birds. Many birds came, among them little Gold Finches, all bright gold except for their dark black wings and a dark black spot above their beaks. To our surprise the feeder wasn't varmint-proof, and one night the raccoons destroyed it. Getting right to the point, they deftly lifted up the glass sides and let them fall. Birdseed and corn kernels were scattered all over the ground.

A few days after, I was in the back of the house in late afternoon light. Through the window, out of the blackness of unlit trees, I saw a small form moving through the woods, parallel to the house and in the direction of the living room. "It's a fox," I yelled to Bill, rushing to the front. The sound made the animal turn and run.

I was home alone the second time I saw a canid out the window. There, lapping at the corn, was a Gray Fox. I kept very still, thrilled, watching this beautiful wild animal. Its fur was a heathered blend of shimmering silvers, blacks, grays, and whites, with a russet blush on its throat. Its eyes were keen, its ears perked and alert. It moved with a hopping motion; this was a lame fox, not the same one we'd seen initially; one of its hind legs was bent and missing the paw at the end. The leg hung uselessly, not touching the ground, the obvious result of a vicious device: the steel-jaw leghold trap. After eating, the fox visitor turned and started for a path through the woods. As it got further away, three raccoons edged back down the tree trunks and resumed feeding. (Years later, Bill would meet the individual who worked on an adjacent tract of land and had found the fox in the trap and let it out, and who had fed it awhile until it disappeared. We would never know who had set the trap or exactly where, but in this area of the country, hunters range around in the woods. For a long time after our forest became populated by us and our neighbors, we all had to run occasional gun-carrying intruders off our land. Some even pulled up to our mailboxes and seeing our driveway and obvious signs of a nearby house, began shooting anyway.)

The fox began coming back every evening and Bill named it Hopalong. I can't recall exactly when we decided to feed it, but we began tossing table scraps and chicken leftovers out the window, and it started coming earlier to avoid the quarrelsome raccoons. Feeding wild animals is usually a bad idea, as they become dependent, and wildlife advocates highly recommend against it these days. But this three-legged fox was at a huge disadvantage when it came to hunting its natural prey; it really couldn't move very fast. Humans had injured this animal, and it seemed right that other humans should feed it. Foraging for bird seed seemed a sure sign of lean pickins. In the natural flow

of nature, the strong survive and the weak die off, but there was nothing natural about the way this fox had become disadvantaged.

We began collecting restaurant cornbread, otherwise known as "corn
sticks." We lunched with friends and our employees (who were also all our
friends) at a country-style cafeteria in town. Bill had a tendency to park
across the street and cross without the benefit of the corner light, and, in a
numb work daze, we all followed him one day, only to become stranded in
the middle of the street with traffic coming both ways. "We'll get run over,"
I exclaimed, and he replied, "It's not my karma to get run down in the middle
of the street." Gary quipped back, "Doesn't saying that change your karma?"
We did survive, and I sought out street corners and waited for lights from
then on.

Corn sticks are a fast-food type of cornbread that came with every meal
at the cafeteria. I've actually had some delicious home-made cornbread, but
"fast" can do in the appeal of any kind of food. I wasn't much of a cornbread
fan to begin with, and nobody else ever ate the cafeteria cornbread, not even
Bill, who likes cornbread, so we always had plenty left to wrap in thin nap-
kins and carry home every day. Bill would even ask other patrons of the restaurant if he could have their uneaten corn sticks for "his dog," avoiding the
whole lot of explaining that "his fox" would have evoked. Asking other patrons yielded a good haul since no one else ever ate the stuff, either.

But corn sticks were an absolute favorite with Hop, who rarely ate it on
the spot, but took it off and came back after a few minutes to watch the window until we tossed more. She would pop up each time from an entirely different direction, cleverly establishing no pattern. We began buying dog food
and leaving it out for the fox. We tried dog biscuits, too. Food for canines
was the closest we could come commercially, since wild fox food wasn't
available in the local grocery. (I found out years later that it's actually available, but only by special order.) Hop liked both dog food and dog biscuits,
and we had neighbors come and leave out the dog food once a day if we
traveled away from home for a day or two. But corn sticks remained a great
favorite with this animal. If cornbread had been around when humans first
threw scraps out to wolves, it would have hugely sped up dog domestication!

Although foxes are canines, they are a different species from wolves and
dogs. Gray Foxes are scientifically called *urocyon cinereoargenteus*; the genus name joins "tail" and "dog," the species name translates to "silver."[8]
They are the only American canines that can climb trees,[9] and after the young
leave their parents in the fall, they still come back to visit at times.[10] Gray
Foxes are native to North America, and unlike the Red Fox in Europe, they
can't run for long periods and aren't much good for fox hunts with horses

and hounds. The colonists imported Red Foxes (*vulpes vulpes*) from Britain[11] because they are good runners who rely on their speed and cunning to elude predators and can therefore be hunted in the traditional way. Although in America the goal of such hunts is not to the kill the fox, it does happen on occasion. Even one rare occurrence is too many for me. I'd prefer it if the hunters would take the dogs out for a run with a fake lure and the horses out for a gallop. They would be preserving the legacy of moving through the landscape and fresh air in the company of well-trained, fine animals, without harassing the little wild things. Despite his seemingly carefree lifestyle, I do not believe that the Red Fox enjoys being chased by predators.

There are some naturalists who think that there actually was a species of boreal Red Fox indigenous to America, larger than the British reds. Imported foxes were released in the temperate areas, and with range drift, the two species have interbred to produce the fox seen in America today. Red Foxes have been seen in rural areas in Alabama, too, but they and the Gray Foxes seem to range in different places. The Gray Foxes like places with dense cover and trees they can climb to escape predators; they are also homebodies who like to stay in their dens. The Red Fox likes open fields and wooded areas and will even rest in open places in the grass or brush, spending little actual time in the den. Anecdotal reports suggest the Red Fox is much less shy. He or she is built for speed and has thick paw pads for distance running. Extraordinary smarts enable him to manipulate his scent trail and confuse predators through stratagems such as backtracking, leaping onto fences, and making use of waterways. Their dens can have up to five entrances, making this fox difficult for predators to dig out.

Each of these foxes, Gray and Red, have the necessary skills and escape mechanisms to live their respective lifestyles and survive well. The Red Fox is often found resting out in the open on fox-hunting days not because it enjoys being chased and terrified by hounds, but because that's the way he or she lives. Red Foxes are frequently photographed sleeping in the open on top of the snow, with their plush tails wrapped around them for warmth.

I would look out the window for Hop, our fox, while eating toast to show it that I was not hunting, as I had already caught my toast. Keeping the room quiet, with no sounds from the television or conversations, was best. Slowly we got the little wild thing to come closer to the window; it would run up, grab the food, and then run off really fast. Evening meant the careful air-sniff of the fox. While some tend their window boxes full of flowers, I tended my window fox.

We didn't know for sure if our fox was a vixen, although when a second, larger fox showed up one day, we suspected he was the male of the pair. We named him Bob for his bobbing head movements. He had an eager look and an aura of slaphappy levity. When Hop began barking and biting at the raccoons, looking thin and acting hungry and snappish, we suspected the foxes might have cubs out in the forest. And when she brought two teenage cubs around at the end of the summer, we knew by the way they followed her that Hop was a female. We wondered if one fox parent was the hunter and the other was the baby-sitter, or if they shared these tasks. Bob, like Hop, would watch and wait outside the window for us to notice and toss cornbread. Both foxes began to bypass the dog food and dog biscuits and would wait, looking at the window, for corn sticks. Only when we'd tossed all the cornbread would they eat the dog food and treats.

On occasion Bob would nab some cornbread, make barking sounds, and run the cornbread out to Hop, who was waiting at the edge of the thicker woods. Sometimes he would have to make a squealing signal before Hop would come closer to him to take the food. We even thought we saw Bob carrying a cub in his mouth, momcat-and-kitten style, but the gloom was too thick to actually tell. We spent many hours gazing at them, and sometimes, when I was drawing at the table in front of the window and felt a presence, I'd look up and see Bob watching me, and I'd feel like maybe he was observing and studying us. I couldn't shake the feeling, as I basked in his glance upon me, that his interest was greater than cornbread. We had a scholarly fox out there. If we glanced out and the foxes weren't seen, we still felt something, some sort of presence in the mottled glaze of forest colors, full of hidden alertness.

A large number of raccoons also began coming for the food, including young ones, and at times, a few possums, too, so we had a wildlife party in the yard every night, illuminated by the floodlights we had installed to light up the trees in the dark. We had front-row seats. There was rivalry for the goodies; the fox would snap at the raccoons, and once in response, one of them swung his great brown bulb of a behind around and sat down directly on the food. These other visitors, like the foxes, favored the cornbread. The raccoons didn't appear to be afraid of us; they just looked at us. At first there were about four, a masked ball going on outside the windows. Numbers grew, traffic increased. From time to time various local health departments will air-drop baits full of rabies vaccines over the forests, hoping the foxes and raccoons will eat it. "They ought to use cornbread for the bait," Bill says. Hop and Bob began coming earlier than the raccoons' regular time to avoid the maskers once we started putting chicken leftovers out. We could tell from occasional sightings of scats when foxes and raccoons alike were chowing down on ripe blackberries from the lakebed in addition to our canine biscuit and table scrap entrées.

Eventually, we also had *beaucoup de possums* out there. During the day, other forest dwellers came for the food, too; turtles, a clucking scold of a Ladderbacked Woodpecker, and crows. The crows made music; they had a repertoire of sounds, like musicians. There were squirrel-like sounds, jungle bird sounds, mewling sounds like cats, *caws, click-click-clicks*, the sound of a car door slamming, and noises almost like human voices. You don't realize these sounds are from crows until you go outside and see that the only thing around is, crows. Crows have incredible variance of expression in their voices and the ability to mimic a wide range of sounds. I suspect sometimes these sardonic wits are laughing at me and at all humans from their lofty heights in the sky, although I never actually catch them at it. Using their smarts, they would come to eat the dog food during the day, before the foxes could get there.

We'd round up Cat before fox time and get him into the house every night. But one day Hop came earlier in the evening than usual and encountered Cat in the yard. I rushed out to collect Cat. They looked at each other about ten feet apart for a few minutes, and then the fox turned to leave while Cat advanced and stopped, me holding my breath. Both soon went about their respective business while I stood on alert to run the fox off if need be, with a piece of restaurant cornbread in my hand. The fox left leisurely and turned to give me a long look, as though thinking, *so that's who you live with*. Cat had certainly seen the foxes and raccoons out the window many times before and he seemed unruffled by them. But he was, as I've said, a particularly serene cat.

Bill had made an ant-proof feeder for Hop with a moat around it. At one time he surrounded the feeder with wet sand, hoping to get a track from which he could make a casting in plaster of Paris. But Hop would have none of this; she turned and left, snoot in air. Bill ran out and moved the food, and she came back and ate. You cannot outfox the fox!

One morning, we found that something (we suspected raccoons) had dug the sand completely up the prior night, and there was one fox-like print in it. Bill smoothed it out, but again, Hop would not step on the sand. In fact, she and her cubs wouldn't even eat food that was next to the sand, preferring the food on a large flat rock, the location they were accustomed to. Picky, wary little wildlings, used to keeping their guard up all the time, relying on the known. I start taking notes on their behavior, calling it the "Fox Dossier."

As I gazed out the big picture window one afternoon in spring, there was another startling sight. Two large, wild canids were making their way down the path from the lakebed towards the house at a trot, single file. I froze in astonishment. They were medium shaggy all over with grayish, sandy, and brownish tones. When the leader got close to the window and saw me staring at them, he or she turned, and with near imperceptible motion, both spun around and ran off back into the woods. In all likelihood, they were coyotes. That's what everyone I talked to about it thought. Coyotes co-exist with humans in many areas of the United States, and indeed, years later we would hear groups of them yipping on the lakebed at night, especially after trains had gone by blowing high-pitched whistles that likely irritated their ears. Even in the center of town, where there are seven acres of woodland, there are now frequent reports of coyote sightings. I went through all the nature guides; I'd only seen pictures of coyotes before then, and I had no idea what an actual coyote would look like in person, as opposed to, say, a wolf.

To the best of my recollection, the animals I saw that day were larger and burlier than most coyotes I've seen in photos. I thought surely that they were wolves. But there are always exceptions, and possible hybrids, and other friends who've seen coyotes report that they are large. I had not yet heard the many stories of coyotes killing domestic cats, or else I would have been extremely alarmed by the encounter. In this way I still had the naiveté of a city person who hadn't actually lived in the wilds for long. In my world, in my mind, wild animals and domestic ones were just separate, and I pictured coyotes preying on wild rabbits, not people's pet cats. I never saw any large wild canines in our woods for many years after, and I suspect that pair I saw may have been moving through, as opposed to being permanent residents. Still, absence of animal sightings does not always mean they aren't skulking around. I was coming to realize that many more animals were watching us than were allowing us to watch them, and in retrospect I can only hope we did not alarm them too much, but rather just kept them entertained.

I realized in later years, after hearing about coyotes becoming bolder and attacking domestic dogs and even humans, that I had the perfect kind of moment with them. It was as though they had said, *okay you saw us, but we're wild, we'll just be going now,* before they sprang off at warp speed. Large wild animals that are too comfortable around humans can be hazardous.

William Faulkner's work referred to wolves in the Mississippi wilderness. That was most likely the Red Wolf, *canis rufus,* which once ranged throughout the southern United States but is now very limited in range and population. I once thought of it in connection with the canids I saw but eventually ruled out that possibility. More scholarship is coming to light about hybridization of coyotes and dogs and wolves resulting in so-called coywolves. These animals are moving eastward, according to some reports

I've seen. There may or may not be new species forming, but hybridization could account for the large size of the two particular canids I saw.

Chapter 6

The Scream[1]

During one of those early summers in the forest, around 1985 or 1986, we worked late one night at our print shop in town. We drove up to the house around 9 o'clock in the evening, just after dark. As soon as we opened the car doors we heard terrified screaming in the woods that sounded desperate and tragic. It came from the direction of an old road down to the dry lake bottom, so Bill sent me in the opposite direction, toward the house, as he hurried back down that way toward the screaming. He thought someone was being abducted and murdered.

"Who is that, what are you doing here, who are you?" he yelled as he advanced. The screaming just kept going, starting on a low note with the second elongated syllable going very high and loud, ending abruptly. It came from the bushes at ground level. The night was moonless, ink-spill dark, and Bill could not see or locate anything. After several unvaried repetitions, he realized it might be an animal, possibly raccoons. And he knew the fox was raising another litter of cubs that summer; he thought maybe the neighborhood dogs had gotten into the fox den and were killing the cubs. He'd also heard that sometimes a rabbit will scream. He came back to the house, grabbed a flashlight, and looked for anything he could use as a weapon. A broom was the best he could find, and he went back out the door to try to illuminate whatever it was and to rescue fox cubs if need be. Only he didn't have time to explain to me that he thought it might be an animal rather than a distressed human. I patted Cat's fur for reassurance, hearing the thing that I feared was a person still screaming. We waited.

Out in the brush, Bill kept after the screamer — if the screaming stopped, he'd throw a pebble or a stick in the direction of the sound, and it would start again. He kept slapping at the bushes with his broom, thinking cubs were being killed. The noise would let him get about twenty feet away, and then run off, stop again, and scream, over and over. Bill could never get the flashlight on it. Once the animal got to the lakebed, the thing sped up, retreating rapidly across the flat ground. Bill went forward on the path while the animal took its own course through the brush. He lost it but could still hear it, and again it stood its ground and shrieked and shrieked until he approached, then bolted, keeping a safe and invisible distance from the broom bearing human.

On the lake bottom, Bill quit thrashing the bushes and throwing things. He kept on advancing until the screaming crossed the creek and went up the steep bluff on the other side, probably following one of the little gullies that ran down to the branch, where there was still cover. If it had climbed the sheer cliff face, Bill probably would have seen it, but after that he hurried back and jumped in the car, again without explanation to me. I was still sitting with Cat and still thinking that murder and mayhem were about. Bill drove off to the highway and around to the neighbor's land, where the road to the house ran along the edge of the hill that the screamer had scaled. He parked and got out, still hearing the disembodied screaming. He threw a few sticks, but the animal was over the next hill and too far away. So Bill came home.

"It was an animal," he began, relieving my fears as he relayed the incident. We puzzled about it. One of his questions was why had the thing not just run off right away? Why let Bill get close and then sprint off, again and again?

Bill re-walked the route the next day looking for tracks, but it was a dry year and the ground was rocky besides, not good conditions for tracks to impress. Later that day he told the tale to our neighbors up the road towards the highway. It had been under one of their houses last night, they said. The screaming woke them up. They thought that their young son had gotten out of the house in the night and gotten hurt. The sound was so convincingly human that they didn't even stop to check the boy's room but went rushing out with a flashlight to rescue him. Out from under their rather large crawl space, the thing had whooshed past, a big tawny animal with a long tail. Happily, their son was found safe in his room; he'd never gone outside, never been injured, and never made any noise. In another house, another neighbor heard a scream sounding like a lady.

But a few days later, driving through a hilly subdivision just beyond a little gas station nearby, a friend's mother saw a big, yellow cat run across the road in front of her car: a cougar, she said.

And weeks later, the local newspaper reported the experience of a woman who lived about thirty miles away, towards Birmingham. Her dogs were going wild with alarm and she looked out and saw a cougar on her porch. She called a game official, who came out to investigate and to look for tracks or scat. As we recall, one track was found but he said she'd just seen a German Shepherd; cougars were officially "extinct" in Alabama. I read nowadays that sightings are frequent but still considered anecdotal evidence, likely to be a case of mistaken identity. Authentic proof is considered to be documented tracks, scat (a "close encounter of the turd kind"[2]), a road-killed carcass, an illegally shot carcass (cougars are protected), or a photograph. None of which will show up if your cougar steps lightly, is constipated, or is nimble and wary enough to avoid cars, hunters, and the paparazzi.

Seriously though, we concluded after the fact that we had a mountain lion passing through. Bill would never have given chase if he'd thought he was after any animal more formidable than a raccoon or a neighborhood dog attacking rabbits or foxes. He had walked the woods, both ours and the surrounding neighbors' land, many times, and he had never seen anything to suggest that cougars, or even bobcats, were out there. But the reliable sightings from neighbors and friends, along with a sighting to the north by an individual who had no knowledge of our own sightings and encounters and who was therefore not influenced via hearsay-driven escalation when suddenly *everyone* starts seeing a large cat, constituted solid anecdotal evidence. We felt that there really had been a cougar screaming its way through the woods that one night.

Bobcats once ranged throughout Alabama in various places, but they were always rare and elusive, night hunters who were seldom seen. Farmers tended to shoot them to protect their chickens, as artist friends who lived on a farm in a county north of us had told it, and they had an explosion of rabbits eating up their gardens as a result. But the long tail on the intruder under the neighbor's house ruled out the possibility that it was a bobcat, which is a short-tailed animal.

Back then, everything we knew suggested cougar was the correct answer to this mystery. Bill was from an area of southeastern Alabama very close to the Florida line. When he was growing up, everyone talked about Florida "painters," that word no doubt a variation of panther. Painters were like cougars in every way, went the buzz, except they were black. Bill's best friend was fishing in Florida and saw a black one cross the road. In the mid-'50s, his Aunt Lola, who lived in the deep woods in Florida, also spoke of black painters, and Bill's mother, who grew up in farm country nearby, said many times that you could hear painters screaming in the woods at night. Everyone, Bill recalls, said that they sound like a woman screaming. He also recalls that everyone said they were black. In the history of the area written by Bill's father, Eddie Alford, he notes that if wagon parts weren't kept properly oiled, they would "squeal like a panther."[3] Rick Bragg, in his book on northeastern Alabama in the '60s, notes that panthers were in the area; he also says the big cat's vocalizations sound like a woman's scream.[4]

The books we had also supported our conclusion. In the 1980 *Audubon Society Field Guide to North American Mammals*, the range map appears to cover Alabama and parts of the Appalachians and says that screaming is a mating call described at times as being like a woman's scream.[5] The 1981 edition of Leonard Lee Rue III's *Complete Guide to Game Animals* also includes Alabama and lower Mississippi, as well as larger areas of the Appalachians than are depicted by the Audubon guide, in the cougar range. Rue also indicates that melanistic, or black, cougars exist in Florida, and he writes that the mountain-lion scream sounds like a woman's scream, citing a description that matches Bill's experience: a cry starting at low pitch that slowly ascends.[6]

The pattern of Bill's chase with the unknown animal, his ability to get within twenty feet repeatedly before the critter moved off each time, also matches the description by the late animal expert Roger Caras of a chase through the Florida Everglades after a Florida Panther. They kept missing the cat by seconds, as the animal advanced just far enough to avoid being seen, time and again. This, concludes Caras in *A Cat is Watching*, is the way cats like it; watching you, letting you approach to a distance of their choosing, and letting you watch them only when they want to be seen.[7]

A reliable acquaintance who had been hunting in the Sipsey Swamp back in the days of Bill's broom chase had once watched a cougar in the swamp through a telescopic rifle sight.

We've never doubted that Bill chased a mountain lion, cougar, Florida painter, catamount (a New England term, but I've seen it elsewhere), or whichever of its hundreds of names you want to call it, through the lakebed and up the hill that night. Maybe Bill's aggressive chase convinced that rather secretive animal not to settle down in our woods, since we never heard one or had any other indication of cougar presence again. That was fine by me, for the protection of our own house felines, our small wild animals, the deer, and ourselves — although cougars usually prefer to avoid people, fatal attacks on humans have occurred.

Furthermore, a friend also reported a cougar sighting in Marengo County many years ago. Almost all boys who grew up in the country hunted as children, usually small birds and squirrels, also known as tree rats. Rural life back then was different from modern life, either urban or rural, and those boys were well-schooled in using guns. In those days, no child would have dreamed of using a gun improperly. (Things have changed and modern times are different, and I believe we now need tighter regulation of firearms.) My friend and his cousin were out on a hunt when they saw what they thought at first was a deer lying in the grass. But when it rose to its feet, they saw it was a large yellow cat, and those kids dropped their rifles and ran. As it turned out, they escaped unharmed. (The usual advice is to never turn your back or crouch, but to back away slowly, making yourself look as large as possible.) They also heard the scream. Nowadays, our friend still hears cougars screaming and occasionally finds a track on the same land, usually in the marshier areas. I absolutely believe, in this case, that our friend knew what he saw. People who grow up in rural areas learn keenness of observation and wilderness smarts early, and they know how to pick out details way off in the landscape where the unschooled might only see an indistinguishable jumble of vegetation, shadows, and beasts.

More interesting anecdotal evidence: Word-of-mouth reports placed cougars in a nearby neighborhood, close to Hurricane Creek, as recently as a few years ago. In Greene County, we heard reports in 2007 of tawny cougars being spotted in that mostly rural area, and there are even older tales of "black panthers" being seen in the backwoods there. In addition, a trusted local veterinarian reports that thirty years ago, a man brought in two sick cougars in need of vet care. He said he had raised them from cubs found in Alabama.

Years after Bill's chase, there's a flood of information and discussion online about cougars, along with a number of disagreements and controversies. But about the scream, there's a consensus. Like house cats, cougars have a wide variety of vocalizations: *yowls, hisses, growls, purrs, mews, chirps,* and sometimes a whistle or a *trill* and, most sources say, a scream. It's found on many serious wildlife information sites, and it's often compared to a woman's scream. Some seasoned outdoorsmen say they've never heard it, but others describe the chill of hearing it for the first time. Some literature indicates that the scream occurs during mating season; smaller members of the feline family certainly turn into opera singers when mating, with lamentations and celebrations late into the night.

Lions, and tigers, and cougars — oh my!

Felis concolor, meaning cat of one color, once ranged throughout all of the United States, but with habitat loss, it became extinct in the East by about the early 20th Century. In his 1962 novel *The Reivers,* William Faulkner describes bear, deer, wolves, and panthers as existing in the relatively untouched swamps and wilderness of late 19th Century Mississippi,[8] but by 1905 bears and panthers were gone, and still later, the wilderness became cropland.[9]

Cougars are known by more names than any other mammals, including one of my personal favorites: catamount, a term that is also sometimes applied to a lynx. Many of those names are First American and the word *cougar* means "false deer" in Tupi, an Amazonian language.[10] (Wild animals do combine visually with the landscape and are easily misidentified in the wild!) They were called panthers and tigers by early settlers in Florida, and the name panther lasted somehow, though mountain lion is more common out West.

Panther, the term used mainly in the East and South for these big cats, is not to be confused with the black panthers in zoos. Those are black (melanistic) variants of the leopard found in Africa and Asia, and if you look closely at black panthers at the zoo, you will see the leopard spots visible on their coats. They are just dark leopards. Panther nowadays more commonly refers to these black leopards, which is a completely different species from the cougar. But in early America, and even in literature of the early 20th Century, panther was a general term for large cat and was also applied to cougars. Somehow, as words do, that term fell out of use, except in the southeastern United States.

In keeping with the older meaning and adding somewhat to the confusion, the original classification by Linnaeus of all cats as the genus *Felis* has now been changed in some cases: *Panthera* is now the genus for big cats; the species of tiger, for example, is sometimes called *Panthera tigris* and the lion is *Panthera leo*. The cougar is not a part of the *Panthera* genus, but the older use of the term "panther" has been grandfathered in by popular parlance, as in the name of the Florida Panther. Since I've come to frequent the Internet, I've learned there are those who would probably say that panther is only "correct" when used to mean the black leopards seen in zoos. But the older meaning refers to any large cats, as the new taxonomic practice reveals, much like lion is also used in "mountain lion."

If language was a frozen rather than a liquid and mutable entity, then the original/older term might carry some weight as the most "accurate" use of the word. But one is not more correct than the other. There is only the way people actually speak. Regional speech ways are not "ignorant" or incorrect. As for the cougar, I've seen it called *Puma concolor* rather than *Felis concolor* these days. I'm interested in how this change in panther terminology came about. The Wikipedia page acknowledges both meanings but doesn't say much about the older, original usage. When I was a child going to the zoo in the late '40s and early '50s, the change had occurred and the black leopard was called "panther." In 1943, the black leopard at the zoo in Val Lewton's film *Cat People* was also called a panther. In a curious and possibly cultural blend, a piece of rural-obtained knowledge from those who lived up-close with cougars is reflected in the movie when Irena describes the scream of the zoo panther as being like that of a woman. And although the theme of the movie is the panther/woman who shape-shifted back and forth, I feel that direct knowledge of screaming cougars likely figured into that idea.

Nowadays, since the first decade of the 21st Century, people are calling black domestic cats "panthers," "mini-panthers," "parlour panthers," or "house panthers" to be expressive. The song "Panther in Michigan,"[11] written by Michael Peter Smith, came on the radio one lonely autumn night long ago and drew my attention from across the room. It appears to detail a real-life account of a cougar roaming (and screaming) in Michigan, and it makes me wonder if panther is actually used in rural Michigan, or if the songwriter used the term because he had spent some time in Florida. Whether it's used artfully or as part of an authentic record of a big-cat event, the song is truly haunting.

As time has gone on, melanistic African Servals have been documented occasionally and links about this can be found on the Internet.[12]

The term "panther" has certainly danced and shifted within the general family of felids! However, I have recently been annoyed by the way the word "cougar" has made a quantum leap to the realm of human behavior, coming rather quickly to mean a woman involved with a younger man. Language always changes and the "cat is out of the bag" on that one, so I'm resigned but never thrilled when natural history terms are applied to human behavior.

Making sense of what we heard in the forest

The Florida Panther, *Felis concolor coryi*, is one of twenty or thirty cougar subspecies. It's protected, and schoolchildren once voted it the Florida state mammal. Because the animals were getting hit by cars, panther underpasses have been built in that state.[13] But outside of Florida, say that cougars have been seen recently around the Eastern United States and disagreements begin. Numerous sightings have been reported, and while there are many believers, there's plenty of disbelief and sometimes even derision, too, especially if the reported sighting is a black cougar.

Sorting all this out isn't easy. Identification in the wild is difficult; size is hard to judge and color, too, in the varied lighting situations of nature, and there's an absence of documented proof, of tracks, scat, or roadkill. People are seeing either escaped captive animals or dogs, say wildlife officials; Black Labradors are the official verdict when the reported sightings are black cougars. I'm not going to take a strong stand one way or another here; I'm hardly up to a hissing contest. But although I favor carefully documented scientific effort, I also believe in carefully investigated anecdotal evidence that's found credible. And, if you've spent time with housecats, you know that cats don't move like dogs.

As for me, with my practiced eye I think I'd know cat-slink from dog-trot or dog-amble anywhere. Mistaken identity is of course possible; imagine

an actual cougar coming around, with a housecat's self-importance and attitude towards the canine, compounded by top-of-the-food-chain arrogance,
thinking *take me for a dog, will you?* There's an interesting suggestion that
the jaguarundi, a small and secretive wildcat that's seldom seen even in its
known territories, actually ranges much more widely in the South and accounts for the numerous "black panther" sightings. The jaguarundi, or *Puma
yagouaroundi*, is slightly larger than a housecat, its body long and low to the
ground. Living mainly in Central and South America and in southern Texas,
there's a feral population in Florida of escaped pets that dates back to the
'40s.

The literature differs on the color of the species, mostly describing just
two variants: a reddish-brownish and a dark grayish. Some include a black
phase, however, and notably, the *Audubon Field Guide*[14] and others note that
black is the color of the gray individuals' winter coats. Whatever species (or
fancy, if you will) the reports of black panthers might be, I've noticed sightings are frequent enough for many official information sites to take the trouble to say that "no, there are no black Florida panthers or black cougars; they
have never been authenticated, photographed, captured, or killed, etc." But,
says one site, melanistic bobcats do exist, and experts in general give cre-
dence to the possibility of melanistic bobcats, which are noted as having been
documented in Florida.[15]

Regarding tracks: in *The Tribe of Tiger*, Elizabeth Marshall Thomas ob-
serves that cats are indeed light steppers and don't usually leave good tracks.
Cougars, bobcat, and lynx will select ground that is hard-packed and step
around short stretches of snow to avoid leaving clear tracks because, as hunters, they know the importance of stealth and of not leaving a trail.[16] So a lack
of tracks does not always mean there are no cats around.

In 1999, *Alabama Wildlife Magazine* published an article called "Cougar,
Alabama's Native Lion."[17] This very balanced treatment says that at one
time, Florida panthers of the regular sandy/tawny color were native here, and
the article points out that around the state there are many panther place
names, such as Panther Creek, Panther Branch, Panther Hill, and Panther
Knob. In fact, there's a Panther Creek mentioned in Eddie Alford's book.[18]
But, according to the article, there has been no actual evidence verified by
wildlife professionals for decades.

Sightings, however, come on a regular basis, and although some can be
assumed to be bobcats, some can also be assumed to be cougars. If so, they
are either escaped captives or passersby, and there is not likely to be a breeding population in Alabama. Florida's known group of panthers get hit by cars
and illegally shot, and there are no reports of that in Alabama. Although we

have plenty of deer around, which are the cougar's main prey, our forests are fragmented and unlikely to provide cougars with the wide range and distance from humans that they prefer.[19] The article certainly sounds sensible, and the cougar we heard was a passerby, since we can reasonably assume from a lack of further encounters that he or she didn't settle in our woods. Bill wondered if it was an escaped captive since it came so close to the houses. And, well, there was an outdoor catnip patch in the neighborhood.

The *Alabama Wildlife Magazine* article goes on to say that belief in the black cougar in the South is part of local folklore that is widely believed.[20] Another article by Mark Bailey in the summer 2003 issue, "The Myth of the Black Panther,"[21] again points out that there's no evidence of black cougars in Alabama and that we may have jaguarundi; black panther stories are just part of the South's charm.

If we hop the pond to the *Messybeast Cat Resource Archive* by Sarah Hartwell, specifically to a very detailed article called "Mutant Big Cats," we'll find a statement that makes sense to me: housecats have all kinds of color variations, so why not big cats? Hartwell notes that a possible reason is that in the wild, such variations are less likely to survive. Pumas, which are normally tawny, have also been reported as black, leucistic (white), albino (lacking pigment) grey, and dark brown. The two familiar forms of leopard coloration are tawny with black spots and the melanistic form that's often called "black panthers," but Hartwell indicates that many variations have been found, including reddish with chocolate brown markings and some with white and/or albino fur. Of course, these are found infrequently.[22] It all gets very colorful, when you take a look around at documented rare variations. And, many sources indicate that black jaguars do exist.

Again, I agree with experts that we've probably got no breeding cougar populations around in Alabama; if we did, those of us living in the country would hear the shrieks of mating painters. I also think that some reported cougar sightings, whether tawny, black, or other colors, are in fact mistaken identity, but I know also that some other sightings are not. Bill chased one screaming, ochre-color cougar that was briefly holed up under the neighbors' house, and that's no folkloric tall-tale.

He continues to charm people with the story, as he did during a New Year's Day party in 2006. A visitor from Ireland made some comments as Bill recounted the events: "See, that's the difference in city people and coun-try people, country people run toward the horrible screaming," and "The cougar's thinking, 'Why chase a deer, these humans are running towards me?'" Did he believe Bill's story? He seemed to, but then again, who knows. History and its perceived veracity are sometimes formed by whatever attitudes shade the receptivity to the stories told. But as for me, I actually heard the thing scream.

Then there are those who say the wildlife officials do know that cougars are here, but they just deny it so that people don't go out shooting them out of fear or as trophies or as perceived threats to domestic fowl, the way people do that other important predator, the bobcat. To further muddy the waters, a friend also reports that another mid-sized cat was seen in Marengo County years ago; it was not a short-tailed bobcat but was about the same size, twenty or thirty pounds heavier than a domestic cat, with a long tail. Our friend called the animal a "wildcat." It was either black or a tortoiseshell color, mostly black with highlights of red. How this fits into the wildlife picture I don't know, but hybridization seems like a possibility. I tend to think that often there is more out there in the forest than meets the eye, and that sincere, savvy rural people are often right about what they see.

Time has passed, but on the Internet controversy about the existence of cougars in Alabama continues. Reports continue from people who claim to have seen them in Alabama, and reports also come from other states where they supposedly do not exist, according to wildlife officials, and some of these large cats are said to be black. However, it is always difficult to know if an Internet report is credible and authentic. That's not to discount the veracity of the many good people who post their accounts, but everyone knows there are some tall tales to be found around the web, and I count myself among those who do not believe everything I hear.

That said, the only way to pick through these reports is to hope you have some sort of instinct for the ring of sincerity and authenticity. Numerous anecdotes are from people who do come across as being real hunters who have spent time in the woods, or from persons who dwell in rural areas. Still others are from those who have seen these large cats since childhood and who had no idea that sightings were ever questioned until they posted their own on the Internet. Many of those living in rural areas report having heard cougar screams, and I'm inclined to believe the reports of persons who spend lengthy amounts of time in the wilderness. I don't necessarily discount the reasoning of the professionals and other naysayers, as it is still true that no formal documentation has occurred recently. However, I have noticed that some, though not all, of said naysayers are focused on informing everyone that a black panther is actually a black leopard when it comes to discounting black cougar sightings. This tells me that these folks likely do not understand that "panther" in the South is a term that is correctly applied not only to the cougar sub-species living in Florida, but also to any large, cougar-like cat. And yes, we do understand when we go to the zoo that the panther in the cage is actually a black leopard! And then, there are always those large cats that are killed and proven to be escaped or released captives, victims of the disgraceful practice of keeping wild animals as house pets or in unsuitable outdoor enclosures.

Since the rise of social media, I am now seeing continuing *beaucoup* reports by people who say they have seen cougars, including black cougars, not only in Alabama, but in regions of Western states where pumas are also said to be extinct. And, in 2011 a tawny cougar was hit and killed by a vehicle in the State of Connecticut. As noted before, numerous long-ago anecdotes about seeing black painters came down from Bill's southeastern Alabama family and community. The U.S. Fish and Wildlife Service believes the Eastern cougar subspecies has been extinct since the 1930s and that strays from the western variant or escaped captives account for the many sightings in the eastern United States. They don't believe eastern states have any breeding populations of cougars besides the Florida Panthers in Florida, but not everyone believes this.[23]

In February 2014, a photo appeared on social media of a large cat that looked to be a black cougar, taken in a small community about ten miles away from us. It's not anyone we know and reactions to the photo vary. Many post that it looks edited, which is also Bill's opinion, but the general consensus is that even if that's the case with this photo, there are definitely cougars and, some say, black cougars, in Alabama. In one discussion, a number of people reported having seen them and called them panthers. The same conversation included jokes about Bigfoot and a post of a photo of The Pink Panther.[24] The statements about panther viewings sound credible, but that particular photo is a little questionable. If it's altered, it's very well done, though one of the criticisms made about it is that the sheen on the black fur doesn't look right. I disagree as I've photographed blue highlights on the black fur of Alabama mini-panthers often. Regardless, if someone is photo-editing fake cougar pictures, it certainly doesn't help anyone who's trying to either establish or disprove the veracity of cougar sightings in this state. Not funny, y'all!

On a lighter note, there are some persons who will somewhat justifiably spread exaggerated reports of the animals they've seen around for the purpose of keeping people who needn't be there, out of the woods or wilderness around their homes. A person who's so inclined might well choose to report black panthers for a nice, scary effect. That usually occurs mainly on a local level, but maybe those who employ that particular home-grown security technique are now using the Internet rather than just word-of-mouth.

At the ShukerNature Blog, in "The Truth About Black Pumas — Separating Fact From Fiction Regarding Melanistic Cougars," Dr. Shuker displays artwork and one historical photo depicting what appear to be black cougars, and he refers to anecdotes. His conclusion regarding reported sightings of black cougars is that they are totally without substantiation.[25] But recently I have encountered a few persons who say they have seen black panthers in the wild in Alabama and I believe these are reliable accounts from reliable people. So while I've presented the anecdotes, the scholarship, and thoughts of others, I don't know what it all means and will refrain from forming definite conclusions of my own. All cat mysteries are welcome!

Since it is at least possible that panther-sized cats are around in a wide variety of locations, it may be important to emphasize here that no one should ever approach or follow a cougar. Bill entered the woods thinking he was coming to the assistance of a human under attack, a situation in which it is appropriate to disregard your own safety. Later, when he determined there was no human under assault and the screamer was an animal, he pursued something he thought was no bigger than a dog. Cougars have attacked people, sometimes with fatal results, and even a fleeing wild animal is dangerous when cornered. Indeed, no wild animal, large or small, should ever be approached. The most common advice in the literature about encounters with cougars is to face the animal, leave it an avenue of escape, and back away slowly. Turning your back and running is a behavior of prey and is likely to trigger the animal's run-down-and-capture response. Instead, make noise and throw things if the cougar shows signs of aggression and fight back if you're attacked. There is anecdotal evidence of cougars following people into the woods, such as hunters and others, seemingly out of curiosity. I have found no advice on what to do in this situation, but I suspect that keeping calm and not running applies here, too. The best thing to do if living or vacationing or hiking through areas with wildlife is to consult local professionals in advance about how to handle animal encounters. As humans encroach more on the living spaces of animals, this precaution applies more and more to populated and partially populated areas. A cougar is a particularly dangerous wild animal and should never be pursued. Cougars will definitely kill housecats, too, so I'd actually not be pleased to have this magnificent beast for a neighbor.

Looking back, considering that the scream of the female cougar is likely a mating call, we wonder if there might have been another, undetected, cougar out there the night Bill chased her! And as with so many topics in this book, over the years, new information has turned up. For example, in 2015 after four confirmed cougars in Tennessee, a state official said that it wouldn't be impossible for cougars to be in Alabama, too. (These are thought to be recently migrated western cougars, though, so this would not apply to Bill's encounter.[26])

Several years before the night chase, while we were still living in town, I was feeling wistful and looking into the darkening foliage, and I wrote these fanciful lines: "Stands of trees, crouched and black in the twilight, themselves become the panthers they are rumored to disclose." At the time I never envisioned we would have a close brush with the actual animal. Those panthers of the imagination are the ones I'd prefer to live with!

Chapter 7

A Midsummer Cat's Gleam

Gray Cat was an animal who knew his way around not only the forest, but also around civilization, hearth, and home. His viewpoint was, of course, that he and not the foxes should be the animal of fascination.

He had not gone unnoticed.

It was summer 1986, and from the direction of the lakebed, from far up a forest trail that both we and the foxes used, a glowing fluff of a cat suddenly came up at a fast trot, bellowing, trumpeting, singing *hooray, hallelujah, I have found it!,* making a bouncing, happy, sustained chirp-warbling *meow ruh ruh ruh* of greeting. It was as if he'd been lost out there in the woods awhile but had also studied the house and, instantly or not, recognized that the house contained a cat, along with people who fed that cat and would no doubt feed him, too. After all, by his lights, that was only right. Or maybe he just thought I was his long-lost friend; his greeting was like that of a soldier returning from a long war, or of a weary traveler come home. Maybe he'd seen me through the window or moving around in the yard. He ran up to me as though it was my destiny to feed him; how could I not heed his exuberant, blaring entreaty? I was soon out the door with a bowl of food. He was a flaring, gleaming shape moving up, a long-haired, creamy-white undercoated cat with a dusting of orange overlaying the cream, heathered deep down into the white fur on his back. His eyes were gold.

He was a tough guy who seemed used to fending for himself among the raccoons and the foxes, perhaps even eating the food we put out for them; but who, although a shade wary of us at first, warmed up quickly to his own bowl, kept full. He had to stay outside until we got him vet checked and vaccinated, but he moved from eating in the clearing with the wild animals to eating on the porch landing. He was unlike the wild critters, a cat, savvy about the wild but also canny about maneuvering himself closer and eventually into the same cushy house situation that Cat lived in, which he was no doubt observing daily through our windows. He began staying on the roof frequently. Cat got slowly used to him by looking through the glass door at the landing where the new cat sat smugly, possessively, and expectantly. After a few cussfights through the door panes, things settled down. It wasn't long until they were stretched out and lounging on the back of Bill's car together. We called him Orange Cat and Cat became Gray Cat.

Orange Cat's cheerful personality matched his pumpkin-glow coat. He had two-way fur. He looked either like pale moonglow or florid pumpkin glow, depending on which way the fur was ruffled at the moment. His over-bite gave him a bright and inquisitive look, and his tail was a plume of blended orange and buttermilk white. He was gregarious and friendly to all who came in. He became a lap cat. When beside people on the couch, he loved to lie on his back, pawing and scratching at the air, glancing at visitors to make sure they had noticed, he was cute! And they did notice. "He was the one who would talk to us," the receptionist reported when we picked him up after he, Gray Cat, and Minx spent a week at the vet while we went on vaca-tion. He was indeed talkative and would actually converse with me. He was caught on film getting picked up by a visiting child, carried to the couch, and petted by both the child and his father at the same time, resulting in a huge orange purr! Orange Cat was a sweetheart, a honey, and a peach.

This cat was so used to people that it was likely he was a former pet or someone's barn or yard rodent patrol who got dumped. His point of aban-donment may have been along the Interstate or the two-lane highway, where the forest flowed to those roads' edges. He came from that direction and his familiarity with the stretch of woods closest to it suggested this route. He would have made his way up the hill, through the forest, and back down to the swampy areas next to the creek. To actually cross the branch, he would have had to find the rapids, where he could step and jump from rock to rock when the water was low until he was on our side of the water, the way we often did, crossing back and forth during woods walks. Then, he would have moved through more trees, a discordant, moving brightness in a world to which he did not really belong, an undergrowth full of small, earth-toned mammals easily mixing with the patchy, deep tones of leaves illuminated with stippled, sunny spots. It was a world where his color shrilled his pres-ence against the foliage like a hunter's orange cap or a swatch of Day-Glo paint, as did his gold, night-glow eyes. For how long had he been lost? How many weeks, months, or years did he traverse the unbroken woodlands? Our house may have been the first human dwelling he'd found, just cause for a shout-out. Nevertheless, I think he waited, studying us, cagey, before holler-ing out that *we are the ones!* It's our world that he fits.

I found out later that either we weren't the first household he approached or he was two-timing us while he was still outside. Neighbors reported a pale, long-haired cat who had come up wanting food and who would jump on their cat. Not very nice, but that's the way cats do when they feel they have to compete for resources. Conflict with their cat meant the neighbors could not keep him in their household, so I was happy that we were able to take him into our family and eventually contain him so he no longer went around fussing at the neighbor cats.

Shortly after we got him, while he was still spending his nights outside, Orange Cat had a close call. We'd put a flea collar on him and the next day as we were leaving for work, I saw him from a distance and his mouth didn't look quite right. We rushed to him. He had somehow gotten his lower jaw under the collar and it was wedged in his mouth, which was swollen. We removed it and rushed him to the vet, and all was well. He perked right back up. He had to be a tough cat, the vet said, to weather this mishap so easily. That was the last time we used a flea collar. I ordered a flea comb instead and combed little vampire vermin off the cats daily. (Breakaway collars now help cats escape when their mouths and paws get caught up in collars or when collars get tangled in branches.)

We didn't know Orange Cat's age, but he was fully engaged in tomcat business. He was seen all over the neighborhood, and when a neighbor's cat some distance away had kittens, orange spots turned up on them. A mannerly cat like our Gray Cat, Orange Cat never sprayed the inside of the house. Cats who are practicing tomcattery can be tough customers, but Orange Cat was genial with Gray Cat and, later, with Minx.

Orange Cat would take a walk with us. I recall one day when my mother came for Christmas, and we had some of that moist, balmy, southern winter weather. Mom and I took a walk down through the lakebed to the creek. Not all of it was on our land, but the neighbors weren't particular about borders. Orange Cat came too. He ran ahead on the path, frisking around. These were his haunts, the direction he'd come from during that first appearance. We leaned down and petted him. We sat beside the rapids he must have crossed, and he sat there, too, as we took pictures. With his flared, orange-white fur, he sparkled against the wet haze of muted winter colors — vine sepias, dark pine greens, and clay-red browns. He lit the landscape up like the colors of Christmas lights pulsing against deep December nights. We lingered at the creek, watching the cold frenzy of the rapids water, which pattered loudly and with voice-like effects. Taking in the view, Mom said to me, "This is what I've always wanted you to have." She kept an orderly house in Maryland and was content there, but she knew I needed the wilderness, the seeming disorder of the natural world. When we got up and headed back to the house, so did Orange Cat, skittering along the path in front and alongside of us. He was joyful; he had an Irishness about him, we just loved him!

In those days we were still carnivorous ourselves, having drifted in and out of vegetarianism for years. I aspired to be a vegetarian, but never was able to do it quite correctly. By that Christmas, we had reduced our fat intake and we no longer ate chicken skin, instead giving it to the foxes or a little to the cats. Orange Cat liked it so much he would slyly ignore his regular cat food, holding out for chicken skin.

A second generation of friendly foxes

Hopalong came around for about five or six more years after Orange Cat appeared. A fox's life span in the wild is about six to ten years, and we didn't know her age when she first came to us. Little yappy sounds at the edge of the wood always made us think that the fox kept having cubs down in the very creekside brush we walked through sometimes. The fox would come to our yard repeatedly, run off to stash her cornbread, and then come back by a different route to nab yet another corn stick, run off with it again and, presumably, cache it.

One night we saw another fox far out in the woods waiting; then it came a short way out into the clearing with Hop. It lurked there a few evenings, and Hop tried to coax it to come up closer to the house to eat, turning back to touch muzzles with the second fox. But the kit stayed out at a distance in the woods for a long time; if it crouched or sat down, it would seem to evaporate entirely into the dense underbrush. Eventually she came close, and we named her Spooky.

Spooky started showing up at later times alone. One night she crouched down on the large flat rock on which we placed the food, and commenced to roll over on her back and rub her head on the stony surface, like a dog might do. Was it exuberance, deposition of a claiming scent, or a food-affinity celebration? I didn't know.

I once got Hop and Spooky to come up and eat while I sat outside only about fifteen feet away; Hop kept looking up at me anxiously. I could hear their teeth crunching the biscuits, and I could see many more colors in their fur without the window between us. Hop had several litters, the largest one being four, and I remember one cub who had particularly huge ears and another we named Shorty because of its short legs. The pups, nearly full grown when they finally came around, would quickly learn to stand at our window and wait for us to toss cornbread or dog biscuits — after all, they'd been raised on it. When startled, the kits would take off running through the forest with rapid, high leaps, sometimes two in succession. They had racehorse-long haunches and slender legs that ended in rather large pads for jumping; they spotted the night-darkened greens of the forest with their quick, glowing, roving young-fox eyes. The sight of them made the heart soar as they flashed through the blue-green shadow and leaf frieze. Out in the twilight, they waved like smoke streamers.

Bill would hear them out in the woods, communicating with each other with high-pitched whistles. He thought these signals amidst wild canids might be similar to the use of whistles by humans to call dogs. At summer's end they'd all disappear for several months, and Hop would come back to the yard alone. Like Ligeia had once tried to do, foxes pack the kids off to college to be on their own once they reached a certain age, a behavior known as dispersal in natural history descriptions. The young foxes did come back now and then for a visit. We learned to tell Hop from Bob by facial recognition alone when they were sitting on their haunches. Their markings were identical, but he had a comical look, while she was more serious. We also knew when Hop had evidently broken up with Bob because she brought a new boyfriend around, and we just knew he was not Bob. We called him Mister Fox, and he would take our food and then pause to look at us as if in acknowledgment. Sometimes, Hop and Mister Fox would curl up in the yard, muzzles snugged in tails, waiting to be fed.

One summer night we saw Hop and Mister Fox nuzzling and nipping at each other's face and ears. They were as before, taking cornbread and dog biscuits out to edge of the woods, where the pups waited in shadow to be fed. When the pups ventured closer, all the foxes would sniff the air back in the woods before entering the food area, and they would come all at once but each from a different direction via circling maneuvers to nab the cornbread. We were out in the yard cooking barbecue one evening when Hop came up about five feet away from me; we kept very still. She raised her gaze to mine, and we looked in each other's eyes a long time. To her I must have appeared tall, like a young tree. She turned and left but did not hurry away. Another barbecue day, we both froze when she came again, and when she left, I went back in the house to complete the dinner. She came back, and she and Bill exchanged a long glance before Hop began calmly munching the goodies at the feeding rock.

We began to suspect her of having the human and feline trait of deep, reflective curiosity. How much did she know about us? Maybe she was just doing what the cats did with their long glances, wondering, asking, *would y'all give me some of that barbecue?* It was an eerie feeling to exchange glances with this wild, wild thing, to have her in the yard like she was our dog or some other pet. We were concerned that she was getting too used to humans, but she was in a large area of neighbors who were animal-friendly wilderness advocates. Feeding her probably kept her close to our area and hopefully within our no-hunting and no-trapping zone. (A fox can have a range of ten square miles, but Gray Foxes like to live where there is cover. According to Rue, they are naturally wary and don't usually take domestic fowl because it means more exposure than they're comfortable with.[1]) We noticed that although Hop was somewhat accustomed to us, the younger foxes would bob their heads at the windows as they attempted to scrutinize our movements behind the glass. But as they relaxed, this motion became rarer.

At least one acquaintance, with eyebrow raised, voiced a complaint that the foxes weren't getting their natural diet because of us. But the fact is, dog food is sometimes recommended for foxes that are kept as pets. And the diet of the Gray Fox in the wild is quite varied. They eat rabbits, hares, birds, eggs, snakes, insects, fish, rats, mice, voles, corn, apples, persimmons, nuts, cherries, grapes, pokeweed fruit, grass, blackberries, and some grains.[2] So cornbread is not that much of a stretch for them. The foxes were no doubt still doing a bit of hunting in the forest, too.

Bill eventually found an uprooted tree stump with deep tunnels leading under it, and he speculated that this might be the foxes' den. It wasn't far from the house, and Hop may have been studying our household sounds to determine when we put out food without leaving her own front door. That could explain why the foxes would pop up at the feeding rock looking perfectly dry after a rain. "They don't call 'em foxes for nothing," as Bill says.

In the fall of the first year we saw her, Hop and her cubs disappeared for two months and then came back. Bill had also noted that the fox tracks by the stream vanished with them and then later returned. When she came back, Hop's tail was a plume, not scraggly like it had been in the summer. All the foxes were really bushed up for the winter. In February of the second fox year, we saw Hop acting in ways we had not seen before, arching her tail and prancing around playfully with the others, the males, no doubt. According to the mammal guides, that month was the beginning of their mating season.

We had some very familiar moments with the foxes, waving at them like friendly neighbors while operating within the parameters all parties had worked out. Bill tried to get Hop to take cornbread from his hand, but she never did, and she never came closer to me than five feet, and just that one time. Only in one vivid dream did Bob jump through the open window into the house where I handed him dog biscuits and rubbed his fur. They were never pets, or even companion animals. They were roan phantoms in the twilight, who sniffed the air from the deep woods before approaching the clearing where the food was.

Although the foxes seemed more cat-like in many ways than dog-like (they even climbed trees), those little wild animals stayed wild, as they should. When the foxes stopped coming, I suspected that Hop had lived out her days and died. She was a wildling who needed our assistance, but her boyfriends did not, and when she was gone they did not regard us as a food source; they either moved on or just made themselves scarce.

Several years later, I saw one Gray Fox pass by the corner of the house and then vanish into the forest. It hurried away from me, so if it was related to Hop, it had lost any sense of familiarity with humans from being fed by us. That fox had not come for food, but was going about its own fox doings. Eventually we had not left food out, but had tossed it out upon visually sighting a fox in the yard waiting; they had learned to wait. This had also eliminated the nightly raccoon conventions and made for a smooth transition towards a state of total no-more-feeding-wildlife when the last of the foxes ceased to come around. The vanishing Gray Fox signaled that the era of cornfed foxes was over. We also grieved for a Gray Fox we saw hit and killed on the road during those years, although it was not one of those we had a personal acquaintance with.

We were very sad once it became evident that our fox would come no more, and that she and her boyfriends and pups had all melted back into the forest. Her aliveness had cut a sharp impact into our psyches in the solitary woods. Our evenings of waving at foxes were at an end, as were our barbecues when we never knew if a fox would be in attendance. We missed her, and we grieved. Like all little animals, wild and domesticated, there was a natural limit on her days, and she had lived them out and faded back into the shadows and trees. It is just the way of things. It is also the way of myself to still miss her every day. We'd had informal fox-watching parties for years. Friends had waited quietly with us at our windows at night, for the foxes to make their entrances. They are still missed by a community of friends. We now go to bed foxless.

Hopalong had done very well for herself. She'd found a fella, raised cubs, then found another fella and raised more cubs. She'd gotten good eats from several humans. It was a fox life of satisfaction.

Not all neighbors are charming: Our challenges with country vermin
When you live in the country, Kingdom Animalia is divided into critters and varmints. A species (and even an individual) can belong in both categories, or change from one classification to the other, depending on your mood, the moment, the time of day, your experience with the animals, and even who you are. As Bill puts it, the difference between critters and varmints is similar to the difference between plants and weeds.

The coyotes, when I saw them loping up, alert and sniffing, were magnificent critters at first to me, but they turned to varmints as the moment passed and I realized they were a hazard to our cat and to other small wildlife. Bill, though, still calls them "God's dogs," which was originally a First American designation. Cotton-mouthed water moccasins and rattle-snakes are also varmints to me, but to Bill, they're critters; they just need to be moved to a more remote location where the woods are wilder and woolier. (Well-versed in snake handling and with the right equipment Bill can do this; however, no one should try this at home!) Rat snakes, the nonvenomous sorts who eat rodents, are also just critters to him. However, rats themselves and mice are varmints, except for the moment after you humane-trap a field mouse for relocation, raise the trap for a look, and notice how cute it is.

Raccoons are the most subject to frequent re-classification. They're charming and cute, but one chewed through our sheetrock, got into the wall between the living room and kitchen, and reached through the exposed unfinished studs to grab a line of Christmas lights, which ended up yanked partly into the wall. One night as we heard scrabbling noises, the strand of lights jumped around as the varmint tugged on it.

Everything in the woods wanted to come into the space we dared to call ours, and finding no ingress, the raccoons had made their own way through the walls. We took various steps to keep the varmints out, but if we succeeded one season, by the next year, the squirrels, mice, or whatever else would come back. In all fairness, we had moved out there to live with all those varmints, both small and large; we had intruded into their turf. (If we and the other surrounding landowners hadn't acquired this land and preserved this forest, the area probably would have been logged and developed by now.)

Rural dwellers are all-too familiar with the difficulties in keeping omnivorous raccoons away from crops, gardens, and trashcans. These critters always know the exact moment of supreme ripeness in watermelons and dig into them the night before you are ready to pick the melons. Back in the '80s, the era of county dumpsters, they were no doubt raiding them and indulging in all manner of home-style "people food."

Like raccoons, the Virginia Opossums, often called possums in Alabama, are also omnivores. The Audubon mammal guide notes that corn is in fact a favorite of the opossum,[3] who also benefits us by eating insects such as roaches, and snakes. This durable animal has been around for seventy million years and was on Earth with the dinosaurs.[4] Sometimes one will open up its huge mouth and display its fifty teeth to try to encourage other animals to leave the food. Bill has heard that possums are immune to snakebite, and research suggests they do have some immunity to pit-viper venom.

They are also highly resistant to rabies. Their low body temperature makes it hard for the virus to develop, but it's not impossible, and indeed, rabies has been found in a small number of opossums. Their small brains might indicate they are not the brightest of animals, but they are certainly one of the hardiest and most unique, being North America's only marsupial.

A possum around your house sounds like a man walking and can spook you. Ours come in a variety of colorings. Typically, they have white heads and dark bodies. But we saw one that was completely dark on both head and body, and another that was totally white. One mostly white possum had dark brown ears, little brown pits around his eyes, and at least one foot that was dark brown to the shoulder. There was once an especially big, mean possum who snapped at the other animals; he was not even afraid of us. He would turn and run when we approached him, but not right away, and not very quickly, either.

We were in a position to observe these animals carefully for any signs of abnormal behavior, which never turned up; it's certain there was never any rabies in the animals that came to our yard. We were constantly keeping up with any reports of rabies that were even remotely close to our area. Every year, rabies is found in a small number of wild and domestic animals throughout Alabama and, indeed, throughout the United States. In 2001, for instance, Alabama had a total of 66 cases. Most were in bats, with raccoons coming in second. Also mentioned were foxes and wild skunks. Domestic cases only numbered six: three in dogs and three in cats.[5]

Usually these don't involve our county, but on October 5, 2006, a dead bat was found that tested positive for rabies in a place just one county over from us. These cases also likely don't represent all the rabies that's out there in the wilderness that never gets observed or detected. In hindsight, we might have done a lot of things differently and should not have been so eager to draw the wild animals into the yard. They should certainly never be handled, and if they enter your yard and become a nuisance beyond what you can handle, animal control should be called if you know you can trust your local animal control to capture and release in wilder areas. And wild orphans should be turned over to professional wildlife rehabilitators. Rabies aside, wild animals often carry parasites, some no doubt dangerous to humans and domestic pets; possums in particular can carry one that causes a serious disease in horses. We had great encounters with animals in our early years in the woods, but we were amateurs, city folks who had moved to the country and had to learn. These days I would no longer be charmed by the sight of the raccoon that walked in through an open door, grabbed a bag of dog food, and tried to drag it away.

But I can look back and laugh at an incident that could have turned tragic, when Bill walked from his workshop back towards our house and into a group of half-grown raccoons rolling and tumbling about in his path. In the swift and sudden way of all things wild, one of them jumped on his leg and began to climb his trousers, while starting to squall. Suddenly, the mom raccoon appeared, bristling with concern. He had called to me to see the junior raccoons, and I had come out barefoot and could do little to assist with this rapidly developing dilemma. Just in time, Bill managed to run off and shake free of the little varmint and thereby absolve himself as the cause of the ruckus in the eyes of ferocious SuperMom. Any wild-animal mother, of course, will attack if it feels its young are threatened, even when she's in perfect health.

Eventually we felt overwhelmed by the raccoons; I called them "total bums" on occasion because they expected to be fed. They would come up and tap on the windows of the door, placing their dirty paws on the glass and the doorstep. They used their mouths to grab moths off of the windows, who skittered there for our indoor light. I personally hand-fed a raccoon when they first began to come up on the landing. He reached his nose out and nipped onto the dog biscuit I was holding really fast, and then he ran off with the goody. Another one snuck up from under the little porch-like landing where I was sitting and with his hand would try to knock the biscuit out of mine. A possum came up on the landing, too, and pressed its face to the glass, and then went sniffing all around.

One of the raccoons actually took over Bill's open-air workshop one summer, having her babies in a box there. Raccoons look at you uncomprehending when you block their access to some part of your home, as if to say, *I only want to move in with you, to live close and be chummy, if only you would just wise up and stop trying to foil my attempts.* It might be said that we had made the raccoons dependent on us for food; however, once you remove the food, raccoons soon learn to go elsewhere. They are extremely resourceful and they tend to approach human dwellings that are in rural areas anyway, raiding whatever trash can and pet food bowls they can get their chops on.

From the eastern shore of Maryland, where my mother was living at the same time we were entertaining the forest animals, comes this story of just how intelligent raccoons actually are. My mother's neighbors had a two-story chimney, and one summer a raccoon mom had her babies inside of it. She decided one day to move her nest underneath Mom's house instead. The foundation was bricked in but had two openings on one side. Mom watched as the raccoon came out of the chimney six times, carrying a kit in her mouth each time, climbing down the chimney, and walking over to the under-house "den" with it. There had been a rabbit living under there, but the bunny left when she saw this.

Mom wanted the raccoons to leave. She called animal services but didn't like any of the ideas they suggested, such as putting something with a strong odor the animals would dislike under the house. She was afraid this might harm them. So she called us, and we called around to local animal groups, but we didn't find any acceptable eviction ideas. About all I could offer was a comment that raccoons are awfully smart. Mom decided to have one opening, and one only, bricked up in the daytime, leaving the other exit open. This had the intended effect on the mother raccoon's feeling of security. That evening, Mom watched the raccoon take her brood out the remaining gap one at a time, and then she walked away down the path with the kits tumbling and rolling after her. The way Mom told it, the mother raccoon did not look at her, as if to say, *hmmmppphhh, you don't appreciate us, you aren't worthy of my notice.* The brickmason came back the next day to seal up the other opening. The rabbit watched him work; she knew the raccoons were gone and she would have liked to get back under the house, but overall, it was better for everyone for Mom to close off the space.

We gradually withdrew from feeding the wildlings once Hop and the foxes were gone. But even though we did draw the wild animals in a little closer to us, our experiences were not so different from those reported by many other country dwellers in our area, who see raccoons and possums come up and eat out of the same dishes as their outdoor cats. We do, after all, live in the woods, and the forest critters are out there, whether they venture under the yard lights within view of the windows frequently or only once in a while.

Years later, the Internet delivered information on a parasitic roundworm disease that many raccoons can carry, called *baylisascaris procyonis*, which doesn't harm raccoons but can cause truly serious diseases in other species and in humans. Although human cases are extremely rare, consequences are serious and even fatal. So I would urge caution around these animals and their feces in any sort of encounter whatsoever. It's odd that we had never heard of the disease before, but at least one source indicated that it's less common in the southeastern United States. Had I been a parasitologist, I might never have moved to the woods. That profession is not for the faint of heart!

Only for a brief time did we ever suspect a bobcat might be out there somewhere, too. We heard some fierce snarling, growling, and snuffling in the woods one summer. There was some commotion and then an absence of fox cubs. Bill also saw a strange track in the mud, and we wondered. But true to the literature, if this critter was there, it didn't show itself. It remained an inkling in our minds.

A lot goes on that is masked by all that foliage. We only sense the strange little clues.

Lessons learned from our fox-feeding experience

Wild should stay wild; that is the way it should be. I look back from to-day's standpoint and question our decision to feed the wildlife, but not only did those foxes have a large area of wildlife supporters around them, there was also, at that time, a vast area of woodlands surrounding our enclave of former '60s persons. Foxes and raccoons had a lot of room out there to roam in relative seclusion back then.

Despite my perception that foxes and other wildlings don't tame easily, I have found some recent literature noting their comfort in the presence of humans. These anecdotes usually involve Red Foxes, who are so bold as to enter campsites and grab food items. In Virginia, an old farmer once told us that he had located a Red Fox den, pulled out the cubs, and played with them. I wish I could have talked to him more, to find out if the vixen had then refused to associate with the cubs or later relocated the den. These are the results I have always expected with wild animals; even very tame cats will move their nests if you mess too much with the kittens. However, rural people have more direct experience with foxes than I do and may be used to a very familiar relationship. I did spend time in the Virginia countryside as a child, but the most I saw of a Red Fox was a quick, ruddy blaze through tall grasses.

We found that our Gray Foxes were quite adaptable towards us in a setting in which their habitat was preserved. The raccoons also lost much of their reticence towards us over time. County rabies information sheets say that wild animals who aren't afraid of humans are a danger sign. This is no doubt the safest advice to broadcast, and I too advise all to be cautious even towards the smaller wild things. Never approach and never corner them.

Yet we had our experiences, and our daily knowledge told us that these animals were behaving normally and with no sign of illness. There are anecdotal reports of Red Foxes behaving in a more familiar manner with humans. Reds are increasingly living in suburbs and even in cities in both the U.K. and America, and I've seen reports of foxes waiting in yards to be fed, as well as interacting in play with humans. There must be many more rural persons with such anecdotes. Surely this is important data, too, and would have significance in science, as in the Russian study aimed at breeding friendlier foxes. When I let my imagination loose, I envision "our" Gray Foxes peering through the windows at the cozy life of domestic cats, viewing it with some envy, consulting with outdoor cats, and thinking, *hey, we could catch mice too, why not us, why can't we have the humans, too?*

By contrast, Gray Foxes like the heavy cover of the woods. They den up much of the time. They are regular homebodies. We moved into their grove, their preferred haunts, their regular fox town.

Again, older and wiser now, I would advise against feeding wild animals. This is a "Do as I say, not as I did" sort of narrative. In our defense, the for-est-tucked households here were already used to the wildlife coming around, so we weren't encouraging them to bother neighbors any more than they al-ready were. No one ever suggested the Alabama Wildlife Rehabilitation Cen-ter to us, which we didn't know about at the time, for our fox. The center was in another city, and I don't think many people knew about it. I'm not sure what they could have done for her, though. As for the idea that we had all invaded the territories of the wild animals: that is true, but as noted before, the alternative to our neighborhood for this particular patch of forest was selling it to logging companies and, therefore, the end of the forest. One thing we definitely observed was that we did not make all of the foxes de-pendent on us by feeding Hop. When she ceased to come around, so did the rest of the foxes. It could be that Gray Fox society is organized around the locale of the vixen and her den, and so they are nomadic. That would make sense for a wary species of fox like the Gray, who likes to remain hidden from predators.

Refocusing our attention to our indoor wildlings

Orange Cat came in with an occasional bite wound from fighting with other toms. He would then get antibiotics from the vet and a lot of petting and up-talking from me. He always came back strong, so strong that one time, the vet told us, it took six people to hold him for his repeat antibiotic shot. Gray Cat, for all his adventures, was still a model of catly decorum and genial serenity around the house. And except for his scrappy outdoor life, Orange Cat followed his example. In short, the two toms ran an orderly household. But as noted previously, all this changed in the House of Minx.

When Minx came, she trusted everybody in the house right away, sleep-ing belly and paws up. She'd get right up in the boys' faces and cuff them into tangling with her in play, and then she'd sleep up against one or the oth-er of them. She bounced and levitated and ran up me to paw-tap my face a zillion times. When she slept and purred, it was mostly me she sought out. A photo shows a half-grown Minx sitting with Orange Cat in an open window, extending her paw to rest on his chest and holding him off at a distance. Or-ange Cat was a good-tempered fellow; intact tomcats will some-times kill kittens. This unpleasant fact has to do with reproductive rivalry, removing the kittens of another tom so that the female(s) will mate with him and have his kittens instead. As shocking as it is to our sensibilities, it is a fact for us to guard kittens against while not passing judgment on the ways of the wild. My purely speculative thoughts are that this is more likely to happen if the nursing or weaning momcat is still in the picture.

Not all tomcats do this, though, and Orange Cat lived with Kitten Minx with no sign of excessive aggression; in fact, he seemed fond of her. Her covering of the tomcats' scats in the box may indeed have been a dominance move, as she would certainly grow up to become a supreme alpha cat. She was fast and bold from the get-go.

The cats were increasing supervised when outside, and one day as we stood with all three cats in the yard, a squirrel dashed out right in front of them. Both Orange and Black jumped for it, and Black got it, sadly, a harrowing predatory moment that is so difficult for lovers of all animals, like ourselves. It happened so quickly that we had no time to make our usual moves to distract the cats with a noise to knock them off their game.

In the Poe story of "Ligeia," the title character comes back from the dead, and it was tempting to say Minx was our Ligeia come back to us. But that was not true. This was *so* not Ligeia's muzzle. Ligeia's face was angular, while Minx's sloped down from cheekbones to muzzle. It was not a rounded face, like that of the purebred black Bombay cats, but something between round and the more squared-off face of Ligeia. Minx had a sort of golden mean of curved-line, catface beauty. She was somewhat short-legged and mesomorphic, and her medium-length fur was textured to scatter the light into silvers, blues, and reds amongst the dark shades.

Each cat is shaped so differently; there are no identical cats, in physical traits or personality. I recall Ligeia as a sleek panther, steady and uncomplicated, the domestic huntress who raises kittens superbly. Minx deflected description. She was complex, a wily ingénue, foxy, suave, temperamental, a prima donna, a sprite of the mountains — all these words, and nothing pegs her. Cats slip through and step around words. As much as they like to hear words and praise spoken to them, descriptions always seem less than catworthy. No wonder they are so hard to name. And so hard to fathom without scrutiny. I may have not even painted Ligeia correctly; maybe I was too busy with school and work in those days to make an exhaustive study of her depths.

Gray Cat became Bill's lap buddy after Minx had come, and although he would sometimes still sit with me, it was understood by the entire household that I belonged to Minx. Gray Cat would turn slightly over as he settled on

Bill, exposing his belly. Bill gave him tummy rubs with such expertise that Gray Cat would soon radiate contentment all over the room. Bill has a flair for finding any cat's sweet spots and eliciting a rousing purr, a head tilting back with a grin, and paws flexing and curling in the air.

Early in 1989, we saw a remarkable sky one night, with fast moving clouds and many layered, many patterned colors of grays both ashen and smoky, plus grays faintly blue-toned; all whorling and moving around together. In another area, sunlight started to brighten a little behind the haze and a partial rainbow came in view, with slate tones in the background, luminous smoke-white grays. At 3 a.m. in the morning, I woke up from horrible nightmares, hearing loud thunder and seeing continual lightning flashes, and Minx started scratching and pulling and calling at the bedroom door. In this land, the rainbow always has the threat of severe weather in it.

I agonized over having Minx spayed and denying her a natural life, and I gave it much deliberation. I asked at least one vet if the alternative tube-tying surgery suggested by Desmond Morris was available, but he said no. The general consensus of opinion still seems to favor spay/neuter for population control, and there are also good reasons for just keeping cats inside.

But on one point we are in complete harmony with Morris[6] and many other cat advocates and writers: we will never have a cat declawed. This drastic, painful surgery involves the removal of bone — of the actual toes — and leaves the cat defenseless and fearful. Some cats respond by starting to bite. Furniture in our house has to take its chances; it comes second, and we don't worry about the tatters. It's possible to keep furniture covered if you have pieces you really value.

Furnishings, after all, are inanimate things, and cats are living creatures. We've never been wealthy enough to just toss furniture when damaged and buy new, but we do value our live cats above utilitarian objects. The beauty of our house is reflected in the splendor of the healthy animals living here. Years ago a book came out called *Why Cats Paint*.[7] Our kitties never painted, but they definitely sculpt: "Tattered Couch" makes a statement about the transitory nature of all fabrics. Our furniture became the masterworks of many talented feline sculptors. Among our three sculptors' many projects was a two-by-four supporting the sink, part of a new and incomplete kitchen cabinet. It was a long-range project. The three used their claws to refine their work. "Fallen Sink," when done, had a Dadaist feel to it. And Minxie's "Afternoon With Paper Towels" was kitty floor collage with found objects.

I made sketches of the cats with some difficulty, as they always, without fail, move just as you begin drawing or right before you finish, no matter how sleepy and immobile they appeared when you began. That year, I placed their portraits in a design with a fox and a raccoon, along with some pine trees as background, and made them into Christmas cards. Although they were done in black and white, I got more compliments and comments on those cards than on any I had ever sent. Cat intrigue seemed to work for many situations, so I began designing my own cards, featuring the cats every year for about five years. Now years later, we have friends who say they still have those cards.

After Minx was spayed, we reluctantly changed away from our old veterinarian. Our first vet was a person of great feeling for animals, but he'd moved his office farther away and shortened his hours. We felt very sad about it, but the increasing demands of our business dictated the need for closer proximity and longer hours available for cat care. (It is important to note here that this first vet of extraordinary compassion was from a rural area in the southern part of the state. I note this in order to counter a pervasive bias about rural Southerners that I've seen on the Internet whenever animal issues come up. I've also heard tell of bad circumstances for animals, sorry conditions, found nationwide.)

Our new vet also had great concern and feeling for her patients, as well as an understanding of the deep bond we had with our animals. She remained our vet until she retired. There was an unadvertised practice that everyone in town knew about: pet owners who found strays would take them to vet offices for rehoming. The vets would keep the animals a week or two while trying to place them with their clients, an at-hand pool of good pet owners whose animals were obviously getting vet care. If no one took them, the pets would be euthanized, but they were given more time to be homed this way than if they'd been taken to the city shelter. One thing that helped me decide to stay with our new vet was that she provided this same service for her clients, but she said she could not bring herself to "euth" a healthy animal. She would keep the homeless animals as boarders for however long it took to find them homes. Sometimes she asked for help with boarding fees from the folks who brought in the animals, and sometimes not. Over the years, we would home many strays with her help.

Orange Cat received a lot of fight wounds in his prime, and one became a very serious abscess that our previous vet had overlooked initially. Orange Cat had a very hard time with that particular bite, and I gave him lots of extra attention and tender loving care. But as usual, he came back roaring, wanting to go out again. Once, he came back with long scratches all over his head, which we thought were from a raccoon but the vet said were from another cat. It seemed he was getting clobbered in these fights. He was ranging far and wide, as reported by neighbors, and one time came back with some kind of black gunk in his tail. Motor oil, maybe? I didn't know, but I had to clip out the affected fur.

He had been a seasoned tomcat when he came to us, and his routine was so well-worn that at first we had hesitated to interfere with it. But now we decided that for his safety, we had to get him neutered. And also to keep the cats inside, unless both of us could be outside to watch them. I struggled with issues of cat freedom, but it was the safest thing, for both them and the wildlife. As the years went by, we heard coyotes yipping on the lakebed with greater frequency, not just during their dispersal time in the fall; all the more reason to make the cats homebodies.

Coyote concerts, which I thought of as "A Little Night Music,"[8] could be dramatic. We would hear a series of rapid, extremely high-pitched *ooo ooo ooo ooo ooo ooo* sounds then another brief, lower pitched *arf arf* then a repeat of the *ooo* sequences and on to the fast *arfs*, over and over for a long time. They were canine noises, but they darn sure weren't dogs. It scared the fire out of me! I became a strong advocate of the indoor life for cats, but I still feel wistful and nostalgic about the times they seemed a rightful part of the outside. Whether it's countryscape or cityscape, there's nothing like the sight of a cat gliding along across a lawn or languishing on a porch, regarding you with that special way of looking they have. A walk in a city alley that's full of pet cats from the surrounding houses lifts the spirits.

For awhile when we drove our route into town, every sunny day we would see a big black-and-white cat curled up in the same grassy spot beside the road, taking in the afternoon's slanty rays. He brightened up days that were otherwise likely to be routine and drab. But I feared for him, too. There were too many horror stories involving cars, domestic dogs, coyotes, and even evil people who would harm animals. Bill had chased the cougar, I'd seen the two large wild canids, and neighbors had seen a hawk dive at one of their cats. Owls, which we could hear hooting at night, will take cats too.

One cloudy afternoon as I walked past our hall windows I became aware of, and astonished by, an enormous owl perched in a small tree fifteen feet from the house. Two-feet-long and wide-shouldered, out in broad (if gray) daylight, it could have easily overcome a cat. It matched the picture of a Great Horned in the bird guides.

The woods had other dangers for our cats, too. Raccoons never bothered our cats, but they can be formidable fighters when they do become scrappy. And although we were always careful to keep antifreeze off of the ground, you can't control or know the level of care with which others handle it; there are many cases of domestic animals drinking this deadly poison. During an outing when we were escorting her, Minx was once chased and bitten by a roving tomcat who emerged out of the shadows as if from nowhere and took after her so fast we couldn't stop it.

We decided we would never let our cats out again except under the most carefully controlled and supervised conditions. The cats adjusted to indoor life and stopped trying to get out every time the door opened. We put a "Cats Stay In" sign on the door, inside and out, to keep our friends reminded of the new policy. Without that sign to cue the visitors, those smart little feline stinkers knew they could play an unsuspecting guest who didn't know the new routine. One droll visitor added a comma after the word "cats" to suggest jokingly that they could actually read it and take heed; the latter was the bigger stretch of imagination, in my opinion. I still miss the fresh air in good weather, when we used to leave all the doors open. But then there was that time I came into the kitchen from the back yard to find a raccoon just inside the kitchen door, dragging the dog-food bag outside. This was amusing in the early days, when country life was new, but I evolved to prefer that raccoons keep their distance after they tore into our walls and chased other animals off. And while I don't mind if the cats keep the rodent population down, I also prefer they not consume these not-so-clean little vermin, as their heritage destines them to do whenever they're left to range outside.

A new direction: selling the shop and finding my creative focus

As time went on, we continued to hire our friends and/or become friends with everyone we worked with in our screen-printing shop. For example, we were honored to work with a wonderful lady, Ernestine, who had marched in Selma with Reverend Martin Luther King Jr. She and Charlotte, another friend of long-standing, had voices of silk and satin and would sing duets: "The Times, They Are A-Changin'" by Bob Dylan; songs about dogs named Blue; and Peter, Paul, and Mary songs. Ernestine and I also both liked birds, and we talked of bird experiences. Elise, a young artist, cut commercial flyers into collages to hang on the side of the T-shirt oven, and she even worked in paper clips of various colors.

Humor remained a keynote of our working days. Somehow we'd acquired some realistic rubber "palmetto bugs," large cockroaches that cover the sidewalks in the summer at night. We each took turns placing them in the coffee mugs of other staff and watching their reactions.

When I mentioned to Gary that reading William Faulkner from the age of fifteen had changed my life, we both glanced around and, reacting to the drudgery of the work, I said, "Obviously, not enough," and we both laughed.

Even some customers became friends with Bill and me and the employees, and there were days we'd all be joking around and laughing together.

But early in 1989, about fifteen years after we'd started it, we sold the screen-printing business, with the proviso that the present employees could stay on if they so chose. It wasn't live-the-rest-of our-lives-money, but it was a good start to just selling printing rather than doing it ourselves and moving on to other, more agreeable work that we might develop. We continued to live modestly but allowed ourselves each one big, luxury purchase. Bill chose a video camera, and I chose a huge, encyclopedic dictionary. I love reading dictionaries; could I possibly be more of a nerd?

On the last day before turning over the business to the new owner, we were under a tornado watch, which caused me to contemplate the possible huge irony of dying just as we were about to move on to an easier way of life. In the mid-'70s, there had also been a tornado watch my last day at a job I didn't much care for. I've read that the geography of the United States, with two mountain ranges running north and south, the Rockies and the Appalachians, primes the southeast for a high rate of tornadoes because upper-level winds are contained and bounced between the two mountain chains. Oddly, this joins in an oblique way with a statement I heard years ago from a local with no particular training in meteorology, who said that tornadoes were formed by winds hitting the Appalachians and "being thrown back." Warm air coming up from the Gulf of Mexico meets the cold air coming down from the Arctic is also a factor in severe weather. Tornado formation in the southeast may be partially geography-driven. Having seen severe weather follow similar tracks through this area for fifty years, I think there may be something to this.

Leaving the print shop was more of an adjustment than I thought it would be. It had become an alcove for independent spirits in a town that was essentially conservative in the business arena. We dressed how we liked; Bill had long hair and the clothes I wore in that inky warehouse were old and comfortable and felt appropriate to the work. Some looked askance upon me, but what could they say? I took *it may be old, but at least it's paid for* to heart, and I even thought of putting it on a T-shirt after a few "bum's rush" experiences. I'm easygoing but I still do what my Mom called "the slow burn" about a few things. Pomposity and elitism, they bug me. But at our own place, I got respect.

Our office was messy and outrageous to middle-class tastes, but we did the best work in town and customers came anyway. I could put environmental stuff on the bulletin board and no one could say a thing because the shop was mine. Much as I had better things to do, this place had tied me to the workings of the real world and the pulse of the town. We printed for all the events: sports, arts festivals and openings, concerts, family reunions, countercultural pig roasts, and crawfish boils. I experienced the life of the grind in the work I did inspecting and counting and handling and packing T-shirts and printing. I was essentially a blue-collar textile worker, a mom-and-pop shopkeeper. We hung on only by ingenuity, succeeding even though it wasn't in the creative fields we'd wanted. The equipment built by Bill in our backyard was welded together roughneck-style, from pieces of metal still scattered in the yard that friends would handle and clink and fiddle with when we held barbecues.

The new owner wanted to scrap our old oven, cobbled from dirt, from nothing, from scratch by stubborn, eccentric do-it-yourselfers. That was of course entirely his call, but to us it was the end of something. Starting from nothing, while economically challenged, even forgoing medical appointments, we had made something. And now, for a price, it was gone. Made with our hands but no longer ours. I didn't know why I felt that way. During all the hospitalizations for the surgeries I'd had, Bill had taken phone calls regarding the printing of T-shirts that were due; at times it had been torture, but it had been ours. Somehow we had outfoxed the cards that were firmly stacked against us ever improving our income. By living sparsely, we had survived, treading carefully. Odd thoughts came with the passing on of the business.

Then there were moments like the one when we stepped out of the warehouse at twilight and saw long trains of traveling birds. Those hundreds of slight movements made black, writhing sheets against the sky. When they came low, all their wings made sounds of rushes and hisses, the sounds of feathers by the thousands fingering the winds. They swarmed, they boiled up, out of the no-place in the distance, the vagueness of horizon.

We had a hard time getting started in the alternative business, but we did have what felt like a real chance to start over. This meant more drawing and writing for me, and more hand-forging of art ironwork for Bill, a process involving an actual anvil and coal-fired forge. He experimented with an array of other new products and inventions; he wrote a pamphlet on silk-screening printed circuit boards. I had an edition of a machine-lithographed print of one of my drawings made and hand-colored them to sell. The phantasm of success doing something we loved, that we had chased all our lives, was finally taking some shape before us. I considered going back to school to get a master's degree in folklore or linguistics, or learning American Sign Language to earn a degree in deaf education. I dreamed of starting a state-of-the-art, no-kill cat shelter, as the radio played and a now-grown Minx graced my lap. We were working at home, which had always been the most productive method for us. It meant being with the cats more for both of us. These were probably the best of our times.

In the large, sunny picture window, I hung two prismatic ornaments that split the rays into rainbows, or spattered hues, all over the floor. On the windowsill was a row of frog figurines that friends had given me over the years because of my frog and toad fixation. (People continued to give me frog art pieces until they were about hoppin' off the shelves!) House wrens entertained the cats, landing on the air conditioner as they tended nests under the eaves. Out in Bill's shop, a pair nested in his hollow-tube, gas-fired blacksmithing forge, and he suspended all work in deference to the brood that would be raised. But one morning the nest had been destroyed, pulled every whichaway, the eggs gone. This was the work of raccoons; only they could have reached into the long, small aperture of the forge.

I typed out letters on behalf of distant rainforests and made drawings that were fantastical aggregates of imagined rainforest leaf-shapes and deep gloom using the observed nearby imagery of the southern pine-and-oak forest I lived in. I daydreamed excursions to those forests even further south, packing big, old spray cans of "Jaguar Begone." I named my drawings things like, "Eve in the Tropics" and "Diana in the Tropics." A series of small, female wood-sprite-looking things was called "Little Witches." It was all good clean fun with archetypes, not to be confused with a more serious focus on witchy stuff one sometimes sees today. These were simply pictures of populated thickets.

I did portraiture that slipped and became two-dimensional masks. I used small, multiple-hue configurations based on ways I could scramble, fracture, and reassemble the spectrum and play with the permutations of refracted light. I drew huge vistas of imaginary frondescence. Eventually my colors moved towards neons and fluorescents. At times my art really seemed living to me, to receive light and cast shadows like natural, wild things do. I even had dreams in which I was in my own pictures, walking around.

I still fantasize sometimes and joke online about journeys to places like Belize and Costa Rica, places that I will never get to see.

After starting to write fiction around the age of thirteen or fourteen, I wrote only term papers in college. After first reading Faulkner at the age of fifteen, in college I re-read his major work, as well as most of Shakespeare's. I had kept on drawing and painting all through my working years, but I stopped writing for the most part after college, until the early 1980s. Cats hadn't ever been a prolonged study or a writing subject for me, but rather a learning, an experience, and a re-living of the moments we shared.

When I started writing again I had long been a student of language and human communication, and I went deep into ruminations on the ways these intertwine. Faulkner and Shakespeare and the Romantic poets were the main influences of the day. I was early in my understandings of the flow between cats and humans, which appeared so effortless. In writing I aimed for high lyricism and cavernous imagery, and that took work. Not everyone can make instant narration. I had a lot yet to learn from those voices on the porch about pacing stories and dialogue. I had been taught in English classes to write essays and literary criticism, but not how to tell a story. In the South, so many come by that facility in some seemingly natural and innate way.

Despite major efforts, I only produced a few shards of poetry strewn across days and weeks and months and years, unraveled and left as lint, willy-nilly, here and there. I would find this fluff usually when I wasn't looking and could never gather enough of it to really spin full yarns. I had a few dusty jokes and froth thoughts, skimmed quickly off the pond's surface. On some evenings I would be spirited away by an unknown Muse to romp in the shaded seclusion of unfettered image-making and thought-forays into unexplored territories, where a stampede in my brain would sling the earth around like percussive animal feet, obscuring the finery of "rationale." Thoughts would then swirl like sun-struck silt in stirred-up creek beds. There was always a cat nearby, sleeping on some papers, *hmmm.*

In poetry I wanted to liberate word nature, to evoke each word's entourage, all struttings, connotations, meanings, intimations, hitchhikers, picked up, festering and stewing, along the way by that traveler through time: everyday language. But I was shy, introspective, and somewhat isolated, and you don't learn social skills that way. Conversation has often been a puzzlement to me. I'm not good at it, and so often I have seen it flow via the workings of arithmetical blends of charm and words that dye the facts, rather than through deep formulae of understandings and insights. I didn't know all those prefabricated jigsaw-puzzle gestures and words and cues that interlock perfectly with every move other people make socially. I was both envious and skeptical of smooth talkers. And no matter how you dressed me up, there was no way to conceal the wolf eyes, the mark of the outsider, the frequent separation of psyche and society.

Learning to translate the language of my own mind — and to read the "words" of cats

I have fought alongside many, but ultimately, I fly my own colors. Yet I like company, both country people and artists alike. I have always wanted to get past the shallows with others, to build an apex from several slants of

mind. I am a fan of the easy-going and the down-to-earth, worried about elitism that might occur if people got too full of themselves and their sharpness.
While the expectations of some have had me grazing in various paddocks, I
have actually leaped the fence into unseen landscapes, and all anyone can
hear are my fading hoofbeats. Perhaps I've chosen the wrong fields and the
more populated ones are greener! If only I can sound the right notes! In the
past, I've felt eclipsed by parlor talk, an umbra that, for me, could only be
breached by feline company, or by writing and viewing with introspection.
Thus, I framed my feeling of apartness.

I'd grown up never really learning how to talk to people, and I was socially out of tune. Cat-to-person dialogues are so different from human to
human ones. With humans the strongest, most harmonious voices will be
noticed, the most polished presentations, the best use of language, because
we know all about it. Exclusionary situations sometimes develop. With cats
and other animals, though, we don't know what to expect; it is all outside of
the realm of the usual. We are more forgiving and inclusive. Well-socialized
animals aren't judgmental towards us at all, so long as we extend kindness
towards them. The dialogue is much more open to improvisation. The route
to unconditional friendship is more direct. It is always a great comfort, when
words fail to connect us to other humans, to sit and purr with the kitties,
while their rapt eyes of blue, gold, and green look into ours. Is there a language barrier? They have no recognition of such. Science sometimes says
their meows and vocalizations are not actually language.[9] Yet it's enough to
create deep rapport. Watching us, with their canny eyes, is part of it all to the
kitties.

While I could have used a course in conversational conversation, there
were a few times I could make people laugh in my younger years. There
were moments when I was "funny ha ha," though overall, most people probably thought I was "funny peculiar!" While some were thinking I had a wry
wit, others were thinking *her wit's gone awry.* The "funny ha ha or funny
peculiar" quip is a slang phrase I recall from when I was growing up in mid-
Atlantic country. Tracking origins of phrases that were tossed off as commonplace has become of interest to me, because they had to start somewhere;
some person had to be the first to speak a clever phrase that became popular.
Diversions aside, there is no doubt that I, a shy introvert, learned a little
something about conversation from the easy congeniality of Southerners.

Yet I was determined to infuse my own utterance with my own orches-
tration. It was all a way of getting back into significant dialogue, to deter the
heavy feeling of "otherness." I wanted to join conversation to literature.
Whatever our poetries are made of, that's what I was grabbing at. I found

that language is your mind; you drape and hang your consciousness from it. I was searching the folds back to the source and it was arduous. Cryptic words were mere cipher for being and might be translated for secrets just as riddles are, just as cats are cryptograms of their own deep selves yet might be discerned. But mostly, the realities of human communication could never be "decoded," and remain mysterious to me.

Words are inadequate nets in which to catch thoughts, nets that might act as veils. Some concepts, things, I had never seen, like nightingales, magpies, and ravens, but they had holds on my psyche that I couldn't explain; they had gathered mystery from some detailed beginning as they aged and festered and stewed in the implications of that traveler through time, everyday language. Storytelling even in one word's struttings, one word's entourage. The whiff of originality could not always at first be spoken of; it took my descriptions some time to catch up with recognition. Analogy was also at-large in the world, still roaming through more than paintings and books, and I hadn't tracked it down, not yet. It was elusive in every way. Wordy wisdom is not the same as worldly wisdom.

Over time, I became more of an essayist than a fiction writer, more interested in chasing the twists and turns of actuality. The cats watched me as I mused, with knowledge glinting in their little eyes. They were poetic floor lions. They took their inspiration from the Great Feline Reconnaissance, that immense moment in history when, through looking at and to us, they discerned that they could eyeball us into giving them food, and thus their future became intertwined with our own. It was their version of a phenomenon we would call a Renaissance. We're always trying to tell the stories our way, in the words that drape our consciousness, but the cat, like a wordless cipher, derails us every time. Odds on their statement will be *meow*, whichever way we write it. We feel it, profound and eloquent, but it's defying our definitions. Cats are storytellers with tails.

It was an ongoing challenge toward achievement in art thought, to actually make something by using language to strip-mine the mind, to use this forced classification of *grunts* and *hisses*, *howling* vowels and *tittering* consonants, this air, this ink, this English. The polarities of my thoughts seemed about to burst grammar with a bit of some out-of-the-way rhetoric, or a word working a double shift, on occasion. Disrobing parts for metaphor, but only taking stuffing, pieces, surfaces, and word phantoms that appeared to my mind just as uncertain apparitions appear to the eye, I was fortunate when I sometimes captured a field of oddities, fresh thoughts, poem parts, pieces of spring. But I didn't even have a grasp on whichever flag I fought under when

I claimed this unknown, fecund ground. I only knew that melodies of cele-bration seemed to clang overhead through the branches.

I became fond of those grammatical aberrations abhorrent to English teachers, and I began collecting the surrounding colloquialisms of the region, as well as American slang dictionaries. Not in ignorance, but in tribute to fading native languages, particularized dialects now being altered as lan-guages always are through the talking and talking of a more mobile society. I forgot how I was supposed to talk. I had a fresh start, a cleared air. I did not know where it would all aggregate, so I waited, in the company of the cats who purred alongside of me while I recorded these thoughts on writing and talking. Meanwhile I mingled verse and converse when I could. I grew fond of obscure words and phrases that were part of language history and lan-guage making.

Eventually I would try to recover all the conversational idioms of both the region I live in and the region I came from, because it is in everyday talk-ing that language lives and grows. After those early forays into linguistics and wordplay, I have now become a more "down to earth" student of lan-guage. The cats have watched and witnessed all this artistic process. It pro-truded into their, our, lives, so there was a certain amount of winding around it they, we, had to do, as they sat on the papers or reached paws up to tap the books I was reading. They purred quietly, but they didn't speak on it. Odds on they would have said meow if they'd a mind to. If we could have translat-ed, maybe it would have meant that all this was all way too "purple," or I was just overthinking things. They were ahead of the times, processing eve-rything as "bites."

Cats will lead your imagination off to romp, sniff, and soar your way through starlight, but they will also bring you right back down to sturdy, practical, earth. They were just waiting in their own feline ways for their sto-ries to surface. Theirs were always the voices underfoot, from the home and hearth, everyday. I was waiting, as I look retrospectively, for the cats to teach me more, to show me the way to write this book, the way "real life" goes into the stew when you're making literature. I was never to really learn the art of conversation with humans. But while I was struggling with my own language as a writer, I was also learning the cats' nonverbal ways of communicating. I was eye-witness to the lives of the cats and am forever challenged to make narration out of feline contemplation. One advantage of writing your first work of significant length with cats as the subject is that it's a detour around the beginner's trap of every character being yourself; you've got to bridge differences between separate species to create and describe your cat charac-ters. Current literature requires complex protagonists; with mine, it's more dazzle and confuse. They are perplex characters. Make that *purrplex*, on a lighter note. My earlier ruminations on language served me well later, when all my neurological functions would need practice and re-tuning, and I had to grab for concepts by stacking words and pushing them around.

Being a pleasure-seeking creature, not unlike a cat, I concentrated more on drawing and painting, which were much more recreational for me in the years after we sold the shop. Painting is a geometry of the mind, worked out in a finite space. I felt it was my destined and watchful otherness, my place to act, to play with the colorful earths that were paint, with freedom to on impulse spring pell-mell down side streets after some indigos if I felt like it. I thought of painting as making new lamps of parted spectra. I thought of it as painting a sly leopard of a scent. My best painting ideas have always come to me not as a result of steady daylight, but as a sudden cloudburst in the air; that thought pits and roils my mind like huge raindrops on dry earth, and then soaks in. Yet even painting employs a language of line and form and color symbolic of actualities, just as words are. My markings were rife with ulterior motifs. They were tricks upon one's sense of reality, slight shifts in things, after effects, the distortions of the everyday which are half attended to, unnoticed until seen in the finished pictures, the opening of a sudden potency of items in the world with wary senses applied. There were times when artmaking seemed just a coating, a cover, but there were others when it was multiple sentience, like a snake's ability to "see" heat, a dog's range of smelling, and the resonance and reflexes of a cat.

Paintings and writings became recollections of my life and thought. Canvases resounded like drums with my psychic history. They were just as much a practice as playing a musical instrument; they kept me in tune for later work, even when they failed as finished pieces. Looking at drawings became a social event in those days, and there were always a few confluent souls who would have an uncanny, empathic experience from one's work, a flaming reaction in the same idiom, the same language. There were surprisingly few cats in my drawings, but writer, artist, and musician LaDonna drew hybrid hordes of imaginary animals, some Peaceable Kingdoms and some predators remaining predatory, hence snappish and aloof. Still others were renditions of eager canid and introspective felid eyes. Her beasts, actual or invented, are privately grazing, running, sleeping, or just watching us with curiosities equal to our own. They were so affecting that it was tempting, in the mornings, to check the positions of these patch-worked creatures relative to one's recollections of them the night before! Regarding cats, LaDonna says, "I like black cats and stripey cats and red cats that shapeshift to foxes." Other artists in my world spun poetry fast and with fervor and painted pictures particularly telling about the spread of night. So there developed a unique, supportive society that was accepting and southern and artistic.

I have included these tidbits of my writing and visual art thoughts at the time not because they're exciting and action-packed, but because they are just as important as the daily routines of our workshop and household. For all this elaboration on language that I was exploring, I was also daily in the long, slow process of learning the feline stories and ways of communication, the language of the Mau. Although I will often describe things in my own intrinsically anthropomorphic terms, shaded with my own goofy slants, I always keep an eye on the natural history texts, which so often offer the best cues to understanding the domestic cat.

Natural history, for me, goes way back to my childhood, to the Smithsonian, to Virginia, a state known for its natural beauties, to "up close and personal" acquaintance with nature in farm country. I still have recurrent dreams in which our farm house is filled with books and one room is a library; that never happened in real life, but it symbolizes the life-long learning experience that sprung from being in the wilderness and an agricultural community for a short yet formative stretch of time. Coming south then brought me into contact with even wilder spaces.

For those readers who feel that this prose has gotten too many shades away from sweet violet and closer to purple for awhile: I'm using the language of the '80s and a few decades earlier. Stick with the cats and me here, and you'll see the style morph into the sparser language of today.

Our last days with our feline trio

Orange Cat got a cold soon after the work transition and began coughing and sneezing. The vet checked him out and found nothing wrong besides the sniffles, and it didn't seem to slow him down any when it came time to lunge for that squirrel that Minx caught.

We met yet another cat who needed our assistance. One night in early summer of 1989, as we exited off the highway, my eyes went roadside to a fast-food fried chicken box that someone had tossed out a car window onto the grassy area by the ramp. Drawn by the smell, a white cat was pawing at that box for what paltry food remained. Some jerk had thrown out this poor, possibly pregnant animal at the edge of the woods. The exit ramp was the perfect place, like the ramp where we'd found Minx, to slow down, stop, and push an unsuspecting animal out of a car to be left alone to scrounge for food and shelter. We stopped and Bill was able to capture her easily. She was tame and it wasn't hard to get her into the car, although she got a little spooked once inside and hid under the front seat. We brought her home and she stayed with us, outside, for awhile.

I fed her on the side landing of the house, through the door from the kitchen. Bill's path to his shop went by there, and she would follow him to the shop and back to the house for companionship, moving like a slinky ghost through the green. Her steady food source was well-established on the side porch; she was never fed anywhere else. I spent what time I could with her and gave her many pats when I fed her, but clearly, she wanted even more contact with us and therefore went where Bill went, every day. Much has been written about the behavior of cats in the wild, how the only time they are with other cats is during the earliest stages of their lives, with mom-cat and their siblings, after which they emerge as fully functional, individual hunters for whom survival does not depend on association with any other cats or beings, except at breeding time. This contrasts with dogs, whose wolf ancestors live and hunt in packs and are never solitary, and thus, dogs are believed to form bonds with human "pack members" instead. Scientists question whether cats really form bonds with people; do cats really love us, or do they simply regard us as a food source? In my experience, though, cats repeatedly seek human company even when it is not necessary to do so to be fed or to survive, like the white kitty did. I'm all for science, but I'm also a big fan of well-scrutinized anecdotal evidence; I've seen many such instances of cat sociability and love.

With Gray Cat, Orange Cat, and the young Minx comprising our household at the time, we weren't looking for a fourth cat, so we felt we needed to find this new kitty a home. About a week after she came to us, a friend suggested we give her to other mutual friends who wanted a cat. They didn't mind that she was pregnant and would find homes for the kittens and then spay her after she had this litter. With these assurances in place it seemed like a good match, so we took the cat to their house. We visited awhile, letting the kitty sniff and adjust before leaving her. She walked around and finally found a place to sit quietly. When we got up to go, so did the cat. She trotted after Bill to the door. Reluctantly, we left her there and felt immediate pangs of regret. Awkward as it would have been at that point to say we'd changed our minds, we've always wished we had just scooped her up and taken her back home. Cats are resilient and practical, and they can adapt to new people after losing the old, but they also do love us deeply. This one made a dramatic gesture to let us know she wanted us, and I now think such an indication from an animal should be heeded. We had missed the cue. It had all happened so fast we had not realized that we were nearing point-of-no-return bonding, but the cat already knew it. She knew we had saved her from starvation. Both Bill and I still mention the white cat to this day and how we wish we had kept her. We checked up on her afterwards and we felt assured that she did adjust, as cats always do to new circumstances after a time. She got a good home, just not with us. We really felt we had enough pets and that rehoming her was for the best, but that decision has always haunted me.

That summer, the year after we found Minx, we took another week's vacation and drove up to D.C. to do the Smithsonian; this time we boarded the cats rather than have a neighbor care for them. On the way up we stopped and viewed Natural Bridge, Virginia, the first time I'd ever seen it. We saw a really great exhibit of the work of surrealist painter Joan Miro at the National Gallery. There have been some strange patterns in my life, and who can say whether they are unlikely or not? I never could seem to get away from Alabama and the South after I began college here. I went to New York one summer, and I ran into my art history professor from UA coming in the door of the Metropolitan Museum of Art as I was going out. And the summer I took a Shakespeare course at American University in D.C., I ran across a guy in the library who recognized some of his friends on a poster I was carrying of the band Hourglass, whose members Duane and Gregg Allman would later go on to form the Allman Brothers Band. Then, during the second D.C. trip with Bill, I went to the National Museum of African Art while he stayed at the Smithsonian Folklife Festival. As I was walking back across the expansive lawn between buildings to meet up with him, our friend Rick from back home in Alabama walked over to me. He was spending the summer in D.C., sitting with friends on a blanket spread out over the grass. And later during that same visit, I was in the Natural History museum and suddenly found myself in a group of motorcycle enthusiasts all wearing T-shirts announcing they were from Huntsville, Alabama. I was so shy I didn't bother to identify myself that time, but now I think I should've hollered "Roll Tide!" I reckon you could find a rational reason for these summer encounters away from home — it's likely the whole state leaves to avoid the heat down here!

On the way back, we stopped at a restaurant near Natural Bridge. As we were leaving the eatery, a group of women were talking to the restaurant supervisor about a hungry stray dog out back looking for food in their trash bins. The supervisor tried to assure them that she would see to it the dog would be fed something. All this was to the good, but the person doing most of the talking couldn't resist taking a high-horse tone and engaging in some regional hauteur, shrilling, "We feed animals in New York!" I wanted to buy another dinner for the dog, go get the pooch and take it home with us, but Bill felt we couldn't delay further and he was confident the pooch would be well taken care of.

Then, as we were driving back, somewhere in Virginia, we saw a black kitten that had been run over by the side of the road. Any road-killed animal is a heart-wrenching sight, but this seemed personally painful in light of our successful rescue of Minx the year before. Was this supposed to have been our next cat? Or our next rescue? Had we somehow missed in the timing? Events such as these are the reasons I can't be too quick to declare happy sense in the story of finding Minx, or in the stories of others that work out well. So much ends with sadness.

Back home, we went to the vet to pick up our cats and asked how it had gone. It was okay with Gray Cat who weathered all things amiably and borderline with the cranky Minx. Orange Cat, however, had been a joy. He had played, talked, and bantered with the staff. Once home, though, all three were disoriented and walked around with annoyed looks, Minx growling. They didn't like being left at all, first off, and left alone of all places at the vet's. They were displaying their opinions, and it was a regular storm of annoyed feline rhetoric.

Eventually, though, they forgave us and the household went back to normal. And once again, whenever I was sitting down, Minx was in my lap. Not only when I was drawing or watching television, but when I was eating, too. She'd use her position as a vantage point to go for my food. Her dark muzzle took aim at the steamed broccoli, advancing until I handed her some off my plate. She took it and ate it, so for several months I'd say "Broccoli, baby," and she'd flare with excitement and come trotting to me rapidly to take the broccoli from my hand and eat it. And then, just as abruptly, like a fickle teenager, she suddenly lost all interest in broccoli.

Often when I got up I had to carefully unseat Minx, and this did not please her. At times she would growl, spit, and even try to scratch during removal. She was both a Minx and a cat, the basic cat viewpoint being, *how dare you remove me from the place I have chosen for myself?* Whenever there was a note of trouble or sorrow in my voice, though, Minx would come rushing to me and attain my lap if I was sitting, or just hover sympathetically if I was on my feet. And after I became ill in 1992, she was always there on my lap.

When we let the cats have an outing in the yard, Minx loved the patio with the ferns and wildflowers that Bill had planted beside it. She'd run from one side to another, back and forth, and sometimes she'd lie down and roll and rub frantically on the bricks, like a catnip reaction. We had planted no catnip, and the area had been woods before we cleared it. But in *Catlore*, Desmond Morris indicates that valerian and several other plants cause catnip responses.[10] I know this must be true. I don't know as much about plants as I should, considering that I live on their turf, so I wouldn't know if we had valerian, but we did have something out there that made Minx crazy, catnip style. This unidentified plant presence, with its potent under-human-radar aroma, suggests an answer to those who think giving catnip to cats is like drugging them. In their natural state of free-range roaming, a cat might encounter such a plant and experience its pleasures. The cat did not have to go out of its way to do so; it only had to travel in its normal manner. Surely such plants were intended gifts from the heavens for felines, who are so adept at pleasure. To me, catnip is somewhat akin to the intoxicating effects of the odors of wisteria and honeysuckle on humans. Once at a cat show, I bought some industrial-strength catnip. This caused Minx to have such an excessive reaction, rolling and rolling frantically and for such long times, that we decided it was wisest to end the catnip parties. The other cats enjoyed it but did not have such strong, excessive responses.

The cat show was the first one I'd ever been to, and while the purebreds were gorgeous, the array of merchandise was also fascinating. I hated having to settle for mere catnip and Mylar-tasseled shaking toys when there were such elaborately constructed cat towers that could even be custom-made. But, those things were pricey. During our vacations, I had sometimes marveled at the sight of a long expanse of Siamese colors stretched out in the back windows of cars. At the cat show, I was astonished at seeing many times over a swath of a calm, feline purebred riding on an owner's shoulders like a scarf, being carried all through the show. Any of our cats who set one paw inside that auditorium and viewed the scene and heard the murmur of the crowd would have evaporated right over the horizon in streaks of fluff. I didn't have travelin' cats.

Saying goodbye to our sweet Orange Cat

I was home alone with the cats in August 1989 when an unease came over the whole house. Gray Cat and Minx became nervous and alert, looking out the door as if something was out there. The cats normally did this off and on all day in response to passing wildlife and wandering cats, but I saw nothing out the windows. I, too, felt spooked and chilled. We all knew something was wrong, but we didn't know what.

About an hour later Orange Cat suddenly howled and vomited, began screaming, and ran for the back of the house. I ran after him. In the hall, he fell down breathing hard and still screaming, but then he went still and silent. I stroked him and tried to gently lift him, but he was limp — he had just died right there at my feet. I screamed for a while, and then called Bill. There again, the shock of sudden loss, the heart ripped out.

We had him necropsied to make sure he hadn't had anything transmissible to the other cats. The vets said, as near as I can recall, that it was a heart and lung problem, something to do with "lung worms." Nowadays I realize they were talking about heartworms, which are a hazard to cats as well as dogs; in cats, the worms migrate to the lungs. They're transmitted by mosquitoes, and Orange Cat had spent a long time living outdoors before he found us. It was untreatable, so we couldn't have saved him even if we'd known, and only a few months earlier, a routine vet checkup found nothing wrong with him. His appetite and general spirits had been good right up until the time he died. With time comes greater veterinary knowledge; more recent scholarship about heartworms in felines is in the note.[11]

Our garrulous tough guy with the bright mane had been with us for too few years; we didn't know his age. At least it had been a natural passing, and possibly after a long life. But it still left a big, empty chasm in my heart, and big, empty spaces around the house. "You have two left," said a well-meaning friend when we went to the Chukker bar later that night, but no cat ever "replaces" another. They are not all alike; they are not interchangeable. They are individuals to all those who perceive them carefully. But no one really knows what to say at such times, things are said oddly and taken oddly, and slack needs to be granted all the way around. Orange Cat left my mind full of thoughts I didn't like having. Life is fragile and fleeting. The only answer, although it feels not enough, is to enjoy each day before there are no days. Cherish those you love. Orange Cat had shone like the moon in the forest and then in our house. We buried him out under our trees.

So then we had Gray Cat and Minx. And we went forward. One reason we'd placed the white cat in another home was that we felt three was enough. We never know what's down the road. Because no cat can replace another, having her would not have eased the pain of losing Orange Cat. But the cat took the initiative in choosing us; we should have kept that white cat.

Around the drawing of Orange Cat on that year's Christmas card, I collaged a half-tone dot pattern (before Photoshop) that looked like a nimbus. Everyone immediately understood that it meant he was gone.

In December there was another sad case of animal abandonment not far from us. On his way to town one morning, Bill found a freezing, starving puppy by the side of the highway, after a night when the temperature had gone down to eleven degrees. He checked with people in the nearby houses, but the "basic hound dog" had not come from there. This dog had been put out on the road by someone, just as the white cat had been. One woman who Bill talked to said it was because whoever had done it didn't want this girl dog, who would keep having puppies. It took us by surprise when Bill brought her into the house, bundled completely up in his coat except for the cutest little black and white puppy head looking out at me.

Nonetheless, we weren't prepared to keep a dog, and neither were Gray Cat and Minx, who were so upset when we put the dog down by the heater that they momentarily tangled up with each other, squalling and cussing mightily. We quickly got them separated and calmed down by gently placing a broom between them, taking care to keep hands high and out of bite range while watching their movements carefully. Meanwhile the puppy had gone for a "treat" in the cat box, a common dog behavior, as I quickly learned. We were able to get this away from her and feed her something more appropriate. Bill later found a lady who took the puppy as a Christmas present for a child. We still went by Bill's instinct on people in those days; we were not so suspicious as we know we need to be now. In our earlier and more trusting days, warm eyes and a pleasant manner most assuredly meant a good heart.

Chapter 8

The Ascent Into The Meow-Storm

I sit here writing with Minx the Muse on February 25, 2005. Orange Cat, the moonshine rascal, all peaches and cream, is long gone and after sixteen years, I still miss him. In three months Minx will be seventeen.

For a few of her early years, Minx was a lithe and sleek young cat. Then she grew portly. Cats who have been strays have a tendency to gobble their chow because they remember when food was not always forthcoming. The Minx was no different and around the age of three or four she became slightly obese. "She looks like a meatloaf with a head," laughed our friend Charlotte. We got her diet food and rationed her kibble. Minx was full of sass, too. She was, as we used to say with affection, "fat and sassy," meaning healthy and buoyant. She had a genetic predisposition to weight gain, which became evident when she gained weight on the same diets that kept our other cats in fit and trim shape. Diet food and diet regimens over the years would help her, but only so much. She stayed a butterbean, and she got flea-combed more than anyone else, as the fleas liked the ranch-style living on her expansive back end. (This was before the anti-flea topicals came out.)

Not long after Orange Cat left us, we saw a stray calico cat hanging around the laundromat we used in town; the attendants had been feeding her. But the kitty was gone when we went back with the carrier to get her. We left the staff our number, but we never got a call.

In February 1990, a predicted storm came late at night, a fierce one. It went right over the house with a breathy, roaring, pulsing sound, sort of like *wheh*, pause, *wheh*, pause, *wheh*, on and on for fifteen minutes. With the power knocked out, we ran in the dark to the front and sat between the couch and the wall at the strongest part of the house. Along with the wind there came a series of booming sounds, tall trees falling to the ground. The last sound, during the most ferocious part of the storm, was the loud cracking of a tree breaking apart. The transistor radio told us the storm was now out of our area and on its way to Birmingham with 90-mile-an-hour winds. I jumped when the phone rang an instant afterwards — the neighbors wanted Bill to help them get the downed trees out of the road so they could drive to town and repair damage to their store. The excitement was supposedly over.

I went to bed, and both Minx and Gray Cat came and snuggled beside me, clearly still frightened. They might have slept, but I didn't. At daylight, Bill came back from tree clearing and we finally all slept for a time. The next day we found about six big pine trees down around us, with no damage to the house. The power was out for four days. In areas to the south of us, friends said, large portions of forest were just flattened. It was supposedly all straight-line winds, but I could swear that what we heard was a tornado going right over us, up in the air. The sound and the way it was pulsing — straight wind just doesn't sound that way, to my knowledge. Mom had just moved down here to be close to us, and huge trees had fallen all around her house in town. Storms in this area of the South are now technically known as "severe" and are far worse than anything Mom and I ever saw when I was growing up in and around D.C.

The foxes had stopped coming by that time, and in midsummer that year, we began seeing a strange cat out in the woods. Those first glimpses were brief, and then he began to come closer, out in the yard, but he'd still move off quickly. When I saw him standing by the barbeque grill on the patio, lapping at a can we used to catch the drippings, I knew he was hungry and likely a stray. So I set a bowl of cat food out whenever I saw him; he came right up to me for it, and I found I could pet this big, black-and-white fellow. He was friendly — he wasn't feral. He was maybe a tomcat on a wander who got lost after the spring mating season when toms travel far and wide. (It may well be called "cat redistribution time.") Maybe he was a cat someone had ditched on our country road. Or he could have meandered from a small neighborhood down the highway that adjoined the edge of the forested expanse we lived in. It was behind a gas station where the county dumpster sat, drawing random visits of strays and ferals, including semi-tame yard cats living in the community. One evening at dusk as we drove by the station, I'd seen a gorgeous black cat perched on the dumpster edge. As we passed and I turned to look, I saw two sharp neon glints of its green eyes through the gray haze of the coming night, as bright as the street lights. It was one of those delicious and mysterious sights that happen quickly on a routine drive into town. Now, it appeared, one of that cat's relatives had shown up in our yard.

A few weeks after the new cat showed up, a friend came out to visit us for Fourth of July. So did the cat. A party gazebo had been built on the site where the old Lodge had burned two years before. We took a walk down to it, the black-and-white cat following us every step of the way. I asked the neighbors gathered there if they knew whose cat this might be and they said they had never seen him before. When we left the group I said, "Come eat, kitty. If you're going to be my cat, you've got to come eat." He thought that sounded like a bargain. He followed us back to the house and ate. He became, as he had already intended, yearned for, and tried to tell us, mine. Ours.

This cat was thin, showing evidence of having been out in the forest for a long time. The unbroken woods of our neighborhood were so vast in those days that there was only a remote chance he was someone else's cat gone missing, once we established that he did not belong to any of the friends and neighbors on our road. Lost cats tend to seek the closest possible safe place to re-establish their territory. Even feral cats who lose territorial battles will go to proximate areas. The cats who showed up at our door belonged to several groups: cats socialized with humans, but recently abandoned in the woods; cats socialized with humans but abandoned some time ago, finding us after having lived in the forest awhile (like Orange Cat); true feral cats who had been out there for who knows how long; and wandering, intact tomcats looking for ladies, like this new black-and-white guy. Cats in this last group might be either feral or socialized with humans, and may have become confused and gotten lost. But the possibility of an owned cat with a long-term home becoming lost in this way does not seem high, given the frequent stories of cats who find their old home grounds after being moved great distances from those grounds. I would never have wanted to recklessly adopt someone else's cat, but we felt we had done due diligence in trying to find his owners; Bill also asked around at the gas station if anyone from the nearby neighborhood had lost him. We felt confident that the kitty now before us did not have anyone waiting for him.

Black-And-White stayed outside for awhile, since introducing cats is a lengthy and uncertain process. Gentleman though he was, Gray Cat was really on the warpath about this new face looking through the panes in the door. He howled, and Minx did, too. While they were getting their minds right about it all, I thought carefully about a name. Bill had crossed species for Minx's first name (Spirit Bird), and for this name I wanted to cross from Kingdom Animalia into Kingdom Plantae. This works well with humans, with such traditional names as Rose, Violet, Lily, and, of more recent origin, Heather and Sequoia. But those names felt suited to girls. Not that I'm especially always for the flowery side of naming girls; I can go with the newer trend toward names like Madison and others like it. But I had a rugged, forest-dwelling rogue of a tomcat to name.

I had a special fondness for wisteria, that frothy lavender that climbs, floating in the tree-tops here in the country, scenting up the air every spring. In town the smell is even stronger, where the vines web around porches. That, plainly, would not do for this boy, but while on the subject of vines, it came to me: Kudzu. Kudzu is a climbing vine from Asia. You'll find a lot of fact and fiction about it, and James Dickey even made it the subject of a poem. Most accounts date its entry into the United States to the 1920s, 1930s, and 1940s, when it was introduced in the South as a cover crop to prevent soil erosion and as forage for cattle and other animals. The first official appearance was in 1876 at the Philadelphia Centennial Exposition, as a forage crop and ornamental. The Civilian Conservation Corps planted it in the '30s, and farmers were paid to plant it in the '40s.

The thing is, kudzu grows better in the southern United States than in its native countries, and it has no insect enemies here. So with its large, green leaves, it took over like wild, growing up, over, and around trees, and then back down and onward. It engulfs large areas of forest and can kill the trees, blocking them from the sunlight and growing about a foot a day in the summer. Kudzu has overgrown large areas of the Deep South: roadsides, forest edges, steep slopes, backyards I've seen in Atlanta, and other cities, too. So whatever its insect enemy is in its native lands, that's a beast I wouldn't want to meet! Kudzu roots are a massive seven inches or more in diameter, six-feet-plus-long, and may weigh 400 pounds. And here's where kudzu legend comes in: I've heard the roots are so tough, they've even been used to reinforce concrete!

It's awfully hard to get rid of, and kudzu was eventually declared a pest and a weed by the U.S. Department of Agriculture. Older herbicides couldn't touch it; one even made it grow faster. Now the county sprays and kills it back every year by the roadside, and I shudder to think about whatever chemicals they're using. It's been known to cover abandoned cars and buildings. James Dickey's poem makes it sound sinister and almost sentient, implying it will enter a house through an open window.[1] In later years as we were all aging, a friend walked up our drive with us and quipped that he was slowing down and all those plants out there were making him nervous. "I hate to think that kudzu's moving faster than I am," he said. Most people likely think of it as the fire ants and stinging wasps of plant life.

Kudzu is a plant of many uses, though. In China and Japan, it's been used to make medicines and flour for centuries. Health-food stores carry it in capsules or as small bags of flour. Jelly and syrup are made from its blossoms. I've heard of deep-fried kudzu leaves and kudzu quiche. I've also heard that only the youngest tips of the sprouting leaves can be harvested to make such dishes, so I'd never just grab it and start cooking without thorough research. Many plants require precision cooking instructions to be edible for humans, so don't just go out and eat it! It's a plant of mystery, of complexity.

It can also be used to make baskets and paper. When I became interested in papermaking for art projects, I had plans to try making kudzu paper. There's long been discussion about using it for cattle fodder, although it is difficult to harvest and bale. But it certainly isn't difficult to grow! There would be no problems with fertilizer or pesticide residues, which may end up in the milk or meat of cattle that consume them in feed crops that are subjected to such chemicals. More recently, it has been considered as a possible source of ethanol, though again, harvesting the large, deep-growing roots, especially from steep hillsides, would make that difficult. But ethanol from kudzu would not encroach on one of the world's major food sources the way ethanol from corn reportedly does.

A lack of sunlight in the woods keeps kudzu mainly confined to the roadsides. It's also said that deer and other forest animals munching on kudzu keep it from going into the woods. It's hard to believe that's enough to stop it once those tenacious, ferocious root systems get entrenched, but I've never actually seen it in the deep woods. Maybe it also thrives on car exhaust!

Near our house, where the dirt road joins the highway, a huge kudzu patch grows down a steep embankment, which houses a groundhog colony. Presumably, the groundhogs feast on the kudzu. We can only spot them in early spring when the vines begin to sprout the leaves that quickly cover all the entrances to their burrows, and the entire hillside. (Each groundhog sighting is a source of great joy.) But no kudzu has yet managed to cross the creek into the woods — it stays on and near the roadside. However, I have seen it engulf the first post on the bridge that goes over that branch, waving its tendrils towards the forest.

Friends who drove from California to visit here found that after they had returned home, kudzu started growing in their yard. It had somehow attached to their car without being noticed and "hopped off" when they got home. However, it stayed in a small space — it did not grow rapidly or take over their yard, as it does here. Presumably it does not enjoy the climate of California as much as it does ours. It might certainly make fine cattle fodder, if the nutritional profile is right and if ways could be found to bale it more easily. And I'm actually rather partial to it, as long as it stays on roadsides. A stand of trees covered with kudzu appears as an area of rounded and smoothed-over shapes, like leafy green clouds. You can imagine figures and faces in it, like when viewing sky clouds, or that somewhere in the vines is a hidden entrance to a home of elves or leprechauns. In reality, the interior probably houses some intense snakes and other crawlies. Still, I'm rather fond of kudzu, weed or not.

Both the plant itself and its name seemed masculine enough for a tomcat. Once it gets in your yard, it takes over. Kudzu the cat had come into our yard and was now busy taking over. He came into our hearts, too, and took over. And like many cats, he was a lover of full sunshine.

I'd take a bowl of food out and yell "Kudzu, here kitty, kitty, kitty," and he'd come running. He rapidly learned his name. Kudzu was, in color and pattern, a classic tuxedo cat — mostly black but with a white blaze down his chest and on his underparts. He had white whiskers and white paws, and his paw pads were black against his snowy feet. His eyes were the deepest green I've ever seen on a cat, deeper than the typical, light-apple-green of calico and tabby eyes. He may well have been related to the twilight raider of the dumpster, the one with eyes that had flashed emerald like bar-sign neon. Kudzu's face was heart-shaped, his nose very prominent. His whiskers were huge and widely curved. His muzzle and his lower jawbone were extraordinarily long, almost a dog-like muzzle. Long-limbed and rangy, his front legs were a bit bow-legged. Like most white-footed cats, Kudzu had a smooth and even line separating white paws from black legs, but on his hind legs above that line, he had a sort of dusting or feathering of white fur amidst the black. At times, he looked somewhat homely, at other times bashful, at times the handsome, roving tomcat he was. He appeared to be about a year or two old when he arrived. In his later years, some shorter, stubbly whiskers on his stunningly long muzzle turned white, giving him a wise, wizened look. The fur inside his ears also whitened with age, adding even more to his white/blacker-than-Minx contrasts. His short, thick fur was indeed a deeper black than Minx's, with even more of a lustrous dark sheen. Lean and lanky, he was the picture of healthy cat youth. Seen from the front, his large lower jaw gave his face a lion-like look. He was my lion-faced boy.

Kudzu first met Minx outside. He loped purposefully right up to her with a lilt in his step and an awestruck look in his eyes, sniffing to make friends like he'd just seen the most beautiful cat girl on earth. I mean, his dark face lit up and his eyes sparkled; he was Romeo seeing Juliet for the first time, and his eyes said, *She doth teach the torches to burn bright.*

Pffsssst! she spit. She turned away and would have none of him.

Cat Romeo expected that he would wake one day, sniff the spring air, and detect Juliet of the Catulets' first estrus cycle in the wind. Spraying the nearest wall, he'd set off and track the scent to Cat Juliet's door. He'd crouch and watch carefully until she appeared high up on the balcony. Cat Romeo would have no trouble whatsoever climbing up to that balcony and going *hssssst* at the nurse. Swift and vocal cat romance would instantly occur. End of story.

Throughout their association, Kudzu would pursue Minx and she would elude him. He would strut around her, rubbing his scent on nearby furniture, then rolling on the floor in her path until she growled and spit and started slapping at him. Over and over, we had to interrupt his courting overtures, which persisted even after his neuter surgery. Two other female cats would join the house later, but Minx was the only one he kept romancing. You wouldn't ordinarily suppose love between cats, but this was a tenacious, eternal pursuit. You might say this was just territorial behavior with the unquestionably dominant Minx. But it was the way he looked at her; I'd see him look at her with the same love-struck-teenager gaze as the first time. "Kudzu!" I'd say to try to distract and stop him, because I knew the look meant he'd start rolling around. So he learned to try his courting when Bill and I weren't present. I'd return from the bathroom to the sounds of the Minx growling, *rerrrr, rerrrr,* along with whisking sounds, *whisskk, whoosh,* coming from beyond the couch; Kudzu was rubbing and rolling against furniture and the floor in front of her. I'd rush to intervene because I knew the outrage that Minx was voicing could result in a nasty claws-out swipe to his face if things went too far. *Ain't keeping company with no Kudzu!* was always the unmistakable Minx message. Even though everyone else had soon learned it was best not to vex a Minx, that one never got through to Kudzu.

In retrospect I sometimes wonder if Kudzu's behavior was at least partly territorial, but it did not match any other territorial confrontation I ever saw between the cats. Usually the cat wanting dominance would take at least one claws-out swipe at the individual he or she wanted out of his turf or way, or such a cat would advance in a hostile manner. But Kudzu was, we always felt, definitely sweet on The Minx. Something had turned the plain fact of biology ornate between them, at least in Kudzu's eyes.

One day when he was still outside, I called him but Kudzu didn't come. On into the night, I went back out with the food and called again, and still no Kudzu. So we searched our neighborhood, with no results, and posted a photo on a poster board at the gas station, by the dumpster with the little rural neighborhood behind it. Bill had gone to town for something when I got a call. Some boys said their grandmother had found him dead under her house. I tried to tell them I was half a mile away with no car and had to wait for Bill to come home and carry me up there, but they insisted their grandmother wanted me to come now. I hung up the phone and screamed and cried. We had not had Kudzu for long, but it does not take long to bond inextricably with a cat. I found a box and started the walk along our dirt road to the other dirt road leading to the highway. Soon after I got to the pavement, after a considerable walk, Bill drove back from town, took me home, turned around, and went on to meet the boys who had called.

Turned out, the dead cat was not Kudzu, but some other poor black-and-white cat. Bill helped them out by removing this deceased animal for them, but my wandering boy was still gone. About three weeks after he disappeared, one day Kudzu showed up again on the doorstep waiting, stretching up to meow and rub on my hand when I opened the door. We were elated! And wondering where he had been and what adventures he'd had! Kudzu, with typical feline composure, acted as though nothing had happened. No doubt he had been out on tomcat business and had a picaresque tale to tell. But Kudzu never meowed much and was a gentleman besides. Not long after, Kudzu was neutered and brought in out of the chlorophyll. Our busy schedule had meant we hadn't been as fast to do this as we would have liked. We started him in the back of the house at first to extend the introduction time. He was the best sleep cat I've ever experienced. He settled right in, didn't move all night, and although he may have risen early, I didn't know it, since he was not disruptive as he left my side.

Kudzu had powerful hind legs and was both a runner and a jumper. After he blended in smoothly with everyone and was let into the front rooms, I found him up near the ceiling on a ledge by the attic fan that pulled air through the whole house. He had to have jumped there from the wood stove, which was out of use for the summer, a distance of about eight feet. While I pondered how I was going to get him down, he came rocketing down by himself, landing on the wood stove with a resounding, metallic *thunk-ring*. He never jumped to the fan ledge again but he remained a climber, using the back of the couch as a launching pad to scale the tall bookcase, just as Minx had.

Kudzu also had a great sense of humor. He was like one of those comedians who makes you laugh even before speaking, who projects an inner funniness just by standing around. Sort of like Jack Benny. He had the risibility of the countryside, at once direct and sly. I saw him play a prank on the next cat who became part of the household after Kudzu did, an excitable little calico that Kudzu considered an awful fusspot. One night she was sitting on her haunches on a table in front of the window, looking and listening at the night with her back to the room. Kudzu, on the floor, crept to the table on the other side where she could not see him. He slowly raised up on his long hind legs, tapped her on her rear with one paw, swiftly oozed back down, and darted off silently at a slinky, low-profile, fast trot. The calico spun around, a yelping swirl of color looking to swat somebody, but he was long gone. She got a puzzled look on her face; she did not know who, or what, had tapped her, which is exactly as Kudzu had intended. "Like a little boy pulling a girl's pigtail," Bill said when I told him about it.

This shows, to me, a complex level of understanding and thinking, something beyond what most people think a cat can attain. Although Kudzu might have teased either female cat, it seems that he understood from many encounters the squally character of the calico. In an instant, he saw his chance and planned both the swat and the stratagem for getting away with it. Kudzu understood that getting out of visual and slapping range would, to the calico, be understood as a slap from nowhere and/or remove him from consideration as the guilty party. Also, he knew he had to make his escape swiftly. And, knowing her fussiness, Kudzu knew it would be what in human terms is funny; he plotted in advance, pulled the prank, and enjoyed the joke. These are the kind of events which convince me that cat communication, intelligence, and inter-relationships are far more complex than we humans have yet discerned. Several cognitive activities we may not associate with cats, such as advance planning, recognition of opportunity, perception and awareness of the character of the other cat, and basic humor were all employed in the ruse.

I, too, was learning from the cats. I saw Kudzu sneak up on the calico and knew he had something in mind, although I didn't know what it was; I didn't startle him off of it because I instantly and almost inexplicably knew that his intent was jocular, not hostile; in that respect, we communicated in sync as he carried out the prank. Had I given him some wordless indication I didn't even recall, informing him that I'd play along with this? He learned not to court and spark Minx in front of us, but he pulled the joke on the calico with me sitting right there.

The old saying "enough to make a cat laugh" fits into the pranking incident. Based on the outward fact that cats don't laugh, the saying implies the deeper observation that cats take themselves really seriously. I can agree with this, but maybe they don't take other cats nearly so seriously and can't resist teasing them. Kudzu wasn't laughing at Spotty, but he was coming close; he was, most assuredly, smirking on the inside. Kudzu showed through this incident that he was a master of timing — maybe with a little more encouragement he could have had a career doing standup! Seriously, though, Kudzu helped teach me just how intelligent cats really are!

Kudzu wasn't especially talkative, and he had a soft meow and a soft purr for such a large cat. He was not, in his early years, a lap cat, though he would tolerate being placed there for short periods. I can recall only one instance when this shrewd, long-legged, long-muzzled catboy with the twisted sense of humor jumped up in my lap and went to sleep. Not all cats are lap cats, but such pets are responsive in other ways, and just as warm and expressive if you watch carefully for the eyes that follow you and the ears that swivel as they track you leaving the room. I recall an evening when Bill suddenly said, "You know those times when you miss one more than the others?" and he went and scooped up Kudzu for some snuggles. Kudzu either humored him on that occasion or understood and shared the feeling; he stayed with Bill for awhile longer than usual that night.

Kudzu was sort of like an old cowpoke, bow-legged and full of his own 'druthers. He didn't like the flea comb, and he was a little nippy about his dislikes. When we went into the yard with the cats on a supervised outing, he'd head straight for the dusty spot in the road and roll with happiness. Like Gray Cat, he loved a dust bath. When I swept up the house, Kudzu would roll in the dust when my back was turned and scatter it all over again. After he appeared several times covered with a mysterious gray dust that looked oddly familiar, I finally caught him rolling in a freshly poured litter tray. He knew somehow that he wasn't supposed to do that, even though I never fussed at him about it and only wiped off the dust so he wouldn't swallow it when grooming himself. I'd hear a sudden crunching sound and see him doing a rapid lope away from the box, with a guilty grin on his face and a fresh coating of clay particles in his fur. He'd snuck into a pristine box and gotten his dust rub in when I wasn't looking.

Despite his mischievousness, Kudzu was a cautious sort; at the first sound of raindrops, he'd wiggle himself under the couch. From living outdoors, he'd learned that rain sounds meant wet fur unless he went under something. Always expecting it to rain into the house, he never changed this reaction to storms. When handling trash sacks, we inadvertently found out that he was afraid of rattling plastic and would bolt away at the sound. When you adopt an adult animal and you don't know its history, you're tempted to interpret such things. Had he been chased out of yards by persons taking their trash out in plastic sacks? Or worse, had some mean person sacked him up in one as a kitten? Such speculations may be futile and inaccurate — Kudzu may simply have been reacting to unfamiliar sounds. He was, in some ways, shyer than the others, much easier to shoo away from the door to the back, for instance, because he would not push or jump past you when you tried to guide him away. Once we learned, from some unremembered source, to hiss like a momcat lecturing kittens when trying to discourage a cat away from people food or to stop any bad behavior, we had a technique that all the cats responded to, at least a little bit. At worst, they might stop and give us a quizzical look, *just who do we think you are? You call that a hiss?* before going on about whatever shady doings they had been up to. Of all the cats, Kudzu was the most easily deterred from naughty behavior by the hiss. When I combined it with a saying my Mom used during my childhood, "Scramezvous," he learned the meaning of that phrase.

Whereas I thought Kudzu was funny and a real comedian, Minx plainly did not. But she did fairly well considering he was the first new cat she'd ever had to accept into her realm. (The white cat never entered the house.) Gray Cat, who had wailed like the tornado siren at Kudzu's first appearances, came to accept him and they sometimes snoozed together, snuggled up like kittens.

This was 1990, and in March I'd had an odd dream that I wrote down: a friend had a Day-Glo, chartreuse kitten, a color not natural to felines, and I wanted it. There were frequently vivid colors in my dreams, nothing odd there. But was it a portent of the coming of Kudzu, and of the next kitty we'd see peering out of our forest at us?

Spotting the newest addition to our household

October of that year, another cat appeared in the woods, cautiously haunting the edge of the patio. This was a small calico, somewhat seasonally camouflaged as she moved among fall leaves, gliding and undulating with careful steps, her gaudy face turned toward us. Most calicos are girls; male calicos are extremely rare, have an extra X chromosome, and are infertile, so we assumed this was a female. The cat called and called to us as if pleading urgently for our company, but she was also wary of us. She would *me-yowl* in a sort of screechy, whiney voice, come closer, and call again. Food drew her close enough to sniff my extended hand. Slowly, she began to accept pats and scritches. Up close, her splashy colors were captivating. This was one of the most distinctively marked calicos I'd ever seen. She had so many patterns that Bill called her "pixilated," followed by "she's all mixed up." She had the same white bib, underparts, and feet of a tuxedo cat. Although her right eye-lid was edged in orange, around that edging was a gray ring fanning out to cover her ear, like an elegant half-mask held obliquely and coquettishly over one side of the face. Her lower face and muzzle on that side were white. Directly above her nose there was an orange streak — the nose itself was white, but the "nose leather" around her nostrils was gray, as was the muzzle on the left side, while the orange of her center forehead came over the left eye, with a few gray streaks through it. The backs of her ears were marbled colors but mostly gray, while the front ear fur was white.

She had somewhat prominent little cat lips: on the gray side of her muzzle they were gray, and on the white side, they were pink. The two lip colors met off-center. Her whiskers were white, and her right front leg, on the white side of the muzzle, was mostly a mottled, pebble-like gray pattern, except for the white foot. Under the dark half of the muzzle, the leg was more white and a paler orange, with a little heathered gray on the outside. From her ears on back to her tail-tip she was a feathered gray and orange, with a few some-what distinct patches of either color scattered here and there. Her hind legs were mostly light orange and white. She had eyes of pale green. Months later a visiting neighbor kid said the calico had hung around their house for awhile but had not become their cat, instead moving on to us. "I'll never forget that face," he said. Other friends commented on her, too; she was so beautifully marked.

Everyday assumptions while we're speaking can sometimes be a little off the mark. When Bill called Spotty "pixilated," I assumed he was referring to the pixels of present-day digital images. Indeed, *pixel* is said to mean "pic-ture element." But there is another possible meaning or origin that I came upon through the circuitous route of the social-media page of another cat book author, in 2014. In Tom Cox's article, "A Walk on Dartmoor, Face to Face with a Homemade Grim Reaper," he notes that "pixie-led" or "pixilat-ed" means being led astray by the pixies.[2] Variations of this word go back to the 1600s. Who knew? This too, could be said to describe our Spotty "to a T" or down to a pixel.

Clearly, the stray cats knew to come to us. Orange Cat had sounded his huge *Eureka!* to the skies the day he claimed us, and undoubtedly other strays smelled our cats and their food and knew that cat feeding was ongoing here. Other neighbors also had happy, well-fed, loved kitties, but some had to live with dogs in the household, so I can see why strays did not go to those houses. It's almost like some careful appraisal process had gone on with Or-ange Cat, Kudzu, and the calico, as well as others later who we would place in homes. It was as though they might be scouting and scrutinizing carefully before choosing us. Maybe they were looking through the glass door when our backs were turned, seeing us petting or talking to our cats as well as feed-ing them, and maybe they sensed the general reverence and deference we had for cats. Perhaps each one looked carefully and thought, in some cat-thought way, *I will not be ignored here, I will get attention, I will be rubbed and cud-dled, and well-fed. Granted that's true elsewhere, but here I may even be able to run the place.* Then, the vanishing into the viridescence of summer, or the color-splatter of fall, to bide their time, waiting for the optimum cat moments to reveal themselves and to carefully contemplate before deciding on us, forever.

However she came, the calico joined us and then we had four. She had a huge need for attention. The first night she was brought inside, she slept in the back room with me, and in the morning she would not leave me alone. She was all over my chest, neck, and head, rubbing her face on my face. Trapped in a supine position, with about three-fourths of the cat sprawled across my neck and pedaling claws-out with her front feet on my collarbone, licking and nuzzling my face, I tried to lift her up and away so I could rise, but her claws tangled in the covers as she scrabbled to get closer. I almost called to Bill for help. About a year or two old, she was impossibly cute, at some higher, more intense level of cuteness that not all cats attain. She was simply the cutest little cupcake of a cat I had ever seen.

There was another calico cat in the neighborhood, with larger patches of orange and black, named October. In a way, that name suits a calico well. Ours had arrived in that self-same month, so Bill named her October also, and she would remain registered at the vet that way. I never quite liked it though. It was too many syllables, too ponderous, and there were no doubt a zillion calicos by that name. Calling out "October" to a small animal didn't quite ring true to me, and any shortening for a nickname, like "Octy," felt awkward on the voice.

I didn't really set out deliberately to change it, but several months later I was petting her and musing, letting my thoughts flow freely, playing with words. A bit of silliness some might say, but a technique I've found that can lead to new phrases and word-depths and insights into word origins. Looking at her front legs, I described her astounding mixed markings aloud, saying, "You have one white leg, the other all spotteddy." For awhile she became Spottadee or Spottatee, and then a guest heard it as "Spotty" and called her that, and she came to be called Spotty by everyone, forever. Eventually I decided Spotty was short for her given name SpottaLee, in the grand old southern tradition of fused names, such as LindaSue, BillyBob, and Janelle. When emphasis was called for, I'd say "Spotta*Lee!*" or "Why Miss Spotta*Lee* Spot!" Another way of pronouncing SpottaLee might give it an extra air of sophistication if spoken fast, with even emphasis on each syllable, like "Natalie." There were a lot of occasions to call out one of the variations of the spot-based name. There was "Spotta T. Spot." There was also "Little Bit," a nickname due to her small size. I've since heard some-where that the double name in the South was always given to the second daughter of a family. If so, it was fitting because SpottaLee was the second female to join our clowder at the time, Minx being the first.

Colorful descriptions for colorful coats

Spotty's colors were slate gray, light orange, and white. When I learned more about cat color nomenclature, I found that there are several names for her color identity: blue-cream (dilute) tortoiseshell with white; dilute calico; or blue tortie (tortoiseshell). Usually a cat with a fair amount of white like Spotty will have larger and more defined color patches, and Spotty had some of these, but she also had blended and heathered areas of blue and cream. Such admixtures are also known as "brindled."

Tortoiseshells are sometimes called *calamancs* or *calamancas*, after a patterned cloth made in the 18th and 19th Centuries.[3] Cat colors are variations of two basic genes, black and red. Black color variants are browns, light browns, and dilute black. The result of a gene for dilution, dilute black is a less-saturated color that would be called a tint in painting, gray. Red color variants are oranges and reds. Dilute red is a result of the same gene and if a calico has dilute black (gray), the red will also be the lighter color, a pale red or orange, which is called cream. Dilute black, or gray, is called blue, and a mutation of the gene for black that appears brown is called chocolate or chestnut, while dilute brown is called lilac or lavender. A lighter brown that is again a mutation of the gene for black is called cinnamon, and dilute light brown (cinnamon) is called fawn. Now, in Spotty's case, her admittedly lighter orange in no way resembled the color I think of when I think "cream," which is ivory or off-white, and may have only the tiniest tinge of orange or yellow or brown to make it "off-white." And while blue and gray can be close, they are not the same color. As for lilacs and lavenders, I really need to get out more and get a look at some of those cats.

It would seem that the naming of cat colors is a thorny undertaking.[4] At least, it was for somebody, back when these designations were chosen. My apologies, but I'm a painter; there's bluish-gray, there's grayish-blue, there's gray with a hint of blue, but I'm sorry, gray ain't blue, and there are no blue cats! Gray fur can have highlights of blue, but that's just the compound nature of all colors, as described earlier. To go scientific on this question, gray color in cat fur is actually dilute black, the color of which results from eumelanin, or black pigment, on the fur shaft. There are no cats crossed with blueberries!

Linguistically, we have to draw the line somewhere. Everyone knows the difference between blue skies and gray skies; try calling that one wrong and imagine the reactions. If weather forecasters suddenly spoke like cat fanciers, think of the consternation and chaos! And it would be so disappointing to imagine the ancient Celts in a blue war-paint that was actually the color of granite. We had only to gaze into Gray Cat's powdery cerulean-blue eyes, a color like the skies of Renaissance paintings (though it would be much later than the Renaissance when a pigment of that name was placed on the market), to see how the color differs from the ashy gray fur on the face of this supposedly "blue-point" Siamese mix.

Anyway, as a painter, seeing gray called blue makes me crazy. That said, I do admire much of the terminology of the cat fancy, such as the elegant and apt term "mitted" for white gloved paws. Crossing over into dogland, much as I love all pooches, terms like "blue-tick hounds," blue merle dogs in the piebald pattern, and dogs named Blue add to all the confusion! Even so, I do rather enjoy the Blue Dog paintings of George Rodrigue.[5] And according to the book *Bright Earth: Art and the Invention of Color* by Phillip Ball,[6] in ancient times blue was actually not recognized as a color separate from gray. So maybe there's some historical precedent and traditional, cultural practices behind these terms. But, as fascinating as the classics can be, color nomenclature has shifted over the centuries; color naming has far outpaced prior eras and should keep on going, with no looking back.

Color skewing doesn't only affect terms describing animals. I can remember when the very purple iris in my childhood yard in D.C. were called "blue flags" by Mom, her grown-up contemporaries, and my grandmother. Oddly enough there's even more blue confusion in several languages that, in early times, did not have separate terms for blue and green. Differences in individual color perception may also have had a role in color nomenclature and sequences of color name emergence. This reminds me of a rhyme from childhood: "I never saw a purple cow, I never hope to see one, But I can tell you here and now, I'd rather see than be one,"[7] which was oft-quoted by my grandmother. My sentiments run counter to those of the rhyme. I'd like very much to see these naturally purple cats, the ones described as "lavender" or "lilac."

All joking aside, I can go with the notion that the cat fancy uses fanciful names, and I myself enjoy lavish names for colors. I can actually see it in the case of blue and lilac and lavender, but I find "cream" really misleading in the case of "blue-cream tortoiseshells." I might instead suggest "peach," a color much more akin to pale orange, but still a term with a twist. It goes with the general theme in naming red colors, as when dilute red is acted upon by a dilute modifier gene, which only affects colors that are already diluted, and the resulting lighter color is called apricot.[8] Even a jump within dairy from "cream" to "cheese," would describe Spotty's orange spots with more precision!

All that said, I do understand the need for fixed terms to sort out, encompass, and define the incredible array of coat colors in domestic cats, which are produced by a wide variety of complex genetic factors. But the color of a cat sometimes does not indicate the correct term for the genetics that underlie it. For example, there is a dark-pointed Siamese called a seal point, whose points are visually brown. But genetically, it's a black cat! Color-pointed cats are the result of a color restrictive modification gene, and they are technically solid-color cats.[9] The brown tabby is also genetically black, with genetic factors such as the agouti gene, which causes variations in pigment distribution and density that in turn result in visually differing colors. Though "brown tabby" is a good distinguishing term, such a cat is, essentially, a black tabby. Once again, knowledge undercuts those old superstitions about black cats. Our perceived colors are often illusions and misunderstandings when compared to the facts of nature.

(Here's one more fun fact about calicos: in 2001, the State of Maryland named the calico the official state cat; its colors match those of the state bird, the Baltimore Oriole, as well as the state insect, the Baltimore Checkerspot Butterfly.)

Anyway, if I ever have another gray cat, I'll probably name him or her Cerulean or Ultramarine as a little joke of my own.

Cat colors emerge in ways very different from paint mixing. These complex facts are described with slight variations on the *Messybeast Cat* website by Sarah Hartwell, "Solid Colors and Dilutes" by Heather Lorimer, and "Cat Color Genetics" by Orca Starbuck and David Thomas. Cat colors are all produced by two forms of melanin: eumelanin, which is black and brown, absorbing most of the light, and phaeomelanin, or red and yellow, which reflects red, orange, and yellow light.[10] Eumelanin is spherical in shape and phaeomelanin is more elongated.[11] In a black cat, the eumelanin granules are round and laid down on the hair shaft thickly so that the hairs appear as an opaque black.[12] Chocolate and cinnamon colors are produced by mutations of the gene for black.[13] According to Lorimer, chocolate coloration results when melanin is laid down in a thinner layer with granules that are more oval and therefore more transparent, admitting some light to produce brown. Cinnamon is the result of even thinner granules, a color that is lighter and more towards orange.[14] An even redder example of this is seen in "ruddy" Abyssinians, who are actually genetically black.[15]

Chocolate and cinnamon cats are found more commonly in the purebred population and rarely among random breds, though black cats, of course, are everywhere. The above three colors are called "dense" colors, and Lorimer notes that although the granules of dense color cats are of different thicknesses, under a microscope the hair is smoothly and evenly colored. Another gene that has two alleles, one for dense and one for dilute, controls how evenly the hair is colored. With the dilute gene, the granules are no longer smoothly and evenly spaced, but rather clumped together in some locations along the hair shaft while being sparse or absent in others. Under the microscope, black pigment bands will look haphazardly mixed with off-white bands, which produces "blue" color. The same effect produces lilac (also called lavender or frost) as the dilute of chocolate, and fawn as the dilute of cinnamon; these are paler colors.[16] This is known as "maltesing."[17] According to Hartwell, another gene called the dilute modifier acts only on already-dilute colors, causing further lightening called "caramelising."[18]

Note that these are all black-based colors. The agouti gene causes each individual hair to have alternating bands of light and heavy pigmentation. The light areas may be yellow or orange in color, but if the hair shaft is pigmented with eumelanin, the effect is produced by sparse granules of black. You will not find phaeomelanin (red) on the same hair shaft. These "ticked" hairs are found on tabby cats; all of the varying coloration of brown tabby cats is caused by eumelanin granules distributed in differing ways. Brown tabbies and black cats are produced by the same elements.

So by starting with black pigment, nature has economically produced a variety of fur colors that we admire as beautiful, not the least of which is the astonishingly beautiful black cat itself. The non-agouti gene will result in a solid color cat, which is usually black. Several sources say all domestic cats carry the tabby gene and therefore the tabby pattern is sometimes not totally suppressed, meaning there can be faint tabby markings on even a solid black cat. But the agouti gene must be present in order for the tabby gene to be expressed in one of the full tabby patterns. Tabby patterns include the ticked, the spotted, the mackerel, and the classic. From Lorimer: "Phaomelanin, red, is dense, meaning intense red, or dilute, i.e. cream, in the same way as the above explanation for eumelanin."[19] Again, the dilute modifier makes dilute red cats appear apricot.[20]

However, the non-agouti gene does not affect red pigmentation, and red cats will usually have at least some markings on their tail, legs, and forehead, or they'll have a darkening along the spine. Breeders try to select for rufousing polygenes that intensify red and may mask the contrast in the tabby pattern, but most solid reds still produce the "M" pattern on the forehead. This also applies to the dilutes of red, such as cream cats (or peach, to my way of thinking). The gene for white spotting produces the bi-colored white markings on solid color cats, tabbies, and tortoisehells, as well as the "piebald" patterns, with patches of solid color and large areas of white. Again, with only a few genetic materials, nature makes an astonishing variety of colors.

The red gene is carried on the X chromosome and is therefore considered to be sex-linked. Usually males will inherit only one X, along with one Y, so if a male gets a red X (an X-carrying red) he'll be a red cat. A female has two X chromosomes, so she needs two red Xs to be a red cat. Red males are more common, and there are differing opinions as to how rare red females are.

When a female gets one red-carrying X and one non-red X, the result will be red and black patches, or tortoiseshell. This occurs because of a process called X chromosome inactivation. One or the other of the two X chromosomes is inactivated, while the other is expressed. This occurs in a totally random way and shows up in the pigment-producing skin cells. The result is a mixture of reds and blacks in the coat. This only occurs when two X chromosomes are present, hence, usually there are no male tortoiseshells or calicos. When the rare male gets both these colors, he will have two Xs and one Y, and evidently the Xs will therefore go through the same random inactivation as happens with a female. The incidence of XXY is uncommon, and these males will usually be sterile. The explanation for why X chromosome inactivation occurs opens up many questions in my mind. My own curiosity craves answers, but those answers are more technical than the scope of this book.

Sometimes, a tricolor male (with white spotting) or a bicolor male is not an XXY, but is instead a chimera, a situation in which two separate fertilized eggs have fused during development. Such a male may be fertile, and this is actually a form of mosaicism, because there are two different cell lines from two different eggs. Another form of mosaicism that may result in a male tricolor can occur when there is a somatic mutation in an individual who develops from one egg, resulting in two separate cell lines within that individual. This type of mutation will only affect body cells and not sex cells, so the mutation will not be passed on to the offspring.[21]

In my own observations and in others that I've read, there are more male black cats than female black cats; I have yet to run across a scientific paper describing the reasons. I would speculate that the reasons are the same as those affecting the red male/female ratio; the gene for black color might be on the X chromosome, so a male would need one black X to be black, while a female would need two black Xs to be black, and so red X and black X pairings would reduce the chances of two black Xs being inherited as a pair. I'm sure it's much more complicated than that, so y'all don't quote me on this!

A meowful of meaning: the art and science of cat-speak

Spotty, bless her sweet little heart, was a neurotic, jealous, whiny fusspot of a cat, who we loved to distraction. She had a piercing, screeching *me-yowl* when she called for food and attention, or when she was just plain irritated. She would do this when either one of us was on the phone, or even when we talked to each other. Many were the times Bill had to explain to friends or business callers at the other end of the line why they were hearing those shrill *me-yowls*. She meowed throughout an entire conversation I had with a doctor once, as she stood right by the phone. "You need to feed that cat," said the doctor, "it sounds hungry." Little did the doc know, dry kibble was set out all the time; Spotty was just jealous.

In contrast, when gratified, petted, spoken or sung to, she could produce the most beguiling series of musical trills and short, bark-like sounds. She'd first emit a curling, coiling *skirulle-ulle-ulle,* rising to *myet! twet! me-yet!* once she had attained your attention, pats, or lap. If one of us petted or talked to another cat, she'd rush over, look up, and let out a petulant, sharp screechy yowl, as if to say, *Me, too* or *Me, not him or her.* At times it sounded like a *me-or yowwelelel* in a drawn-out drawl as if she was trying to say, *Ya'awwwlulull, pat me nooowww.* The harmonics in the noise of rushing water can cause you to think you hear voices; Spotty's unfurling sounds were almost as potent and sibilant with half-heard words and whispered meanings as the rapids down at the branch.

Many books on cat behavior indicate that adult cats seldom meow to other cats. Instead, meows, or *miaows,* are reserved for humans. According to "The signalling repertoire of the domestic cat and its undomesticated relatives," by John Bradshaw and Charlotte Cameron-Beaumont in *The Domestic Cat: The Biology of Its Behavior,* meowing is definitely a cat-to-human communication. The meows of one cat vary widely and meows differ from cat to cat. Cats learn to meow to humans and seemingly learn to innovate variations.[22] Cats don't come with a standard meow. As seasoned companions to cats, we knew this so well; we have lived it and witnessed the distinctive meows particular to each cat growing, improvising, expressing.

Therefore, I conclude that a real vocal-virtuoso-of-a-meower like Spotty, with her large fund of variations on the meow theme, was trying really hard to communicate with us. The Minx had her own expansive set of beguiling sounds, also delivered with eyes trained on one of us. Trying to interpret the meanings of the vocal (and other) signals that cats present to us daily is a constant source of intriguing thought. And as one who has spent years observing cats, I can agree with the experts that I've never seen a cat meow to another cat, outside of kitten-to-momcat and momcat-to-kitten conversations. In keeping with the idea that cats learn various meows in the company of humans in a continuum of communication, studies are now being done to determine if cats detect and pick up human rhythms of conversing; in other words, can cats hear differing human accents? I would say first, that U.S. Southern accents do have a different rhythm than those of other U.S. regions, and second, that SpottaLee, with her drawling, sprawling vocalizations, definitely meowed with a southern accent.

We can't begrudge Spotty her nervous, high-strung, and clingy nature. Not only does it fall within the range of personality that an animal might be born with, but we also didn't know what she had undergone in that year or so before she found us. She may have been feral, but she had likely been abandoned, and even if she'd simply been someone's ignored and neglected yard-cat and wandered on over to us from a great distance, it was clear she'd had a very hard life. Until she found us, that is. It was Bill's theory, or wisecrack, that Spotty's "mixed-up" coat meant a mixed-up mind to match. Calicos, I hear, are often divas.

I would frequently recline back somewhat when sitting, which was the perfect stance in which to accommodate more than one cat. If Minx was half in my lap and half on my chest, Spotty would climb above her, closer to my face, and settle there, even if she was just about on my face and/or sprawled across Minx's head; Spotty would do anything to be closer to me than Minx. Once she attained this place, she would *chirp* and *trill* with happiness and triumph. She craved attention from other cats, too, and would lie down with Minx on the couch and thrust her head at Minx's face repeatedly, until Minx would begin grooming Spotty's tri-color noggin. Spotty would sometimes tend Minx's face in return and would not hesitate to place a paw firmly on Minx's head to hold her down as she groomed the black ears. If Minx groomed Spotty's sensitive skin too vigorously or just rubbed her the wrong way, Spotty would swat her one upside the head and the girls would quickly disentangle.

I would sometimes engage Spotty in a long conversation by calling her name in all its variations, interspersed with a few meows that I'd learned over the years. She'd answer back and forth for a long while, and we'd have a *meowlin'* good time. Once we had such a talk entirely in meows. On my end, it was completely my interpretations of meows that I'd listened to over the years, probably with the wrong emphases and accents, but Spotty was cordial enough to respond to me all the same.

Minx had accepted Kudzu and Spotty reluctantly, but eventually they became partners, along with Gray Cat, in various around the house takeovers. Minx was the ringleader. She'd pull the door to the back room open, and I'd find all four of them snoozing on the bed. Or Minx would leap onto the drawing table and shoulder her way among the ink bottles until she'd arranged a place for herself, and then the others would follow. The others lost their good manners as she led them into ruination. The cat sleeping would often be so profound that I'd just work around them. I'd feel bad about moving them if I had to, and it sometimes took two of us humans to defelinate a bed, desk, or room. Drawings produced during this era were done around, next to, and among the cats in tight proximity. The presence of such discerning and wise creatures would only improve the work.

I recall one particularly difficult defelination at the drawing table. I had to sit on a stool about three-feet-high to reach the drawing surface. One day I was there with Minx on my lap and Kudzu and Spotty jammed together, somnolent and directly in front of me on the table. I was using a stiff cardboard under my drawing to lean on for support. Next to Spotty was an open bottle of ink. Suddenly Spotty's rear, with herself still in deep slumber, rolled off the table towards me. I took one hand off my drawing board and supported small little Spotty with it. She was then suspended between my hand and the table, over the chasm of the three-foot drop to the floor. I couldn't let her down onto my lap because the Minx was there, and they might tussle if I tried to crowd them both onto me, but I also couldn't edge her onto the table one-handed because Kudzu had oozed closer when Spotty's butt slid off the edge, leaving no room. And, there was the open inkpot to consider. Meanwhile, Minx was getting restless as Spotty's feet dangled over her. I didn't want Spotty to fall, especially while half conscious, and I also knew that a cat who starts to fall is going to reach out and dig claws into the nearest solid surface, which in this case might be my flesh, or the piece of paper situated under the ink bottle. I hollered for Bill's help; he gallantly came from the back, carefully lifted Spotty straight up and off, and eased her down; by the time her paws touched the floor she was fully awake and chirping happily at the attention.

At times when Spotty saw Minx on my lap, rather than join us she'd just walk up to Bill and voice a *sca–reeeeeee* yowl of a complaint — Minx had a lap and she didn't — until Bill would lift her or moved to allow her easy access to his lap from wherever she was standing. Once snuggled in and petted, a celebratory song came from Spotty's diminutive muzzle, notes curling around each other, rising, falling, twirling; part flute and part bagpipe, ending in brisk *tweets* and *chirps*. I wish I had a recording of all the cats' vocalizations. Each one was different and I always knew who was meowing, even if I couldn't see the cats. If Minx had my lap, Spotty must at least have Bill's if she couldn't have mine. And the fact that she at times sought out Bill first instead of demanding to sit with me may have been a concession to the fact that even she knew I was taken by Minx.

Bill would break off little pieces of potato or corn chips and feed them to Spotty, who would pull them into her mouth with her tongue and crunch them up noisily in her teeth. "Want some kitty chips?" he'd say to her when he started. Soon, whenever Spotty saw Bill with a bag of chips, she'd head his way, sit next to him, and start working on him with a look that was both imploring and smug. He would always respond by giving her kitty chips. She'd try it with me, too, and I'd sometimes oblige, but I wasn't as patient about feeding her chips as Bill was. Chips aren't the best things to feed cats, of course, especially if they contain onion, which is toxic to cats. Raw potatoes are also on the toxic-to-felines lists, although cooked 'taters are said to be fine and are used in some commercial cat-food formulas. We instinctively avoided those with onion for Spotty, but still, chips mean carbs and cats really don't need many of those.

Those were still the days of supervised outdoor yard time, and we discovered a curious disconnect between indoor Spotty and outdoor Spotty. Indoor Spotty was a lap cat, friendly and demanding of attention from us or from anyone who walked in. She would approach company by standing at their feet, locking her glance on them, and issuing an irritated, piercing *me-or-yowel* until she was noticed and babied. But outdoor Spotty seemed totally twitchy, fearful and as though she didn't even know us. There was no coaxing her and no catching her — she'd run if you even took a step towards her. If we opened the door and avoided standing in it, she'd come back in eventually, and a tuna trail up the steps and into the house would bring her in faster. Once back inside, Spotty was all sweetness again, head butting and rubbing against us and seeking our laps. Spotty was just plain strange and unique in many ways, but she had also lived for an unknown time homeless in the woods. Dogs, raccoons, opossums, territorial neighborhood cats, the occasional coyotes we heard yapping on the lakebed — all those perils may have made her fearful of everything outdoors.

She did become paranoid inside when we tried to give her medicine. If we didn't get it down her by surprise on the first try, she'd run frantically all over the house, trying to dart into her various hidey holes while we tried to head her off and block her access to those nooks that only she knew how to create. She'd screech whenever she was caught. Bill joked that it was as if she was yelling, *Oh, I always knew it! You're going to cook me in the pot and eat me!* Besides, it was an affront to her catly status to take something not of her choosing. Seconds after medicine time was over, she was all peaches and cream, buzzing with purrs again. She was complicated, full of the blended contrasts of wild animal: panicked and distrustful of humans one minute, and the next, absolute waif cuddlepuss, wailing-in-your-face, pouncing on your lap, demanding your full devotion to the tasks of stroking and snuggling her. Cats use their paws in many ways to obtain or express things they want — to catch prey or to slap another cat who's in their way or just a furfaced irritant at the moment for some reason. Spotty used her paw, with claws sheathed, to tap my hand as though she were jump-starting a motor whenever she wanted petting. I knew that was the right interpretation because as soon as I would pet her, she would stop tapping.

Driving Spotty ten miles into town to the vet for her first checkups was an ordeal for all concerned. Most cats I've known have disliked car rides, but Spotty was so terrified that she screeched at the top of her voice the entire way. Having me sit and talk with her made some difference, but not as much as we would have liked. Once there, though, her eyes would get big again and she'd smile and strut for the new people to impress and get pats from them. But back in the car, she'd resume the yelling until we turned off the highway into the woods. Then she'd sniff and sniff, knowing the forest smell meant home. The forest was another world, different from the highway, and the cat's keen nose detected that immediately. She yelped less on those trips as she got older, but she still showed agitation and fear.

Like Kudzu, Spotty proved a skillful climber. One day I walked through the kitchen and discovered her high up on top of the kitchen cabinets, nestled in and looking well-pleased with herself. "Spotta*Lee*, however did you get up there," I tilted my head back and asked her. I soon observed her coming down from above via a very narrow ledge around the sink; she'd slide her front feet down the cabinet while holding her hind end on the top edge in a springing crouch, and then she'd jump on down, landing on the ledge and strutting; she knew she was agile. She would go back up the same way, leaping first to the counter, then trotting around the sink with a determined demeanor as though she knew we'd rather she didn't, then she'd launch from the ledge, grabbing the ridged top of the cabinets with her front feet and digging her hind claws into the wood for leverage to help push herself on up. It was a distance of four feet. The claw marks are still on the cabinet where she used her hind feet. Minx had tread the sink ledge, too, in pursuit of whatever food smells or tastes were around, but she had never climbed to the summit of the cupboards. Spotty was lighter than Minx, and she had long lived outside where climbing trees and houses meant safety from ground predators.

Every country house has mice, especially houses in an unbroken forest. All the best houses have them, in fact. Spotty was one of the all-time great mousers. She was little and quick and very patient. She'd sit, profoundly still, by the place under the sink where the mice had a trail and would dart into an opening into the wall, an oversight because our place was still unfinished thanks to the hectic pace of our self-employed life. Why the mice even attempted to come into this house of cats I don't know, but they seemed to waltz on in. We'd frequently wake to a commotion out front and find Kudzu and Spotty growling at each other, one of them with mouse-in-jaw as the other two cats circled around those two. Bill would rescue the mouse if he could — if a cat dropped it or he could manage to distract the proprietary cat of the moment, which was usually Spotty. We preferred trapping mice alive and relocating them to a less populated wilderness down the road. To her horror, one night my mother witnessed Spotty dispatching an unfortunate mouse, sailing in ahead of Kudzu. Kudzu was good at mousing, but Spotty was better. In fact, she had goddess status when it came to mousing. Spotty was the Diana of my floors. (She was the first to pursue lizards that came into the house, too. We preferred to rescue lizards by slapping a cup or a bowl over them, carefully sliding a stiff cardboard under the bowl, and carrying the whole thing outside. They were then evicted to our yard.)

One night, when the door to the back was open, we heard noises from the hall. Spotty was after a mouse. It was zig-zagging back and forth and had lots of cover from boxes stored in the hall, so Spotty didn't have a clear shot. Our appearance in the doorway blocked the mouse, who did an abrupt about face and ran back up the hall. Spotty had been in furious speed but suddenly she plopped down on the floor with her feet extended out from under her. She had trapped the mouse under her belly. All of us froze for a moment. Spotty just looked at us as if to say, *Well, what now?* She couldn't move to use her teeth and claws or else the mouse might get away, and she wasn't having that. Bill finally managed to nudge her up gradually and trap the mouse in a cloth himself, then give it safe passage to the release area down the road. Spotty was, I'm sure, perplexed and annoyed. As usual, she had done all the work but Bill, not she, had ended up with her mouse.

We bragged on Spotty's mousing prowess enough that friends in town who were troubled by rodents jokingly asked to borrow her. But cats, of course, would never perform normally on such a visit, and we would have never lent her out for any reason, mouse duty or otherwise.

Spotty brought color, excitement, revelry, pizzaz, and at times, exasperation, to the house. She was high maintenance. When she first came, she drooled a little at times, and I just wiped it off with a tissue whenever I saw it. Hyper salivation can be a sign of nutritional deficiency, as well as many other conditions. Six or eight months of cat food formulated for optimum cat health — rather than whatever she'd found to eat as a stray — likely helped to stop her drooling. But nothing ever stopped her tendency to chew on any string or wire-like items around, so Bill had to keep wire for his electronics projects put away. I took down the prisms in the window, because she would stand on her hind legs to reach the fine wires holding them and chew. She also liked to chew on plastic. We didn't mind a little extra trouble for Spotty. We were smitten with her, and a pet is family to us. You do whatever you have to.

We had 24-hour nibbling in our house in those days, with diet food in the mix. Cats taken into your home who have lived on their own and have gone without food prefer a constant food bowl and they tend to overeat. You could say they totally stuff their faces. Minx with her tendency to gain got a little round from time to time, and the others had a bit of extra padding at times, too. So we worked out yet another diet with the vet, taking up the food except at certain feeding times, thereby controlling random nibbling. One night as I lifted the food dish to put it up, Spotty's eyes were on me. She walked to the spot where the chow had been, *miaowed* and paced around. "Sorry, girl," I said, making no move to restore the food. She then strode purposefully to the place under the sink where the mice habitually ventured out of the wall and sat there watching it fixedly for a moment. She turned and regarded me with a withering look that was partly perplexed and partly offended, which plainly said, *If you're not going to feed me, I'm going to catch something.* Although I have manufactured these words for her, I am convinced that cats use visual and aural demonstrations to get their points across, and that this was precisely the message Spotty meant to convey.

I would see this time and again with her and with the others. Spotty observed me taking the food away and registered concern at this atypical, new action. She may even have read the negative lilt in my voice after she sounded off and stepped around about the matter, showing me she liked the food bowl in its old place. If her purpose in walking to the mouse entrance had been only to hunt, she would have locked her gaze on the rodent ingress without looking at me. I had seen her waiting to ambush enough to know that her steely, iron gaze and pronged ears would not shift direction from the spot where she expected to sight her prey. Spotty had to have made an "assumption," or simply have had an understanding or an impression that, as members of her group, even the big, clumsy humans would have noticed the things that were common knowledge in her awareness, like the place where the mice come in. She also had to somehow regard or recognize us as intelligent or perceptive enough, in touch with her enough, to understand the meaning of her demonstration. Spotty by that time, having had several caught mice taken away from her by Bill, may also have understood that we did not *want* her to catch them. This may be stretching things too far, but if this had been the case, she may have been implying, *feed me or I'll strew mouse guts on your pillow.*

All joking aside, having lived with these animals, I am convinced that they are not aloof and that they do communicate with us and regard us as being in a dialogue with them through body language, visual cues they give us, and a range of vocalizations, both meow-based and others. Of course some cats are better and/or more frequent communicators than others. Spotty was downright eloquent. She was a master of feline diatribe. If you are inclined to say that Spotty's look couldn't have meant all I said above, well, you just had to be there. I've seen such things often enough to be able to translate from the multi-faceted language of Mau. At least partially, that is. No human will ever totally capture the thoughts of cats or grasp their intentions. But it was Spotty who inspired me to say one day to Bill, "These little things are so smart."

If another cat blocked her path, she'd do the *screechy* sound. She'd try to chase the other cats away from us and the food. When she saw one of us or another cat heading for the kitchen, she'd jump down and run ahead of them, trying to shoulder the other cat out of the way or block its path. Once when she tried this with Kudzu, he simply jumped over her. But sometimes when she and Kudzu met going opposite directions in a narrow passage, they would have a spirited debate about it until one yielded. Cats who have been strays tend to regard other cats as rivals, because they no doubt did compete with each other for food while fending for themselves. In fact, most if not all cats frequently regard other cats that way. But Spotty ran contrary to every general notion. She was an enigma. For serious napping, Spotty liked company and suddenly she was everyone's pal. She'd place herself up close to the snoozing Minx, who would usually, but not always, stay while Spotty stretched against her and slowly snuggled more and more into Minx space. Kudzu often trotted rapidly by Spotty when he encountered her, and you could almost see him shaking his head at what a fussy, prissy, little scold she was, but she would cozy with him, too, and he would put up with it, no doubt pretending not to notice. A photo from this era shows her jammed up against Kudzu and looking well-pleased with herself, since she probably on some level detected his opinion of her and enjoyed flying in the face of it. She would often wiggle herself closer and closer to her sleeping companion, until their feet and legs were all sprawled around and over her, making a jumble of cat feet and a splatter of her rumpled, gaudy-quilt colors against the black fur of Minx or Kudzu. It was white foot city when Kudzu was her snooze buddy. He would sling his huge hind foot right over her and into her face.

Spotty, too, liked my singing, which made her flex her paws, purr, and call to me in her sweet voice, those curly, curving musical sounds. She enjoyed my entire repertoire, plus a song that sprang into my head one day that was all Spotty's own, a rewrite of the chorus of "By the Beautiful Sea,"[23] with "Spotty and me, Spotty and me, by the beautiful sea. We'll eat fresh fish daily, you're spotted up so feyly." This song worked in the good times, as well as helping her get through the times she would be ailing. I can't say I never sang it to another cat, but it was mostly Spotty's song.

When the litterbox was in need of a bit of cleaning, Spotty would walk to a bag of litter and scratch at it with her paw, claws extended to make sure we heard as well as saw. That girl knew where the clean litter came from and how to tell us to use it. One of her quirky little traits was that every time we came into the house after being gone, Spotty would take one look at us and then head to the litterbox to wet a little. That one we never could quite figure out, unless it was territory marking and she wanted to show us every time we had been gone that she was still the boss here and should get the first attentions upon our arrival.

As near as we could tell, Spotty was one or two years old when she came to us. Bill voiced the idea that Spotty, because of her orange patches, may have been our old Orange Cat's daughter or descendant. That old moonglow rascal had gotten around these woods for a long time before he was neutered. She could have wandered over from the little neighborhood behind the gas station up the highway, or any other area our old, roving tom had been. But someone looking for a secluded area could have dropped her off at the edge of any road around here, under the mistaken notion that cats will survive all right by themselves in the woods (or out of a complete lack of caring what will become of the kitty). From the many directions that stray cats could have come from, we were not the first house on the various routes; we were fairly remote. Regardless of how she arrived in our forest, whether by careful study or by a bit of cat clairvoyance or both, Spotty had come to us as if she knew we were the right place.

We knew that the house where her face had made such a lingering impression had come under her surveillance as she shopped around, and had been rejected as her new lair. Resident dogs were no doubt the deal-breaker in that case, since cats at that house were well-cared for and other strays had settled there. Cats scrutinize and evaluate each potential place thoroughly. Either through observation of the in-dwelling cats, or by communication with them, cats determine the level of care received and happiness of animals in a given area. They may peek in the windows when you're not around or go nose-to-nose through the glass with your own cats on furtive fact-finding missions. If the resident cats are sleek and satisfied, and there are no dogs, the newcomers want in, and they shout it out once they decide. Suddenly, *you're the one!* Other strays would also find their way to us, and we would place them in good homes.

There was nothing like the night walks in our forest to glut the senses and fill the mind with reveries. Sootiness here, moonlight there, sliding into the dark spaces veiling the visage of nature, into the blackened frondescense, fingering each caressing twig slinking across our faces, and strong pine scent as needles stuck into the skin through clothing. Near the creek, we'd hear the *plunk-gulp* of something large, raccoon-size at least, leaping into the water at our approach.

On April 10, 1991, we were walking around at night with a visiting friend. There were odd, vivid red patches all over the sky. We checked every possible cause and found nothing that would explain it, except our conclusion that it was a rare, southeastern appearance of the aurora. Even though we didn't see anything in the paper or hear from anyone who had witnessed the same thing, I stand behind that call. It was bright, cherry red, like nothing I've ever seen in the night sky before or since. You never forget a sky color like that! In those days, weather and sky events weren't tracked as carefully here, and we didn't have the instantaneous reporting of experiences that we have now through social media. Later there was a rare appearance of the aurora documented in Alabama on October 24, 2011, which establishes that although rare, it's not impossible for the aurora to be seen here.

Although we still had occasional supervised outings with the cats, they were mostly indoor animals by the late 1980s and early 1990s. Among other good reasons, we and other neighbors had a history of experiences with snakes. One neighbor opened up a dresser drawer to get ready for a routine work day, and it was filled to the brim with a coiled-up snake. And once while working in his two-story shop, Bill became aware of a sound like someone coming down the stairs and looked up to see a snake flowing down the steps. Fortunately, this was a striped and mottled rat snake — a beneficial snake that goes for rodents and is not aggressive toward humans.

Then there was the snake in a piece of 4-inch diameter, ten-foot-long pipe that Bill had gone to use in some of his constructions one day. When he pulled the pipe out to cut it, out stuck a snake head. When Bill moved, the snake ducked back into the pipe. Bill called for me and somehow I heard him all the way over to the house. He told me to bring him newspapers. I did, and he wadded both ends of the pipe with crumpled papers. Then he loaded up the pipe and drove to an uninhabited area. There he cut a sapling, tilted the pipe upwards and ran the long stick all the way through the pipe, but the snake would not come out. Bill recalled that during the Rattlesnake Rodeo in Opp, Alabama, near his home town, every year when rattlesnakes were rounded up, the catchers poured gasoline down the "gopher holes." Gophers meant turtles, whose hollows had been taken over by the snakes; the snake couldn't stand the odor of gasoline and would then come out. Bill had a can of engine-starting fluid, and he sprayed it in one end of the pipe. That snake came out of the other end of the pipe like it had been shot out of a cannon and went on into the woods. (No one should try this at home. If you find a snake around your house, call a professional wildlife handler to catch it and relocate it.)

Life in those days was full of sniffing lions, velvet noses, thrashing fur, and tumbling kitties. During this era, I was one day looking out through the glass in the door like the cats often did, kitties around me, watching Bill plant some hostas around the little patio. And I was overcome by a sensation of bliss and contentment at this supreme juncture of home and cats, man and love.

Chapter 9

Paper Boy

Over the years, Gray Cat's mask and his "points" − feet, ears, and tail, turned a darker, steely gray. He was thirteen in 1991. I remember telling his age to someone else waiting in the vet's office, who said that was old. The vet was there when I responded, "He's old?" She must have heard the sadness in my voice, because she quickly said, "He's not old, he's middle-aged." That had happened back in the winter months. By spring, although he was cheerful and affectionate, he had gotten slower, extra sleepy, and mopey. He lost weight, and then he stopped eating. The vet diagnosed gradual kidney failure. He stayed at the clinic a few days getting fluids to flush him out, and he was placed on a kidney-supportive diet. He came home and did much better, and after about a month he had gained his weight back.

But not for long. He got sick again. The vet gave him more fluids, and he was again better for awhile, but still weak. Looking as elegant as ever, he sat on Bill's lap every evening. He slept with us every night and was very affectionate towards me. I stayed up most of several nights with him. He slept next to me. I saw his bewitching blue eyes cloud with illness. I saw him fall trying to get into the litterbox, and I helped him up. I placed him on the bed. I felt like he was saying *Let me go, I am so sick, I cannot be well again*. I knew he had to leave us. It was very hard to make that decision, but it was also hard to think that Cat might be suffering.

We took the top off the carrier and placed him within it, on a blanket he liked. Outside, Bill walked around carrying him for awhile so he could smell and see the forest. At that moment, I felt bad that we had been keeping him inside. We waited in the vet's office with Cat, talking to him in quiet tones and trying to hold back the anguish that Cat would no doubt sense and be made anxious by.

"Sleep kitty, go with our love," I remember saying.

"Do go gently into that good light," Bill said.

Sometimes, people can be so kind. Another client sitting there told us she had lost her old dog and adopting a puppy afterwards had brought her much joy. I burst into tears and said "Thank you," and she hugged me.

Bill was heartbroken and devastated. He and Cat had been inseparable. After he was gone, we drove back home and a huge bird, probably a wild turkey, flew up from the road ahead of us. "That's the soul taking off," Bill said. I waited in the car while he dug the grave, next to Orange Cat. I looked at Gray Cat's body. The light was gone from his sky blue eyes, and that vibrant quality of his fur, too, was gone. But he was no longer suffering. It was Wednesday, May 22, 1991.

That day on an adjacent small mountain, a black cat belonging to our neighbor Gale Johnson had kittens with a wandering tom, who was also black. There were three black kittens and one that looked exactly like Gray Cat, a light-gray body with the darker-gray Siamese ears, legs, and tail. He even had the faint tiger stripes down his hind legs. This seemed like some kind of spooky sense for sure. No one had seen any Siamese toms in the neighborhood, which of course does not mean they weren't there, and a tom of another description may have had recent Siamese ancestry. Still, this seemingly confirmed what I had heard long ago from the woman who gave us Ligeia, that all black cats had Siamese ancestry. Not only does this seem unlikely, but I believe current genetic theories would make this a bit of cat folklore, albeit one perhaps based on genetic facts about some Siamese color-point patterning being composed of variations of dark pigment. Bill and the neighbor instantly agreed: we would get that kitten when he was old enough to leave the mom. Gale's cats lived mostly outdoors, on higher and wilder ground than we did. These two lady cats had taken up with him a few months ago. While the two grown momcats did fine, the kittens often fell prey to the savage side of the forest. And several weeks later, the gray kitten disappeared, the small victim of a raccoon, hawk, coyote, or even a snake. The other kittens were later either given away or also disappeared. It was another heartbreak. It was the way of nature, but some of nature's courses cause bewilderment.

Our hilltop neighbor worked out of town in the summer, coming back only a few weekends. He asked Bill to take care of his place, check on it every day, feed the cats, take in the mail. At other times Bill had been made caretaker, he had taken whatever kittens that were old enough to leave the mom to our vet, who was very helpful about giving kittens away to good homes. The second cat girl was also black, part of the achromatic group of cats up the hill towards the highway. Her litter came a few weeks after the first cat's kittens had come and gone. One kitten was a black female; the other, a black-and-white male. Bill told me that this boy had a way of looking at you fixedly, as if he was studying you. Cats will give you searching looks, but when I went up the mountain to see the kittens for myself, this was indeed the most pointed, piercing little cat gaze I'd ever seen.

Bill was again in charge of the place after Gale left again, and he decided that to keep the kittens safe he had to bring them down to our house and keep them inside. When he poured out the kibble and called "Kitty, kitty," the boy kitten came right to him, but Bill was unable to locate his shyer little sister. Perhaps she had already fallen prey to the relentless jaws of the forest; she was never seen again.

I started the little black-and-white guy out in the back of the house, closed off from the other three cats. He must have been between three and four weeks. He would eat food, but he would not drink from the bowl of water I got for him. So I fetched him a saucer of milk and guided his nose onto the surface for an instant. The pink tongue started lapping. He quickly learned to lap up the water, too. In the weeks that followed, I went back every day to play with him, shaking a cat toy consisting of a stick with Mylar tassels on the end. The kitten jumped, sprang, levitated, ran, and chased after that sparkly toy. And he stared at us in that way he had, both entrancing and unnerving. His stare could be felt across the room or through a brick wall. Soon we were both completely taken with him and it was apparent he was with us to stay. Gale later expressed a wish that he had kept the kitten, because of the way it looked at you — its affecting, opaque little gaze had gotten to him, too — but it was too late; it was apparent to all that Bill and this kitty had a special bond. My regret was that we had not been able to bring in his little solid black sister, and I have thought of her often, to this day. Not long afterwards, our neighbor had his girlcats spayed.

The first time we brought the kitten into the front to meet the gang, Spotty strode briskly to the side door in the kitchen and scratched at it. She then turned to look at us searingly, as if to say, *If you're going to bring him in here, I'm leaving home*, and then turned and scratched some more. This was the first time she'd had to accept a new cat into the house she had claimed as her own. Cats entering a house always do their share of spitting and hissing at the cat occupants, but it's often low key compared to the uproar expressed by the affronted resident cats whose turf is being encroached upon by a feline newcomer. Minx, high-strung though she was, had done very well in accepting Kudzu and Spotty. With Gray Cat gone Minx was now senior cat, Queen Bee if you will, but she'd do surprisingly well with the new kitten. And Kudzu, for all his grumbling, accepted Spotty when she came only a few months after he did. But Spotty, prima donna that she was, staged this dramatic doorside protest. In *The Tribe of Tiger,* Elizabeth Marshall Thomas has observed household cat groups exhibiting a similar pattern to what we saw with Spotty. Although in the wild, cat groups are often composed mainly of a momcat and her descendants, when a new litter comes along it's technically time for the older, adult/adolescent kittens to leave because it's time for the mother to tend to a new family.[1] That is why an incoming kitten or other adult that's younger than the resident cats might trigger a runaway in a multi-cat family, and that may be what Spotty was saying when she headed to the door; it was time for her to hit the road, by her lights. Either Minx, or Bill, or I was, according to Spotty, head momcat.

There's a seemingly unresolved duality here, as it's also been observed that in large groups of barncats, descendants do often stay with a momcat. Cats have fluidity and individuality. Ligeia obviously did not subscribe to the communal way of life when she tried to run off her eight-week-old litter. So, cats aren't acting up with other cats just because they don't like other cats. I personally think cats will work things out together if given enough time. As humans providing homes for cats, we have to tweak nature a bit. Our homes aren't like a free-range, wild-living situation. Cats are very adaptable and do adjust, and this group of four would oddly enough turn out to be the most harmonious one I've ever had. Eventually, I'd frequently look out upon a scene of everyone peacefully dozing, with muzzles turned aloft.

The new kitten was a classic tuxedo black-and-white, like Kudzu, but his eyes were gold, a much lighter, more yellow gold than even Minx's eyes. He had pink paw pads, except for his right front foot, on which the central pad was a dark gray, along with some slight overlapping gray on one of the otherwise pink toe pads. His mouth was marked dramatically. While his head, including cheeks and upper lips were all black, his chin was covered in white fur that flowed down to join the white blaze upon his throat and chest. When his mouth was open, a black "lining" along his lower lip could be seen contrasting with the white chin. His cheek whiskers were white, except for one black one on the left side, while the whiskers above his eyes were black. His white feet were large out of proportion to his slender black legs; his front feet very rounded, like the hands of cartoon characters. His tail was long, slim, and limber. He would mature into a rather small cat.

Like Spotty, the kitten had a double dose of the unutterable cutes. And like Kudzu, his fur was thick and short, a sleek and satiny black, contrasting with Minx's rumpled thicket, which scattered her blacks into shades of warm, dark tones, just as prisms scatter sunlight into rainbows. Of the three, Kudzu's black areas appeared the blackest and slickest. But the new kitten had the trimmest lines and the contours that, in silhouette, were the most sinuous of any of them. He was a real smoothie.

For a long time, the new one was "the kitten." Sometimes I called him Purrywitten. It mattered not that I'd begun reading Faulkner in high school, at age fifteen, and had read all his major novels by the time I was seventeen. Nor did the massive amounts of literature I'd absorbed in the past and indeed continued to read make any difference. Shakespeare went through my head most of my days; in the grocery store I'd point to an item in my cart and announce to Bill, "That's for tomorrow and tomorrow and tomorrow." When cats flexed their claws and lightly snagged me, I'd say, "Take thy claw from out my flesh," an allusion to Poe's "Take thy beak from out my heart," in "The Raven." Still, the presence of cats had the power to reduce me to blithering verbal nonsense or rather, uh, reorganization. We were both at a loss to come up with something more permanent than Purrywitten to call this astounding kitten.

We went to Atlanta for a terribly sad occasion, a wake for a friend who had died way too young at age forty and was a fellow lover of books and cats. We stayed with friends. The lady of the house, who had grown up in Cajun country, had an artful and comforting touch with decorating. In the morning while I, flattened, struggled to regain consciousness, everyone else went outside. A cat was walking around the yard. "Here, Minou," our hostess called to the cat. This was what they always called cats when she was a child, she said. Bill told me this as we drove back home. I can't recall which one of us spoke first, but for once we were in total accord on a name from the get-go. The new kitten was now Minou.

I loved that it was French, a language I had studied in high school and had always intended to study again. I'd also always wanted to know more about the culture of Acadiana. Later, when it became available in our town, I wanted to join the class in Cajun and Zydeco dance, but that was another thing I would never get to do thanks to illness. Back at home, our friend Olivia, who was a native of France, explained that saying "Minou, Minou," was like saying "Kitty, Kitty." Her own cat was called Minette, the feminine of *minet*, yet another French word that meant, roughly, puss. I liked, too, the fact that I did not see the name Minou elsewhere again, for persons or cats, until many years later. Now in the 2000s it has begun to appear on cat name lists. I also once saw a young woman of French descent on television whose first name was Minou; it's likely the equivalent of the girl's name "Kitty" in English.

A few years later, the friend who had helped us name Minou would name her own cat Gata, the Spanish word for cat. It appears we are all going back to the minimalist way of naming cats, but putting it in another language mixes some spice with the factual. In the old days, literary names had been popular. Friends had named their black kitty Ginsberg, and Mac named a black cat Madame Sosostris, the name of the clairvoyant from T. S. Eliot's poem, "The Wasteland," which seems to be ironic or sensible or fitting in relation to Eliot's firm grasp of the strenuous task of picking cat names.[2] Craig had named his beautiful tabby cat Mr. Christian from *Mutiny on the Bounty*. When Rachel was a child in the late '60s, her family had a black cat named Othello by her father, because he loved opera. Rachel recalls, "He was our first cat among us three children and we thought he was great, partly because he was a CAT, and he was BLACK." Everyone also understood that having a black cat named after a black man was a political statement in those times of the horrible wrongs of racism and Governor Wallace.

Cat names would later come from all the arts as well as literature, and thus extend to the unusual. Craig and his wife Linda would have Man Ray, Thelonious Monk, Ornette, and Yggdrasil, a great tree from Old Norse mythology. And while talking cat names with Craig and Linda at the Kentuck Arts Festival, we would meet Lynda, who had a cat named Katzemire Meowevic, as well as a white cat named Marcel DuChomp — that spelling being intentional! Other kitties Lynda named were Clawed (Claude Lorrain); Caitlin (wife of Dylan Thomas); Grisabella and her three kittens Fearless, Reckless, and Feckless; and a rescue kitty, Isabella d'Este, called Izzy. Another very imaginative name comes from our friend Cathy. Her rescued black kitty was beautiful and talkative; she named him "Buzz!" Davey had a cat he describes as "small, very fluffy, and cloud-white": named Nimbus, she would make a reaching gesture with one paw crossing the other.

Long-time friend Birry named her four beautiful cats Miles Davis, Etta James, Lena Horne, and Billie Holiday, all musicians close to my own heart. She also had another kitty named Ella Fitzgerald, sister to Billie Holiday. Back in our college days, Birry and I went to New York together, saw *Henry IV* in Central Park, had other grand adventures, and came back with fond memories to treasure — and cat-keeping in both our futures.

The black cat with the slightly spooky name of Madame Sosostris, along with her kittens, were great influences on me. That was my first prolonged contact with nice house cats. When I was in high school, I daydreamed of having horses and collie dogs. Somehow during the college years, a shift occurred and the daydreams became all cats. One day, I would name a feral Madame Curious. Later it dawned on me that the two names illustrate the transition I've made since college, from a faintly spooky outlook to a more science-based one.

Our new quartet finds its rhythm

Despite the soubriquet "Purrywitten," Minou had, relatively speaking, a quiet murmur of a purr. Both Spotty and Minx were louder. Kudzu had the softest meow and the softest purr of all — you had to place your ear close to him to hear it. Bill called it his "stealth purr."

Minou was an active kitten and once he achieved a degree of détente within the group, he was pell-melling it around the house. Spotty would hiss and slap if Minou tried to play with her, and Minx wasn't too eager to play with him, either. But Kudzu loved to engage with him in mock battles, slapping, chasing, and tumbling around on the floor together in a flurry of thrashing white feet. Minou was the better strategist and could actually get Kudzu over on his back, defensive. He'd reach one long, slender front leg up to Kudzu's shoulder and pull, and Kudzu would go down on the floor, Minou jumping on top, and they'd smack and tumble around. After a few minutes, Kudzu would jump up and trot off. Kudzu was a gentle sort and just not much of a warrior, not even in mock battles. When Minou was full grown, the boys would raise up on their hind legs facing each other and have a slapfest, as if they were boxing. This was not serious quarreling, but rather playing between two cats who were friends. We watched carefully, making sure claws stayed retracted. If anything ever got out of hand, which was rare, we would intervene. Kudzu was mostly a mentor of sorts towards Minou. A photo from the early times shows six-month kitten Minou resting his head on big sleeping Kudzu's back. And if Spotty blocked his way and screeched in his face, Minou would leapfrog over her, as Kudzu had sometimes done.

Minou could be inventively mean about his play. Once I saw him grab the tip of Minx's ear with his teeth and tug it rapidly back and forth. "Minou" I yelled, but he released her before I could rush over to stop it. Fortunately, he had not bitten but only firmly held her ear.

Minou's creativity could have good results, too. He had a new way of using the litterbox to urinate. He would step in but rotate around to the corner, facing out, and place all four feet on the rim of the box, the forefoot and hind leg of one Minou side on one of the corner's sides, with his other forefoot and hind leg gripping the corner's other side. In this way he could balance his lightweight body on the corner of the box and urinate without a single paw in the actual litter. He would grow into a small cat, never too big to support himself in this manner. Recently I have learned that this is not so unusual, that other cats perch on the litterbox sides, too, but we had never seen anything like it before Minou came.

He was also a foot drinker, like the old Gray Cat. But Minou really liked to splash and splatter the water around with his foot, licking the paw off only once in a while, especially if he was annoyed about something. Even with filtered water, the red-clay earth we lived upon, which the water had flowed along, through, and above, would stain Minou's drinking paw.

Minou, Kudzu, and Spotty were all fond of jumping on the arm of the couch, running up to and then around on top of the back, then scrambleleaping to the top edge of the tall bookcase, and dashing back down. On one such Minou run I was sitting on the end of the couch as he descended at boiling speed and, from the couch back, launched his glide down to the floor. He whizzed past before I knew it, missing my head by about an inch — I could feel the displaced wind on my face as he flew by. It happened so fast I had not heard his approach; any slight shift of my position and we would have knocked noggins. My fault for sitting in his flyway, in his airspace!

Yet challenging to avoid, because Minou took daily flying leaps and arcs across the room every whichaway at crazy cat-speed. But then there were the quieter times, when Minou would turn that knowing gaze on one of us, in deep and bemused reflection. Other glances had a more overt touch of arrogance, as if to say, *And who do you think you are?* He was very self-absorbed, one of those kittens who would lie on top of the food while eating to keep anyone else from getting it. Other times, though, Minou would be making eyes at us, loving the attention it brought him. His gaze applied an acuity beyond anything I could ever attain and return with my own eyes.

The space between Minou's ears was the perfect size to plant a kiss, the most kissable little cat noggin I've ever seen. I started planting one frequently and Bill quickly followed suit, seeing it was the most natural thing to do. In fact, after one of his exams at the vet, she too "kissed his little head," as we called it. No one had said anything to her about it; Minou just had a head that was the size of a kiss, and it was universally irresistible.

Minou acquired a lasting secondary nickname, Booper. This came about when I found myself living in the woods with a new kitten and no one to hear me indulge in another bit of silliness, and I began to sing "Minou Minou Minou," which became "Minouper," and then I rhymed the *ou ou ooo* sounds and scat-sang it into *boopity bip bop boops*. It was only a syllable blip on to "Booper." If Spotty's cunning little self had led to fractured adjectives with cannibalized syllables like "Spottedtee," then Minou's cuteness had lead to a further descent, as shown by the " Minouper booper" song. Just how far was a well-read English major going to sink? There's no telling when it comes to living with animals. At least they make you relax and drop the usual adult pretensions toward rock-hard sophistication. Regardless, the kitten soon responded to both names. He would come to recognize, or "know," several other words.

Minou began a habit of carrying rubber bands around in his teeth, especially the broad kind that come on vegetables, before we learned to guard these from searching paws. As soon as we took band-wrapped broccoli out of the grocery bag, Booper's eyes would light up and follow the vegetable, looking for his chance. Like Spotty, Minou was a chewing cat, and we'd find shards of those rubber bands around the house. We were afraid he'd swallow them, so we always took his rubber band away when we saw him with one.

But he could smell them across the room, and he'd jump up on the counter and snatch one the second I got it off a stalk of celery or a broccoli bunch. Then he'd run away fast, with me in pursuit. Once I was on to this, I would glance up and see Minou's eyes bugging at the scent and sounds of vegetable unbanding, and I'd swoop the bands away seconds before his dash and the leap onto the counter.

Bill would hide them in a drawer, but the drawer didn't fit the casing well and there was a space where Minou could fish them out with his paw. We found other places to store bands away, too, but we kept finding them in his food dish, where Minou had deposited them. He knew we didn't want him to have rubber bands because we took them right out of his teeth so often. He was sneaky smart enough to wait until we weren't looking to do his "plundering," to use a lower Alabama term for rifling through an enclosed space. One day I saw him go and take a rubber band out of a concealed nook under the wood stove. I looked and found a cache of several more hidden there. The clever little scamp had a secret hiding place for his forbidden toys! His eyes got big with concern when he saw me there, but I had no choice but to confiscate his cache and find a more secure place to hide the loot.

Once Minou was allowed out in the front room with the others, we placed the Mylar-tasseled toy on the bookcase when we weren't using it to play with the cats. Minou was so fixated on it that he climbed up on the bookcase and fetched it one day when we weren't home. He chewed it to pieces, so we kept trying to find shelves he couldn't nab it from, but we finally had to hide it in a cabinet or file drawer somewhere. We eventually lost track of it ourselves and had to buy a new one.

We had a home office and Bill often wadded up paper and threw it on the desk or floor. Minou began to run after it when it fell and skittered along the boards; then he would carry the paper around in his teeth. Bill started to throw small, crumpled paper wads in the cat's direction, and Minou would run after them, clamp on the teeth, bring them back, and drop them near Bill to have him throw them again. Bill tried tossing the bunched paper high in the air. Minou jumped and caught it. Bill and Minou did this for twenty or thirty minutes before the kitten tired of the game.

The jumping catch was such a fast action that it took careful observation to see the way Minou did it — he would clap both front paws together on the paper ball and shove it in his mouth before descending, spreading his front feet back out for the landing by the time he got down, paper in teeth. All done at such speed that the action was near-invisible. Then he would go drop the wad at Bill's feet. This agile front-paw action, a trademark of felines, established the paper jump as a cat's game. A dog would, in most ordinary circumstances, have just caught the tossed object in his teeth alone.

When the paper was tossed across the room, Minou liked it best if it rolled under or behind something, so that he had to hunt for it, crooking his paw and scooting it up to his teeth once he found it. Sometimes Minou would jump and with one paw, bat the paper back in Bill's general direction. That meant the paper scattered every whichaway, and we can't recall if Bill ever actually caught it. But he nearly always picked it up and tossed it for Minou again.

Before long, whenever Bill was working or just relaxing, out of the blue Minou would come up with a paper wad he'd found in his mouth and drop it for Bill to throw and start the game. Or Bill would be startled as he sat on the couch by paper rolling down his chest into his lap — Minou would come up behind him and drop it on his shoulder. Bill could start the game himself by saying "Paper, Minou, paper," and soon Minou would come trotting up with his eyes gleaming, ready to play. He had learned the word, paper. Even if he was semi-asleep when he heard it, his ears would swivel and he'd begin stirring. We found we had to spell the word "p-a-p-e-r" if we said it when we didn't intend to play. But when the spelled-out word was spoken, it usually meant I was handing Bill a sheet of paper he had asked for, and Minou would see this, hear the noise it made, and assume it was the first step towards paper being crinkled up for the game. That noise would always get him excited to play the game, too. His sharp mind made the connection between his visual and aural perceptions of paper, along with the spelled word. He soon reacted when we said "p-a-p-e-r," having learned that combination of sounds also meant paper, which to him meant jump-and-chase game. Many visitors watched Minou play the game and were amazed.

I have since learned that it isn't so unusual for cats to retrieve. James Herriot wrote the story "Buster, The Feline Retriever,"[3] and Elizabeth Randolph wrote about training cats to fetch in *How to be Your Cat's Best Friend*,[4] to name just two of the examples from cat literature. But neither we nor our friends and family had encountered any other cats that did so back in those days, and we thought our little "tuxedo retriever" was quite unique. We thought his abilities and ingenuity displayed through kitten antics were near otherworldly.

Unfortunately, we waited to videotape the paper game until Minou had grown slightly past the stage of kittenhood when kittens, as anyone would swear, can fly. It's a rare photographer indeed who snaps a good picture of this little-known, fleeting life stage. With adulthood, Minou grew somewhat less interested in paper, but he still brings us a wad sometimes or perks up at the word, "paper." Our responsibilities have increased over the years and time is tight, but every now and then, Bill and Minou again play the paper-toss game. We still sometimes find Minou putting a crumpled-up ball of paper in his food dish, or we'll find one in an out-of-the-way place that was most likely hidden there by Minou. I've begun to toss paper for Minou myself, and as a fourteen-year-old he will still retrieve, but not jump. He snorts and chuffs as he chases his paper, and he pulls at it with his paw once he's clamped his teeth on it.

One day, Kudzu watched the paper game and showed great interest. He pawed at the wad, batted it, and picked it up and carried it in his teeth. Clearly, he had learned by watching the other cat, sensing that something fun was going on. That would be the only time, though, so maybe he decided it wasn't his style. The incident further convinces me that cats are much more thoughtful and intelligent than people often give them credit for. They can learn through visual cues. For example, it's known in the literature that when a kitten runs up a tree and hollers because it cannot get down, sometimes an adult cat will climb up the tree and show the kitten how to descend by edging back down the trunk itself. In these cases, not only does the kitten learn by watching, but the adult cat knows the kitten can learn by watching and stages a demonstration. I've talked to people who have seen this happen.

Minou polished his hunting skills through this game, so we were surprised by his reaction one night when the other cats had a mouse cornered. Instead of trying to go for it, Minou just looked at the rodent. He was a student and philosopher when it came to mice. But when lizards came into the house, it was another story. Many's the time we had to try to get Minou (as well as Spotty) to release one; then we'd capture it in a bowl to let it outside. They were both keen lizard hounds. With mice, we would foil the cats' strikes any way we could and then Bill would capture the rodents in an old towel, to be released across the highway at an old abandoned wreck of a house by the railroad tracks that we called the "mouse house," where the woods were even wilder and less frequented by humans.

As a young kitten, Minou also learned the word "bedtime." He slept beside Bill at night in those days, and every night Bill would announce, "Bedtime, Minou" and carry the kitten off to the back. After awhile Minou would begin to play a game when he heard "bedtime." He'd perk up, feint towards Bill, and then about-face, run, and hide. Bill would chase after him. Minou's little black-and-white face would peek out, and he would start running again when Bill came towards him. I'd join in the chase, and both of us would try to catch him from different directions. Minou would let us get just close enough for him to bolt and escape, again and again.

Eventually Bill would capture the kitten, and Minou would begin to purr. He wanted to get caught and sleep with us; if left out, he'd howl and scratch at the door like Minx. Minou would later be evicted from the bedroom for getting up too early and wreaking general havoc, as well as for tapping on Bill's nose with a paw to get him up and thereby gain an audience for his sunrise antics.

Once during the day I said, "Bedtime, Minou," to see what would happen. Minou started up and looked puzzled for a moment before staying just where he was, knowing daytime was all wrong for "bedtime" games. I felt bad about deceiving him, but it helped to establish that he truly understood the word, even out of context, and not just as part of the entire set of usual bedtime conditions. I never said it at the wrong time again. On nights when we were up later than usual, Minou would begin hiding when it was roughly our time to turn in.

Around the same time Bill announced "bedtime," he usually took off his shirt. One broiling-hot summer night, many hours earlier than the time we usually turned in, Bill removed his T-shirt, and Minou hid, as if playing the night-time game. This was yet another demonstration that cats can interpret visual signals.

Like Minx, Minou learned how to hook a paw under the folding door and pull it open from the kitchen side. He also figured out how to get through from the bedroom side, so long as the cat lock wasn't in play. I saw him gallop down the hall, raise up slightly on his hind legs, and hit the door in the center with a front paw. It folded open quickly, and he passed through. I don't know how he knew to tap the door in exactly the right spot to make that happen, if he had watched us pushing the door in the center to make it open, or what. He could have used trial-and-error to find the spot. These little cat things are indeed much smarter than they often get credit for.

I had mail-ordered some frog-shaped refrigerator magnets, painted many colors like rainforest frogs. Every now and then, Bill or I would accidentally bump a frog off the front of the fridge with a shoulder in passing, and then the cats might bat it around until we scooped it up and placed it back on the fridge. Minou, having used the magnets for toys on the horizontal, saw no difference in their status on the vertical. He jumped up and knocked one off the fridge while I watched one day, and then proceeded to slap it and chase it around the floor. After that he got a frog down to play with any time he cared to. As our fridge magnet collection expanded with gifts from traveler friends and some of our own souvenirs, Minou also tried to get himself a French villa and a row of San Francisco houses to play with, but the magnets on those were too strong for him to knock them off the door. Minou was also attentive to the television whenever it was on. He would tap all around the screen with a paw; Bill said he was trying to get at the people.

Now that we had four cats, a larger water dish seemed in order. Pebble finish was "in" at the time, and I found one that was actually a dog-food dish that served very well. When I got up in the morning, I began to notice that the dish had been moved several inches from where I had put it the day before, and sometimes the water had been spilled. The first few times I dismissed it as human foot-bump displacement, but when it began to happen consistently, I was mystified. Then I saw Minx one day, pulling the water dish with her paw to get it closer, then drinking. The agile kitty just cupped her paw around the rim of the bowl and pulled, placing the dish where she wanted it.

She was very handy with her paw. She continued to walk up to my face and use it, with thoughtfully sheathed claws, to tap me, and as time went on, she would use it in many creative ways. Minx was the ringleader in breaking and entering into the back rooms, and she was adroit at rattling the door until the cat lock loosened and fell. Then she, Kudzu, and Spotty would go have a snooze together on the bed. Minou tended to be a lone sleeper in feline company.

We would have these four cats as a group, the girls Minx and Spotty and the boys Kudzu and Minou, from the summer of 1991 until December 2002, a little over eleven years. They were joined by only one other cat, and that one not until 2000. Our knowledge of cat behavior, and the unique, quirky dynamics of this particular group, would enlarge, and these four would be the last cats that knew me during my better days.

Like Minx, we had Spotty spayed, and like Kudzu, we had Minou neutered. We had, as noted before, grown to realize just how astronomical the population of domestic cats and dogs is, and there was no letting the girls have even one litter. There were hazards to the boys on tomcat excursions away from home, not to mention their possible contributions to getting someone else's females pregnant. Multiple sources detail the vast numbers of cats produced from just one breeding pair. This was the only way available to curtail the numbers and to keep the cats satisfied to remain at home, where they and the local wildlife would all remain safe.

As Minou became an adult, he gained yet another soubriquet, "Minnow," for his slimness and the way he would slink, like a satin scrap of night, through the house like something darting smoothly through water. Sometimes he'd be called Minou Minnow, or his whole series of nicknames in a row, or a few of them in various combinations. Whatever we said to him, he would listen intently.

It was really easy to imagine conversations with Minou. So I'll add one unreal bit of fancy that popped into my head: Once Minou asked me to explain why the term "Fauvism" referred to an art movement when it came from French for "wild beasts," "les fauves." I was partial to bright colors and wild about Fauvism and was happy to explain. He was a mighty smart cat but he did have a little trouble with the concept of color intensity beyond what he could see.

In August 1992, I had surgery and we were away from the house and the cats for four or five days. We arranged to have them looked in on. The cats were a little standoffish when we came back; they didn't like to be left alone so much, and they liked to make their points so they could stealthily watch us suffer.

Chapter 10

Snuggling Through The Rain

I don't know why we've never seen or heard any sign of bobcats in the area. They are mainly nocturnal and crepuscular hunters, usually remaining unseen during the day, although not always. But there would have been signs if they were around, and I just don't think they're out there in our woods. And I'm glad they're not, since they will sometimes kill and eat feral or house cats that wander into their hunting grounds.[1] Maybe the former fox presence reduced the rabbit population, the bobcats' main food, and therefore the rabbit numbers were not sufficient to attract the wildcats during that time. Other small mammals, such as mice, rats, and squirrels, can serve as prey for both species of cats — bobcats and housecats — making a competitive situation. There are a lot of humans and dogs around our neighborhood, both of which the bobcat will try to avoid, especially the dogs. Most of the neighborhood houses don't keep poultry, an attractant to bobcats, who will snatch chickens when they can. Then there's the coyotes we hear at times; they will prey on bobcat young and sometimes even attack an adult bobcat.[2] Maybe they're a deterrent to bobcats in our woods. But the wildcat is versatile and not entirely unknown near human dwellings, and we haven't seen any foxes in a long time.

Most closely related to the lynx family, the bobcat is also called the Bay Lynx, Red Lynx, American Lynx, or just plain wildcat. Its scientific name is *lynx rufus*, or reddish lynx, although its coloration is not always reddish and can be grayish, or yellowish,[3] or reddish brown. Andrew Garman mentions black or dark bars, tabby stripes, and some spotting.[4] A bobcat has white underparts and a white underside on its short tail. Its ears have a white spot on the back of each and are tufted, but not so much as those of the lynx. The bobcat has a ruff on its face, but again, not so large as that of the lynx. Sarah Hartwell indicates that melanistic (black), leucistic (white), and albino (white) bobcats have been observed.[5] Bobcats range over most of the continental United States, southward into Mexico, and northward into southern areas of Canada. Garman notes their absence from areas of the middle United States that are heavily cultivated.[6] Cultivation can mean habitat destruction and lack of prey species. Nevertheless, bobcats are not endangered; their numbers are estimated to be about one million in the United States. Hunting bobcats and trapping them for fur is permitted in some states. They are highly adaptable and live in any kind of forest or brushlands, as well as in mountains, deserts, and swamps.

Audubon and Rue note that bobcat calls are similar to those of the domestic cats; although they have loud screams, Audubon describes their short bark when alarmed. Rue also notes that they purr. They are most vocal during mating season, when loud yowling occurs.[7] They are also attracted to catnip, which is reason number two not to plant that outdoor catnip patch! (Reason number one: every feral and otherwise stray cat in the neighborhood will show up at your house.)

The bobcat is well-camouflaged and can lie motionless in wait to attack passing prey. It's mostly terrestrial but climbs and swims well when necessary. Both Rue and Audubon note that in stalking mode, the bobcat sees which place to put its forefeet down without disturbing small branches or other debris, and then places its hind feet in the tracks of its front feet where it now knows it can step silently.[8] The bobcat is generally said to be more aggressive than the lynx. Truly ferocious, bobcats are hunted by packs of dogs, but a wildcat can kill a single dog. Rarely, humans are attacked by wildcats, according to Deborah Ciszek at Animal Diversity Web.[9] I'll venture to say that these attacks most likely occur in cornering situations, as most wild animals avoid humans if they can.

I've seen this fierce, medium-sized cat in the zoo, where I still go to view animals even though I dislike seeing them caged. The most striking thing I recall is how closely the faces resemble those of domestic cats, except they're much bigger. They make you think, "Kitty, kitty," when you should be thinking, "Back away slowly," if you encounter one in the wild. After all, bobcats sometimes bring down small deer! I have to admit I'm glad not to have seen them around our forest, although I'm glad they thrive in other deeper, darker woods. Or, it's always possible that they are in our woods watching us, and we just don't know it. They're just that clever, I'm sure.

The bobcat has been trapped using catnip as a lure, a dirty trick. When the Convention on International Trade in Endangered Species banned trade in the fur of most spotted cats, bobcat fur became valuable. Populations are sometimes high enough for hunting and trapping to be allowed and regulated. Canadian Lynx fur has also become popular, and they are now harvested for fur, with regulations, although they are not as numerous as bobcats.

I, for one, am astonished that anyone is so eager to rip the fur off some poor wild animal. Humans no longer need to do this for warmth — synthetics now keep us toasty in cold weather. There's nothing glamorous about the processes involved in obtaining fur; it's ugly and cruel from day one, equally so when the animals are farmed rather than trapped wild and not endangered as a species. Human artistry has now provided us with faux fur, although you have to carefully peruse the labels to find out which products use deceptive language and actually include real fur. We have dazzling arrays of elegant, non-animal-hide-based designs in clothing and home décor, as well. Why not shine with the light of wild human originality, inspired by natural forms, creating our very own patterns using fabric instead? There's nothing more pathetically unoriginal than slicing the skin off an animal and slapping it on our bodies. That's destroying what we should be celebrating. It's one thing to use an animal motif, made from plant or mineral materials, as a signal that we are somehow part of nature and that we ponder our place in the natural world and the universe. But we betray our own imagination if we decorate ourselves with the dead animal itself rather than crafting our natural references with the innovations of cruelty-free construction techniques that employ and reveal the full potential of the creative human mind. My experience with the foxes shows me that one live moment with these creatures is bliss. I can't imagine a lifetime or even a moment of wearing dead coats that belong on live animals. That's vain, empty, and cruel.

According to the International Society for Endangered Cats Canada, the bobcat has been the most harvested and most often sold of all the cat family. About half of the cat pelts in legal world-fur-markets were bobcat and lynx in the early 2000s. (Most recent numbers are available in the note.[10]) The bobcat also faces increasing habitat loss and persecution by farmers. I mentioned earlier a case of farmers shooting bobcats in rural Alabama, and the resulting surge of vegetable garden-eating rabbits.

The Convention on International Trade in Endangered Species of Wild Fauna and Flora (CITES)[11] is a voluntary international agreement to try to regulate the harvesting of endangered species worldwide. Countries have agreed to be bound by its regulations. However, local regulations to protect endangered wildlife are still needed. Domestic legislation needs to be in place to facilitate the regulations of CITES. There are 169 countries that have signed on. Appendix I of CITES lists species threatened with extinction, and trade in these species will only be permitted in extraordinary circumstances. Appendix II includes species not immediately threatened with extinction but for which trade must be controlled to avoid over-harvesting, which would reduce populations towards the danger zone of near-extinction. Bobcats and Canadian Lynx are listed on Appendix II of CITES. They both should be further protected by national and local governments. The surge of coyotes in the U. S. has been written about frequently. A few articles I've seen suggest that coyotes may reduce bobcat numbers by preying on the kits and outcompeting bobcats for the same food sources.

Taking comfort in cats while struggling with chronic illness

I have been trying to say as little as possible about "The Illness." There may be those readers who view talking about it as complaining, but facts are facts. I'm practical and straightforward about reality. Catastrophic illness changes your life. It limits, describes, and defines the household in which these cat stories unfold. It has to be talked about. I can't tell the stories of the cats and ignore momentous events in the lives of the people.

For a long time, I had ignored subtle signs of not being robust, but I was always cleared by the doctors. The signs had actually been present from early childhood. They were the precursors of an illness that manifested when many factors came together. In 1988, I recorded that I felt a ripple in my formerly keen awareness. Every reaction felt slower and less sure, and I had some dizziness. There was some trouble with my memory; things would just stream through my mind and get gone. There were lapses of attention, oddly combined with my usual sharp attention to detail. During late 1991 and early 1992, I continued to have a series of health problems. By the latter part of 1992, I was experiencing a long, slow onset of a rare disease with neurological effects. Not much is known about it, there are few treatment options, and there is no known cure. The lack of known information is why the doctors of earlier years could not detect the condition. It can only be managed; the treatments keep me semi-functional but go only so far in relieving my discomfort and disability.

Because so few doctors, far fewer than exist nowadays, were studying this ailment at that time, it took us until September 1994 to make our way to several subspecialty clinics in various areas of the country, where the doctors could give me an accurate diagnosis. What savings we had rapidly hemorrhaged away into the medical system. A trace of America's greater post-war prosperity came to the South very late, really not until the '80s. We had started in a low-income situation and worked our way slowly out of it. But twenty years of the hard work by two persons went out the window with astonishing speed as the bills came in.

My activity level was greatly reduced due to extreme, crushing fatigue, loss of fine motor coordination and balance, as well as difficulty with focusing attention and multi-tasking. Sometimes I felt I was in a kind of diminished consciousness, a walking coma. Artwork and writing, as well as daily tasks, became difficult actions that wore me out. Because of weakness of my hands and a loss of fine finger coordination, I all-but-stopped doing art. I became limited in both indoor and outdoor activities. I became about 90-percent housebound due to fatigue and the fact that it was difficult to walk around by myself because of problems with coordination, balance, depth per-

ception, and higher chances of falling. I had perceptual concentration problems that meant I couldn't keep my balance, and concentrate on seeing vehicles coming towards me while crossing a street at the same time. And I had
to get used to — and weather each day — a certain amount of discomfort for
which there was no relief, not to mention getting used to an amount of disability and idleness that was hugely frustrating for a person of many interests.
The fatigue and limitations on my activities were some of the most frustrating aspects of the disease. I learned to pace myself so the energy I did have
could go towards basic care of the cats and myself. I would do small amounts
and then either rest or do a less-taxing activity. Stringing out the chores ena-
bled me to still get the cat feeding, medicating, and litterbox tending done.

To fully describe this disease would fill another book, one I hope to write
some day. There are old news articles on the Internet about the disease that
quote me, and although the writers of the articles did very well indeed, this
complex illness and the differing ways it presents in each patient cannot be
defined in short spaces. Bill conveyed to the reporters a general, symptoms-
focused description of the illness that does not completely apply to me. I say
this due to our direct experience of having those past articles cause misunderstandings about my illness, which is not unusual with any complex medical condition.

I will briefly try to explain it: The main dysfunction is called Chronic
Intestinal Pseudo-Obstruction (CIP), a failure of the gastrointestinal nerves
and muscles to move and process food in a correct and timely way. CIP
means that the intestines behave as though there is a mechanical obstruction
when there is not, hence, "pseudo-obstruction." It can be myopathic or neuropathic; mine was diagnosed as neuropathic via full thickness biopsy as well
as accompanying neurological symptoms. The autonomic nervous system
regulates gastrointestinal function, and CIP patients frequently have other
autonomic dysfunctions besides the gut failure. There are frequently neurological symptoms. Various allergies are often present. There are wide variations of symptoms among adult-onset CIP patients, and the relationship between seemingly disparate altered physiological functions is not well understood. Essentially this disease means that food and fluid consumption cannot
be normal. I live on nutrient formula. This disease is entirely physiological
and is not the result of psychological causation.

Life can change in an instant. I never saw this illness coming. During
those "best of our times" I mentioned earlier, we couldn't see what was down
the road. I shunned doctors' offices whenever I could, putting up with things,
such as a lot of stomach distress that others would have sought help for, by
using over-the-counter remedies. I was just too busy for doctors, and I hated

spending time in their windowless offices. At the print shop, Bill had installed (at my insistence) a small window by my main work area. It only revealed a few, rough-textured leaves of a vine and a postage-stamp view of sky, but it kept me sane and satisfied. I had inherited my grandfather's aversion to needles and blood and shots. I could never have envisioned being in an illness situation and frequent creep-outs of blood draws, intravenous lines, and shots. Ironically, at onset time, I was trying to do everything right health-wise. I was using more fiber in our diet and less fatty foods. I was fixin' to study up on how we could become vegetarians in a healthy way. I restricted alcohol to two beers on Saturday nights. I recycled every product we used, dropping off items in bins that the local health-food store had in the alley at its back door, which they took to city recycling at regular intervals. I was trying to live healthy, with everything in harmony.

I had a lot of plans during this time. I had gone from painting to drawing, using images and designs based on the natural world. I had begun hunting the textures in some of my drawings and cutting them apart, to fit and collage into other drawings entirely. To expand the range of trim and textures for this, I'd planned to begin making my own paper. Handmade paper can be worked into a huge variety of differing surfaces.

This was never to be. When the illness came, I lost too much strength in my hands, fine finger coordination, and ability to render spaces accurately to even construct basic drawing images and materials. Oddly enough, I had done only an occasional sketch of the cats, usually for Christmas cards, which were not my main artwork. Rather than subjects, the cats were my fellow onlookers and observers as I took from the natural world to reconfigure imaginary places into little pictures. I had also wanted to start a no-kill cat shelter and a paper recycling business. Both were intended to employ people, and of course, accomplish so much more. Another dream had been to make a moth garden, with neon-light sculptures. (As green industry opens up more work opportunities, it will be a popular alternative to polluting industries. I think environmentalism will win fans that way.)

But the illness kept me in the house most of the time, where cat observation took place in-depth, almost continually. No doubt my bonds with them deepened due to such prolonged, close proximity. But I'm not one to talk about silver linings in rotten diseases like this one. Winning the lottery would have put me in the house all day, too, and life would have been so much more agreeable! I'm a person who likes contrasts, and the way I like to pace my day is to go in and out — going into the world among people and then returning to savor home, hearth, and cats, my mind pleasantly saturated with outside-world experiences. I can no longer do this most of the time. Bill takes me to visit my mother in town and to a few shops I know well enough to get around in quickly to get health food and cat food, about twice a week. But visiting in town with friends or going to events is something I now might do two to four times a year. Chronic illness, especially rare illness you have to explain continually, has no upside.

Business had not gone well for us since the sale of the T-shirt shop, and there was no replacing the funds we lost due to medical bills. I had worked full-time and beyond in our mom-and-pop business, but without a salary. Our accountants had advised us that this was okay, but there's a little-known glitch for wives or other family members in such businesses. As a result, I did not have enough payments into the social-security system to be eligible for disability checks. This oversight in the social-security laws leaves those who worked for self-employed spouses without salary, as well as those who were unable to work much for whatever reason, totally in a bind. There were no "wrong" moves on our part; there was simply no language in the small-business guides of those days on this issue. (Since that time, the guides now indicate that family members who work in a business and share in the profits are to be considered "partners" for tax purposes and should file partnership taxes, even without a formal partnership agreement. This now helps others avoid the snag but does not help us.) Although we let it go, this soured Mom on accountants forever. They'd given us a "bum steer" in her words, an old idiom for bad advice with a nautical history that refers to the difficulty of guiding a ship while it's backing up. With Mom, one bum steer means your advice is forever scorned.

One of the most disappointing effects of the scarcity of our resources was that I could not do things I wanted to for the cats. I'd wanted to buy them cat furniture with towers and scratching posts and perches to play on, but there was no doing that now. We became busy researching, dealing with insurance companies, and going to doctors, and our supervised outdoor times with the cats were phased out. Even in our presence outside, Minx had been chased and bitten by a visiting tomcat. So ending those outings may have been for the best anyway. But in their absence, I wanted to build the cats an enclosed outdoor space, with screen and wire around it to keep them in and other ani-mals out, so they could still enjoy something of the outside. I envisioned that years ago, and such spaces are now called "catios." Due to illness-related glitches, we were unable time-wise or money-wise to make it happen. The cats did adjust and stopped trying to get outside eventually, but I know they missed out on some high times around the yard.

Isolation increased not only because of our remote location but because we were unable to go out on many of the excursions our friends invited us to or to expand our limited space into a more comfortable setting for company. I had a useless feeling while researching this book and reading over old copies I kept of my outgoing letters to family and friends, revisiting the full life the letters convey, the life I used to have.

I hasten to add that acknowledgment and thank-yous are due to our many friends and family members who have overwhelmed us with their help, generosity, and kindness. I want to express heartfelt thanks to those who have understood the illness and responded with support and just plain keeping on like always. You called to see how we are, visited, invited us to visit when we can, and continued to invite us to events you know we can't possibly attend, making me feel I'm still part of the world. You kept our names on rolls of organizations and mailing lists. You walked down to visit, bringing beautiful flowers from your gardens. You brought me a crystal from an Arkansas mine. You told me where thistles are blooming, when I said I missed the ones that once grew in the yard. You passed along information you think might help, donated airline tickets to get me to experimental treatment centers, helped cook for Bill when I couldn't, and helped with repairs on a family house. Artists at the local arts festival in town have continued to greet us effusively, although they know we can no longer afford to buy their work. Some of y'all have given us discounts on essential goods and services, or traded with us by barter. There are too many details of your goodness to list, and I can never thank you enough. Y'all know who you are. A special shout-out is due to our neighbors who took Bill to the hospital in later years when he became critically ill and helped me with rides to and from the hospital, kept our animals fed, and gave me all kinds of assistance and support until Bill was able to come home. I get misty and overwhelmed about the warmth that has come my way and helped me get through this, and I deeply appreciate you all. Many strangers, too, have sent information and done things that astound us with their caring. I am forever beholden to so many. All this kindness uplifts the sagging spirit.

That said, a sick person would much prefer to experience the camaraderie of friends, family love, and kindness of strangers from any other cause than being sick. And conversely, there are a few friends, and even some family, who just don't grasp the seriousness and the ongoing and incurable nature of an ailment they have never heard of. The concept of illness that most people are accustomed to is of something treatable that goes away and does not last, like a cold or flu. Or, if it's more serious, it's something you can treat and hopefully bring to a full recovery or manage to a full life. I myself had never thought much about illnesses that linger with no resolution and little improvement prior to getting one myself. This is outside of what most persons think about illness. The most familiar ailments are those that heal, resolve, or are cured, and so some persons are put off by what they cannot compute. Others no doubt avoid you because of the depressing gap between what you were and what you are now, or because your limited energies mean you don't get around much and you have less to talk about — and what you do have to talk about is medical, not anyone's favorite topic. You are a "buzzkill." And there are store clerks who look at you funny because of occasional balance loss or lapse of attention, which they might attribute to drunkenness, even in a person who can't possibly consume liquor for health reasons. And there are persons who don't understand that your opinion should not be dismissed just because you now have a speech defect and a slower-on-the-uptake way of speaking and reacting.

Misunderstandings have also occurred due to the fact that I cannot do what I used to or what others can, and also from the fact that just because I can do one thing does not mean I can easily do another or another. I do things slowly and with rest breaks and breaks to get nutrients and to feed cats. I've had persons respond with anger when I didn't react on social media as fast as they felt I should, but just because I've clicked a few things doesn't mean I have sentence-making speed at a given moment. I have to pace myself carefully and if I'm going somewhere on the weekend, I rest the week before and do not make phone calls, because talking tires me greatly. Dealing with insurance companies is a full-time job and very draining. Doctors specializing in this rare illness encourage you to research, especially Bill with his science master's degree, because they're overtaxed by just maintaining people and need our help and input; a few doctors still don't get it and react badly to the idea of proactive patients who want to stay involved and do research, despite the fact that they themselves have no more ideas that will help. The list of downsides goes on and on. Striking a balance between talking too much about the illness and conveying a clear picture of my shifting abilities and disabilities is near impossible.

I love my adopted town in many ways, but I could not be correctly diagnosed here. I know what a few people are thinking, that the South is always behind, but in fact, the doctor who finally diagnosed me through a series of comprehensive tests he developed himself was a Southerner who was practicing in Memphis, Tennessee, at the time. And by becoming involved with support groups, I've found that patients with this rare disease have had similar experiences with uncomprehending medical personnel nationwide. My views on why the medical world often functions this way and the consequences of it for patients would fill another book.

I also must reiterate that I eventually found a few stellar local doctors who have the right blend of knowledge and open-mindedness to advance science, combined with pleasant and caring attitudes towards their patients. When you travel to a subspecialty clinic, you have to admire the dedication of physicians who take on the commitment to diagnose, keep patients alive, and seek new treatments for an elusive disease. They are simply overwhelmed. Thus, through no fault of their own, when they recommend something that might help in some small measure, there are scant opportunities for follow-up. Our resources for traveling to see them were running short anyway, and it was a bit like back in those early '90s: "Take twenty thousand of these and call me in the millennium."

Rare illnesses do not get much funding for the huge amount of research that needs to be done to find cures. Research dollars go towards those common ailments affecting the most persons; no one can argue with that necessity, and I certainly feel for anyone who has any kind of medical problem. But there should be some way of accomplishing research on rare conditions, which are currently known as "orphan diseases" for obvious reasons. At present it is frequently up to patients and their families, who are scarcely in a position to add extra activity, to raise funds and generate interest in the rare diseases among both doctors and the public.

Over time, our finances were completely wrecked. Usually with this particular illness, most of the person's resources are gone by the time the correct diagnosis is reached, with little left for maintenance and management. As in my case, most patients are too ill to work and replace those lost resources. You can indeed go broke in the United States from a serious illness. As marvelous as our medical system is, with its sophisticated diagnostic and curative technologies, there are many who cannot afford treatments or even the basic care; this may be a revelation for those who've never been seriously sick. Add one severe illness to a middle-income household, and you're sunk.

We found ourselves skipping basic tests considered necessary for persons our age. And should some miraculous cure for the ailment that affects me come along, I don't know if it will be available to me or not. One bit of good fortune is that Bill, like many persons raised in the country, is a mechanical wizard who has always been able to keep a series of old, clunker automobiles going. And my own ability to carefully manage our resources and make do with less has kept us from getting to the point where we would have lost our home if we'd been less skilled in those areas. My blood boils when people say that poverty and homelessness exist because people won't work. No, these issues exist because salaries often don't cover basic living expenses these days, let alone catastrophic illness.

There's nothing like a serious, long-term illness to make you feel like a lost child, alone and abandoned, and all the actual abandonments of the past are magnified, and those who are absent are missed, mourned, and/or resented more keenly as you cling to your corner of the world, thinking of old words like "waif," wondering, and waiting, for what? You don't know with a rare and unknown disease of no cure and uncertain outcome. At the same time, those who call to ask how you are, those who communicate on social media, and those who visit are exalted and cherished in your mind and affections. Enhanced and praised also are your pets, with their immense rapture of love for you, who are always there for you.

When someone I know is in the hospital, no matter how bad I feel, I make a point of visiting them, because I've been there. A rare illness and one that is "invisible" (i.e. you don't "look" sick) is especially hard for people to understand, but it's there and it's true. Friends need to stick with an ill person. I do understand that when the sick person gradually vanishes from friend circles (due to their shrinking energies or from a lack of comprehension of what's going on with the ailment), that person can seem to fade to nonexistence. We are not interacting with friends enough anymore; the isolation we experience is very sad and not our fault or our doing.

Chronic illness is a whole 'nother way of life entirely, one full of daily peril and obstacles that are not envisioned by well people as they go about their lives. I'm angry about becoming sick, which isn't necessarily a bad thing; according to what I've heard, anger helps you fight. I also cope by keeping busy. With a shaky hand and while feeling fatigued and foggy, I thought about writing this book and jumped right in. Some other patients in a support group have questioned whether I should spend my feeble strength taking care of cats and I answer, "Absolutely." It gives me something outside myself to dwell on and care for, extends my horizons, and provides both cats and me with companions. Cats, like humans in a distressed household, are all about ensuring that their home turf is defended and will survive.

It takes time, patience, and a watchful eye to fully experience the profundities, mysteries, and revelations of living with and knowing cats. I'm sure that's true of other companion animals, too. Without the cats, I would have gone stir-crazy long ago. They helped me to feel useful again because they appreciated what I did for them, at a time when the things I could do in other arenas was decreasing.

A snowstorm and when it rains, it pours

During the year 1993 while the CIP onset continued but before the diagnosis the convergence factor was again in play. In March, there was a snowstorm here. That was unusual in itself, but this one yielded thirteen unbelievable inches. The rare storm covered much of the eastern United States and dumped snow as far south as Florida. It would come to be known as "The Storm of the Century."

We'd had advance notice and were stocked with food and had firewood handy for our wood stove. The cats, all major heat seekers, would always head towards a newly lit wood stove at the first pulse of warm air that rose from it, all of them seeking to claim the most advantageous sleeping space stove-side. We knew, too, that on our dirt road off a dirt road, we'd be snowed in awhile, which would delay my doctor's visits. That night as the snow fell, it became a rare thunder-snowstorm; it also dropped an especially soggy sort of snow that didn't happen all the time, even in areas that saw a lot of snowfall. That heavy, wet mess brought down hundreds of branches all over the forest. All night long, we heard them cracking and thudding down, while the storm boomed. The accumulating snow meant a light bounce to the lightning flashes; they glared whiter and brighter, splashing quick illuminations into the bedroom through the uncurtained windows. I didn't get much sleep!

In the morning we weren't just snowed in: we were branched in. Every road was piled ten feet high with a snarl of branches, edge to edge. All the power lines had been downed by falling branches. We stored perishables outside, as it was freezing cold, and cooked on the wood stove. We brought snowballs in and watched the cats sniff and try to paw them. We videotaped the cats with the snowballs. The whole neighborhood was silent that first day. If anyone even tried to get out their front doors, they didn't get much further than their yards. We had checked — everyone had stocked up well in advance. The second day, we heard the neighbors' chainsaws and they heard Bill's. Neighbors came to visit after the road was cleared of branches (but not snow) to their houses, which were even more remote than ours. By about the third day, the one-lane dirt road was passable as far as the hill up to the highway, but we heard someone speed up and then spin their wheels trying to drive up the hill itself. It would take four days for two groups, friends working from one end and branched-in residents working from the other, to clear the road to the most remote house in the neighborhood. The power stayed out for about four or five days. Eventually, we all drove out.

Meanwhile, we took way too many snow pictures. Our old albums are full of rare southern snowscapes, more, in fact, than of the land in its more usual bewitching lushness during warm weather.

The snow was the storm before the storm. For the rest of that year, in addition to coping with the worsening illness, we were engaged in maneuvers to keep gas wells off our land and that of our neighbors. None of us owned our mineral rights, and our land sat over an enormous coal shelf. The energy industry had developed a new method called hydraulic fracturing, or fracking, to extract methane gas from the coal. They had also bought up all the mineral rights in the area. When the corporate powers came expecting to place wells anywhere they wanted to, a conflict arose between the rights of the surface owners versus the rights of the mineral owners. Every day, Bill made numerous phone calls, looked up records, met with people, and compiled information. I helped organize copies of papers when I could. (Fracking has more recently come to the attention of the rest of the United States, but it actually started in Tuscaloosa County long ago, as far back as the '80s or even the '70s.)

There was a lot of tension, which happens when two urgent, thorny matters of uncertain outcome collide. Working with city governments, Bill, with the assistance of our neighbors, helped to draft city ordinances regulating this new industry; there had been no such regulations in the entire state before. Eventually, we were able to keep gas wells off some locations but not out of the neighborhood entirely. There are still some wells close to us, raising concerns about safety and environmental effects, and access roads were created that have opened us up to more automobile traffic. The industry got what it wanted, but it had to make some deviations from its original plan. All this happened as I was slowly becoming more fatigued and losing more function, with no real answers to my medical questions. "Everything happens at once" is a living, walking, stalking, cliché around my house.

When my fatigue became such that I could no longer keep up with all the postcards and pictures and information from organizations festooning my bulletin board, I felt I needed to simplify every aspect of my life, and I took everything down and packed it away — except for two pictures from Greenpeace of their ship, *The Rainbow Warrior*. Under one picture was printed this statement, attributed to a Native American prophesy: "When the Earth is sick and dying, all over the world people will rise up as Warriors of the Rainbow to save the planet." I left those two up on the otherwise empty corkboard.

We also took down my drawing table where the cats and I had spent so many happy and productive hours to make way for a computer — *a bad mistake?* murmurs my inner Luddite — to aid in our medical research. For me, that was one of the saddest days of my life. It crushes my mood still when I think back on it. As noted earlier, effects of the illness means I haven't been able to draw or paint since the onset, beyond a little hand-coloring "within the lines" of a mechanically produced art print I did a few years back. I was just hitting my stride creatively, in both visual artwork and writing, when the illness hit me.

Life had become about survival. Mental life each day in our living room of books and cats became much simpler. With greatly impaired motor function, I was focused on getting through each moment, getting one foot in front of the other without tripping, and getting things accomplished in the kitchen without accidentally running my hand into the side of the cupboard. It was the old reptile brain thinking, *survive*. Getting the cats fed and the litterboxes cleaned, getting the checks written and signed — these were accomplishments.

Settling into a cat-focused life

Each of our cats had a distinct personality, and they mixed together with as much drama and complexity as any group of humans. Although altered, the girls and boys still displayed differences in behavior. The boys were always playing and tumbling in mock battles, the girls watching them from the couch with airs of superiority and disdain. They had their own "girl biz" to attend to, and they would slap at the boys and maybe hiss or just slink on their way if the boys got too near them with that tumbling nonsense.

Kudzu, more than Minou, was the flirt and tease. The girls were offended by it, and Minx would go positively ballistic whenever Kudzu tried to romance her. The few times he tried it with Spotty, she would *screech*, *hiss*, and put him in his place, too. The girlcats would nab turf away from the boycats, grab food off humans' plates, beat the boys handily at mousing, and in general, snort at the boycats from their lofty perches, or strut past them with fuming eyes to come snuggle with us. Oh, could they snuggle! All of this was done with those airs of smoldering grace that only girlcats can exude by the bucketful.

Spotty would run the others out of laps and chairs and away from food when she could. The others all seemed to wish to avoid her fussy ways. Kudzu would just lope away and you could almost see him shaking his head, going *ummm ummm ummm* at her prissiness. But they all learned to stand up to her when they wanted to; Spotty was just all hot and hissy air.

The boys were the sentinels, the first ones to go to the door in case of a noise, scent, or another animal. Every time we'd been out and drove back up to the house, the two of them would be visible through the glass, checking out the motor's approach. They'd be side-by-side and at night the headlights revealed them, four floating points of eye-shine, white blazes gleaming, with their perked black ears discernable as plush little cones on the darkness. They would be on alert, with protective intent, the much bigger Kudzu next to the little Minou. They looked striking when they occasionally sat on their haunches in the same position, white feet forward, like a feline chorus line "Puttin' on the Ritz."[12] And I told them so, on many occasions.

Both girls were lap seekers; the two tuxie boys, not so much. Minou didn't like being on a lap at all and would only go on rare occasions. He would sit on Bill's computer chair all day and move to Bill's lap when he came home and took the chair over, or he would go into Bill's jacket as he sat back in a recliner in cooler weather. (The only perk to cold weather I could ever see is that it puts cats on your lap.) Kudzu only occasionally went for a lap during his younger years, too, and neither boy could ever tolerate being picked up. So, we avoided picking them up unless it was absolutely necessary. Both Orange Cat and Gray Cat had been major lap cats, so Minou's and Kudzu's lap avoidance was not a sex characteristic but rather an individual preference.

Minx and I, of course, had our sublime bond and she was always on my lap when I was sitting, even more so after I became ill. She had come dashing up as a kitten to my face with paw taps that pointed me out and said, *here we are.* As an adult, she would still climb to my face, nudge my chin with her head, and I'd rub my face on her. If I left the room, I'd feel her eyes on me as I walked off, and I would turn to look back and she'd be watching me.

I talked to the cats, I admit it. They liked to hear me address them, and I spent a lot of time out here in the sticks alone and in their company only. I had to say something now and then. It wasn't all "Purrywitten" and "Minoup Minoup," either. I spoke in a regular and serious voice, asked what they thought and what they wanted, asked for advice, and spoke flattering words about their smarts and their beauties, anything to catch their ears. This may sound silly, but many persons have observed as I have that they listen. They respond sometimes, with their own vocalizations, and they enjoy your voice. They turn towards you and direct looks of such seeming comprehension that some persons feel they've learned your language and/or "get" you, with some sublime, transcendent feline understanding not possible in human-to-human conversations.

We can't quantify and know this with certainty, but cats know, at the very least, that you are interacting with them and giving them attention, and they like it; they want it from us, an odd fact in itself. I see them approach each other to play, to nudge, and to groom, but I don't see the same amount of direct looking at other cats — or responses to their meows — as they display towards us and our utterances. They seemingly engage with our eyes and voices, knowing these are our modes of communication. Vocal inflections and volumes may convey your moods, which they show signs of recognizing. I'm not one to think that they understand a great many words, but they do appear to recognize their names and those of the other cats, as well as a few other terms. Demonstrate to them that "Kitty, kitty" means chow, and they will come flying up when you say it. Of course, when a cat fuss begins, "Y'all quit," is futile — I have spouted it off, with a string of other advice, on many occasions to scholarly cats who suddenly haven't the foggiest notion of anything I said. "QUIT, y'all qui-it" is equally ineffective most of the time.

I could swear that Minou, once grown to an adult, didn't always care for the "Minoup Boop" scat song anymore. His lack of response was like a visible wince. He was not a kitten anymore! He was a small cat, slightly taller than Spotty, but glossy and sleek like the shine on anthracite coal. He was the most like a kitten of all of them — and the most likely to elicit a kitten-appropriate response from us. I tried to curb the "boops" to accommodate his young-adult sensibilities. No grown person likes to be treated as a child, and cats are no different. But he still answered to Booper, and Kudzu, so much larger than Minou, sometimes got called the Big Bopper. And everyone feline, especially when seemingly in need of comfort, might be called "Kittums," which I originated and Bill took up. "Kittums" would sometimes serve to address the whole group collectively.

Minou was now due an adult song of his own. Since he was the Cajun kitty, I composed words to the tune of an old Cajun song called "Grand Texas" (Hank Williams employed the "Grand Texas" tune when he wrote the words to his song, "Jambalaya") to Booper spontaneously, without much thought or effort. It just flowed. I'd sing: "Do you remember when you were my Purrywitten? And we would play, Chase the sparkly," then I'd go into some meows and *meow-boops* and *boopity meows*.[13] He'd flex his paws, curl up his body, and swivel his chin upwards, knowing it was his song.

Cat-related patter tumbled through my consciousness, along with the resonance of Shakespeare and Faulkner and Shelley and Keats, each day. Humans may think cats made me babble, but the cats never intimated any disdain. They loved it. And if Winston Churchill could turn to his black cat, Nelson, during the Battle of Britain and say, "Cat, darling," I can be forgiven for a few "boops" on plain days.[14] (Churchill's cat was named for the great British admiral, Lord Nelson.)

Sometimes I'd answer words I thought the cats might be trying to convey to me through their actions. When one of them had vomited up a hairball, very often he or she would stare out the window and fixate on a bird or squirrel as if to say, *eating that would settle my stomach.* "Yeah right," I'd find myself answering, "you little predatory beast." Words supposedly meant little or nothing to the cats, but the kitties liked the voice-sounds and I'm convinced they discerned my moods and attitudes from my inflections.

I've always heard that cats are jealous animals, folk wisdom likely derived from their nature as solitary predators who are rivals in the wild for food and resources. These four were certainly green-eyed. Talk to one of the group, and three other sets of eyes were instantly upon you. They looked at once cross, puzzled, and wounded. *What about me? What am I, chopped liver?* Spotty would come and yowl at you to include her, too, along with *don't talk to Kudzu, talk to me!* She'd do the same if Bill and I talked to each other, and if one of us talked on the phone, she wanted in. She'd come padding over, meowing and reaching a paw at you, trying to pull you away from that mere inanimate object that did not merit your attention and conversation in any way. The others didn't mind the phone or the talks between Bill and me; they were just attentive to the talk that went to other cats. Even if they were out of visual contact when human-to-cat talking occurred, they would often still have the look of compound resentment, as though they could hear and discern the difference in talks between Bill and me from one of us talking to another cat, without actually viewing the conversation.

I know they recognized each other's names, too, having heard them mentioned so many times when we addressed each of them directly. Petting one within view of the others elicited the same reactions and hard looks, and if they were all on the couch I'd rapidly pet one, then another, and another, and another, and switch back and forth, wishing I had four or five arms as portrayed in depictions of Hindu deities, to get everyone petted at once. I'd get a rhythm of pats going as I moved my hands from cat head to cat head, with a counter-rhythm of cat glances following each pat as it went around the couch, cat by cat.

Having four cats in our living area gave me a sense of abundance. Glancing around at them perched, snoozing, and snuggled in and around the room made the house feel like a living jungle, a cat city, a place with a pulse of living and doing, which became even more important once illness restricted my doings. The view was not same ol' same ol'; the house was not static. I was stunned daily by the sight of them — they were glorious! When they stampeded to the kitchen together for canned food, it was a breathtakingly beautiful sight of colors and patterns, like a herd of wild horses running. Arriving, four furfaces tilted up at me, mewing and trilling. I loved feeding them; it made them so happy. Even their incredibly uncouth eating and drinking sounds, *smack, munch, slurp, lap,* and *splatter,* gave me a profound sense of peace and tranquility.

When it came to food, Minou had, as a kitten, flung himself over the plate. As an adult, he still ate rapidly, gobbling the food; he was my little "goblin" at the food dish, a real feline vacuum. He loved canned food, and after bolting his, he would nudge Kudzu out of his dish; Kudzu was an extremely slow eater. I'd have to put one of them in the back room and secure the cat lock to make sure Kudzu got to eat his, or just give Minou, the insatiable feline chowhound, another helping. The girls would be close to finished when Minou made his swerve from his dish to one of theirs, and they were both better than Kudzu about standing their ground when that two-toned mouth came muzzling in. Kudzu was gentle and self-effacing about it; maybe he still regarded adult Minou as the kitten he had mentored.

Minou much preferred canned food. At times he would shake his tail in annoyance when he entered the kitchen and found only his same old dry staple. Then he would look at me, puzzled and cross. Spotty would shake her tail for the same reason and give me much the same look. Minou also had another way of getting his point across. He would patiently paw at any fabric in the room — couches, throw blankets, or the very shirt Bill was wearing — until he pulled up fibers, and then he'd try to eat those fibers. I even saw him paw at the occasional spiderweb around the room, pull a strand of spider silk to his mouth, and gobble it down. Like the petulant child who doesn't get his way and chants "Nobody loves me, everybody hates me, I'm gonna go eat worms," if Minou couldn't get the canned food he wanted, he would go eat worms, preferably right in front of us. He would look around at us with hot gold eyes, to make sure we were watching, then turn back to pawing and eating. We'd fuss and scold and hiss at him when he did this. Clearly, Minou was black-cat-mailing us. Bill laughed at that the first time I said it; I love to make him laugh.

Unfortunately, at the time Minou started doing this, we did not have the means to replace the furniture with surfaces that could not be pulled to fibers. He'd get to them before we could stop him, and then he would walk up to me and stretch open his mouth and make a straining, swallowing motion as though they'd become stuck in his throat. I'd jump up and fetch him some flavored hairball remedy gel on a spoon, which he really loved, to grease up his gullet and pass any fibers on down. After we did this over several weeks, he began coming up to me when I knew he hadn't eaten any fibers, making the same mouth-stretching motion. He wanted a taste of the cat laxative and this was his signal to get me to supply it to him! Minou's wool-sucking behavior subsided when we began serving canned food twice daily and keeping cat grass available.

As for Minx, she loved to chew on plastic, which we had to keep stored away. And I found out she had developed a sudden taste for a throw blanket when I began to find it in her stool. So the blanket went into the closet away from Minx teeth, too. Spotty was especially keen to chew those yellow plastic ties on self-tying trash bags, and we had to make sure they were out of her long and artful reach. We were always on plastic alert because of those two.

Spotty liked to cozy up for a snooze with Minx or Kudzu. They had been here when she arrived, but never, ever would she cozy with Minou, who was the only one who had entered the house after it became her domain. At times if he got too close, she would run past him and squall as only Spotty could. She wasn't wild about Kudzu either, and she might avoid him in waking. But her need for companionship was so great that she would nap with Kudzu. With either nap partner she would snuggle closer and closer, and sometimes they'd have legs thrown over each other, paws all jumbled together every whichaway.

Minx never sought out another cat for a nap, only me, but she would accept Spotty's nap overtures most of the time. Their mutual head grooming was usually at Spotty's insistence; she would thrust her head repeatedly at Minx until she obliged, but it could result in a fuss and separation if Spotty, who had sensitive skin, decided Minx groomed too vigorously. Once Spotty went smack-fest, slapping Minx with a rapid-fire paw about six times so hard I could hear it going *pop-pop-pop-pop* on Minx's head from across the room. By the time I got there to intervene, it was over, and Minx was fortunately unharmed. After that, the girls were on the "outs" for awhile, no napping together and both huffing off curtly when their paths converged or crossed.

Despite Kudzu's bemused opinion of Spotty as a terrible scold and a shrew to boot, he would accept her as a sleep partner. Minou snoozed mostly alone but also, at times, with Kudzu. However, Minx preferred me as a cushion so much that I could scarcely sit down before she was on me. Many times I'd have to balance a plate or mug of tea above her head, or work on art or writing with Minx on me. When she got older and stiffer, she had trouble climbing up on her own and would expect to be lifted. She somehow knew to come and turn her back to me, standing up straight so I could place one hand under her chest and the other under her round belly, spreading my fingers to equalize pressure on her underparts as I lifted her. Over and over she'd come to me and get in this "lift-me-up" position, and every time, I'd oblige.

Frequently when she got down from my lap to go eat, she wanted me to walk with her to the kitchen, and she'd turn around and look back to see if I was coming. Usually I was, since kitchen runs or runs to the back of the house were frequent as I went through my day. But sometimes, I'd go just because Minx wanted me to tag along.

Often, I would enjoy just watching them sleep. Cats sleep about twenty hours out of every twenty-four, or about eighteen out of twenty-four, depending on the source, so sleep is serious business for cats. Nevertheless, they can spring up from deep somnolence into instant action. There may be a strange cat or a raccoon in the yard that you actually see or hear, or you may detect no sign of the critter that the cat has sensed. At least part of the time, there is an undercurrent of alertness during cat sleep. I know I've seen a kitty slyly open an eye just a crack when asleep or flick an ear, and I realized they must be keeping tabs on us. I do think they always know if their people are around, through smell and/or whatever other mysterious cat radar they have, and that they are glad we're there, even when they seemingly ignore us. I know I felt Minou and Kudzu in particular feeling and taking comfort from our presence and checking our positions in the room with brisk glances, even though they are not lap cats.

At night when we were in the back and the cats were in the front, Minou would call mournfully at the door. In our house, they did not behave like the solitary and independent creatures they are said to be when living in the wild. I think they've always got a track of some sort on us when we're around, and they miss us when we go out and leave them alone. I've seen enough of them blatantly turning furry heads to watch me as I move around a room to be convinced. Whenever I made preparations to go to town with Bill and leave them alone, Minx would call to me more than usual and park by the door to the back; it's far away from the door I would leave by to go to the outside and it was as though she was saying, *Here, not there, this is the door we go through to have quality time.* Even in their deepest sleep I could tell that they were aware of everything going on in the room, as well as outside, hearing sounds we couldn't hear, smelling things we couldn't smell. Awake, many is the time they went all alert at the door when we saw or heard nothing, and then there would be the sudden appearance of a raccoon, another cat, or a person walking up to the house. Sometimes we never knew what they'd detected out there in the landscape, hovering invisibly. And maybe it's just as well we didn't know!

For me, cat sleep also elicits human daydreams. When the head turns upward and the cat seems to smile in sleep, I wonder if they are imagining they are the object of adoring crowds and are feigning indifference to it. With one ear folded underneath and next to the couch and the other flicking, are they trying to say, *I can barely hear you, praise me louder?*

A closer look at secret cat behaviors

Cats communicate with us in ways we have to watch carefully to recognize. For example, we learned about "the slow blink" by observation, and then found out from cat literature that it's well known. Cats will look at you, sometimes in a prolonged manner, and slowly lower their eyelids in greeting — and if you respond by slow-blinking back, they will repeat it and respond with another each time you repeat, too. Or, you can be the first one to slow-blink at a cat, and that cat may blink back and repeat blink if you then keep blinking. I've blinked at cats from across a yard and had them come rapidly trotting up to me. I've also exchanged slow-blinks with Anna, my mother's semi-wild former street cat, who would not allow me to touch her at that time. I've since won over that cat, at least to the extent that I can pet her, and it seemingly started with the blinks.

While many call the blinks "kisses" or signs of love, animal behaviorists point out that staring is a sign of aggression in the animal world. Cats use direct staring to gather all needed visual information before they pounce on something and as an "I challenge you" signal during hostile encounters with other cats. Blinking is the predator's anti-stare, the negation of the otherwise hostile gesture; it means: "I'm friendly towards you, I do not challenge you, and I'm not going to eat you, either." It's a sort of feline peace sign, relatively speaking.

Some butterflies have eye patterns on their wings to mimic a stare; this may deter predators who perceive a stare as danger. Human eye contact practices reflect this factor too. A direct stare from someone is usually discomforting and is considered rude human behavior. The steady stare as pre-predatory behavior resonates with many species.

One of the possible sources for the word "cat," as described in Barbara Holland's *Secrets of the Cat*, is the Latin phrase *captare oculis,* "to catch by seeing." This phrase morphed into *cattare* and then into *catus*.[15] According to Budiansky, the cats in Egypt were not named individually, but rather were always called by the name for cat: *myw.* (Vowel sounds weren't yet represented in the written language.) It's fairly easy to see where that one came from! Budiansky also notes that one exception was found in Ancient Egyptian writings: *njm*, meaning sweet.[16] That's a given for me, too!

With our cats, over the years, the blink exchange seemed to evolve from a simple reassurance of peaceful intent into deliberate, affectionate gazes towards us; the eye squinching punctuates the non-aggression we call a bond. Rather than a simple negation of predatory intent, these became love blinks. Minou would then shift his gaze away, presumably to further deflect the direct-stare impact. Kudzu's way of looking at us was always out of the corners of his eyes, with his head slanted slightly away from us. Minx and I tended to look long and searchingly at each other, *blink blink blinking* back and forth. In the wild, the stare is used in the most immediately important communication, *Hey you, get offa my turf, I'm challenging you!* It is also used in tracking and catching prey. In our household, the cats learned to use the direct glance technique in new ways — often they stared when they wanted to be fed, interspersed with friendly blinks, especially Minou. They would direct their glances toward me and the two of us communicated. They added embellishments to this basic "looking-and-getting" tool, with blinks and eye-to-eye contact, which grew into relationships with humans. The same stare that nets them prey in the wild got them fed in the house.

A Minou stare with friendly blink accents could mean any number of things, from "please move aside so I can have my favorite spot on the couch," to "please feed me," to "please freshen the litterbox." The Minou stare-and-blink, with summoning meow accents, also included purr and "pat me" requests. Minou knew he has the predator's hot glare. Survival was his primary instinct and that's how he met the world. But as he looked to me for pats or food, and when our glances mixed, he blinked with me, he was a friend. He blunted his glares. Minou was sometimes atypical about his staring, though. He would look deep into your soul at times, as if he thought, as Bill said, "you were fascinating."

Minx too would sometimes direct at me a gaze of unblinking adoration. The Minx stare and her slow, eye-squinching blink, along with her repertoire of long, loud and entreating *mrrrr-OWS,* elaborately expanded over the years into an exchange of mutual affection and admiration, of purrs and paw pats and hand pats.

In all cases, the cats' motto in dialogue with humans is: "Always let them see you blink." But the direct stare is also part of cat strategies for bluffing each other off, in a way. It starts with each of them calculating as to whether he or she can win the fight. Cats know other cats have the same powerful teeth and claws. Often, yowling results in one cat backing down and edging off, or both may execute a strategic retreat. Contrary to what I would expect according to the sources I've read about wild felids, I've even seen a video of a captive small wild cat, the Sand Cat, blinking at a photographer very deliberately.

Something basic that I used to accept without thinking is that a cat may not have an elaborate concept of what vision and hearing actually are, but it does recognize that our vision and hearing are located in our faces. A cat wanting to be fed will look from the floor up to our eyes to meet our gaze. He or she does not stare at our shins, which stand at its eye level. Meowing, like "The Look," is also directed upwards to our faces and not at our knees, which are more convenient to their height. They know where we perceive their entreaties and directives. They know from where our responses come. It is face-to-face, brain-to-brain, heart-to-heart. They look up at your eyes and meow to your face. They have transferred knowledge from their eyeball-to-eyeball encounters with other cats to their discourse with humans, a much larger animal. Perhaps, as some experts say, cats put up with us simply because they are neotenized, meaning they retain juvenile behaviors that go all the way back to their kitten days and their very involved relationships with their much-larger momcats.

Although there is some advice now to avoid looking directly at cats in order to avoid spooking them, I believe that a developing cat-and-human friendship has to start with brief-glance sallies to open up communication. A friendly cat learns to use stares to contact you, open dialogue, and cause you to bring food. The cat judges your response by the fact that you look back, notice him, and blink to soften the message.

Aloof or just misunderstood? The science behind a cat stereotype

The question of just how solitary cats really are is a complex one. My mother reports that when she lived in a small town on the Eastern Shore of Maryland, three of the neighborhood cats from different houses would take a walk together every day, including her own tabby, Skye. One cat would start off and be joined by the others as their houses were reached on the route. Then they would all go down to the water's edge at the end of the street and slap at fish together. Sometimes a small Lazu-Apso dog would go with them. All three were un-neutered males, those independent types who are usually the "lone wolves," or in this case, "lone tigers." Of course, each one was away from his home turf. In their own territories, they would probably want to keep other cats away.

There is a cultural image of cats as aloof, independent, and territorial. Many animal behaviorists stress that cats don't like living together, because they are solitary in their hunting practices in the wild. But some scientists are now beginning to question this viewpoint. In *Cat Culture: The Social World of a Cat Shelter,* sociologists Janet M. Alger and Steven F. Alger report on a long-term study done primarily in a crowded cat shelter, within which the cats were mostly free-roaming. The researchers found that the cats interacted with both shelter staff and adoptive families, sought their company, and communicated their preferences. There were intricate configurations of buddies amongst the shelter cats, and they tolerated the closeness and shared space well. They even showed empathy for newcomer cats that were caged within the room until they became acclimated to other cats; the veteran cats would go up to the newcomer cages and play with them through the cage windows. The authors point out that cats will form territories when necessary to survive, but not in every situation. A few cats remained aggressive after blending in with the shelter group, sometimes singling out one other cat to bully. These cats tended to be those who had been in homes before being turned over to the shelter, some as a single cat, which suggests that differences in background experience might account for the aggressive behavior, as well as other behavioral traits. The authors also noted that feral cats tend to live in groups. Therefore, cats are adaptable to various situations and do not always live isolated lives, not even in the wild.[17]

Social catalysts: Connecting with fellow cat lovers

I loved the co-existence of life in a jungle of domestic cats. Most of our friends were fellow cat people (except for the occasional cat-allergic person) or at least, they were animal people. Spotty was friendly with everyone. In fact, she seemed eager to gain the favor of any person new to her, going up to them and *me-yowling* for attention, settling into their laps where we hoped her fine, sticky little claws that she extended slightly in friendship, as cats often do, would not rip up their clothing. I remember carefully separating Spotty's claws from a friend's sweater in one instance. (As a denizen of cat country, I had come to wear mostly durable, old clothes, usually denims, around the house.) Spotty was so distinctive a cat that friends continued to comment on her beautiful markings and on her pouty lips.

Kudzu was fine with visitors, but he could be a little nippy if rubbed in some way he didn't care for, which a new person had to be cautioned to avoid. But Minou was a congenial cat who went right up to visitors. As a kitten, he made people smile. Once I had to yell "Look out!" to a friend whose hand movements — as he stood talking with eyes on us and above the cat-realm level — had put kitten Minou in crouching launch mode. A second after my words were out and our friend moved just in time, Minou levitated with kitten claws out, ready to capture and skewer. That was a close one! Grown-up Minou had a nippy tendency similar to Kudzu's; *pet me only in an exact way to be determined, moment by moment, by myself.* These might have only been the love-nips a high-strung cat will resort to when revved up by head-rubbing, but those nips were to be avoided if possible.

Minx was tolerant of visitors when young, but she really only liked Bill and me. As she grew older, she was crankier with new people and would spit if they stroked her, usually right after I told everyone what a sweetheart she was. Once, when a good friend I hadn't seen in many years sat down on the couch beside Minx, who was neatly tucked up there, Minx turned her head, locked her gaze, and opened her mouth in a *hiss* with a wide, gaping display of teeth. My friend was not amused. "She's old and cranky," I hastened to say. "She won't hurt you." (In retrospect I wonder if Minx could have been objecting to the fact that my friend sat between her and myself; in her cat-view, my friend was taking Minxie's rightful place by my side.)

Eventually she'd just hide when any person came in who was not us. She would, however, press her head against us and accept pats, in the best and most intense kitty way, with no nipping — unlike some cats, notably Kudzu and Minou, who easily got over-excited and too free with the love-nips. During the years when Minx was still in a friendlier mood, we had to go on several out-of-town trips to doctors specializing in my disease, and Mom would come to tend our cats every day while we were gone. Once she sat on the floor, and Minx got in her lap. When Mom wanted to get up and tried to move Her Majesty, Minx growled at her. ("That's my kind of cat," said Mom's sister, Aunt Faith, when told the story.) Minx's behavior at the vet was also horrific when she was young, and that would continue as she got older.

I was sitting talking with a friend one day when Kudzu jumped up on the couch arm and walked slowly along the back towards us to investigate her, or so I thought. He was all deep green eyes and long legs, shining black-and-white fur. "What a beautiful healthy thing," said my friend. Kudzu gave me a bashful, secretly-pleased-slantwise look. He may have been showing off for us as much as he had been being curious about the visitor. He was, after all, a huge flirt.

To sit in my house, you often had to move a cat or scooch in close beside one. Either way, you'd get smarmy looks from the cats, their equivalent to raised eyebrows. We'd make the offer to move a cat so people could sit. After all, with so many cats, couch space was often scarce. Some visitors, often but not limited to those who had cats themselves, would forego a prime spot so the feline could remain; those were, needless to say, the favored guests of the cats. When we actually had to move a cat for a human, we'd be faced with either withering looks or beguiling purrs, or both, and would have to employ our most skillful defelination techniques. Also favored by the felines were the ones who petted and talked to them. Some people could charm all the fur faces, even the company-aloof Minx. (One such friend would sing to his own cats. When they had been feeding some strays outside at their house, his wife came home one day and he told her, ironically, "I've done a bad thing. I brought in the cats." A kindred spirit indeed.)

The cats became about all that was happening in my daily life. That made for easy conversation with other cat people, and everyone would ask how the cats were. Everyone knew cats are revered around here. Visitors continued to praise the cats and sometimes talk to them directly. Minou's paper chasing kept many entertained, and for awhile, he was a great show-off.

I became a little cagey around those for whom animals didn't have the same elevated status, and around those who didn't want to hear endless, detailed, doting cat-person stories. Other topics take some restraint on my part, and I daresay, I don't always make the grade. I did okay at one party at the gazebo we now call the Lodge. Friends were talking about politicians' promises in the most recent elections. One said he would do away with the portable classrooms that were used in so many Alabama school systems. "We won't have to go to school in trailers anymore," said a friend. I once rushed a group of students from a trailer classroom to the much safer main school building during a tornado warning. "We won't have to go to school in them," I said. "We'll just have to live in them." That was one occasion where I was able to make my friends laugh, and it felt great. No cats in my conversation that night.

With cat people, though, it's different. They shower the cats with attention when they visit, and I listen spellbound and with complete understanding to tales of the way a certain cat used to smack down a newspaper to obtain the reader's full attention or of the finding of a new kitten. When we went to the houses of cat people, the cats seemed to seek us out. They always recognized us, maybe not such a mystery since they can undoubtedly smell the scents of our own cats. New cat smells arouse curiosity, and they must then check us out.

I had a singular evening at the home of our friends Craig and Linda. Their cat, Man Ray, hopped on my lap and settled with his head facing the group. He was a mostly white cat, with a few small patches of tabby on his head and tail (which I now know as the "van" pattern); he was the most muscular, burly kitty I'd ever seen. He turned his head around and gave me a penetrating *pet me!* look. I responded by rubbing his head around his ears and his throat. Every time I stopped, around came his snowy face with a look of *What!? Why?!* and I'd rub again and he'd snug in and purr. He was insatiable. I petted him for about an hour and a half. It was almost as if he knew a little cat attention cheered me up that night, making me feel needed and useful, as well as being to Man Ray's own benefit, too.

Animals can connect people. Once at a dinner party in a restaurant, we met a new friend, a retired professor who had just rescued four kittens. We had instant rapport with him as we shared our own animal rescue stories. "I like people who take care of animals," he said cheerfully. Sadly, that was right before I became increasingly ill and housebound, and we had few opportunities to visit this newfound friend.

When a friend with only one cat learned that we had four, she let us know, "That's too many," but with a pleasant lilt in her voice. I resisted the urge to answer back, "One is not enough!"

Some cats in this town are cared for in public spaces. Long ago when we used to frequent a bar that drew all the "outsiders" in town called The Chukker, there had been a Chukker cat. Fed by the management and patrons alike, this cat would grace our evenings by strolling through the bar, which he easily accessed through the open doors during the magical warm nights that could happen year-round in earlier decades.

More recently, a semi-feral tabby named Shug began hanging around a space devoted to artists, in which a few of our friends had studios. Everyone began to care for her. When she had five fine tabby kittens, everyone socialized them. While Bill visited a friend at the studios, I petted and scritched the kittens; one little guy fell asleep in my hand! The kittens were all homed, and last I heard, they'd had Shug spayed. I think she eventually went home as a house pet with one of the artists.

In the '90s an animal advocacy group was formed in town. Low-cost spay-and-neuter was a feature of their work; they TNRed a small feral colony that was living downtown and relocated the colony to another location, complete with a caregiver.

Cat naps and claws for attention

With all their fine sensibilities, I am sure that somehow my cats detected the difference between well me and sick me. I tried to keep as busy as I could, but I had to sit and rest a lot, and I could only do about one twenty-fifth of what I had done pre-illness. This was blatantly obvious, but other, more subtle aspects, such as less mental energy and less ability to concentrate, I'm sure they could pick up on, too. Due to the failed gastro-intestinal function, I had a feeding tube for nutrition beginning June 1994. (It was removed in 1996 after I determined that I could take enough liquid formula orally with only a small increase in discomfort.) The first time I used the tube to feed in the living room rather than the bedroom (I would creepy-voice a joke, "I feed at night, *muhahaha*"), Minx came right over and tried to bite the tubing! I wasn't sure how to interpret this puzzling, hostile act. Did she resent the machine being so close to me? Did she somehow comprehend that it meant I was sick, and was she "saying," with a visual demonstration, that she didn't want me to be sick? The formula was not made tasty or enticing as food for any species in any way, so she was likely not trying to gain access to it as a food treat.

The cats took over the large room that was our living area for their sleeping and sitting pleasure. In general, each cat would select a favorite spot for a time — then suddenly, after several weeks or maybe several months, they would change to another spot. They're comfort seekers, so couches were always popular. In summer when the one window with a screen was open, the windowsill was a great favorite, too. At the most, two cats at a time could squeeze in; there were occasional spats over a space when somebody didn't want to share. The front room had a large, south-facing picture window and abundant, splashy sunshine, and the cats loved to snooze in sunlight.

Observant persons who live with cats and who have heard of REM, or rapid eye movement sleep, know that cats dream. Our house was full of rapidly fluttering cat eyes. I'd seen Minx tremble all over in her sleep, eyes rolling under partly opened lids, sometimes even growling as in some fierce confrontation. Back in town Gray Cat had the dream that caused him to meow in a startled querulous tone and leap over to snuggle in my lap for protection and reassurance. Bill saw Minou's eyes rolling while he mewed in his sleep. Nightmare and battle dreams caused those dramatic actions; perhaps sweet cat dreams cause the episodes of pleasurable rolling and stretching they often display in half-sleep. Science knows cat dream.

It pains me greatly that the resource reduction meant we were unable to afford those comfy padded shelves that can attach to windows, allowing cats a view of the outside while soaking up the sun. But we were fortunate to have many sunny spots available around the room, if not right by the windows. Minx's favorite sleeping spot, of course, was me or beside me. The couch in front of one of the tall bookcases, the one that was the launch pad for bookcase climbing, was an older model with a one-piece firm back extending around into arms. I usually sat on it while looking out the window and leaned back on some pillows, the most comfortable position for me. Minx would often sleep on the arm or on the back of the couch near where I sat, as if she was waiting. Sometimes, if she was up there and I came and sat down, she would then step onto my shoulder and descend down my chest to my lap, then step-twirl in a circular motion to settle in facing me. "Hello, Furface." I might say as she parked in my face. Nothing like taking the most direct route!

Spotty, of course, continued to come running most every time she saw Minx attain my lap, sometimes darting and leaping on before Minx or climbing up right after the Minx, even closer to my face. With two cats on me, movement was limited and rising required careful defelination. I could accomplish this alone in most cases. But one time I was stretched out on that couch, head and torso slightly raised, I had the Minx on my lap; Spotty high up on my chest, almost eyeball-to-eyeball with me; Kudzu on my thighs; and Minou on my lower legs. I stayed still as long as I could, but when I finally had to move, I called for Bill's help with the defelination. There was no growling, but we still got a lot of that ol' cat attitude: *How dare you move me from the place I, the cat, have selected for myself?*

In the short story "The Long Cat," the French writer Colette implies that female cats are none too fond of tomcats.[18] This rang true in our girls' disdain for the rough games of our white-footed gang of boys. But in this group, the two girls competed to sit closest and the two boys vied for the most attention. Pet one of the boys and the other guy's ears would prong forward, his eyes fixed upon you. Those rivalries seemed more intense than the rivalry between cats of the opposite sex.

The cats would all use the back of the couch to traverse the room. Kudzu liked to sit on the arm of the main couch nearest the window, looking tall and formal and stately in a classic pose against the greens of the jungle outside. All of them would sometimes sleep with their four feet hanging down off either side of the couch back, slung over it as though draped over a tree branch. Some of their ancestors were no doubt arboreal, sleeping high up for safety from predators. But Kudzu used the couch back in a way all his own. One day as I was sitting there, I heard rapid, breathy snorting sounds behind me. I turned to find Kudzu had crept up behind me with his nose working, sniffing my hair. He was quite adamant about it, working his muzzle through my hair and pushing his snout against my head; he persisted several minutes despite my startled, "What are you doin', big buddy?" It was surprising how loud the sniffing sounds were when they were right next to my ear. Kudzu did this repeatedly over the years, sometimes pawing at my hair vigorously. He was such an old flirt, after all.

By contrast, Minou preferred a place on the seat right by the arm of a couch. He may have liked it because it rose beside him as a sort of shield. He also liked to sleep on his back, bracing with his paws up against the couch arm. He would put great effort into getting another cat, or person, out of whatever spot he wanted for himself. He would sit on his haunches and stare at Bill or me, trying to get his message across. If we obliged and moved, he'd immediately take the spot. Once, after he stared at me for a few minutes, I refused to budge, and the little stinker then gave my arm a nip to illustrate his point. Fortunately, it was not penetrating, only startling. I laughed it off as part of Minou's personality, but I chose not to move to avoid encouraging this rude gesture. However, both Bill and I do move on occasion when Minou, or one of the other cats, has designs on the place one of us is sitting.

Kudzu in particular showed great ingenuity by engineering a spot for himself that he made his most frequent bed for about two years. My mother had given us another couch, which we set at right angles to the first one, parallel to the archway leading to the kitchen area with one end near the glass-paned front door and a view of the forest and yard. The back of this couch consisted of three cushions that fit together, which greatly expanded the cat-sitting area. It was a great favorite with the cats, who interpreted it as a gift to them, not us.

Kudzu chose to sit and sleep on the back of that couch, along the top of one of the cushions at the end near the door. It was prime real estate: he had a vantage point that looked out on the living room, the kitchen, and out the door into the forest; it was the "Lookout Mountain" of home furnishings. Sunshine reached the couch every day from the glass front door. It was also an area of heavy traffic flow — to get to both the kitchen and to the back room, Bill and I had to pass by that end of the couch. My entire day consisted of going back and forth between the kitchen, the back, and the living room. Thus, Kudzu got quick head pats all day long, since he was right at hand level. He'd turn up his lion-face muzzle as I passed, and I'd scritch his head. He also had the warmest spot in the house in the winter, since the fan in front of the heater blew warm air into the living room across that very location. And he had easy access to sniffing and snuggling perks with whatever human was sitting on that end of the couch.

Of course, all this was not unnoticed by the other three, but we made a point to compensate by patting them a lot, too. Kudzu used his weight to make the cushion sink beneath him, and it sank on the top into a bowl shape he could puddle himself into, curling up in an area shaped just right for his body, crafted by his own belly. Always a tease, Kudzu would frequently take a playful swipe at me, with a diffident air when I walked by, and sometimes I'd have to disengage his rather large claws from my clothing. He was content and self-satisfied in this spot he had molded for himself.

Feline Feng Shui

Minou was always quick to find a seat with a view. When we placed a big, cushy work stool beside the kitchen counter, Minou began hopping up on it and watching us in the kitchen, especially Bill, who gradually took over all cooking. Minou watched his every move, even when onions and garlic were involved, foods that cats don't usually go for, fortunately. Onions are deadly toxic to cats, and garlic contains a smaller amount of a related compound found in onions; both are thought to be deadly or at least questionable for cats. So Minou's interest in Bill's cooking was probably much more a study of the cooking process than an actual interest in grabbing the food. Maybe Minou was curious as to how food that smelled so bad to a cat could be prepared in this house, when all food preparation was supposed to pertain to him. *What is this about, how can this be?* he may have been thinking.

When the stool was later eliminated from the house, a new perch was not long in coming for Minou. Bill acquired a freestanding closet, which he set in the archway space between the living and kitchen areas. At the opposite end from Kudzu's couch place, opportunist Minou soon began launching off the couch back and up to the top of this closet with frequency. From there, he could scrutinize both the living room and the kitchen activities, and he mostly chose to focus on the latter. He watched dishwashing and medicine- and nutrient-taking. He pranced around and chased his tail up there in a space that was just Minou-size. He'd snooze up there, too, hanging his black tail down or sometimes a white foot; other times, he'd be tightly curled up, unseen by humans and all the other cats. Bill later built a shelf very high for his valuable workshop materials, close to the ceiling and extended over this closet. Minou then proceeded to use the top of the closet to reach that shelf with his long-legged front paws. He would pull himself up, knocking things stored up there askew. Bill had to re-arrange everything to block Minou's route up to the shelf, but Minou still loved to get a running start and bound up to his new observation tower. He made a big *thunk!* when he landed on the top of the cushion back of the couch coming down; it was exciting for anyone sitting nearby, since Booper moved so noiselessly in beginning this descent. More than once he startled Bill or myself as he hurtled down this way, missing us by inches.

Minx had been known to climb the bookcase and settle on the top in her early days, but in later years, both girls were content at lower altitudes. With Minx, that meant mostly snugging herself into my lap. She'd come running, sounding *ruhuh ruhuh ruhuh* to me, jumping up (in her younger days) or waiting for a lift (in her older ones), walking around on me until she found the right place, facing me to ripple her torso down, tilting her head upwards, *trilling* to encourage head pats, and/or rub her face on mine. Sometimes, I'd press my chin on her head. If I was occupied otherwise, she'd fix her gaze on me until I petted her, and then she'd settle in for as long as I didn't have to leave. I'd place her on the couch when I had to get up, and when I returned, she'd climb up on me again.

She also liked to camp by the door with the sunlight streaming in on her through the panes. She was a gorgeous sight, with her sparkling gold eyes and the sun looking frosty and silver on her fur. During the terrible storms that came when tornadoes were either possible or on the ground somewhere, we'd go to the strongest part of the house, on the divide between the living and kitchen areas. I'd grab Minx and place her on my lap, and she'd stay while I tried to coax Minou and Spotty over, while the huge, translucent winds hollered. Kudzu, at the first sound of the lightest rain even in the mildest storms, would wriggle his rangy self under the couch, so in tornadic storms, he would be under cover long before we were. (He had lived outdoors a year or two before he met us, where the sound of thunder and rain meant getting wet, and he was still having none of that. Not even canned food during a light rain could bring him out.) In fair weather, he wasn't just a couch upper level dweller in his favored personally engineered spot, but had a fondness for the lower regions of the house, too — he loved to roll around on the floor.

Spotty would sit on your lap or nearby and let out her screechy *me-or-yowls, y'aawwwlll* for pats or attention of any kind. Once she even reached out with her paw, cupped it around one of my fingers with her claws at just the right extension to avoid sticking me, and pulled my hand to her. I rubbed her head and she trilled in happiness, as getting pats had been her purpose in grabbing my hand. Other times she'd merely tap my hand with her paw, trying to indicate that hand should be petting her. It astounds me how smart these little things are, but I remain puzzled by witnessing Spotty making overtures to a lightbulb one night. Looking towards it, blinking, she reached out and pawed at it repeatedly, while the glow lit up the multi-colors of her face with its pronounced, two-toned lips. My thinking is that since it was winter, maybe she wanted to pull the warmth of the bulb to her. Or perhaps she shared my admiration for the practical lion-color familiarity of the old one-hundred watts.

Spotty had a phone fixation, too, and once she made a phone call on her own. One night, Bill stayed on the phone a long time with friends. Somehow Spotty waited all that time until after Bill hung up to make a fast beeline for the phone and rub and caress it all over as she had a way of doing. We tried to get back over there to remove her, but it was too late. When we heard the phone begin dialing again, we knew she had stepped on redial.

Being territorial creatures, the cats worked out amongst themselves their favored positions around the room, as well as their time-tables for swapping them out. Usually they wished to be in eye-contact range with us humans for purposes of directing their keen gazes our way at feeding times, and the eye heat from all angles made for a kind of fuzzy geometry. The cats were drawn to sitting, sleeping, and even pouncing on things that we, their people, considered important. This they discerned by carefully observing which things we focused our attention on, and therefore they had a basis for practicing a sort of feline Feng Shui in their ways of placing themselves. They would, of course, sit right upon the newspaper or magazine or book you held in your hands trying to read, but they would also seek out these things for a snooze when you weren't using them. My drawing table, with its colorful pencils and ink bottles, had been a welcome challenge to saunter through, bumping and kicking some of those obstacles out of the way, making it their cat space, as if to have its elevated status literally rub off on them. Or maybe it was the reverse — they were adding real importance, cat importance, to a previously trivial place we'd only thought had significance before. *This is one of our haunts, now it sizzles!*

Our cats sought important work areas and work projects, such as letters and drawings and medical notes, to sleep on. Minou liked to be on, or next to, or pawing, Bill's computer keyboard or posing in classic positions on the table next to the television. Had Minou been a person, he would have been one of those annoying, knowledgeable, younger-than-us computer geeks. As Bill worked on the computer, Minou watched. Not a lap-warmer type, Minou would sit on Bill's lap in only two places in the room: at the computer and in Bill's LazyBoy chair. Spotty was fond of stretching herself over the closed top of my old Smith-Corona typewriter; she would sprawl over and cup her paws around it, getting as close to the machine as she could, even though that put her at a slant. If one of us typed a letter, inevitably, one of the cats would sit on it if given a chance. On the couch where I usually sat, Kudzu also liked to sit, either on haunches or with all fours folded under him on the end that was in front of the window I spent most of the day looking out of, so that he, too, would be gloriously in the path of my gaze.

Cats set a very bad example when it comes to working and getting things done. By sleeping all the time and turning their heads and paws up happily, and purring besides, they make it look like goofing off is intensely pleasurable. By occupying your work places, they seek to divert your work energy. If too much of your attention is being focused elsewhere, they decide it should be re-focused on them; they are the cats! They head for the pools of concentration in the room and soak it up like they do sun-puddles.

From WWII to a pair of Bill's shoes

In a story from World War II, in August 1941, Britain's Prime Minister Winston Churchill sailed aboard the *H.M.S. Prince of Wales* to meet President Franklin Roosevelt aboard the *Augusta*. Although America was not yet in the war, Churchill was seeking assistance from American ships in the escalating conflict. The two ships met secretly off Newfoundland and just as Churchill was about to step off the *Prince of Wales* onto the *Augusta*, the ship's cat, a black cat with white face and paws (named Blackie) came up and tried to go aboard the *Augusta* with him. Churchill restrained the cat and a famous photo was taken. After that, the cat was renamed Churchill. Human Churchill was successful in attaining the aid he sought, and the Atlantic Charter was signed.[19] It is mere speculation, but the actions of Blackie-Churchill suggest that the cat tried to attend a meeting of momentous importance as if he knew it was significant. Cat enthusiasts might say that of course the cat knew. On August 21, 1941, Roosevelt gave a speech to Congress about the Atlantic Charter, pointing out that the document was carefully worded to state that the peace being sought after the war permitted no compromise with Nazism.[20]

Cats were frequently on World War II ships. They were considered lucky by sailors and were useful for rodent control. Cats on ships go back a long way, and sailors kept them even during the terrible times of cat persecution. Usually ship cats were well treated as pets, and sailors went out in small boats to rescue them if they fell overboard. It was believed to be unlucky for a ship to lose its cat. There are several stories that say a cat always returned to a docked ship right before it sailed, and if the cat did not return, the ship would sink the next day.

Hammocks were brought back to Europe from the Americas, and their usefulness for sleeping on ships was obvious. Moving with the motion of the ship, they kept sleeping sailors from being knocked around the way they had been when they slept on the decks. And many ship cats have been photographed curled up in cat-sized hammocks made especially for them. A great favorite of all our cats were the folded-up blankets we placed in various places for them: on couches, or on the floor in front of the propane heater, or in front of the wood stove in winter. When a blanket was being set down, the cats would come immediately, pouncing on it or lying down, knowing it was for them. Minou would be so eager that he'd be stepping on it and sitting on a corner before I could fold it and smooth it down for him.

During the late 1990s, Minx developed a reaction to Bill's shoes. Every night after he came in, she would rub on them, gripping them with her forepaws and claws, tumbling around on the floor next to them, pulling herself this way and that, and getting goofy grins on her face, almost like a catnip reaction. He was out in the yard more than I was, and we could only surmise that whatever plant odor out there that she had responded to in similar fashion years earlier was traveling in on his shoes. Once in a while, she'd go for my shoes, too.

Our cats were content, but I still had regrets about keeping them indoors, although it had certainly cut down on the carnage they used to proudly tote home to us. Besides an outdoor space, I had wanted to build them an indoor recreation area, custom-designed with a cat ziggurat to climb on with gradual inclines for the kitties who were getting older. Again, limited resources, space, and time prevented this. During especially buggy summers when all manner of airborne insects came in the house — June bugs, moths, and katy-dids, as well as the unidentified flying annoyances — the cats were very entertained, locking their gazes on the network of trajectories, giving chase at times, and just being generally "bug-dazzled," as Bill described their finely tuned attention.

Each cat's voice was distinctive although Spotty's was the most stand-out. I always knew which one was sounding off even if I couldn't see the me-ower of the moment. "What chyou studyin'?" I'd address whoever had en-treated me, and find satisfaction either in fulfilling a need, or in an exchange of banter. If the meows came in a chorus, the response was "What chy'all studyin'?" Answering multiple meowed queries could be challenging, but I always found it rewarding.

Finding spiritual wisdom in a simple life

Since life as I'd known it stopped, time seemed to pass quickly. There was not a lot of variation in each day, and one day seemed to melt and fade into another. Sitting and communicating with cats, watching the light of days and nights change together, is not action to most people but only the stuff of an instant, a snapshot, a portrait, a postcard. But for me, I had to be alert to the stories in the most seemingly plain moments. My faculty of noticing had to be heightened. Even a freshly cleaned and newly poured cat box resem-bled one of those textured arrangements of raked, small stones in Japanese Zen gardens. I would use two different litters, which resulted in a "best of both" product performance, and upon the first pourings, subtle color varia-tions resulted, like a painted desert in a box. Of course once one of the cats, who were often hovering to gain first use, employed the box for its actual purpose, all aesthetics of the situation dissipated — until the next box change.

Around 1997, we and a few of our friends were invited to a formal meet-ing with the Dalai Lama in Atlanta. We had been sympathetic to the cause of Tibetan autonomy for a long time, and Bill and our friends had arranged for the Singing Tibetan Monks to appear at the University of Alabama. The friends drove us all to the meeting in Atlanta, held in a large, conference-sized room at a hotel. By then, I'd been ill since 1992.

In the hotel hallway, we each purchased a small scarf to be presented to His Holiness upon first approaching him. Then he would pass the scarf back, along with a blessing to the receiver after holding it for an instant. We went in and sat down, facing the raised platform where his chair was ready and draped in colorful decorated cloths and fitted with pillows. There was a loud buzz of talking, but suddenly everyone fell silent. Nothing had happened in the stage area, and puzzled, we looked around towards the back. The Dalai Lama had entered the room through the back door and was slowly walking down the aisle, making half-bows in either direction. He was smiling, and my first impression was of a friendliness that put everyone totally at ease. He was glad to see us! It was almost like the appearance of a neighbor who is known so well that he just appears in your house without hesitation or knocking. There were no barriers, no concepts of unknown or "stranger." Although he is in exile from his true home, he seems at home wherever he is and brings that feeling of home and familiarity with him across continents and cultures. I felt he had a glow about him, a sort of felt radiance that might be depicted as a nimbus in a painting. He was accompanied by guys in suits as protection, who Bill jokingly called the Tibetan Secret Service.

When His Holiness was done speaking, everyone lined up for the formal greeting. As I waited in line, it became apparent that I had to run out to visit the ladies room. Handing my scarf to Bill, I went out the open door and returned as quickly as I could to find the door closed and two guards with rather grim looks on their faces. "Had I been inside there before?" they asked me. "Yes sir, I had," I replied, but I didn't even have my scarf to prove it! But somehow, some way, they opened the door and I rejoined the group behind Bill, almost at the very end of the line. I almost missed it!

The suited guys were walking along the line, urging us to close the gaps and step quickly. There was another function the Dalai Lama was to attend after this, a fundraising dinner for the Tibetan cause, and they wanted to move things along. (They were also carefully standing within arm's reach of His Holiness as he met everyone.) We observed him greeting the others, and he was laughing and jovial. Bill approached him, and the scarf exchange and handshake took place.

Suddenly, without having planned it, Bill said to him, "My wife is behind me, she has been sick for quite a long time." At that, his face changed from beaming to care and concern. He said, "Ohhhh."

I approached with my scarf and made the half bow, ready to shake his hand as he had with all the others. But then he took my hand in both of his and looked into my eyes for a long time. I was just stunned, and I don't remember everything that went through my mind. I recall being over-whelmed by his kindness in caring so much, enough to take extra time, even with the vibrant impatience of the attendants standing right there. I'm a shy person, and I try not to call attention to myself in public, so I usually keep my cool. But Bill reports that a second after I stepped away, I was seized with great, gasping sobs. Bill helped me back to our seats, where I slowly regained control.

I can't really articulate what caused the sobs, except to say that I am a person with a chronic, rare neurological disease with no known cure, and I feel really hopeless and rained on and alone at times. But I had just looked into the face of the Embodiment, or Emanation, or Manifestation, of the Compassionate Buddha, as the Dalai Lama is described as being; that, plus the effect of directly receiving this kindness beyond imagination from someone I hadn't known an hour before, a person generally acknowledged as having a certain world importance; it just went directly to the emotions. I felt truly moved although I am not a Buddhist; I've read up on Buddhism and attended lectures out of interest, but not with commitment in mind.

The ride back home was a blur: the spinning around the highway circling the lights of Atlanta, the stop at our friends' daughter's home in another city to drop her off, the warm night air, the branches against the sky. I was tired but didn't want any of that to end; it was like the radiance of the experience was still with us in some strange way, as long as we were with the same people. Years later, I like to think that radiance is still lingering in our daily life, its undercurrents and intimations edging our churning thoughts and our difficult times in some way.

I agonized over whether to include this story, as it was a deeply spiritual experience and is therefore somewhat private. Should it be written up for others? I only hope my words invoke love, awe, and compassion. However, my eventual decision to tell this comes after much reasoning, and not the least among those reasons is that this happened in the South, where many outside the region think nothing of cultural significance ever occurs. And no doubt a high percentage of those in the room who met the Dalai Lama were native to southern states.

Minx versus the indignities of aging

Minx was diagnosed by our local vet with a heart murmur in the late 1990s. At our vet's suggestion, Bill took Minxie to a vet school at a college in Mississippi for an echocardiogram. The exact grade of murmur was determined to be not serious enough to require medication at the time.

But in 2000, when Minx was twelve, she began losing weight and drinking more water. She was diagnosed with hyperthyroidism. The excess release of thyroid hormone speeds up metabolism and heart rate and has serious consequences if left untreated. The best treatment option was a low-level radioiodine therapy, available at a veterinary college about a four-hour drive away. She would have to stay four or five days. If I'd been well I would have gone with her, stayed in the town with friends, and made a real pest of myself by visiting at the hospital and getting in the staff's faces. But at this stage of the illness, I was not up to travel. And during this therapy, only clinic personnel are allowed to actually have contact with the cats due to the radiation involved. So Bill and Minx set off by themselves; we put a shirt I'd worn that had my body smell on it in the carrier with her to make her feel as at home as possible.

I wrote a note cautioning the clinic about Minx's appalling attitude towards all things and persons veterinary and to be wary of her. Bill left her at the clinic and came home; he had elder-care issues to take care of here that I couldn't manage alone. We waited. I was lonesome, fretting, stewing, and brooding with worry. Bill called every day and the clinic personnel declared that she was doing fine — and there was one guy she really liked, who could actually pet her! I was amazed. My one-person girl, who didn't think highly of the veterinary profession, had a crush on a guy!

The week finally passed and Bill went down to pick her up. I waited eagerly for their return as the hours grew long; dusky haze suffused the room, then night fell, and wore on. I was foaming. I was more than ready to have my cat back! When I heard the car I shot straight out the door. "I was afraid she'd killed someone," I joked as Bill got out of the car. (Visiting friends around town had delayed him several hours.)

Socially, Minx had done uncommonly well at the clinic. She came back bright-eyed, bushy-tailed, and fuming for awhile, walking around growling her response to the outrage of having been taken away just like that. I couldn't help but feel curious about the vet assistant she liked, since Minxie warmed up to very few people in her lifetime and ended up in later years shunning everyone besides Bill and myself. He must be a real cat charmer; if he was a student then, he must by now be a fine vet or veterinary technician.

One of the great mysteries about cats is why they put up with us, why they take to life with us so readily. They are essentially little wild animals. The sweetest cat will revert to the wild faster than you can get your flesh out of the way should you find yourself too close to territorial fireworks when a strange cat is at the door. For instance, Gray Cat, so civilized, was in a yowl-off with another tom on the other side of the glass one day when Bill startled him — Cat spun around and snapped, missing Bill, thankfully, but he left teeth marks on the handle of a broom standing next to the door. Dogs, with the exception of a few husky breeds, have been very much changed in temperament and morphology from their wolf or wild-dog ancestors by centuries of breeding. But house cats have changed very little from their wild ancestors, according to zoologist Roger Caras in *A Cat Is Watching*.[21]

It's said that cats were drawn to us by the mice that were in turn drawn to our stored agricultural products. No doubt the grain/mice factor had a role in starting it. But to me it doesn't completely explain the great delight they take in having us rub their heads and scratch their chins, nor the way they become so devoted to us. Nor does it explain the displays of contentment and belonging or their sense of entitlement once they take over your house. Some scholars, such as Desmond Morris in *Catwatching*, say that they become kitten-like and enjoy being petted because that is the same kind of grooming motion that mother cats make.[22] These sensible observations from an eminent zoologist still don't quite explain it all to me. Even cats that are semi-wild, cats you can't even touch, will look at you like they're saying, *Bring the chow, that's your job.*

Other small, wild animals may be tamable when raised from babies, and I've heard of housebroken squirrels that use a litterbox and sleep in your lap, as well as tame raccoons that wash their food at the table. But squirrels in the wild are busy with their own agendas and wild raccoons just want to run off with your food, whereas stray, semi-feral, or feral cats will window-shop your house, peering in your windows, and assessing whether you're a good prospect to move in on. They seemingly have had enough domestication to understand that we can be trained to do the hunting for them. I've never had a non-feline wildling raised from a baby, but I can't imagine any other species taking over a household with the same panache and attitude that cats will. Cats just look natural draping themselves here and there in a house, in ways foxes or raccoons or squirrels never could. And I've never had to show any cat the litterbox more than once. They readily move from their outdoor ways of eliminating in any spot with sandy or loose material to eliminating in one sandy spot and signaling you when to freshen it, expecting and demanding it, too. They move from rambler to housekeeper and will change from one to the other and back again all day if we let them go in and out.

Maybe all this is because next to primates, they have a brain and neurological system more like that of humans than any others in the Animal Kingdom, and thus have some natural affinity for us. Information on feline neurology is widely known and available today; I first read of it in Cleveland Amory's *The Cat Who Came for Christmas*.[23] They search the neighborhoods looking for a mind they can meet, among the ones closest to their own. Once they determine that you're the one, they claim you with a mixture of charm and imperiousness. Or maybe it's just that they're smart, heat-seeking, comfort-seeking opportunists who naturally head for our hearths, our food offerings, our ready adulation, and even the intellectual stimulation they get from matching wits with us daily as they move in, take over, and scheme, to put it cynically, to keep us serving their best interests.

There are some who believe cats merely put up with us. But I believe they really want more. In my experience, even if it starts with food, cats develop deep bonds with us and really love us. It may not be possible to know exactly how or why this wild-descended beast will bond with us so deeply. Whatever the exchange, whatever they derive from us, it's in that cat-brain way that is unknowable to us. Aside from momcats to kittens, most meows are directed to us rather than to other cats — meaningful meows as if they were pouring out their heartfelt secrets to us and expecting us to understand, or just voicing greetings full of the joyful intensities of being with us, sitting on our laps purring, reaching out paws to us, sitting beside us, subtly checking with an ear twist or sideways glance to see that we're still there, engaging us in play, turning to us with penetrating and rapt glances as they watch our behavior with even more studiousness than we do theirs. Purring is, according to the literature, never done alone, but is a communication technique often related to attention or stroking; but sometimes it's simply done spontaneously in company. Cats develop a large repertoire of varied vocalizations, each with a differing meaning, and I try to answer what I think each cat-look means. All these things my cats do outside of the kitchen, nowhere near feeding times, knowing they do not have to do these things to be fed.

Yet they stay wild in some ways. It's as if they say, *most of the day we're your cuddlepusses, but when pill time comes around, remember we're wild, and well-armed with teeth and claws.*

As I wrote this, I was kept company by Minx, an old cat who has come to look to me for her every need: the food I carefully measure out to her, the water I hold up for her to drink, the airlift she needs to get on the couch. She even began to turn questioning eyes to me on her way to the litterbox. Yet she'd still smack me if I tried to clip her claws at the wrong moment. The most domesticated cat is never completely tamed to the extent that she will allow you to take liberties with her claws should she decide to be touchy about it.

To some it's a puzzle that these lone hunters, seemingly so independent, will compete for a human's attention when living in a cat group in a house. It appears much more reasonable that wild canines, who are pack hunters, will come to see us as part of a "pack." Behaviorists explain it as the same rivalry for resources being displayed by the independent cat as by a cat in the wild defending its territory from others. But it's also well-known in cat scholarship that when we share our space and live with cats, we exchange odors and come to be regarded as one of their family group.

I'm not sure this explains those cats who have probably had very little human contact and therefore are living an essentially feral life, but who seem to decide to cultivate a human and engineer a takeover of a human's home — and of the human's heart, too. Conversely, a person living in an extremely remote area where cats had been "dumped" by uncaring humans for years told me that the feral domestic cats there had gone irretrievably savage and had killed his tame housecat. The amount of affection a cat will potentially show you may have to do with the amount of human contact it had as a young kitten, and yet, I've seen semi-wild strays become bigger cuddle-pusses than some kittens who were socialized from three or four weeks. Generally speaking, in my experience most cats that grow up feral or wild are difficult to tame and might warm-up slowly to only one person.

I've learned from reading feline behaviorists that if you wait until a kitten is six weeks old to handle them (even in a home with a tame momcat), it will usually never be completely socialized or friendly to just any or all humans. But start interacting between two and four weeks, and you are likely to end up with a fully socialized snuggler who seems fitted to the human home in every way. Just beware of the momcat, whom you must know well when you lightly stroke her very young kittens. She may decide to slice you up if you're not careful, or even if you are. I add this caution because I have heard of a case where a momcat attacked a person she was normally cozy with when a kitten became distressed and started to yell. (In my own experience with Ligeia as a new momcat, she permitted her close human friends to handle her very young kittens.)

Morris explains that the mangled bird or mouse cats bring you, expecting admiration and approval, is akin to the momcat bringing food to her kittens.[24] Could this also be behavior ingrained from ancient times with humans, when a successful rodent hunt around the kitchen would elicit high praise indeed from the cat's humans? Domestic cats are very much like their wild ancestors and their wild contemporaries genetically, yet domestication appears to make some mysterious difference. I've heard tell of bobcat kits who were hand-raised when their mother had vanished; they are reported to recognize those who feed them, and yet they are not "sweet."

Banshee Cat, Carrot Top, and the other forest cats

Our cats were smug and well-fed, and they adjusted to our schedule somewhat by sleeping most of the night. So it was a great surprise to me when I found that sometimes at night, mice had entered and found pathways to evade the cats. The ductwork along the wall of the kitchen leading to the back rooms, which kitten Minx had once used as a secret passageway to sneak back there, was now used by mice going both through it and scrabbling along the top of it. As our storage space became congested, the cats lost good striking space in and around the ductwork. So mice began to enter this House of Cat.

Country mice know how to make good use of cover. I made the startling discovery one year that mice had stored a large amount of dry cat food in a bedroom bookcase, behind the books. They had taken it from the cats' dishes in the kitchen at night; they had stolen it, so to speak, from right under the cats' noses. Since not much gets past my cats, this confounded me and the only explanation seemed to be that the cats had regular sleeping times and the mice knew it. I have to give the mice credit for having some smarts of their own in pulling off the great cat-food heist. Spotty and Kudzu, especially, were no slouches in the mouse-hunting department. Minou was sometimes seen to sit and observe and study a mouse that ran past him — he was a bit of scholar. But all of them would hunt for days once they'd heard a lizard. Even the Booper, who was a persistent lizard hound despite his lax mousing policy.

Our spoiled cats were caught napping and slacking off by the mice, but it requires outdoor cats to really make a dent in the rodent population. Neighbor cats were a help with that. The boldest of them would come up on the porch and look in through the glass. They'd be greeted with hisses from my guys on the indoor side of the glass, and sometimes from my gals, too. In the earlier years, there were three households that had cats between us and the highway. Those cats visited, wanting to know all about what was going on about cats in our house. Cats always seem drawn to and curious about other places that are focal points of cat life, and they are eager to add their marks and spray their scents (peemail) in those locales themselves. Wandering tomcats that looked well-fed and cared for would come by on their "courting and sparking" quests looking for ladies, and also, it would sometimes seem, for lively conversation. They'd come to the door to check ours out and they'd bellow outside awhile, but our girls weren't interested in either romance or small talk with tomcats.

In more recent years, we began to be visited by a huge, fluffy gray-and-white fellow who would roam the woods wailing at night. This sound wasn't the usual tomcat calling-up of females. This was longing and loneliness and lamentation. A possible mating appeal to draw ladies, his wails had the plaintive, eloquent intonations of a medieval singer plucking a lute, pining for lost love. It occurred during times when, we were fairly sure, there were no other pet cats in the area, and no strays had been seen, so we wondered if it was actually about courtship. It may have been about being the only outdoor cat in the area. I called him the Banshee Cat, even though the traditional banshee is female.

Many late nights, I'd hear that mournful nocturne; it didn't even sound catlike at times. The sound would wind about in the woods as he circled the house in the darkness. Daytime, he'd run from me. His head was massive, he was plump, and his coat looked healthy, so we were sure he had a home. He made no moves indicating he was home-hunting, and in fact made himself mostly scarce in the day. He would, however, spray our underbrush right in front of me as he sauntered away, to show me he was boss here. I tried leaving food out, but I never saw Banshee come to eat it. After many years, he just stopped coming.

Minou also had a way of calling at the catdoor at night that was almost as yearning and mournful. It makes me think that cats can have moody times like people do, longings, regrets, thoughts of what might have been, all in their own cat-brain way. Maybe they just miss us terribly when we're separated from them. Maybe it's simply some mysterious cat sadness beyond anything we can ever discern or fathom. It's something that at times, just makes them feel like a good caterwauling cry.

Cats always seemed to know they could come to us for help. Houses closer to the highway had dogs — so did houses farther on down the dirt road, which were even more remote from civilization than us. That was part of the factor in the strays' choosing of us instead of those dog-occupied homes, but it seemed to be something more, too. We were Cat City inside. Our cats were satisfied, comfortable, content, and apparently smug about it all. The wanderers and the abandoned knew that; perhaps smug is an element communicated easily from cat to cat, inspiring some sort of challenge. For example, one summer, there was YardKitty, part chocolate-point Siamese and part tabby, with an "m" on her head, possibly pregnant. She'd approach us but would not get close enough to be touched. But she would roll onto her back with pleasure in the yard when we were out there. We found a home for her with a lady from a local neighborhood who saw the photo we posted at the gas station nearby. The woman thought she was a special cat and was willing to work slowly to tame her, find homes for the kittens, and spay her after the kittens came. By saying she could tell Yardkitty was a "very special cat," this person gave every indication she was one of those Southern rural persons with a "heart of gold." YardKitty was most likely feral or semi-feral, although she may have been an actual wandering yard-cat.

A year later, there was a softly striped, tawny tabby with flaming orange streaks on the backs of her ears. She was a girl, but even so, to me there was no name for her but Carrot Top, after the redheaded comedian. Six months or so old, the kitten started out in Bill's mouse-rich shop, where so many feline passersby dallied, and he fed her there. But she moved to the yard outside the house seeking company to go with the food. This friendly girl was fully socialized with people. She'd wind around our feet when we walked out the door, and she'd park on the doorstep so that when we opened it, she could try to dash in. She almost made it a time or two.

The sudden appearance of an animal so accustomed to humans indicated that she was probably abandoned, furtively pushed out of a car and onto our country road by a heartless former owner. How could anyone do that? She was an excellent mouser, and unfortunately, she caught a ground squirrel that I had enjoyed watching in a certain brushy place on our driveway every day. She was swelled up with pride, and she thought we'd be ecstatic when she placed a portion of it right outside the door. Such "gifts" from one's cats may well indicate a willingness to reciprocally share their catches with us — after all, we're obviously sharing what we "catch" with them. (Ground squirrels, unlike the gray kind that leap through trees, are smaller, browner, and have stripes like chipmunks. They're lawn, garden, and forest-floor dwellers. Local popular opinions differ as to which we actually have here: chipmunks or ground squirrels. I can't find anything called a ground squirrel in the Audubon mammal guide that looks exactly like what we see here.)

We managed to get Carrot Top adopted by neighbors with dogs that had become sleepy old pooches and proved cat tolerance by getting along well with another, newer neighbor's group of three felines. Carrot Top settled in well with them after a few trips back to our place to visit us. Carrot Top's story again illustrates my point that cats really do crave attention and a relationship with people. But Bill didn't want her to become bonded with us, or us with her, since we weren't in a position to adopt her at the time; therefore he continued to feed her only in his shop. She didn't make a home base in the place she was fed. Instead she hung out on our doorstep or in the yard most of the day, trying to entice us to scratch her and pet her when we came out, and to allow her into the house so she could claim us and our attentions, and I'm sure, the companionship of our cats, too. This clever kitten had found a house in the woods full of cats with two big humans in attendance. She knew she was in the right place. She didn't group the mangled chipmunk with her food at the shop, but rather she brought it to the door for us to see, or maybe even to feed to us. Show off!

After we placed Carrot Top with neighbors down the road, my heart was sad with regret. I'd grown very fond of the girl with bright red ears, but we were at catpacity at the time. She kept coming back down to visit but eventually settled in nicely where she was. They renamed her Tiger Lily, very apt as that is a bright orange flower!

Then there was Mister Tom. He was a roving black-and-white tuxedo tomcat. Our neighbor Gale, who had Minou's mother, a small black cat who also visited us at times, fed him whenever he came by and named him. Mister Tom was one of the few local wandering cats that favored and cultivated a household other than ours; it may originally have had something to do with the two un-spayed stray female cats on the hilltop, a huge draw for an intact tom. The time he spent in our woods was scant in comparison. He ranged throughout the forest and was seen by the neighbors at the very edge of it, where a lakeside community bordered the woods. Mister Tom would meander by our place over the years to say *hey there, meow y'all,* and we'd talk to him and pet him and I'd walk with him down our road.

Once, I pulled a tick off his neck for him with the flea comb, a huge tick engorged with blood that had been there a long time. To do this I held a folded up paper towel lightly around the tick and slid the flea comb carefully onto the tick's head parts, pulling gently against the tick's body. Ticks might burst if full and I didn't want the blood to go everywhere, hence the paper towel. I'd wear plastic gloves now, but even with gloves, don't try this at home. Much better to take the cat to the vet to have the tick removed; they are better equipped to make sure they remove all of the tick's head. I could tell by the way Mister Tom looked up at me that he understood what I had done and was grateful. He was very friendly.

Another time, when Bill was sitting with Gale up at his house on the porch with Mr. Tom there beside them, Mr. Tom suddenly shot off and ran about a hundred yards to snatch some mouse or vole or critter that he had detected from afar. It was, Bill said, just like watching a lion spring off after a gazelle on a wildlife show.

Bill believed Mr. Tom was the father of both Minou and Kudzu, and that our two white-footed boys were half brothers. I wasn't so sure about Kudzu, who was, I thought, from the cat tribe with the neon shamrock eyes up the highway at the gas station. They had haunted the garbage dumpster next to the kudzu patch, and then vanished into whatever shadows and vines lay in the gullies beyond it, fitting my intuition in naming him Kudzu. Later, those cats hung out in the little neighborhood behind the ravine after the county went to curbside garbage pick-up. But we knew that Minou's mom had definitely been on Mister Tom's route.

Eventually Mister Tom started hanging around at our place. He came up on the porch, laid down, and didn't move much. Another day passed, and he was on the back of the car, with sadness and trouble in his eyes. Over several days I went out and talked to him as he showed up and sat, immovable, around our yard. Gale was out of town working again, having left Bill in charge of his place, so Bill took Mr. Tom to our vet. He was an old cat, and the vet diagnosed a huge tumor in his abdomen. When Gale came back soon afterward, he took Mr. Tom back to our vet, hoping that surgery would help him. He was very fond of Mr. Tom. But the cat was in pain and dying, and at his age surgery wasn't a good option. It was time to help him move on. Our hilltop neighbor was really sad about losing him. It hurt our hearts, too; it was another one of those sorrowful times. He had come to us when his main person was out of town, knowing he would get the comfort and help he needed. Maybe Mr. Tom had been watching us and our cats all these years. Maybe he'd assessed the way I talked to him and gave him pats from time to time and considered that I'd removed the tick. He made the decision, when he felt himself becoming ill, that ours was the house to go to for help. He was a wise, old, roaming woods cat.

Cat behaviorists say that cats will hide when seriously ill and/or dying, out of the instinct to disguise vulnerability in the wild. I know this is true because I have seen severely ill kitties hide themselves. But there are always exceptions, and Mr. Tom proved that. He had acres and acres of woodland to conceal himself in, and he chose to make himself very visible near our door to get help.

We had moved into this neighborhood about the same time as many of the neighbors. Before that time, there were only one or two households, and the forest was patrolled by a succession of stray, feral, and semi-feral cats. This helped to keep the rodent population down. Once we arrived, we began to take in these cats, or tame them and place them in homes. The rat patrol, formerly living on the edge, now had cushy assignments in various homes, some in our neighborhood. The fact that they were all spayed and neutered reduced their numbers. Our decision to keep our own kitties inside further limited the number of cats outside, while greatly pleasing our bird enthusiast friends, and even though most of the neighbors let their felines roam outside, that wasn't enough to put a check on the mouse population. So we began to swap humane mousetraps back and forth amongst the neighbors. They make the cutest little mouse-sized safe traps these days, though sometimes a larger size is needed for plus-sized mice. Our farthest neighbors had one, so Bill walked through the woods "as the crow flies" to borrow it one winter.

Before the days of YardKitty and Carrot Top, for awhile there had been a dark cloud over the outdoor cat world in the forest. In the country, there is an expectation that dogs will run free. But once, neighbors with dogs took in a stray yellow pooch that turned out to be a cat-killing dog, and he led their other dogs to chase after and attack cats. Almost all the outdoor cats living nearby were killed by the dogs. Another neighbor's cats began hanging around our place to keep away from the dogs, staying out in Bill's shop and on our doorstep, until the neighbor moved to town and took his cats with him. We noticed that we didn't get as many cat visitors as we had before the bad dog days. We seldom heard the air-raid sirens at night that meant our boys were confronting a strange cat through the window glass. I became more vigilant about the door, dreading that ours might slip out. The worst of the killings had happened before we knew about them, preoccupied with matters of work and illness as we were.

Overall, the mouse population soared. Dogs seem to naturally belong in the country but when there's more than one, they can become a wolf pack that will kill cats or, at the very least, keep them away. I believe cats should be kept inside for their safety, but there are many strays and cat owners who will let theirs roam, and those cats will greatly reduce the mice problem if there are no deterrents to feline presence. Although we generally tried to rescue and relocate mice, I recognize the fundamental truth of this predator/prey balance. Mouse-catching by cats has kept humans from being overrun by rodents throughout history and undoubtedly remains a huge factor in reducing stratospheric rodent numbers.

I like dogs and I respect the bonds that my dog-loving friends have with their pooches. But if you live in the country, the local cats need to both thrive and feel encouraged to hang out at your place, or you will have mice. During the cat-killing dog years, we must have caught twenty mice in the house in just one week of an especially mousey winter. This is my anecdotal observation and not scientifically proven mouse population data, as scientist Bill, a.k.a. Dr. Photon, hastens to remind me. But several years later when another neighbor moved away and took his cats, leaving Bill to look after his empty house, Bill reported to me that the house had been taken over by mice — another unscientific observation, but one I have great confidence in.

Eventually the cat-killing dog was run over on the highway by a car, right after Christmas 2002. And I do believe that Carrot Top, who came along about a year-and-a-half after that, was a much-needed addition to the neighborhood by that time. I'm sad for any animal that gets hit by a car, but I was glad to see cats return to the surrounding area. Since they belonged to households where they were indoor/outdoor pets, they helped keep down the mice and were probably safer if they roamed near our neighborhood, which is more animal-friendly to them than wandering elsewhere. With the addition of Carrot Top to one neighborhood household, and the aforementioned new three-cat household, we had fewer mice come in, even though we were several hundred yards away from both locales. We indeed affirmed that it takes outdoor cats to keep the mouse population down. Having cats inside is only the second line of defense against the little mouse twerps that make it to the inside, and indoor cats are not population control at the mouse source. Many people use poisons against mice and rats, which cannot be done if you have cats, as the cats will get poisoned from catching and consuming the poisoned rodents; but more rodents will always come in to the house or the barn or the silo. They're breeding outside, in the woods and trees and in underground tunnels. Using pesticides also potentially poisons any wild predators that consume the rodents. The cat's rodent controlling abilities are still greatly needed in the modern world.

A wolf comes to Cat City

We both liked dogs but lacked knowledge of them. I have joked that they are really wolves, and in a group, they are "wolfpack lite." But in the mid-1990s we gained new canid experience when an actual wolf came to live up the road from us!

Really, it did sound rather romantic: a half-wolf, half-dog hybrid. She was a likable creature; she was friendly, and she was a beautiful animal, looking like a young Siberian husky. She had one blue eye and one gold eye. Watching her ask for treats by stretching up and gently placing paws on someone's back made me smile. She was a well-socialized wolf. Even another neighbor's old lab found her charming, and he followed her down to our house and sat happily in the yard while Miss Wolf went denning under our house in our open crawl space. I could hear her moving under the floor but lost visual contact with the cunning lady wolf for awhile. So the half-wolf roamed the woods of the whole neighborhood, as all the dogs did, as wolves do, and she loved to run, as Siberian Huskies are known to do.

Eventually she disappeared, rumored to have heeded the "call of the wild"[25] and run off with the coyotes. She may have fallen for a handsome coyote dude, as dogs sometimes do according to the literature. I admired that animal and present the story of our acquaintance with wolfie-kind in a bemused spirit. But I do have to quarrel with the breeders of dog/wolf hybrids. Wolves are really not pets, just as various wild species of cats both large and small are not pets, with the exception of *Felis catus,* also known as *Felis domesticus,* the common house cat. Gentle dogs, mutts as well as purebreds, make the best pets or companions for humans; they have been bred until they are far removed from their wolf or wolf-like ancestors for good reasons. Thousands of years it took to domesticate dogs, now they're trying to go back. The work of taking a wild animal and making it domestic has already been done, and I question the need to backtrack. Another point against keeping hybrids as pets is that hybrid animals have not gone through the studies of rabies disease progression that allows us to confine dogs, cats, and ferrets that have bitten humans for ten days of observation before hopefully being declared rabies-free. Local laws regarding possible rabies exposure will vary, but if a hybrid animal bites someone, the animal will probably not be allowed that grace period, but will be euthanized immediately for brain testing.

A family of "cat whisperers"

We met cats everywhere who needed our assistance, and not just at our doorstep. One day I waited in the car in Kroger's parking lot while Bill ran in the store for groceries. I heard a kitten yowling in fear somewhere among the parked cars. I got out and started searching. Another woman had heard it and was looking, too. Suddenly she reached up under the wheel housing of a parked car and pulled out a kitten covered with mud and gray fur. She asked if I would take it and I said yes. She handed me the kitten saying, "She's going to get you muddy."

"That's okay," I replied and clasped the kitten close to me, becoming instantly mud-covered myself. I got back in the car and waited for Bill. Somehow it hadn't occurred to either of us to ask if the owner of the car had lost the kitten, which may have been the most likely explanation as cats will climb under nearby car hoods and into car mechanisms. On the other hand, if they didn't check their yard kittens before driving off, how responsible could they be? When Bill returned to the car, we took the kitten to our vet, who is wonderful about helping us place stray animals. She helped us find a home for the gray, and another home later for a found golden-tiger kitten. Later, she helped us find adopters for an entire litter of six black- and gray-spotted kittens from Bill's parents' yard in the southern part of the state.

During Mom's childhood, my grandmother took in a white cat they called Topaz. Years later, living in Maryland, Mom had taken in a male tabby she named Skye for an island in Scotland and cooked fish for him. She would later tell me, "Oh, he was pretty, he had these black bands on his legs." She never did get around to having him neutered. That was back in the days when the thinking was different, and she said she didn't want to "take his manhood away from him." So he was an indoor/outdoor cat who went out on rounds. One day he came back sopping wet, making Mom laugh. She thought someone had splashed a bucket of cold water on him; back in those days it was the way to cool the ardor of a tomcat who was after your girl kitty. One day, though, Skye never came back. He was not with her very long, and due to our hectic business I hadn't even been able to travel up there and meet him before he vanished. Mom never got over it, and when she moved down to Alabama, she never wanted another pet and the potential heartache of loss.

But soon, a momcat appeared with a litter of five under her house, reported by neighbors to have been abandoned by students. The cat got an occasional handout from various houses. One neighbor fed her on the windowsill. She would bring one kitten at a time up there until all had eaten a share. At first, Mom wanted nothing to do with the cat and kittens; she thought they would go away. But she didn't object when I began taking food out to them. Soon, Mom was taking the food out occasionally herself. One day when we walked outside together, the cat jumped up and came trotting towards me. Because the cat had gone to me first, not to her, Mom looked hurt, completely crestfallen. I could have predicted Mom would react that way; it was almost like the smart animal knew what I'd been plotting all along! I handed Mom the food and encouraged her to give it to the cat. Long story short, Mom kept the mother cat, a softly shaded gray-and-orange patched calico, along with one of the kittens, a silvery-solid gray male. They were all spayed and neutered. Our vet helped us place the other four kittens. There was quite a range of colors and patterns of kittens from this beautiful, dilute calico momcat. Two of the females were calicos, with the same clearly defined patches in soft colors as Callie, the mom, but with much more white on them. One was a medium-length furred, silver-gray tabby with a dark spot on its nose, a girl and just cute beyond belief. The other male kitten, besides Mom's solid gray named Tom, was a solid-gray tux with white feet and vest.

Mom was back in the cat business, big time. The other kittens had tamed up readily but the gray male had remained aloof, essentially a feral cat who had been past the prime age for socializing when found as a kitten. But my mother is a great tamer of small, wild felines. Long before she could pet or stroke or have any real contact with Tom, she called him "the sweetest cat." He never became a lap cat, but she always thought of him as a sweetie anyway. Mom would tell me, "He's a honey." Thus, my mother's tightly organized home slowly became the refuge of wild little felines, the ones who went *oh boo hiss* when originally approached by humans. There were a number of fast food restaurants close to Mom's neighborhood, and whenever she partook of their food, she noticed that her former strays always wanted some. "You see, they've eaten that before," she'd say. She figured they had been raiding those establishments' dumpsters on a nightly basis when they had been on the streets.

When Callie had been outside with her kittens, a tiger male was hanging out with her, just lying there and watching the kittens, with, I'm tempted to say, pride in his eye. I don't know if they were his kittens or if he was just one of those kitten-mentoring tomcats. Mom invented an on-the-spot narrative about this cat being Callie's boyfriend who had helped keep her warm over the winter. "He was nice and furry!" was her ending line. (I so wish I could have caught her performance on tape! A hectic life, a limited budget, and some problems with memory have taken so much away from me.) Callie graced the house with soft colors and a sweet disposition, heralding an age of even more cats becoming part of our family. You know how family members sometimes get their names mixed up? One day I accidentally called Mom "Callie."

Several years later, at Mom's house, two adult cats showed up, completely spooky and feral. According to the neighbors, they were from Callie's first litter on the streets. Winnie was a very un-dilute calico, with sharply delineated patches of intense orange and deep black — a gorgeous cat. The other kitty was a very pale solid orange or cream, who looked like walking moonlight as he made his way down the narrow path between the house and the fence, coming to be fed. Mom named this cat Mary for Mary, Queen of Scots, but then one day I caught a glimpse of the back end and saw that cat was no lady. So Mom renamed him Bothwell for an acquaintance of the Scottish queen. Her intention was to take both of them in, but sadly, as happens with so many street cats, Bothwell vanished after a few weeks. But Mom did manage to get Winnie, the calico daughter of her calico, into the house. Winnie had two black-and-white spotted kittens with her when she was found, and our vet assisted with placing those in homes.

Tom, the gray kitten from Callie's first litter, never became a lap cat and rarely even let Mom pet him. But she continued to call him a "really sweet cat," and this would also be true of Winnie, who had no human contact and had been living a feral street life for a long time. Mom could not pick Winnie up, or hold Tom for more than a few moments, so when either one went to the vet, Mom would buy a fish sandwich from a fast food restaurant nearby and "bait" the carrier with it.

Mom innovated a way of scooping a litterbox that I've never seen anywhere else. Instead of using a slotted scooper and removing only solid waste, she used a large, garden-style scooper with which she could also remove liquid waste. Even with non-clumping litter, the urine formed enough of a mass to be lifted out this way. I began to do this too and found that I learned to angle it so that I wouldn't get too much clean litter along with the waste. For those who find this unwieldy with the poop, you could use two different scoopers. I've found I can shake the clean litter out of the garden scooper without losing too much of the solids, though I may have to use several scooping motions to remove each deposit of feces. The scooper can be cleaned thoroughly with damp paper towels after use.

Mom's cat adventures in her relatively new neighborhood included a friendly neighbor cat owned by amiable students, a huge, fine black cat named Chainsaw. When the students got a puppy, the cat disappeared, only to be seen later in the yard of a posh house down the street, wearing a new collar. He recognized his original people and head-butted and played with them but showed no inclination to go home with them. Sadly, they left him at his new home. Chainsaw just didn't intend to share household with a dog.

There would be other strays from Mom's neighborhood in need of home placement, and our vet, bless her, helped time and time again. Maybe it was those unseen lines of cat communication again: *Cat people here, the best on the block, your gateway to a new house with your own people, if they don't take you in themselves, they'll find someone who will.* Or maybe it was just that my mother's garage was the best shelter in the neighborhood for mom-cats. The next cat to take up residence there was a friendly, expectant white female cat with longish fur, most likely another cast-off from students. Again the vet helped us place her kittens, and the momcat too. Another year, one day there appeared in the garage a black-and-white polydactyl with an elegant, thin white blaze down her nose and simply remarkable cat feet: both front feet had an extra toe, and in addition, there was an extraneous toe growing sideways on the top of one front foot. This animal could be handled and had a sweet disposition, indicating she had probably once had a home but had been abandoned.

I thought of her as "Ms. Black and White Amazing Foot." The vet examined her feet and found that maintenance only required regular claw clipping to prevent the top-of-the-paw toenail from growing into the foot. The clinic staff named her Diamond for the diamond-shaped spot on her chest. After being spayed, she went to a good home. She was a sweet cat that I wish we could have kept, but by that time, Mom had her two cats, and we had our four. Diamond the polydactyl had come with two five-weeks-old kittens, a girl and a boy. The girl was a tabby who was a regular kitten in every way, and the vet found a home for her. The boy was slightly floofy, sleek and all black, except for a white tuft on his throat, with longer tail fur like a dark plume. He had a rare genetic trait. He was not going to be easy to give away, so the end result was that Mom kept him herself. She brought him home, hand-carried him into the house, and set him down carefully. Intensive veterinary observation determined that he was not in pain, and he could have a good quality of life with special care.

Mom said the perky kitten was "one of Alabama's good old boys," and named him Good Old Boy against my advice. Mom was from a time when it was a positive term and did not have the unpleasant connotations of sinister, small-town insular corruption and cronyism that it does today. She didn't understand the shift in meaning. Anyway, Good Old Boy turned out to be his own cat, who never networked.

I have to think the shift of meaning is of a somewhat elitist origin. "The good-old-boy network" really should be something like "crony network." The shift of a formerly positive expression, used only in the South, into something negative nationwide occurred, in my opinion, partly because of stereotyping of Southerners. Cronyism does happen nationwide and no doubt, worldwide. The use is so widespread now that it has lost all good connotations, and I'm not faulting those who readily toss it out that way. Bill still says that when he talks to rural people, he engaged in "some good ol' boy talk about dogs and tornadoes" to help facilitate conversation; in other words, he uses the phrase in the traditional way, as a fairly benign term. The best thing I've heard about "good old boys" lately is attributed to Billy Carter,[26] who wrote that a redneck drives his pick up truck around drinking beer and then throws his empty cans out the window, while the good old boy rides around drinking beer and throws the cans in a sack on the seat beside him, to dispose of or recycle later.

Mom recalls a day she picked up Good Old Boy at the vet. When a staff member called out to her that "Good Old Boy" would be out in a minute, every young man waiting there went alert and all eyes went to the door to the back to see what animal had that name. Mom says they were expecting a big ol' dog and were surprised when the animal turned out to be such a small cat!

Anyway when it comes to cronyism, Good Old Boy turned out to be misnamed. He stood alone; he did not like other male cats, or any other cats at all. He was not a team player. He was not "one of the boys." He did not network. You get nowhere fast in cronyism if you are always trying to bite and scratch the cronies.

He was a small cat, and when he would step over from a nearby table onto Mom for petting, she always said "He's one of the big cats." She felt he had a complex about being small and needed to hear that he was big. He was one of our most arboreal kitties ever, climbing anything he got his paws on. And he moved faster than other cats did, faster than you'd ever think he could, and certainly faster than me.

The joys and challenges of an RH cat

Normally cats have eighteen toes, five on each front foot, including the "dewclaw" toe higher up on the inside of each forelimb and four toes on each back foot. Front dewclaws don't reach the ground when the cat is in the standing position, and none of the hind toes are dewclaws. Polydactyl cats have extra toes, usually one or two on the "thumb," or dewclaw side, of the front feet. Sometimes there are extra toes, but no dewclaw at all. Extra hind toes are less common and usually only occur if there are extra front toes, and sometimes a greater number of toes are present. According to "Polydactylism (Extra Toes)," by Dr. Arnold Plotnick of the Manhattan Cat Specialists, the most toes ever found on one cat was thirty-two. The gene expresses in various ways and toes may be incompletely formed, and/or claws may tend to become ingrown, but these are considered minor problems. The most common form of polydactyly is considered an anomaly and not a deformity.[27]

According to Sarah Hartwell at Messybeast.com, polydactyls were considered good luck by sailors and taken onboard ships. They were believed to have better balance on ships during storms, and also to be better mousers.[28] Indeed, I think their popularity with seafarers may have had a more pedestrian origin than ideas about luck; the more toes, the more claws, the better to skewer rats with. Some owners report that polydactyls use their extra toes with great dexterity. Having ocean travelers as ancestors, they are more common in the United States in seacoast areas and lands closer to waterfronts. (I'm not surprised to see an occasional polydactyl here, as we are about a six-hours drive from the Gulf Coast.) They are thought to have begun arriving as early as the 1600s, and there are many on the East Coast, especially in New England. Although apparently more numerous in the United States, they occur in Europe, too. According to Hartwell, they are found in Europe, Asia, and Britain, especially among Celtic-area cats and in southwestern Britain, where ships set sail for America. In Norway, they are known as Ship's Cats.[29]

Several genes cause polydactyly, and Mom's black kitten had a rare and more disabling expression of one of those genes. His forelegs were affected as well as the feet. This is known as radial hypoplasia (RH), when the radius, a forearm bone, is underdeveloped, or agenesis radius when the radius has failed to generate at all. Sometimes the forelegs are shorter than usual. Good Old Boy had fairly long front legs, but they were bent at an incorrect angle at the elbow. The back legs of these cats are normal lengths, though, and this kitten's hind feet had six toes each. On each of those hind feet, one of the extra digits was a dewclaw toe, located higher up on the inside of the foot and helping to make his hind feet fan- or wedge-shaped.

I've seen photos of other cats with RH on the Internet, most of which appear to have broadly shaped hind feet with extra toes. Good Old Boy often sat up on his haunches in a squirrel-like posture, as the literature describes. He had to walk on the sides of his front legs, with the front of his body in a lower position than is usual for cats; he did not have a typical gait. With his hind end thrust high, he was in a sort of crouch. The sitting-up stance is a compensatory position that takes strain off the spine and weak front legs. Early in kittenhood, he was referred to a veterinary orthopedic specialist, who examined him thoroughly, observed him walking, and determined that he was not in pain and that his mobility was sufficient. For those reasons, the vet decided against surgery to support and straighten the front legs. Surgery for RH was a special interest of this vet, but he thought the surgery-related risks were too great when balanced against the kitten's ability to get around fairly well. (Mom was prepared to spring for the surgery if the vet suggested it.)

During the time frame Mom found Good Old Boy, most of these kinds of kittens were euthanized when found, which in my opinion was needless. Those that are more mildly affected, like Good Old Boy, can be cared for. According to personal histories on the Internet, RH cats with an even greater degree of impairment have been nurtured in homes successfully. The vet specialist used bandaging to support Good Old Boy's front limbs, but only briefly. One evening, when the kitten climbed into my lap, I knew immediately that he felt way too hot compared to any other cat I had ever snuggled. I knew he was burning up with fever, but Mom didn't think so — we all know about trying to tell our mothers something! But fortunately, I convinced her to take him to the local vet the next day, who unwrapped the leggings and found abrasion, infection, and high fever. That was the end of wrapping his legs; the vets found that Good Old Boy's forelegs strengthened as he grew. Cats have very strong muscles.

Back in 1995, the ideas of keeping RH cats and doing surgery to correct their legs were both relatively new. I feel the vet made the right call about Good Old Boy. Surgery is now more common, and my opinion is still that it may be unnecessary. However, every case is different and individuals who have these kittens need to consult with veterinarians on a case-by-case basis. They should seek out those vets who have experience with the condition. Never accept a recommendation of euthanasia from a vet who is unfamiliar with RH cats, or who decides to euth quickly without a thorough evaluation and the benefit of thought. This is inappropriate with the possible exception of only the most extreme cases. A veterinary orthopedic consultation would be a good way to go whenever possible.

Good Old Boy was a great favorite with the vet's staff when he went in for his neuter surgery and while there for recuperation, he was invited to share in their lunches. He happily munched on food from all the best restaurants in town: Chinese, Mexican, and home-style. Mom carpeted her house throughout to give him better traction as he was more prone to slip on a smooth surface. We watched his legs carefully for any sign of abrasion and often lifted him down from high places. His weight was carefully controlled, as an overweight condition would tax his weaker front legs. Fortunately, he was a smaller-sized cat, which was an advantage for him.

This amazing animal was adventurous and sometimes more active than Mom's other cats, getting around almost as quickly as they did. He didn't know the concept of limitation and even somehow found a route to the top of the refrigerator via the stovetop. We'd find him sitting up there, smug and smirking, all legs tucked underneath him. He was actually the only one of Mom's cats to ever summit the refrigerator, though of course he had to be helped back down. Mom tried to block off his route up the fridge, but his hind legs, with their huge, wedge-shaped, six-toed paws had become strong, making him a powerful jumper. He ascended to kitchen counters, couch backs, and the dining table. We'd see him spring upward onto a surface in a great leap, relying on hind-leg thrust. Like many cats, he was arboreal; he liked a high space to sleep on, and he never hesitated to ascend anything in the room he could get his paws on, claiming peak areas for himself.

If I saw him looking to climb up on something and I was fast enough I would lift him, sometimes saying "Upsa kitty," a variant of "Upsa daisy," a phrase I heard in childhood. I'd have to scoot to get there in time, though! We would help him get up and down, but he adapted remarkably to his differently working legs. Instead of easing the front legs down and landing first on them, bringing the hind legs down later in the common cat manner of descending, he used his strong back legs to propel himself into the air in a forward motion, so that he would land on all fours, thus distributing the weight more evenly so that he wouldn't overburden his front legs. I saw him bump his face doing that, since his head was in a lower position than those of other cats as he descended, so Mom and I both rushed to help him down whenever possible. But he would lounge up there on top of the refrigerator, casting big-cat eyes down upon us all, like a leopard up a tree. *Ha ha, I dare y'all to try to get me down.*

At twelve years old, he was still running and playing in his own way and he was beautiful, with the elongated lines of his panther-like muzzle and his

pale gold eyes and his shiny, mid-length black fur. His floofy tail was a wonder. He moved with astonishing speed. If a fly got in he would jump for it
repeatedly in mighty, twisting leaps. The action was so fast, and he was so
frenzied, that Mom and I could not contain him. The best we could do was
try to shoo the fly back outside. But he never showed any sign of distress
after a fly encounter. Fortunately, flies didn't get in very often.

His adaptations highlight the resourcefulness and ingenuity of the feline
species. Often staying by Mom night and day, when she returned after having
been out, he would scramble to the door and roll over on his back, roll back
up, and tumble about in her path as she entered. He was very adventurous
and was always one to run out the door if he got the slightest chance. Mom
and I had to recapture him on several occasions. She called him her "beautiful, black, fox-faced cat." She also said, "He's a honey." I would later see on
the Internet that several other cats with RH have the same long, narrow muzzle as Good Ole Boy. But by being aggressive with other cats, he eventually
came to be called "Stinkpot" by me. "Stinkpot" is an old term from my
mother's and my grandmother's repertoire of expressions, used way back in
my childhood and likely from New England. It's affectionately meant, denot-
ing naughtiness of children and pets. Oddly, the only definitions I found for it
online are unpleasant ones, and apparently, a stinkpot was also once a weapon. But the term wasn't used that way when I was a child; it was more like,
"well, you little stinker, you."

Despite his relatively small size and narrowed muzzle, Good Old Boy
had some of the biggest front fangies I've ever seen in a cat. Unfortunately
for any of us who had not yet learned to be careful around him, especially
when he was riled up at another kitty, he was a cat who never learned not to
bite family. It was also impossible to keep him from going up on the dining
table. He accomplished this by first ascending to one of the chairs, and then it
was just a quick hop to the lateral vantage point from which he kept up a
close surveillance of the plates of anyone dining there. Stinkpot! When Bill
later took over the cooking in Mom's house, Good Old Boy would sit on the
dining table and watch him cook. Watching this plucky little animal cope
with his differing mobility gave me a lift in dealing with my own increasing
limitations.

My more recent reflections are that Good Old Boy reached an advanced
age and had a good quality of life. I am seeing more kittens with RH placed
up for adoption and I want to reassure potential adopters that they are not so
very difficult to care for. You must watch the front legs carefully for any sign
of abrasion and tend the litterbox frequently, especially in a multi-cat household. These cats are not quite as agile about avoiding what's already in the

box as others are. But you want to keep a tidy box anyway, and Mom was the fastest of anyone I ever saw to remove any and all waste from the cat trays. RH cats must, of course, be adopted into indoor homes only, as they are unlikely to survive outdoors.

Cats with Good Old Boy's condition can usually thrive when placed in good homes. Cats with three legs, two legs, blind cats, and those with many other disabilities have fared well when placed with the right persons. The key to success is really supportive care from a committed owner. With a vet involved to evaluate potential life quality, I'm always in favor of giving a special-needs animal a chance at a good life with a caring person. Good Old Boy and other kittens with RH have turned up in the random breeding population of strays and ferals from time to time. However, in the 1990s there were allegations on the Internet of attempts to deliberately produce cats with the exact forearm bone deficiency that Good Old Boy had, through breeding cats affected with RH to each other. There was a worldwide storm of protest among cat enthusiasts and animal advocates. Near as I can tell, this practice is not ongoing today. I, too, object to any such attempts to breed these animals, who have little chance for survival outside in a natural setting without human assistance. This would be a cruel error in breeding programs. I cannot imagine why this would ever be done. Hartwell notes that often this gene produces forelegs so weak and short that the unfortunate cat cannot even use them for locomotion.[30]

Even the most mildly affected cats have to use adaptive stances, such as resting their chest on the lower rungs of chairs with their front legs dangling over to approximate a normal, comfortable cat position and rest the front legs. Although Good Old Boy developed a special mode of descent that was mostly bump-free, some of these cats are observed as having rough landings in which the chest or chin takes the brunt of landing, because the forelegs are too weak to absorb the shock. They require assistance or special ramps in getting down from high places. When these cats are found in stray and feral populations, or turn up in the litters of owned cats, they should be vet-evaluated and placed in homes if pain-free, and spayed and neutered to prevent the problem gene from being passed on. Prospective owners need to be educated in the special needs these cats have, but they can and should be cared for. However, animals aren't novelties and should not be bred to produce this defective skeletal structure, which lacks a main forearm bone, or any other trait that results in such a serious disability. If there's any purpose in breeding cats in a world glutted with random-bred kittens, it should only be to improve cat physiology and quality of life, not deteriorate it.

The Internet has changed the nature of communication, and I now see concern on social media because more and more cats with RH are being placed for adoption. Sometimes called "squittens" because they often sit up in a squirrel-like posture, their greater frequency of adoption and online presence has made some people still think they are being bred. That would certainly be wrong if true, but I can't find any evidence. I am convinced they just show up from time to time amidst the polydactyl population, as described in the literature. They are often unknown to the general public, because for a time, they were euthanized upon discovery or, if born feral, they were unlikely to survive in the outdoors with no special assistance. I have seen no statistics as to how often they appear in the feral cat population, and while my feel for this is that they are relatively unusual, I do see more and more RH cats on social media with their own fan pages. One would think they would be more common in seacoast areas, as polydactyls are. We are a few hundred miles from the Gulf Coast but our vet has only seen one other besides Good Old Boy. (That kitten was white while Good Old Boy was black, but I've seen RH cats in a number of coat colors online. I'm sure the white kitty got a good home.) Recently, another RH kitten turned up in Tuscaloosa, an orange and white; that kitty was social networked and placed in a home.

The greater visibility of these kittens on the Internet has also led to some emotional opinions that are not always based in research. These cats have not have been "released" into the population from breeding programs; they are simply more common in the gene pool than was known previously. Again, the fact that they would have been routinely euthanized at an early age in previous times meant that the public was unaware of them, as we were until Good Old Boy showed up in Mom's yard. Feral-born RH kittens are unlikely to survive in the wild; they have difficulty milk treading effectively, and if they do survive that stage, they are less able to run away or defend themselves. According to Stephen Budiansky in *The Character of Cats*, the population of polydactyls is roughly less than ten percent of the total cat numbers in most areas, in accordance with a general pattern of novel feline colors and traits.[31] Cats with RH, even adults, should not be released back into outdoor feral colonies if they are feral, but rather cared for inside a home. They are just not likely to survive outdoors.

Not just cat lovers: Our dog rescue adventures

We rescued dogs too. There was the black-and-white puppy back in 1989, and years later in the woods, at different times, two more puppies showed up that we also rescued. The first time, I heard a strange truck motor from the turnaround at sunset one cold February day, and I thought that someone was exiting who was lost, who had turned onto our road by mistake. But hours later there was the sound of a frightened, wailing dog — they had driven down our road to abandon him, to drop him in the woods to fend for himself. We found a home for this little black pup who looked like he might be a Labrador Retriever; the pup and I had started to bond, but our life was just too complicated to keep him. When the next puppy showed up, several years later, our vet assisted us in placing the little yellow half-Chow.

The most satisfying dog story is of an old, round beagle that showed up one long-ago summer and had been hanging around a neighbor's house for days. He had a collar, but no one could figure out where he came from. The neighbor walked down our way with the dog following to talk to Bill at his shop, and I walked out there from the house. I approached the beagle carefully since I didn't have much experience with canines. The pooch accepted my pats with one hand on his head, while with the other I worked the collar around on his neck. Up came a brass plate with a name and phone number. A phone call was made and the neighbor drove with the beagle down a road behind the little gas station to take him home. When let out of the car, the dog took off running to greet his elderly owner, who came running to meet him, equally overjoyed. This happy reunion was the kind of heart-melting ending that those of us who try to assist lost and abandoned animals just love.

Friends also took in stray and abandoned animals. LaDonna and Davey, visiting the Civil War battlefield in Shiloh, Tennessee, were startled when they saw a cat on the road near the Peach Orchard. They stopped the car and opened the door. A seal-point Siamese stepped towards them and hopped into the car. She came home with them and became their cat. I assume she had been abandoned in that remote place, or maybe she had escaped from some traveler's car. Named KittyWitty, she once helped rescue a kitten who had climbed forty feet up in a huge tree in the backyard. Davey put a ladder up and said, "Come down," and as he tells it, the kitten said *Naaahh*. KittyWitty saw the kitten, climbed up the ladder and on up into the tree, said *Mrow mrow,* and began to back down. The kitten then, seeing the way, also backed down. I would one day witness myself this exact kind of kitten mentoring by an adult cat, who was a stranger to the kitten.

I understand that people don't always have the means to keep an animal. Speaking from this region, the Southeast is still the nation's poorest area. But I don't understand abandonment. Some people may think cats can live on their own, but that just isn't always true. The strays we've rescued have been extremely scrawny and clearly weren't getting enough sustenance on their own. They are also not so independent they don't care if they have people or not, as has become more and more sharply evident over the years,. Whenever our cats know we are both leaving the house for a time, they give me searching, displeased looks. Cats gravitate toward people and they have feelings that get hurt when they are shoved out of someone's life. I don't need to elaborate on dogs' feelings about being thrown out, as they are less subtle and more demonstrative than cats, and dogs are known for their frantic and sometimes house-destroying reactions to loneliness. You'll see cats do have their ways of letting you know if you're watching for it carefully, and they are just as traumatized by abandonment as dogs.

I would do everything I could to find an animal a good home before taking him or her to a shelter. I've never had to resort to a shelter, but I understand that overwhelming circumstances may make finding new homes impossible for some people. For those unable to keep an animal or find it a new home, the shelters are there. When they can take the animals, the no-kill rescue groups that have sprung up all over the nation are a much better option than shelters that euthanize.

Short-sighted local animal laws

Sometimes municipalities make serious errors regarding animal issues. In the late 1990s, people in Tuscaloosa whose bird feeders were being raided by free-roaming cats complained to the city government. There were also a few complaints about cats that were scratching cars. I am, as I previously said, in sympathy with those who wish to protect birds, but these seemed like matters to be talked out between the bird-watching neighbors and the cat-owning neighbors; the best solution for all concerned would have been keeping those specific cats inside, and finding homes for the offending strays.

Instead, the city enacted an ordinance that infringes on the personal freedom of residents by restricting each household to owning three cats only and saying that it's illegal for cats to prey on birds. The latter evoked many tart letters to the local newspaper, and some wisecracks by me to my feline ornithologists whenever they looked out the window at birds flitting around and chattered their teeth at them. "In town, what you're doing is illegal," I admonished them. But I find the first part equally ridiculous and counter-productive. Whereas there are cases of persons who keep too many animals, resulting in poor living conditions, responsible owners with the means to keep them properly can and do keep way more than three cats in healthy surroundings. The way the animals are kept is the key factor, not their numbers.

Since so many responsible owners keep cats inside these days, all the city has done is to limit the number of cats these people can take in off the street. That plainly leaves more strays outside to prey on whatever they can,

including birds if they can get them. Even given the fact that many cat owners still let their felines roam free, it doesn't make sense to limit the cat
groups these owners can feed and care for. It simply means that, of all the
cats outside in a given area, fewer can be well-fed by those persons who give
cats homes, and more will be hungry strays compelled to hunt. Well-fed cats
still hunt, but not as constantly as starving strays do. This city has had some
fine governance over the years, but this is not part of it. It's simply a bad law
that serves cat lovers badly and has unintended, ill effects for the bird lovers,
too. Such pet-limit laws exist in various municipalities nationwide, and there
is opposition from many pet enthusiasts. Animal cruelty laws already address
the sad issue of hoarders who have more animals than they can care for
properly. Pet-limit laws do not deter those individuals. These limits only re-
strict responsible owners, providers of excellent pet homes who could otherwise take in more of the street-animal population.

Sometimes animals that need rescue are in the wild. During our travels
down to South Alabama, we encountered many turtles trying to cross the
highway. At certain times of the year, turtles are always crossing the roads in
this way, but some we'd find had already been run over. So Bill always
stopped the car when we found a crosser and carried it across the road in
whichever direction it was headed. Usually, the turtle would then head off
into the woods as fast as turtle speed would allow, towards that same area it
was pointed, which we suspected might be the stream or glade where a mate
was to be found. On another occasion, we were driving across the bridge
over the Black Warrior River when we saw a large snapping turtle crossing
the road. Bill stopped the truck in the middle of the bridge and ran out and
grabbed the turtle, lest some car hit it. Then we took it back down to the river. Bill, of course, had passed a lot of time around woods and water and
knew how to identify and handle snapping turtles. No one should attempt
turtle rescue without a thorough knowledge of how to handle these aggressive animals. Snappers have a nasty bite, and the larger ones can even take a
finger off or snap a broom handle in two. Snapping turtles "won't let go 'til it
thunders," as they say.

That said, Bill found just such a snapping turtle on the highway one day,
the size of a frying pan. Since it was likely to be mashed flat if left where it
was, he was determined to rescue it. It had a wide reach with its flexible neck
and was ready to take a big chomp out of any and all who messed with it.
Snapper reach is much longer than anyone would think reasonable or possible. Bill took two hubcaps and picked the fellow up with them and put him in
the trunk. Then he brought it home to show it to me. That turtle had a smell
worse than that of any animal I'd ever scented! As if the shell wasn't enough

protection, the skunk-times-a-hundred odor surely must have sent predators howling off for parts unknown. So much for clean, fresh nature. I suggested we get it to a nearby pond, quick. We drove there and Bill carefully used the hubcaps to maneuver the beast to the water's edge, where it swam away joyfully. This probably wasn't the best way to guard one's own safety while moving a snapping turtle! Anyone finding one should notify a wildlife rescue group so trained professionals can handle the snapper. Anyone helping turtles to cross roads should review solid information on turtle identification and handling techniques.

Bill also once found a hawk roadside, injured and tumbling around. He drove to a gas station and got a Styrofoam cooler. Using a thick welder's glove that covered a large part of his forearm, he managed to get the hawk into the container and placed a towel over it to quiet the bird, like covering the cage of a parakeet for the night. He then drove back to the nearest town and found a vet on-call on Saturday. The vet turned out to have worked with eagles out West and knew his raptors. He'd even once been injured by an eagle talon. The vet used the welder's glove and determined that the hawk had a broken wing. What's the first thing any self-respecting raptor does when popping up from an injury?

With one of those sudden animal moves that are too fast for humans to escape, the hawk wrapped a talon around the vet's gloved finger. The vet wriggled his hand out of the glove, which the bird hung onto. They instantly decided to let the bird keep it. Bill had to go on and leave without the welder's glove. An argument with a hawk just wasn't worth the risk. The vet then sent the hawk to Auburn University Veterinary School in Auburn, Alabama, which is famous for raptor rehab.

Nowadays there's a state wildlife rehab center you can call. You should not attempt to contain a hawk or other raptor yourself but let the wildlife specialists handle the rescue. Moving steel-clawed birds of prey is best left to professionals.

A tornado

For years we weren't nearly as attentive to the numerous tornado watches and weather as we should have been. On January 24, 1997, a tornado hit just about three miles down the road from us. Bill had just driven by a grocery store moments before. A store employee saw it coming and ran into the parking lot to get everyone to go in and shelter within the store. The wind picked up a car and dropped it through the roof of the structure. Along a ten-mile path 200 yards wide, many homes and business were damaged. The tornado was determined to be an EF2. It wasn't even very windy out where we live.[32]

Chapter 11

Answering the Call of The Wily

In 2000 while the cat-killing dog was still around, our closest neighbor still had about five cats living at his place. Some of them were un-neutered toms, although his females were spayed. Bill had built a roof overhanging our side landing and we had stored a jumble of items there. I looked out the window one day in late summer and was surprised by two kittens climbing and tumbling all over our junk. Lurking furtively in the background was the momcat, stepping and sniffing her way tentatively. You could almost read her thoughts as she looked on: *Hmmm, the kits seem to like it.* They might have been living undetected in Bill's shop, which had corners we could no longer keep track of, but they had definitely moved to the house and revealed themselves to us now. They were a family of classic mackerel tabby, or tiger cats — striped, stippled, and splashed with brown, gray, tawny, cream, reddish, and black colors.

We put out food and began taming them. I talked to them, and once they understood we were a food source, Bill would lure them into coming closer and closer by throwing out one nugget of dry food at a time. The tabby camped out a lot under the house with her kittens. Bill had a habit of taking the cordless phone out in the yard during conversations so he could hear without the distraction of television noise. Drawn by the sound of his voice, the cat would come out towards him, trailed by the kittens. The momcat was wary and standoffish at first, but she began coming closer and finally walked right up to him while the kittens tumbled around behind, keeping their distance.

Soon he began calling her "Pretty Girl." I expect he thought flattery would help draw her closer. It worked! Or maybe it was the strong smell of stinky-fish cat food. Or perhaps she heard his voice from underneath the floor, and associated it with the room she saw above her hangout, the one with the four well-nourished, and contented cats. Or maybe she was just reaching out to get a human with a congenial-sounding voice to replace the ones she may have lost. She slowly came closer and let us stand nearby while she ate the food we brought her. After letting her get used to this arrangement awhile we began petting her, which spooked her a little but not extremely so, and we made some slow progress in coaxing her to accept more contact. Judging by her reactions, which were not entirely fearful as with totally feral cats, she may have been someone's yard cat, a blasé relationship on the human side that results in a marginally people-friendly animal.

One of the nearby handsome tabby toms had probably gone for an excursion wherever, romanced, and impregnated her, and she may have followed him back to his home, our forest neighborhood. She may have then discovered the second floor of Bill's unfinished shop, poor in barriers to keep out animals but rich in mice, and settled in to have her kittens. As a result of the urgent time and resource demands from both my illness and that of family, the shop had become Critter Palace, a fast-food restaurant for any stray cat, the place to stroll through and pick up some McMice anytime.

I watched the kittens scratch in the brush around the dogwood trees for insects; they used the pine-needle matting on the forest floor outside the bedroom window as a litterbox. The savvy momcat kept the kittens mostly under the house, or up on its flat roof space at night for safety from the dog pack led by the cat-killer dog. (Thankfully, those dogs usually didn't come our way.) The kittens were about six weeks old. We wanted to get the cat spayed soon, before she went into another heat cycle. But the two kittens weren't tame enough to handle yet. I never even got a really close look at them. We set the HavaHeart box trap, baited with cat food, so that we could get them to the vet. The trap captures an animal safely, without injury. Soon we had three trapped and unhappy felines. Bill whisked the kittens to the vet in the early morning before I was awake, so I could not see them closely and become attached to them. The kittens stayed at the vet to be socialized and placed in homes, but the momcat came back after being spayed. It was supposed to be temporary, while we found her a home. We had our four cats, and we really didn't feel we could take on another pet.

There was one boy and one girl kitten. The vet gave away the boy but herself adopted the girl, who had developed a special bond with her dog. One of the perks of living in a southern city of moderate size, with all its interweavings, is that not only do I know my vet's Mama, who used to spend time at her clinic, I know her cat's Mama. However, we had our work cut out for us socializing the tabby mom, who had thrown a fit at the vet's, broken away from Bill, and climbed some shelves. She appeared to be more of a scrappy, outdoor sort of feral than we'd thought. We felt it best to work slowly and let her live outside until we could handle her more; and we still thought we might give her away. But somewhere along the way we reached that state in which the cat gets its paws wrapped around our hearts. Bill kept calling her "Pretty Girl" as he sat by the ferns, trying to draw her closer with food. This name seemed a little mundane to both of us, but nothing else came up that fit. I thought of Tara, which as far as I knew was Irish Gaelic for earth, because of her multiple earth tones. But it didn't quite suit her and it had become so commonplace as a girl's name that the novelty and twist of it had worn off for me, although I still like the concept and the bit of Irish. (It turns out opinions range as to the actual meaning of Tara: Gaelic or Irish for hill, tower, and/or star, the place where the ancient kings resided; it can also be Sanskrit or Hindi for star. A name with a composite and beautiful resonance, but nothing that really pegged this cat.) Heather, a really lovely name, had a similar overuse problem. I toyed with Fiona, but that didn't fit either and Bill didn't like it. Besides, I'd changed a lot of cat names Bill had come up with. So we had Pretty Girl. I played with it a lot, though. I called her Attractive Female, Comely Lass, Hot Stuff, and Pretty Thing.

Pretty Girl was probably a semi-feral. She would never get used to all humans and would run and hide from people she did not know. She would not have been easy to give away. Most people want a cat that's friendly from the get-go, but we were willing to work with her for a very long time to socialize her, and she would eventually become a really sweet pet.

Unfortunately such cats, the ferals and semi-ferals, are most often euthanized in shelters. Usually potential adopters, understandably, want to begin with cats that demonstrate affection. Although not all ferals can be tamed, many can, and I would like to see them given longer periods of time awaiting adoption so that shelter staff can work with them and bring out their sweet sides. Any animal suddenly captured and caged in a strange place will react with fear at first. Even well-socialized cats react this way; cats are very attached to their premises and dislike and fear being taken out of the places they have chosen for themselves. Patience is the quality that needs to be employed with both ferals and strays. The ideal scenario for all degrees of socialized cats is no-kill care for both friendly and feral cats. For intractably un-socialized ferals, TNR and release back to home grounds with caregivers is the way to go.

So Pretty Girl was fed outside for the time being. I worried about the ill-led dogs, but we rarely saw or heard them here — both the closest neighbor's cats and Pretty Girl had evaded them for a long time. When she came up to eat right next to us, we could now pet her while she ate. This is one of the best times to attempt to stroke a feral; with a head sunk deep into a dish of chow, a shy cat may not mind or notice the petting quite so much. I'd try to slide my hands under her belly to get her used to that so she could be picked up, but she'd sidestep and squirm away from my hands while her face stayed in the food bowl, noisily munching. It was as if she was saying, *hey, a girl works up an appetite living out in the leaves!* She did start coming up on the porch landing, looking in the door panes, working her front feet up and down in milk-treading motion like a suckling kitten does. I'd then go out, and she'd keep looking up at me after I set the food down. *For me? Really?* I'd pet her and she'd keep her eyes on me awhile before lowering her head to eat, as if she craved the attention first, the food second. I came to sense an enormous loneliness about this cat who demonstrated that, although half-wild, she wanted to reinforce friendship with people, as well as eat the food provided by them. I saw the wonder in her large green eyes — she had never seen the beat of this; the giants were taking care of her! She very much wanted the cat life inside our house, where our cats had other cat "friends" and lived with us as companions, with devotion on all sides. She wanted what those other cats had. "Cats are jealous animals," I recall my Mom saying so many times! Pretty Girl may also have expressed her affection before eating as an enticement for me to stay and stand guard against other animals. In her formerly deprived life, other cats or critters may have taken any food she found.

I'd go out and pet her and talk to her sometimes; we'd given away her kittens, and I surmised that made her even lonelier. She was a young cat, determined by the vet to be between two and three years old, and she would scamper off down our driveway about 9 p.m. every night towards the neighbor, who had her tomcat boyfriend and about four other cats. I expect she wanted to play with those cats, but I feared she might venture to the nether reaches of the forest, too. Earlier during those days, when I'd come back from the mailbox she'd run at me, leaping and making playful mock-starts as though she wanted me to chase her. I was so sorry that due to illness, I was unable to run and romp with her. Anytime I heard dogs barking, I'd go out and run them off if they were venturing down our road towards our place. Once I saw a neighbor's cat approaching and ahead of him, Pretty Girl trotting hurriedly up to our house like she wanted to avoid him. Closer to the house, she stopped, turned towards him, and bristled. I went out and advanced in his direction, and he turned and ran off. Pretty Girl gave me a look that was at once astonished and grateful. She clearly knew I had helped her. Maybe she was surprised I'd been willing to help her out, or maybe, cats being somewhat full of themselves at times, she was surprised that a mere human would have the wits to understand the situation and do what was needed.

She was very smart about the way she spent her nights. The flat area on our roof was favored by raccoons, but we heard the tabby up there every night after she showed up; the raccoons appeared to have yielded. She was entirely safe from dogs up there, and when the weather turned cold, the area by the heater vent was warm. At the back of the house stood an oak tree whose branches overhung the roof; she would climb it and go to the roof via the branches. The trunk was right outside the bedroom window, and every morning, Bill would see her backing down the tree with all four long legs wrapped around it, darting him a look of big, green-eyed surprise when she'd see him through the glass. Whenever she heard the dogs barking in the distance, she'd run under the house and make for the back, and then scoot up that tree to the roof.

Every night Pretty Girl would come to be fed and scamper off at about nine. and my heart would sink, fearing she would not come back. But every day she would and she'd sit on the doorstep and I'd feed her again, and she'd try to get inside. Then she'd wait awhile, eyeballing the room, pressing against the glass, wanting us to let her in, before finally leaving with a face we could almost see emit a sigh. In a few more minutes we'd hear her on the roof. Like cats had done for centuries, by night, she was living the wild-cat; but by day, this former feral or semi-feral now wanted the domestic life: hearth, heart, warmth, scent, purr, and humans who gloried at her fur and whiskers.

Pretty Girl was looking in and seeing not only our happy cats, but the two persons she thought were hers alone, sitting and interacting with those other cats. She wanted this prime territory, with two automated cat-feeding machines for her own — no matter how cantankerous those other cats were, no matter how much they cussed her. I did not fully comprehend at the time, but this was the ideal way to have a feral or semi-feral, or any stray for that matter, enter into one's household. The cat finds a place and people that it wants for itself. The place and people then respond to what the cat has decided, its ownself.

This realization is important for new cat owners to make. When a cat is captured from the street or adopted from the shelter and released into a new situation, in no way has the cat taken part in the decision to go to the new space, even though it may like the person who brings it there. This can only result in fear and the assertion of independence at first. The cat will hide and may take time to acclimate. The cat only needs time and space to reach its own decisions about the grounds and people. No shelter should label feline personality based on initial post-capture behavior, although sadly, they frequently do; similarly, no new cat owner should give up on a cat that goes into hiding mode for a considerable time in a new setting. Give the cat time to draw its own conclusions and make its own catly decisions.

We were distracted with many things and slow about getting Pretty Girl into the house and facing the enormous task of a five-way cat acclimation. Fall came, and the weather began to turn cold off-and-on as is usual in our area. On the really cold nights we began having her stay in the bedroom, where she could have a private cat suite. Bill would put her into the carrier outside and take her around to the back door to avoid getting the other cats upset. This worked fairly well, but Pretty Girl was eager to get back out in the morning, so early that she'd wake Bill by scratching at the door and raising a ruckus. So he built a cat door into the window, even taking care to build a shelf on the outside of the window so she would have a large amount of space to step onto when she went through the flap. Pretty Tiger Girl learned to shimmy to the outside through it, but she didn't use it to come back in. So Bill kept boxing her up and getting her in every night.

On December 16, 2000, Pretty Girl came into the house and stayed in. Our dear friends Charlotte and Steve were getting married that evening and we were looking forward to a good time. But we weren't so pleased with the weather forecast, which predicted possible severe weather at about 1 p.m., meaning a storm system was coming and conditions were favorable for tornadoes to form. Spring is usually thought of as tornado season, but in the South, we have a secondary season in November and December. Meteorologists now tell us we are the only area in the world with two tornado seasons a year. Bleh. In those months we keep warming up and cooling down again, and tornadoes are likely to occur when a cold front smacks into warm, moist, and unstable air that's in place, roughly speaking. Several other complicated upper-atmosphere factors also play into severe-storm formation.

So it had been a warmer night, and Pretty Girl had stayed outside. It became even warmer in the morning, when the juicy tropical air came in, with a peculiarly uneasy humidity and low pressure we could feel, that we'd felt before. Definitely tornado weather. But so many times the predicted bad weather weakens before it gets here, or it goes elsewhere or comes later than expected, so that we always hope it won't happen and we just go about our business, albeit cautiously. No one should ignore predictions of severe weather, but forecasters can only state that conditions are favorable for windstorms. Meteorology cannot pinpoint a precise when, where, or if until the last twenty minutes before the storm. After hundreds of tornado no-shows, no one here cancelled plans during a tornado watch. (At least, that's the way things used to be, before April 27, 2011, which changed everything. Now, I watch weather constantly and plan my life around the forecast.)

The temperature was going down to sixteen degrees that night, so we already knew Pretty Girl would be coming in. We looked around for her to get her in early because of weather and our evening plans, but we hadn't seen her that day. As it neared 1 o'clock in the afternoon, Bill was up at a neighbor's doing repair work. Oddly enough, the sun was shining. There was no rain yet. I'd been in the bath and was just getting dressed when all the lights and the electric clock went off and the whirr of the refrigerator stopped. I rushed to the front and looked out through the glass-front door at the trees, and I just knew: the tops were being jerked rapidly around, one way and then another, in swirling ways I'd seen before, ways that meant there was a tornado somewhere nearby, and it could be coming right at us. I paged Bill on the phone, scarcely able to press the right buttons, I was so scared. I used our prearranged code that meant, "Come home now." Meanwhile our neighbor Gale, the one on the hilltop who had Minou's momcat, was paging Bill, too, entering 911 several times. Bill had forgotten about the weather report and thought Gale needed some help, so he called him first. That was how he found out about the storm as "Please, please Bill, come," was tearing through my mind; it seemed like eternity before he drove up, and we went for the "strong place" of the house and Minx stayed with me. Kudzu had gone under the couch, and Spotty and Minou were around the room, and we could only hope Pretty Girl was somewhere safe. The wind blew and it rained heavily awhile and then it was over as near as we could tell — we had no television or radio without power. Then the sirens started. Out on the highway, there came the shrieking of police, fire, and ambulance vehicles. We didn't know it at the time, but five counties were responding to the storm within our county.

Bill called his dad, who had electricity in town; one person had been killed, he'd heard on television. I knew it was too soon to tell what the casualties were, and that there would likely be more. We were about to call my mom when the phone rang again and again with friends calling to check on us, the first one all the way from Salt Lake City. Five people were killed, they'd heard. The storm appeared to be over, but we had to rely on the television weather from Bill's dad to confirm that. Bill called our friends to see if the wedding was on, if the church had electricity. A wedding guest from California answered. Charlotte, who was a nurse, was not there. All off-duty medical personnel in town had been asked to go to the scene of destruction and help with the injured. Knowing the way that people of this land respond to those in need, I imagine no one refused. Her fiancé had gone with her to help all he could. During the storm, they and their family and wedding guests from out of town had all jammed into a closet. They would call us back.

I got my clothes for the wedding out while we still had some daylight, and I made some tea by soaking a teabag at length in some of the last of the hot tap water. Later in the afternoon the friends called and said the church had power, so the wedding was on. I dressed for it with a flashlight and candlelight and a lot of dark. We looked for her, but still hadn't seen Pretty Girl by the time we left for the wedding. I was shaken but I took in the wedding ceremony our friends had put together themselves. Charlotte looked radiant as a bride; her hair was in a swept-up style and was all in place, despite having spent the afternoon pulling debris off of people and pulling the injured along with the ones who didn't make it, out of shredded homes in the hardest-hit area. Later we would learn that eleven people died in town that day, and one down in South Alabama in a separate tornado within the same vast storm system. The path of the tornado was narrow but long, and hundreds of structures in town, including homes and businesses, were destroyed or damaged. Only a few miles away from the path it was sunny and dry. Our friends from California changed their plans to move to Alabama; it was the second time they'd visited when tornadic weather struck. (One previous May, we had taken a walk with them at dusk to see fireflies and heard the tornado siren. We rushed back to the house and had a very tense evening, but fortunately, no tornadoes occurred at our place; my recall is hazy as to whether there were any in the county that night.)

This twister had come within one mile of our house. The next day Bill would go out with his chainsaw to help cut up trees fallen on another friend's yard in a community about a mile up the road. Our friend had seen the tornado coming right over the hill at him, and he had run for cover, thinking he was gone. This at the very time Bill had actually heard the tornado, like a long sustained roll of thunder that wouldn't stop, except he'd thought it was just thunder until he'd called Gale. The tornado had originally come down somewhere near the Black Warrior River and traveled for eighteen miles through the southern parts of the city and out towards our place. After crossing the highway, it tracked generally northeast for awhile and then lifted. Bill went for a walk in the woods not far from our house the next day and observed tree trunks with treetop sections twisted off by winds that had to have been tornadic. We didn't really know until later just how close it had come to us. Also much later, we found out it was an EF4.

When we left the wedding reception the chill hit us, coming on strong with biting, cold post-tornado winds. Bill drove us up to our dark house. Pretty Girl was waiting on the doorstep. She had probably been on the trailer top under the roof during the storm, or maybe under the house. In her animal wisdom she no doubt found the safest spot, some cranny we knew nothing about. Animals always seem to know where to go preceding an impending natural disaster. Without electricity, there was no heat in our sleeping area on this sixteen-degree night. The living room/kitchen heat was propane, which survived the storm. I didn't adjust well to anything except my carefully arranged bed, so I decided to rely on the comforter for warmth rather than try to sleep in the living area. Bill brought Pretty Girl inside using the carrier.

I was talking to reassure her but as soon as she was released in the darkness I heard her claws scrabbling on plastic storage boxes as she climbed up to settle on a high shelf in the closet. To her, coming from outside and nights spent on the roof, safety was as high up as she could get. In the morning, she was on the bed outside the covers, snuggled up against me in the freezing cold room. She wasn't going outside again. With such storms, I wasn't having her out in the wind, hidden high or low. Even if she did know more than we did about tornado safety, it was best for us all to remain together. She could meow her objections at the back door in the mornings all she wanted; she wasn't going out again. It was time for her to become an indoor-only cat.

The electricity was off for four days, because the tornado had knocked out the lights all over town and beyond. Being ill it was extra hard for me to do without power but I wasn't complaining. We had our lives, and others didn't. We had our home, and others now had none. The town responded with every kind of donations and assistance. People rode around in the days after the storm taking food to anyone they saw out working on the debris and damage. Veterinarians, my newly married friend later told me, had rushed to the destroyed area where she had worked that day to take charge of injured animals. A pizza delivery person had used his vehicle to assist in blocking the road into the destroyed neighborhood so extraneous traffic would not enter to sightsee and interfere with the rescue work. That day, with its agony of contrasts, continues to haunt me. The wedding day of much loved friends, marked with love and new beginnings, yet also smeared with death and destruction and horror in my own community.

Pretty Girl stayed in the back for a few months while the other cats got more used to her scent. They already knew her from the doorstep, looking out at her with only glass between them. The howling about that had stopped long ago, but to have her in the house was a different story, and there was some howling traded back and forth from either side of the louvered door to the back while scents drifted easily through the spaces between. She could be disruptive at night, getting up early and running around, but I didn't have to get up to work, so it wasn't a problem for me. She found herself a spot on the bed alongside me and was careful to stay in her own area, and I found it comforting to stir in the night and stroke her fur, or to wake in the morning to the sound of her purring.

Nevertheless, we had to combine her with the rest of the household. We took each cat to the back one at a time to meet her face-to-face, both of us standing by. Despite the ongoing five-way smell exchange from proximate quarters, there was spitting and slapping and sniffing noses. The first time we took Minou, the instant he saw her he spun around and tried to hide. He repeated that many times. He had become a more cautious, easily spooked cat over the years. Pretty Girl was bigger than he was, and of the resident four, he was the only one who had never before had to accommodate another cat entering the household. Sequence of introduction to territory within a cat group is crucial, I've come to believe. Minou had no fear of cats already in residence when he arrived as a young bristling kitten, and he had accepted mentoring from Kudzu and made his way around the girls, even if he didn't especially like them. But a newcomer to his established turf presented an entirely new scenario, one much more difficult for any cat, especially an older one, to adjust to.

It was a long slow introduction with all four, and once Pretty Girl was out front, it was apparent that she very much wanted a kitty friend. But none of our others would pal around with her. She'd try to snuggle with them and they'd leave, and Minou actively avoided her, waiting to eat until she'd left the kitchen, turning around and backtracking if she approached him head-on. I felt very sorry for my lonesome tabby. In other circumstances, I'd have considered adopting a kitten on the chance it would be a friend for her, as well as for the joy we would have in raising a kitten. But with our dwindling resources, I could not consider another animal at that time; a person needs to think about providing for the pets in the future when adopting animals. Pretty Girl kept on approaching Minx, grooming her head, and sometimes she even got a brief return grooming but never an open-ended, cozy-with-me-any-time deal.

Wild colors: The unique camouflage of tabby cats

The tabby pattern is similar to the coloration of the domestic cat's ancestors, and variations of it are found on many wild cats. The description of most of the wild guys will be at least partially reminiscent of tabby patterns; some are minimally marked with a few face stripes, leg bands, and tail bands. Some patterns are camouflage for forest dwellers who are both hunters and hunted. Under cover of vegetation, these cats can move in places where leaves, in all their randomly patterned designs, will break the sunlight up into slanty, glinty spots and irregular patches among the subdued greens and browns. Andrew Kitchener notes in *The Natural History of the Wild Cats* that various configurations of bold stripes, blotches, and spots are examples of disruptive coloration, because they make it hard to see the outline of a cat in forested surroundings.[1]

Disruptive coloration only partly duplicates background patterns, while also offering other random patterns to confuse the eye with pattern-against-pattern. Two of the tabby types found on domestic cats, the classic, blotched tabby with broad whorls like marbling and the mackerel tabby with thin stripes, both on lighter backgrounds of banded fur known as agouti, incorporate these elements in their coats, which would represent disruptive coloration, if the cats were living in a natural forest habitat. I have witnessed something like this in action, especially one recent winter when there were several shy tabbies that I'd encounter when I walked on the road, neighborhood cats who would turn and enter the tangle of pastel grayed forms in the winter woods, leaping and vanishing into visual confusion as I still tried to keep eye track of them, the brisk crunching sound of their flight on dry leaves fading away as I called, without effect, "Kitty, kitty."

Whether part-cryptic coloration, in which the animal matches the color of its environment and becomes less visible, as well as part-disruptive coloration, or of a completely disruptive pattern, these cats were well-camouflaged. This natural phenomenon seems to work indoors, too; at my mother's house two mackerel tabby cats are difficult to see for an instant if they are reclining on her Asian-style rugs and viewed when daylight is muted. A third tabby pattern, the "ticked" tabby, is also known as the "agouti tabby" or the "unpatterned tabby." Agouti hairs are each banded with pigmentation varying in lightness and darkness and hue; this results in a "frosted" appearance due to a gene which obscures all other tabby patterning. Ticked tabbies may have a few thin stripes on their legs, tails, and faces. The Abyssinian, Somali, and a few other breeds are examples of ticked tabby coloration; it can also occur in random-breds. The Abyssinian fur is often said to resemble that of the African Wildcat, now Near or Middle Eastern, which is a major ancestor of domestic cats.

The spotted tabby is a fourth type. It's not known whether this is a separate pattern or just a modifier gene that breaks up the mackerel tabby stripes into spots or the larger blotches of classic tabbies into smaller spots. These have been seen in random populations as well as in several breeds.

Mackerel and blotched tabbies have a background of agouti hairs, while the darker hairs tend to be solid color, as do the dark bands and markings on the tail and legs and face. They also have the "M" on the forehead and tend to have spots on the belly. They are found frequently in random-bred and feral populations.

Overall, tabby is a coat pattern and not a breed; tabby markings can appear in many breeds. The word "tabby" originally comes from Arabic; *atabi* is a type of watered silk that was produced in Baghdad. Mackerel tabbies were called "tiger cats" in the Mid-Atlantic area where I grew up, but they are generally called "tabbies" in the South. Most sources indicate mackerels are the oldest pattern of tabby. Green-eyed, brown-mackerel tabbies are said to be the phenotype, or most commonly expressed genetic type, of the domestic cat species. Therefore, from their large numbers within the cat population, I surmise there are a lot of them out there needing homes.

The tabby who has stripes on the head and down the nape of the neck and back may resemble a snake from the air when moving fast and may, therefore, fool the eyes of large predatory birds. Pretty Girl had this appearance, and Bill sometimes called her a "snakey-headed thing." He also thought that the dark, mottled streak on her back and tail resembled snakes. A coiled-up tabby cat against a surface of shed leaves might indeed look like a snake. Mom's take on tabbies is this: "Tabbies all look alike but each have their own charm."

Whereas outdoor cats in the wild instinctively use camouflage to hide their whereabouts from predators, indoor cats safe in our homes seem to develop a kind of sense about how to make themselves cute and attractive by rolling around with paws up in positions that would make them vulnerable in the wild. They artfully use the colors and patterns of the home as backgrounds to enhance their beauties, which might endear them further to their humans. I swear if they could have careers, they would make fine interior decorators! These are my own unscientific musings, and while I have no doubt that wild cats and feral cats have been observed relaxing and playing just as domestic cats do, I can't shake the suspicion I sometimes get, that in our presence, cats are really hamming it up at times.

Pretty Girl was a distinctive, beautiful, tawny, mackerel tabby. Her fur was a jamboree of earth tones; she was like a mobile winter forest. Her nose was russet red with such subtle gradations of colors and depths that it reminded me of a Rothko painting. She had a small reddish streak on her head and one streak slightly behind her shoulders. Her light green eyes were outlined in black, with a trail of contrasting brown color from the corners to the sides of her face, like the eyes depicted in Egyptian art. (Maybe they got the idea from their cats!) Scattered throughout her mostly white whiskers were several that were black at the base for a short while until they changed to white extending to the tips. One whisker on her right face side was all black. The whiskers over her eyes were white. The shape of her ears was an especially pleasing curve, and on the points she had black tufts that were especially long and lynx-like. Although a few longer hairs can be seen on most cats' ear tips, hers were extra prominent.

She had a wide face with a perpetual smile — her forehead was very flat, and her mouth was broad with her two long fangs set far apart. So broad and smooth was the expanse between her ears that in complete flights of fancy, you could almost imagine setting a Dixie cup or a *demitasse* up there when she was sitting in certain upright positions. Her lower jaw was wide and flat, and her mouth and lips were lined with a dark color against her gray and cream undercoat tones. By "cream" here I mean warm off-white, not the pale orange of cat-fancy terminology. Her shoulder blades were set far apart too.

At first she'd been scrawny, but when she bulked up, she was broad from the shoulders on back to the hindquarters; she was built like a semi tractor-trailer truck. The bottoms of her paws were a dusky, dark color that hovered between burnt-umber and black and seeped up between the toes. The fur on her feet was a silvery color tipped with black. Her hind paws were patterned with the dark color, pale cream, and silvery tones in gorgeous, natural asymmetry. On the right hind foot only, the cream flowed up over the tops of her toes. The paw pads on this foot were softly mottled with two colors; three were mostly an ashy gray, with a spot or two of pale pink. The second pad from the right was mostly pink with accents of the ashy gray, like the way colors will speckle pebbles, or the way pebbles vary in hue under creek water. One of nature's marvelous random displays of irregular pattern! Anytime she was standing or walking along, she carried her broad-based tail aloft in a straight-up position, with the last three or four inches sailing about in contrast to the other cats, whose tails waved up, down, straight, curved, all over the map.

Our vet told us that Pretty Girl's kitten also carried her tail upright most of the time, a trait either learned or inherited. She had this really sultry, slow walk with a rippling motion that traveled through her form. As she made her way between furnishings that concealed her body, you'd see her straight-up tail-tip waving to-and-fro rhythmically as she moved along through the room. Reading the Cat Fanciers' Association website, I learned that Pretty Girl's reddish areas and two-toned feet indicate that she should probably be called a "patched tabby" to be absolutely accurate.

High fives for our newest cat

Like many cats that have lived out on their own, Pretty Girl over-nibbled because she never forgot the times when she didn't have enough to eat. When her abdomen enlarged out from the truck shape, her tiger stripes spread out across her behind. Her dark lines flowed down her head and neck like rivulets, then pooled in the shallows of her shoulders and went on to spread and ripple out into the Delta of Tabby. Cats that tend to add pounds, even former strays that nibble a lot, must surely have a genetic tendency towards weight gain. Kudzu, Spotty, and Minou had never gained too much during the times we had food set out 24/7; even though Minou was an absolute feline vacuum, gobbling everything in sight, he never lost his slim, smooth minnow-like profile. Only Minx and Pretty Girl showed the tendency to gain, no matter how carefully we controlled their diet. Pretty Girl was slowly becoming an obese beast and would later be placed on a diet.

In 2004, four years too late, I thought of naming her Lynx for her ear tufts — then we'd have had Minx and Lynx. But Lynx did not quite suit her, though. Pretty Girl's wild looks, the basic tabby pattern of the cat's wild ancestors and the earliest housecats, meant that I sometimes called her "Wild Thing,"[2] singing the title and the first line of the old song. One way or another, Pretty Girl kept defying description.

There are many joys in rescuing and taking in a stray animal. Not only will you have a friend to care for, but you may come across a sublime rapport like Minx and I had, or some delightfully quirky natural patterning, like the colors on Spotty's face and Pretty Girl's paws. If you watch pets carefully and learn their ways and respond to their subtleties, they will keep you entertained. Close, daily life with the animals I exalt continually enhances and expands my views and knowledge of them, and in this way I find I slide easily from moment to moment, never finding myself bored.

For nine years since Minou had come in 1991, we'd had the same four together. Now there were five. It slowly sank in. It was cats galore at our house. This was a new ripple in the flow of the group. Pretty Girl had looked in at our cats and desired everything they had. She now became insecure and lonely when none of our others would play with her. She wanted to play so much that she had even tried to frisk around with her slow-moving giant, me. I wanted to but was not capable of such lively activity. She wanted to be included any time another cat got attention, and like Spotty, she became a huge buttinsky when other cats got their pettings. We tried to reassure her by giving her plenty of her own pats. But she was even envious when Minx would later get vet-prescribed home medicine injections, and she would come over to check out the action and get in on it if she could. Bill joked at such times that Pretty Girl was just a country girl and didn't know any better.

Right away Pretty Girl found Lookout Couchpoint, Kudzu's snazzy arrangement at the end of the couch on the cushion back that he had snuggled into so hard to shape just right for himself. One day when he vacated it, she took over the spot. Kudzu looked at her balefully for awhile as she sat there but he didn't challenge her, being a rather non-confrontational sort. For several months she made it "her" spot. Like an explorer on the shores of a new land, she was staking her claim. When she changed to another place, as cats often do after a spell of favoring a particular spot, Kudzu never went back to it. I did feel sorry for Kudzu. As much as I would have liked to, I don't think there was a viable way I could have changed this for him. There are some cat events in a group that you cannot settle yourself; you have to learn to let some disagreements between disparate personalities alone. If I had nudged her out of the spot, it may well have been beneath Kudzu's catly pride to acknowledge that he needed the assistance. He may well have been indicating, gruffly, that he had never really wanted it anyway by refusing to take it back over after her blasé abandonment. Spotty was beneath Kudzu's notice, or so he let on, so it stands to reason he also wished to show, or feign, indifference towards the antics of this new striped intruder.

Pretty Girl didn't manage this real estate anywhere near as well as Kudzu. She pushed her forefeet against the backing, and the pillow cushion would drift out and begin to tilt, eventually falling over while she sank farther into the cavern between. Or she'd rest on the back supporting panel of the couch and extend her feet out towards and over the cushion, and this, too, tended to push the cushion over onto the seat. Either way, I had to lift up the cushion to fix it, again and again. Only Kudzu had known just how to work this arrangement and keep it balanced. He meanwhile took to sleeping on the chair behind his former vantage point or underneath it, giving me his regular swat from those areas every time I walked by.

Pretty Girl would go on to displace other cats from their favored niches, too. When Minx liked the bottom shelf of the television console, Pretty Girl would either take it herself when the Minx wasn't there or try to cozy up to an in-residence Minx, crowding her out of it. She'd do this with any current occupant, as the other cats went through their phases of enjoying that place. All four had each taken turns knocking the pesky videotapes stored there every whichaway to gain the space for a den, like the small lions they were. (Sometimes you have to give in a little to their whims.) The shelf also made a cool cave retreat in the summer for whichever cat was claiming it at the moment.

I felt sorry for Pretty Girl when her every attempt to make a cat friend failed. She'd try to play with Minou, running at him with a spirited side-step in her gait, and he'd just turn his back and walk off. The others had some years on them and just hadn't been into active jumping around for some time. I really wished I could have gotten her a kitten, in the hopes the two would have bonded. Pretty Girl turned out to be even more green-eyed than Spotty, coming up whenever another cat was patted or even talked to, sitting partly on our laps to be in on things. She was slow to become comfortable placing her entire self on our laps, and it would be several years before she became Bill's lap cat. Even so, from the start she loved attention. She'd project a front paw towards a person, arching her leg and putting her foot up straight with toes out and claws visible, too, like she was going for a high five. I started touching her paw with my fingers, avoiding the claws, saying "High Five, Pretty Girl." If I brushed the claws accidentally, it would be a "Sticky High Five."

These greetings were for Bill and me only. Visitors terrified her. If my mother came into the house, she'd run to the kitchen. Gradually she began to venture out a little bit when Mom was there, but several visitors at once, with animated conversation, would send her to the door to the back, scratching at it frantically. I'd open it and let her through, since the best thing to do for a scared cat who wants to hide is to let that kitty hide. On those occasions she sought the comfort of the high shelf in the closet like a wild thing, just like she had so wisely spent her nights on the roof when living outdoors. It would be a long time after the company left until she came cautiously creeping out into the kitchen to satisfy herself that the loud ones were gone. The winter that she came in we saw no sign of the usual mouse invasion, probably due to her time spent prowling the roof and the grounds in the previous summer and fall, which illustrated my contention that outdoor cats make the difference in rodent numbers.

She was thoughtful about her actions. Set canned food down in front of her, and she'd hesitate a minute before eating, sometimes still expecting a pat first. Or, I'd see her sitting by the litterbox, just looking at it. She had a perpetual smile, and she contemplated. She was like Buddha, but she lacked serenity.

In color and pattern she was my jungle girl, my wild thing, the cat that looks the most like the small, wild ancestors of modern housecats. In sunshine she's a myriad of colors for maximum camouflage value in the compound hues of dappled forest shadows. At night, she still scampered around the house like she used to scamper off down the road for adventure when she was outside.

New recommendations for handling stray kittens

In the summer of 2001, we almost added a sixth cat. We found a stray with kittens under Bill's dad's house in town. We used the low-cost spay-neuter program through a local animal advocacy group to have our savvy vet spay the momcat. She was a tabby with white feet, blind in one eye from a cat fight and even more people-shy than Pretty Girl. It wasn't likely we could give her away, so my Mom, who lived next door to Eddie, took over feeding her and eventually took her inside with her cats and named her Anna. We placed an ad in the paper to give away the kittens, who were at four or five weeks, a shade on the wild side. Bill and I worked on socializing them. I would scoop up and pet one kitten after another when I was in town; each little fuzzy guy would settle on my lap for a spell. They were all gorgeous. The only female was a tabby of a rusty, light-orange color. There was another tabby of the more common grayish-brownish tones like Pretty Girl, with the boldest stripes I've ever seen — he was a handsome fellow, a true small tiger. Two black-and-white boys had tiny amounts of white on their feet, near tuxedo pattern but not quite; they, too, were sharp-looking kittens.

The fifth kitten was really unusual. He was a classic tuxedo cat with white feet, white underparts, and a white blaze down his nose. But instead of his dominant color being black, or tabby pattern, he was mostly a deep, mahogany brown. Both Bill and I wanted him. I would have sprung for him, but Bill felt we could not have six cats in our small space. Yet I couldn't stop thinking about him, and I almost spoke up about it. The very first respondent to our ad chose him after Bill described all the kittens to her over the phone, so I was resigned to the inevitable. I typed and copied a note for Bill and his Dad to give out with each kitten, saying that if you find that you can't keep the animal, don't take it to the pound but bring it back so we can place it elsewhere. We also gave out a copy of the local animal group's information sheet on their low-cost spay-neuter program to each adopter.

Still, when the young woman who wanted the brown kitten didn't come for a few weeks, I secretly hoped she wouldn't. But eventually she did come and take the kitty. The two tigers, the rusty orange girl and strongly marked boy, went to a family together, as did the remaining two black-and-white boys. It's always sad to let go of kittens you nurture to be someone else's pets. A few tendrils of attachment were already in place.

When the momcat came back from her spay surgery, she looked all around for her kittens, calling out and hollering, and we felt so sorry for her. Unlike most momcats, when the kittens were six to seven weeks of age, she had evidently not been ready to give them up. She did soon settle down though, with my mother's loving attendance. More recent recommendations are to keep kittens with the mother cat for about twelve weeks to ensure a smooth separation of kits and momcat, as well as proper socialization. Kittens learn their social skills from interaction with each other, as well as from the momcat.

I'm aware that animal advocate groups now recommend against advertising kittens and other animals in the newspaper. It's certainly possible for the wrong persons to answer the ads, with dire consequences. Shelters and adoption-room personnel are trained to ask certain questions and to recommend spay/neuter and indoor homes, discuss potential problems, and say a few other things that might be viewed as pushy if coming from an individual who's giving away free kittens but are routine and acceptable from shelter staff. I endorse this route for placing animals when it's at all possible.

However, Bill has keen insight into people's characters, and we made efforts to cover the necessary topics when meeting potential adopters. A person can go to a shelter under false pretenses and give insincere answers to the questions, and I believe tragedies have been known to result from shelter adoptions. The most excellent training programs cannot always screen out the wrong persons, and almost anyone can be deceived. Without a home visit follow-up program, which the public often views as invasive, there is never a guarantee. Students here in this college town used to be notorious for abandoning animals on the streets when they moved away. Yet I've seen students being allowed to adopt kittens in local adoption rooms, and in a university town it might be difficult to deny them adoption. In contrast, I've seen "Free Kittens" ads in the newspapers that also say "No students."

When the first two of Anna's kittens were given away, I was at home. Bill called me to ask which kitten was the only female. A woman had come with her daughter, wanting a girl kitten. When the kittens played together, the little girl said, "Oh look, Mama!" and Bill quickly said, "If there's anything cuter than one little kitten, it's two little kittens." So the lady took the tiger boy as well as the orange tabby girl. This adopter called Bill about a week later to tell him how well the kittens were doing in their new home. Another family came with their two daughters and gave both the little black-and-white boys a home. These two cases were ideal, as it's good to keep littermates together for at least eight weeks so they will learn restrained play interaction from each other.[3] Kittens learn to temper play-bites from the squeals of their siblings. Our kittens were about six weeks old at the time, and I felt very confident about these placements, as well as the match between a young nurse and the brown kitten. I was confident in Bill's canny radar into human character. Nevertheless, as an official position, I favor leaving animal placement to the professionals and to those associated with well-seasoned rescue groups. Nowadays it's recommended that those who rehome animals charge small rehoming fees to ensure the adopters are serious about caring for the animals.

Some rescue organizations have extremely stringent standards regarding such things as income and ages of children, as well as required home inspections and visits. Whereas I respect the good works they are doing in saving animals, I do think at some point the requirements become too tight and limit possibilities for homes to an extreme degree. This works at cross purposes. Loving hearts exist at all income levels.

The cosmos sends back a favorite kitten

I've meant to detail mainly the lives of our cats, with a few sidelights of the lives of we who have loved them. And I've tried to discuss mainly animal issues. But no chronicle of this time period can proceed without noting the events on the day Bill woke me to say, "We're being attacked."

September 11, 2001. That rotten day was about a week after we gave away Anna's litter of kittens. Like everyone else, we were shocked, stunned, and heartbroken. I have no doubt that, sitting in front of the television with us, as responsive as the little cat creatures are, they sensed our troubles and they felt the altered currents in our psyches. Our one small and distressed household in the forest felt overwhelmed by the enormity of events. Barely hanging on as we were, here was another concern crowding our jam-packed load of cares. I added "My Country 'Tis of Thee," to the group of songs I sang to the cats around the house.

On the weekend following September 11, there was a local tragedy. Thirteen coal miners were killed in an underground mining accident. We hate to hear of this happening anywhere, and this time it was not so far from where we lived, although we did not know any of the families. I feel tremendous empathy when hard-working people trying to make a living are injured or killed on the job. I was in complete agreement that better safety regulations should be put in place immediately, with no delay, and that in fact, this should have been done years earlier, from the get-go.

Bill's insight into people was sharp, and I knew he'd allowed only good folks to have Anna's kittens. Nevertheless, I always thought about our given-away animals afterwards. I knew they always got good homes in every conventional sense, but the kind of high veneration and exaltation that we had for the animals in our own home (the kind where people came running if a cat sneezed) wasn't universal. So six months later, I found myself thinking of the kittens, especially the brown-and-white one and how much I'd wanted him. I couldn't shake him out of my mind. That was the week before we celebrated Eddie's 85th birthday party at his house. It was an afternoon party and that day, the house was full of people, Eddie's relatives and some of our friends.

About an hour passed, and there was a knock at the door. Bill answered it and went out on the porch. I peeked out between the blinds and saw him standing on the porch talking to a young woman with her hair in long braids. A few minutes later he came back in, carrying the lanky brown-and-white, now six-months-old kitten, who was wearing a bright blue collar his lady had bought for him! His person was moving to a new apartment that would not allow pets, and she had remembered my note saying she could bring him back if she couldn't keep him. He looked healthy and well-cared for. Bill told me when she said good-bye to him, she had tears in her eyes. Just as I had supposed, he had adopted this kitten out to the right person.

Eddie wasn't thrilled to see the kitty that day. He thought we'd never told anyone they could bring kittens back, since he never looked at the paper I wrote. He asked one of the relatives, does it cost money to put an animal in the pound? "This family doesn't take animals to the pound," Mom chimed in quickly, while Bill and I hastened to assure Eddie that we would incur all costs and do all the care of the cat until another home could be found. *With us,* I was thinking as this went on. Eddie agreed to let him stay until we found him another home. Since this felt like one of those assorted, spooky destinies that I just can't ever evade, I said we should take him home to the country and keep him this time. Bill was reluctant and it was all in limbo. The kitten hid immediately after Bill placed him on the floor, but after awhile, after the guests left, he came out.

The kitten stayed at Eddie's longer and longer, presumably until we could introduce him into our household. And then we began to notice odd things, like Eddie smiling at the cat and Eddie petting the cat, who was stretched out and luxuriating beside him. Eddie buying cat food. Eddie and the cat playing "chase," walking from room to room of the house. In their later years down south, Eddie and Abbie, Bill's mom, had made pets of a few yard cats, including a tabby who ran around, moving her tail in such a way that Abbie named her Twister. And earlier, they'd had a cat named Streaker, for the way she streaked around the place. But Eddie had never had an indoor cat before, underfoot and in your face, so he'd never had the chance to carefully study their ways. Once he did, he became fascinated. To our great surprise, he became very attached to the animal. The cat followed him everywhere and kept him amused by being playful and curious. The cat would knock his empty food dish around to create a noisy signal meaning, *Fill this!,* and Eddie said he was the smartest cat he'd ever seen, and his mood would brighten when he talked about the cat, saying "This morning he took every step I took." It made us smile to see the elder and the cat take to each other.

This young kitty was strikingly handsome. His coloration was unusual in random bred cats; his fur had a deep sheen like fine furniture. Even so naming him was no piece of cake. I thought of "Hershey" for the chocolate color, but overall "Mocha" seemed the best fit. When the vet said she had several Mochas, even though I expect most of those were Chocolate Labs, this name seemed a shade commonplace but what can you do. Eddie called him "Pesterhead" or "Bub." Since the cat appeared to Eddie to be swelled up with his own self-importance, he also called him "The Supreme Court Cat." So, it all worked out. The shiny brown cat was staying. Again I find myself unable to comment on the existence of precognition regarding the return of this kitten. Like the case of Bill's dream before we found Minx, I just don't know. This sort of thing doesn't happen to me consistently, although I do often think of people right before they call, a commonly reported phenomenon. But there is something a little mysterious here, I think.

I can comment, though, on landlords who don't allow pets. I'm in strong disagreement with this unfortunate policy. Well-kept pets don't damage places. Studies show that they lower blood pressure and improve health, making for happier, more agreeable tenants. The person who tends a pet carefully may very well take better care of the landlord's property. Children learn responsibility in caring for a pet, as well as how to respond to the needs of another individual, and therefore they, too, grow in empathy and compassion. All of this makes for a healthier community, which always means less property damage. I feel safer in a neighborhood if I hear an occasional dog bark, which can also deter criminals. Criminal break-ins will damage a landlord's property, too!

Although rodents can be poisoned, that's a hazard to children and the environment. It's always the houses in town where pets aren't allowed where the rodent population soars. Mice and rats cause substantial structure damage, including house fires due to chewed wiring. It may well be that companion animals are a fundamental human need and provide constant instruction and fine-tuning for a person's ways of living harmoniously with his fellow creatures, including landlords. While I'm far from having all the answers on the purpose of our existence, I do feel strongly that the existence of animals is as meaningful as our own. And dogs and cats are meant to live with us in some grand, cosmic-scheme-of-things way.

Watching Mocha grow older — and the other cats, too

Mocha was as unique in character as he was in color. He had a strange affinity for water, and he loved to jump into the empty bathtub and play with any water dripping from the faucet, or jump on the sink and do the same. Like Gray Cat and Minou, he was a water-stepper, using his foot to scoop up water and drink it by licking it off his paw. (Cats who do this may not want their very sensitive face whiskers to touch the insides of the bowls or the water.) He'd drink from a dripping faucet in similar fashion, by catching the drip with his paw, and sometimes, he'd just lap at the drip with his tongue.

Eddie was right about him being a smart cat. One day Bill called me into the bathroom to watch Mocha, who turned to look at us and emitted a rare meow; he almost never meowed. He was sitting in the bathtub trying to get water out of the faucet by placing his paw on top of it and patting all around it. Then he started swiping with the paw at the steady drip from the faucet. He caught one, licked his paw, swiped again, and missed; then he watched, got another drip, licked it off, and suddenly learned the exact rhythm of that particular drip, catching every one, lapping off his paw, and catching the next one, and the next, and the next. Bill and I stood stunned, wishing we had a video camera at hand to record this astonishing moment.

Mocha loved to get a running start through the house and would end with a leap into the bathtub, and Eddie reported that on one run when the tub was full, the cat splashed in, did an about-face, scrambled out, and ran from the room. He also missed a jump for the tub once and tumbled end-over-end. Mocha tended to miss-jump now and then. He had grown enormously, and was the largest cat we'd ever seen. He was extremely rangy and, in fact, his body was almost disproportionately long in relation to his slender girth. He was swaybacked when standing in some positions. Bill decided therefore that instead of being clumsy, when he missed jumps Mocha just "couldn't judge his mass." Because of his unusually long and swaybacked body and the swift growth spurt that preceded it, I thought perhaps he had a pituitary condition that caused excess growth. However, in a few years his growth did seem to stabilize, his back muscles strengthened, and his morphology became like that of other cats, even after he gained a bit more weight.

When his food bowl was empty, Mocha would bat it around on the floor or hook a paw on the edge and pull it around, until someone noticed the noise and filled it. He was deft with his big, white paws and would lift up a kibble of dry food and drop it into his water bowl before fishing it back out and eating it. He liked his kibble dunked! The kibble we fed him back then had an X shape and was therefore paw-grippable. We missed the signal somehow when Mocha began flipping his water bowl over with his paw, a dilemma that I solved by bringing a sturdier basin in from the country to use as his water dish. I now believe he was telling us he wanted his water freshened. He came running whenever I refilled his bowl, liking the taste of water untouched by any cat tongues, even his own.

When he and Eddie would play "chase" around the house, Eddie would walk around the corner and into the next room, with the cat continuing to run after him. Mocha came running up whenever Bill and I entered Eddie's house, eager to see visitors. Bill would lift him high, to chest level, and hold him, and he'd purr when I stroked his head. While held aloft, he would look around and sniff around at the upper level of the room that he could not usually frequent and smell. He'd flop onto my lap when I sat down, only half on; he was so long that while his chest and front feet were on my lap, his abdo-

men and hind legs had to rest on the couch or chair. In fact, that was the way
he had to sit on anyone's lap. He had grown so big that he inspired an attempted wisecrack on my part, about a chocolate bobcat coming through
town and romancing his mother. I also called him "CatZilla" and "Cat
Kong." The jokes may have fallen flat, but his size is not to be ignored. During those times when Eddie went on visits out of town that lasted several
days, Mocha was left alone, with Bill going in to feed him and check on the
house every day. Mocha would be absolutely frantic for attention at these
times, again proving that cats are not the solitary creatures they are reputed to
be. They require company even if they play it cool about showing it, and they
develop deep attachments to their people; Mocha and Eddie were pals. Mocha had already lost his first person and was probably afraid, whenever Eddie
left town, that he'd lose him, too.

Mocha's white nose blaze was offset, and he had two tones on his nose
like Spotty. About a third of his nose leather was dark umber, under the
brown area of the nose; the rest, beneath the white blaze, was pink. On that
same left side, his central front paw pad, the metacarpal pad, was a lighter
brown color, a sort of bronze. The back central, or metatarsal pad, was also
bronze, as well as part of one toe on the hind foot of that side. On the right
front paw, he had one lightly bronze toe. The rest of the paw pads were the
usual pink. He had white fur in his ears, like Kudzu in his older years. At first
I thought his eyes were going to be a pale gold, but in maturity they became a
pale greenish-gold color that I'd never seen before in cats. It was so light and
clear, many shades away from Kudzu's intensely emerald eyes and even
Pretty Girl's opalescent green.

The house Eddie lived in was built around a central wall with two rooms
on either side of it; all the rooms were connected to each other so that you
could traverse the house in a circle. Mocha invented a floorplan-dependent
game. He started by posturing and challenging Bill and Eddie: he would bow
up, tail afluff, and come sideways towards them, crab-like. They would rush
towards him and he'd tear away, and then he would run around the house
through all the rooms with one or both guys in pursuit. With Bill, Mocha
took the game to another level. At some point during the chase, the cat would
hide under a bed or a chair, or in the closet, where he thought Bill couldn't
see him, but of course Bill knew where he was. Mocha would jump out at
him suddenly, playing at being scary, and Bill would make a show of jumping and running. To see what this highly imaginative cat mind would do next,
Bill took things a step further and let himself be drawn into a game invented
by a cat. Bill would hide behind a door where the cat couldn't see him and
peep around time to time, waiting Mocha out. Mocha would eventually

emerge, creeping around slowly and carefully, looking for Bill. Bill would then jump out at him, and Mocha would take off like a shot, running around the house again. They would each take turns hiding and jumping out at the other. Bill and the cat developed a game that kept Eddie amused and smiling.

Over time, the name Mocha morphed into MochaBud and then just Bud. Bud grew, and grew, and grew. He's now about twenty-inches-long, from head to base of tail. His noggin is the size of a grapefruit, even though his mother, Anna, is a small girl. So I was thinking to myself, *we've seen possums and raccoons in the town neighborhood, why can't there be bobcats out there?* Of course, a bobcat is much more likely, upon seeing a domestic cat, to think "dinner" rather than "dinner date." And I'm actually sure there are no bobcats in town. Bud's a domestic cat, just a really big one. Bud's play can be rough at times, so he not only has the size of a bobcat, but the manners, too.

Back at home in the forest, cat stuff went as always: lots of snoozing, chowing down, purring, and careful selection of the next napping space. When we came home from being out, the cats would sniff our clothes and shoes to read the news of where we'd been. Sometimes they would make the open-mouthed grin called the "Flemen's reaction," which enables them to more thoroughly investigate odors. The look really fits the South Alabama expression "grinning like a mule-eating briars." They no doubt smelled the cats at Mom's and Eddie's respective houses. "What a story I've got for you to smell," Bill would address Minou, as the cat carefully worked his nose. At either parent's place, the resident cats would also check out our clothing, learning the news of our household cats and our travels.

Spotty was being her petulant self, trotting into the kitchen whenever I went, viewing my every excursion there as a chance to sing for canned food, shaking her tail when I was there for some other purpose. With only a slight stretch of imagination, her screechy soprano drawl again became *"me-ya-awwwwuuulllll* meaning *y'all pat me now folks, pat me nooooo-ooowwwww.* Spotty was all chirps of happiness and slow-blinking eyelids over chartreuse eyes once she was fondled and patted, even if it was while sitting alongside another cat who had been the snuggled object of her envy the instant before. Spotty addressed these vocal forays towards our language, the plural *y'all* to us as a group, like a true southern cat. (Hearing "y'all" said to one person drives me snakebit crazy; but Bill claims to have heard this as a traditional use. One humor site I saw said y'all is singular and "all y'all" is plural. But the most sensible information I've seen says that "you" is singular and "y'all" is plural for up to four persons, and "all y'all" is for groups greater than four persons.) In the kitchen, both Minx and Minou would look at me and lick their lips to signal they wanted canned food. Minou would walk around meowing and doing his "Give me fish please" strut.

Minx was proceeding up my torso when I reclined at a slower pace than in her mad gallop kitten days, but even with a bit of hind-leg stiffness, she was still tapping my face with her paw before turning this way and that, feeling for her best seating arrangement for looking into my eyes and suffusing the air around us with the rumble of her purr. If facing away from my gaze, she'd tilt her head back towards me and again and again, I'd rub my chin between her ears. Sometimes she'd climb up me and nudge her head against my face. After I became ill, she became even more adhered to my lap. Getting up meant a slow and delicate series of maneuvers to gently lift Minx from me to the couch space beside me, and then a quick rise before she could scramble back on. She would re-claim me repeatedly, even though I had to keep unseating her due to chores and frequent restroom trips. The day we watched Mocha learn to catch water drips in synchrony with the pace of the drip, Minx had gone around meowing mournfully that evening after we got home. I thought maybe it was because she hadn't gotten her daily quota of pats due to the loss of pat-time while I was in town; and she was making sure we heard her discontent.

Minx would often stretch a paw up towards me, toes and claws flexed outwards like Pretty Girl high-fiving. If she was sitting on the couch facing me as I watched television, she'd do a fast claw retract as she arced it back down, resting the paw on my hand, and she'd sleep and we'd sit there together, hand-in-paw, for long lengths of time.

The boys were still alert and watchful, even as they grew older. Minou liked to sleep in Bill's computer chair all day and when Bill came home he'd park in Bill's lap, after Bill managed to edge himself onto the seat, with the Booper still taking most of it. Minou would turn his intent gaze on the computer screen, although never long enough for me to get a photo. I always joked that he was trying to figure out how to order seafood and have it delivered to the door. Mature Minou now began again to respond to the "Boop Boop Minouper" scat singing. He was over the young-adult touchiness and disdain-by-nonresponse, and was more in the "I used to be young, too" phase. He liked to hear the sounds of his kitten days, strutting and pressing his face on us when we sang it. At least, that's all I can figure to account for the change.

Bill burst into song one day while looking at Minx, with a lyric that fit any cat, from "Sea of Love" by George Khoury and Phillip Baptiste, and laughed. While meaning something else, the song told perfectly of instant connections between humans and pets.[4] When older Kudzu and Minou rose up at each other, about to box, Kudzu would place his big front paw on Minou's head to hold him down, albeit temporarily, before Minou wriggled around it. His flexed-out white paw filled the space between the ears on Minou's smaller, still kitten-like head.

At some point Kudzu had begun to chase and pounce on shadows. There were many windows in the main living room, and one wall was almost all window, a south exposure to the woods. On sunny, breezy days, shadows shifted and danced on the floor everywhere, cast by room objects and from the dense branches growing close to the house outside. Kudzu would run after the shadows, batting and pouncing, even going up on his hind legs and coming down *thunk!* with his forefeet, capturing the squirming shade. He nailed most of them. Bill had the telephone on a long cord and he would sit back and talk while the cord dangled about. Kudzu began to chase that shadow, too, and Bill would bounce the cord around and make the shadow motion lively and frenetic for him, while Kudzu went pouncin' crazy.

Spotty was sitting on a chair in sunlight with her back to us one day, waving her tail in annoyance at something, perhaps her inability to catch a distant bird outside that she could see and hear but I couldn't. Kudzu was on the floor behind her, chasing the shadows cast by her flicking tail. When she stopped wagging it and the tail shadow was suddenly still, he looked up at her colorful back end for a minute, and what I saw on his face was comprehension and recognition. He reached up with his big white front paw and tapped her on the rear to make her start waving the tail again. She did, and he went right back to chasing and pouncing on the shadows it made. I gawked in amazement. I knew cats were brainy, but even I would not have expected Kudzu to comprehend so absolutely the link between Spotty's moving tail and the moving shadow tail on the floor. Bill called this "calculated logical reasoning." It was unlikely Kudzu had encountered that exact configuration of sun, waving tail, and shadow before. But upon this very first encounter, he had instantly perceived the cause-and-effect relationship, not something I believe the experts expect of these animals. Certainly cats seem to understand the difference in real prey and toy prey for playing, and we can wonder further if Kudzu understood that the shadows were even more insubstantial than, for instance, a stick we waved with shiny tassels. He certainly seemed to understand that once he had landed on a moving shadow he'd gotten it, and that he could grab it no further as he would have done with the tassels, tousling them with a series of rapid fire grabs. With shadows, he would just move on to pounce the adjacent negative branch image, and then the next. We can also speculate, was it possible that maybe, in chasing the silhouette of Spotty's tail and knowing it was connected to her, he was symbolically jumping on that fussy little spotty thing he considered such an annoyance? Or was she finally just being "good for something" in his view? Of course, we can't answer those questions.

These amazing moments with brainiac Kudzu all happened when I was alone with the cats and there were no other witnesses. *Aha!* Some readers will say that I am a teller of tall tales. But I can assure you that these are the absolute truth, no fiction involved. When it was just me and the kittums, I was more aware of their every move. Having Bill home would have meant the other distractions of conversation and watching movies and television shows, and less intense cat watching.

Pretty Girl was still lonesome and trying to find a friend, but she was mistrustful of laps and only sat with her front paws and chest on me. Eventually she would climb on Bill and radiate bliss as he rubbed her face and stroked her back. I don't know why she would not do this with me, but it may have been because with Minx in the house, there was a palpable feeling that I was "taken." Orange Cat and Gray Cat had known it, and so had Spotty, Kudzu, and Minou. Pretty Girl was more jealous of the attention Minou got than of any overtures to Minx, as though she had some degree of not respect, but resigned acknowledgment, of Minx as matriarch or queen bee. Whereas Spotty was satisfied once she got attention, Pretty Girl had some deeply insatiable longing that no amount of attention and pats could calm. She evidently had never recovered from being abandoned and left alone.

Neither could our attentions deflect her resentment towards other cats. Cats that have lived outside on their own for a long time usually regard other cats as rivals for food, and tomcats may have been a threat to her kittens. That may account for her seeming greater jealousy towards Kudzu and Minou. My heart went out to my lonesome tabby every day when again she would demonstrate that cats are not the feline equivalent of "lone wolves;" they do experience prolonged suffering when they lose their human friends or even the acquaintances known to semi-feral yard cats.

I had a friend who was an incredible painter and colorist. He never worked with black straight out of the tube, but instead mixed colors in with black to make it what he termed a "rich" black, rather than a plain, ordinary tone from the tube. My three predominately black cats — Minx, Kudzu, and Minou — were three distinctly different shades of the same vibrant, spectrum-haunted night color. It was obvious when you saw them all together. The natural world has an infinity of subtle variations for those who will bother to notice.

Good and persistent lap cats can increase your observation skills, but they can also make your work ethic shrink up and scuttle away into oblivion.

Cats make indolence look elegant and satisfying, even productive. In our house there was a condition called "being catted." It meant having one or more cats reclining upon one's person. Having two was described as being "double-catted," and etc. It was a great way to get the other person to wait on you, as in, "Will you get me such and such, I'm completely catted down." The cats, after all, preferred not to be disturbed, and we both respected that. Of course, if the cat took a notion to jump off, he or she would completely destroy one's "catted" status, and likely one's pretense to helplessness, too. The rare evening when three or more would be parked upon one person was a golden opportunity for complete indolence and required the other one of us to tend to schlepping meals, drinks, books, and changing the television or fetching the clicker after we acquired that technology. It was complete incapacitation via cat load and could even require assistance with the eventual defelination, such as those rare times I had four sleeping on me. Once, they caught me in a half-reclining position, first Minx installed herself on my abdomen and purred and then Spotty sprawled across my chest, placing her muzzle in my face; not to be outdone, Kudzu leaped onto my upper legs and settled in and then Minou stepped onto my shins and weighted them down. They had me good, and they knew it, those smart-aleck cat brats! I couldn't move. Not wanting to disturb anyone I waited as long as I could, and when I finally just had to get up, I had no choice but to ask Bill for assistance.

I spent long days at the house when Bill was out working, because employment wasn't possible for me. If you live in the forest, you had better like the color green, and I've got that part down. In late summer, looking through every window of the house there are festoons of leaves interspersed with bits of sunlight; green in rivulets, clumps, veils, curtains and spottings offset by the darkness of receding areas, all with an overwhelming, verdant tinge. There's all kinds of breathtaking, natural beauty in every permutation of every season in the forest. But the isolation I didn't handle so well. I couldn't slip out of the house and spend an hour or so in town anymore, or even take a walk to a neighbor's, as I could no longer walk very far. During the day, everyone else was working. I could not have existed there without the cats. In fact, I cannot imagine living anywhere without them; even in the most entrancing social whirl, I would still require my cats.

Sitting around with a bunch of cats, I admired and aspired to their vigilant serenity. Many times I'd sit there gazing at them and suddenly along would come an unbidden sense of awe and joy and rhapsody in their presence, a wild and mad love for the little things, sort of an "Ancient Mariner"[5] moment, or a "cleansed doors of perception"[6] moment or, like in the Blake poem, "To see a world in a grain of sand, and Heaven in a wildflower."[7] And

I'd think, we have had such terrible luck in so many ways, but the finding of our alley cats, randomly turning up on highways and in the forest, has been incredible good fortune, with so much love and adventure and comfort coming to us from each one. Years ago a neighborhood child who visited told me so; looking around the room at Gray Cat, Orange Cat, and Minx, he said we were lucky to have three cats; he only had one. I might add, though, that even on a mundane day, a sudden glimpse of even just one cat can plunge you into a lengthy contemplation of all that is catness and grace, so impossible to detail in words. This magnificent creature, who confounds endlessly, may then break the spell with the familiar comfort of a resounding bellow that means, *Feed me fish, now!*

The cats we've had have definitely been "come home to" critters. They have not been the "go with and do" types. Short car rides to the vet elicited howls that rivaled the sirens of emergency vehicles in volume and urgency. At the clinic, they would go all fizz and vinegar at the new place and the new people. Transported to Mom's house and left undisturbed in a room to settle in, they hide for days and *might* creep out in the deepest, darkest hours of the night. Detailed in three books, Peter Gethers's cat Norton went everywhere with him and shared his adventures. Not so with my couch potatoes. The closest we ever came to the exciting life of Norton and Mr. Gethers is when I sang "Sur Le Pont, D'Avignon"[8] around the living room with the cats. I missed them when I was out and about; rare occasions these days.

In August of each year there is a blues festival in a town about half an hour's ride south of here, where some friends of ours live. We used to catch it all the time when I was well, and one mid-'90s summer, we decided to pack up my nutrient supplies and catch it again. After the festival, we had a wilderness experience of an area even more remote than the one we live in. The Sipsey River runs a long way through Alabama. The northern part is a National Wild and Scenic River System, and part of it is protected. In areas closer to us it winds through wetlands, cypress swamps, and hardwood stands, which contain a wide variety of wildlife. Johnny, one of the friends we visited that day, had some land along the Sipsey River in really wild country, where bear tracks have been seen. After the festival, in the long summer evening, we went there with a group of people.

We bounced along on a dirt road far more rough and rugged than our own. Stepping out of the vehicle, we had a ways to walk, past a stream and into another world. Everyone assisted me and stopped frequently so I could rest. We ended up in a scarcely disturbed forest of rolling terrain beside the river. There was an embankment of about eight feet along the shoreline. I walked to top of the rise. Bill had already slid right down to the water's edge with Johnny, who was yelling up, "Don't come down here!" and I saw why; they had sunk six inches into the viscous mud on the banks. With every step taken, they pulled up a foot coated with slimy mud about to the tops of their socks. "Otter!" they shouted back up to us, reporting on tracks. I found a little clear space amongst some leaves to sit. Overhead, the trees made a sparkling haze of the daylight's fade. The stillness was overpowering. We were far away from the small towns, farms, and other beaten pathways. There was no hearing a car or a train go by, as we did when at home in our forest.

Our party was ongoing. Music came from a truck radio. Our friends drank beer, and I raised a can of liquid nutrient. There was the sound of slapping rapid thuds as two members of the group ran past, getting a big head start, and jumped into the river for a swim, sending up plumes of splatter. Slowly, dusk thickened in the canopy above. Late at night, using flashlights, we negotiated our way back out. There's nothing like being with friends in the remote wild places of Earth. I daresay it's rare for a person with a sickness of this magnitude to be able to go to such a remote wild river. I only thought I lived in the wilderness; the Sipsey wilds were so much deeper.

The cats had waited up for us, the boys at the door with white ruffs gleaming, the girls folded skeptically on the couch, anxious no doubt, as we were very late. A perfect ending to a perfect evening. I was still sick, although while in the deep woods with friends it had been almost possible to forget. We said a few words to the cats to convey our outings, knowing they didn't really understand the speech. But they may have detected in our demeanor, the lingering afterglow of a really fine evening along with the satisfaction of finally being home with your cats, those heart-lions who stretch and purr.

Living in the country, you'll hear gunshots, both in and out of hunting season. Sometimes we had to run people off who would stop at our turnaround, and despite the mailboxes indicating nearby houses, start shooting — just to be shooting, I presume. That was enough of an irritation, not to mention a danger to those of us who walk in the woods or even just live there. But I also can't help but wonder why it's considered sporting to shoot an unarmed animal with a technologically advanced weapon. Arm the deer and the wild turkeys with high-powered rifles, and then you'd have something more like an even match. Seriously, though, if the "sport" is in the skill of tracking and getting within sight of the animal, then why not capture its image with a high-powered camera instead? That way you'll have the same thrill of tracking and stalking something, of crouching in the brush and taking aim to snap the shutter, and the pleasure of owning and tending a precision piece of equipment. You'd even have the photographic trophies to display proudly, and they don't draw moths. You'd have satisfied the yen to match wits with wildlings and you'd have a memory and a tale to tell, rather than a carcass. If it's your marksmanship you want to flex, go to a shooting range and nail inanimate objects.

These objections apply to sports and trophy hunting only; I do understand that there are still people who have to hunt in order to have enough to eat. This sad situation shouldn't exist in the United States, but it does. Ethical hunting of non-endangered species, when the animals are used for food by hunters or donated as food to charity, gets a reluctant pass from me. It's not something I would ever want to do myself, but I really can't say for sure that it's crueler than slaughterhouses are. However, hunting large game for the thrill of it, known as trophy hunting, and the photos of those who think this gives them some kind of prestige, still sinks my heart and sickens my stomach.

I don't actually advocate spontaneously running into the wild to photograph wild animals. No one should enter the wilderness without first consulting wilderness experts and learning about terrain, climate, indigenous fauna (especially snakes), and specific instructions for encountering each kind of animal. It's best not to approach or corner a wild animal. Using long-range lenses is probably a possibility, but you need expert advice as to what distance from an animal is safe. All animals are aggressive during the seasons of mating and raising young, even herbivores like deer. We ourselves entered the deeper forest only after years of our own experience and only while in the company of others very seasoned in woods-going. Take precautions so no one has to go in after your carcass.

And whatever you do, don't fall out drunk on a fire ant hill. I've heard tales of people that did and all they found later were skeletons! Although that's probably just a rural folk tale.

"Finally you got to the real starting point of the book, when I came along. Everything before that should be scratched. And all the Othercats." So says my Editing Cat, Bud.

"Um …"

"And I never missed a jump. I staged all that. I'm a comedian. I'm here all week, folks. Take that part out."

"Um, no …"

"*Phssssst!*"

"How would you even know about comedians?"

"Well, *phsssssst*. I just now read it in your book, doofus. Holler at me whenever you decide you want to edit for reals! I'll be napping."

Chapter 12

Splendor In The Grass[1]

I'd known for some time that all of our cats were getting older, and that one day they would leave us. You raise one from a kitten or take in a young cat at one or two years old, time passes, and suddenly they are older than you are. The chart that compares human ages with cat ages is disconcerting; you can see they're getting white hairs in their dark fur and long toenails that click on the floor.

One of Minx's all-black whiskers turned white in 2002. On the left side of her face, it had the curve of a handlebar mustache, and I trusted it still retained its maneuverability and sensing capacity. Kudzu, too, had grown short, spikey white whiskers all over his lower jaw. These older kitties slept a lot and they didn't romp all over the house, crackling with excitement as they did when they were young. The barn dance was over. They were not required to entertain us. By then we had learned the art of stillness and contemplation from them anyway, and we enjoyed watching them sleep, as we did when they were young. It was time for us to join them in finding a sunny spot and stretching out. The deal was that we would care for them when they were old and no longer action-packed. We revere them through all their ages; it's part of the agreement to share hearth and home.

You feel a sense of having seen and shared a lot of things with an old animal you've been with a long time, and even if you acquire one with some age on him or her and the time you've had together has been shorter, there's a sense of shared present instants, and caring. Older cats sometimes become more affectionate, seeking laps out more often. Even cats that weren't lap animals when younger might discover, as seniors, the comforts of lounging on you and keeping you catted down for their enjoyment. Seasoned cats really show you how contentment is done. No animal expresses the art of being comfortable like cats do. They seem more aware of ambient sounds, movements, and presences in sleep than do many persons while fully awake. When cats sleep longer hours, it doesn't represent a diminished life; it's just an expansion of the hidden side of their alertness. Just what do they take in from the outside and monitor, and what do they dream while asleep? We can only watch and speculate or wonder. It's a secret, a cipher. It stimulates the mind.

Saying goodbye to Spotty

Spotty had never been robust. There had been the drooling when she came to us, which cleared up with good nutrition, but we didn't know how long she'd lived homeless and malnourished, and what health damage she may have incurred from those years. She'd been through spells of vomiting that the vet found no cause for, and the only thing to do was to nurse her through, soothe her with singing, and after a few hours, when she would begin to pull out of it, give her electrolyte solution. The savvy little thing knew that she had to refrain from eating and drinking for a span of hours, giving her system a rest to recover. As far as I know, that was before the days when food allergies were well-known in veterinary science. I wish we'd thought of that for Spotty, but it just never crossed our radar before the Internet. However, the cats' diets were fairly consistent at that time, and the irregular sequences between episodes didn't suggest that she was having a reaction to specific foods or ingredients.

She'd had skin problems, too, and in the past, a large mast cell tumor had to be removed from the surface of her flank. Before surgery, the area had been a "hot spot" that she licked persistently despite attempts to dissuade her. She required a vet-ordered Elizabethan collar for six weeks to keep her from opening up the wound with her teeth. The concern was greater than the usual stitch-pulling mischief that cats will get into in a flash before you can stop them. All of her extra loose skin in the area had been used to close the incision, and if she did too much tissue damage to the site, she would have ended up with a wound the vets could no longer close. Rather than leave her collared up 24/7, my mom would come over to help watch and we'd take the collar off and pet and play with her, occupying her every minute to keep her from irritating the wound. She'd turn her head often trying to get at the sutures with her mouth, and we'd have to deflect her head away from her back end.

Cats don't like to be contradicted and she gave us some looks and *mroowls*, but good-natured as she was, she never tried to bite or scratch us. Instead, she basked in all the attention she was getting. We both had the free time so we kept her preoccupied and un-collared for large spans of time out of every day, all those weeks until the vet declared her completely healed. Nowadays there have been innovations in keeping cats from disturbing their stitched wounds: stockings, stockinette material, and baby onesies have been fashioned into barrier garments as an alternative to the old "cone of shame." Usually mast cell tumors in cats are benign, as Spotty's was, and easily treatable. She had a great outcome from her procedure, and no further trouble with this sort of skin lesion. That was back in 1997.

Her weight had gone up and down. For awhile she was a comfortable plump, but in early November 2002, although she was eating well, her weight was down. White hairs had been creeping into the slate-gray side of her diminutive muzzle for some time. She had become crankier with the other cats and jumped on Minx, and although most of the time she'd still run around like she had lots of energy, there were other times when she acted feeble and frail, and she had increased her water intake. (Many older cats develop chronic kidney disease; increased water consumption can be a sign of this ailment.) Then she decreased her food intake. I began to fear losing her, and I felt heartbroken and overwhelmed. I talked to Bill about it, but I delayed telling my mother. We phoned the vet and obtained a high-calorie gel. I began giving it to Spotty to try to increase her weight. Fortunately, Spotty loved the taste and would cheerfully lap it off a spoon.

On November 26, Bill took Spotty to the vet. She got frantic in the car. At the time I thought she was about thirteen years old — she'd come to us in 1990, a little less than twelve years ago, and I thought she was maybe one year of age when she arrived. But the vet said she was as least fifteen years old, and that she was just old and failing. Heart or kidney problems could be making her thin. She was still perky that evening, but she wouldn't take much hi-cal. The next day she stayed hidden until night — and then she was better, but feeble and eating less than before. She sat next to me on the couch and purred and purred. For a small cat, she had a very loud purr. By November 29, the day after Thanksgiving, she was hiding even more, only showing herself now and then. She'd lost more weight and took less hi-cal, but she did eat with gusto the turkey Mom sent home for our cats. That girl could always be counted on to relish a treat.

The next day the woods were shining with the bright, sunny light of the late fall. Bill had to get Spotty out from under the couch. She had stopped eating her canned food but she did eat a small amount of turkey. She stayed out from under the couch and blinked at me from across the room; I went over to her, sang to her, patted her, and she meowed and meowed back using her wide range of beguiling notes. She seemed unsteady on her back legs, and I knew then she was in the process of leaving us. Nonetheless, she was out in the room most of the next day, too; she ate turkey and a little dry food, but nothing else. She got lots of attention from both of us, and even though Bill said she was just fussy about food in her old age, I later caught him looking really sad.

December 2 was a bad day for me because it was a bad day for Spotty. She staggered and could hardly walk for awhile, and I went and sat with her and sang and talked. She meowed and flexed her paw and was responsive and walked better for awhile, but then she went and hid again. *She's a plucky little thing,* I was thinking. *She's come back from illness before maybe she can do it again.* But I also thought, *if she has to go, I hope she'll go easy and at home.* December 3 was another bad day for her, but the vet's suggestion that it was a possible kidney infection, which was a treatable illness, plus an appetite stimulant to rub on her ears gave me some hope. I kept singing to her as much as I could, and she kept up her loud *purr* songs. On December 4, Bill talked to the vet a long time on the phone. In the afternoon, a responsive and alert Spotty went to the vet with me sitting in the backseat of the car with her to pat and talk and calm her. She had bloodwork and turned up a low calcium level, with treatable hypocalcemia as the possible cause, again giving me some hope. Mom by then knew Spotty was sick, and I even told her we had some hope.

Bill went that evening, after it was already dark, to take Spotty to a clinic outside Birmingham, with all its sophisticated equipment, for further tests. But those vets didn't confirm calcium deficiency. Instead, they prescribed anti-inflammatories for her gut and said to force-feed her with a syringe, and we did and she kept it down. They thought she had high blood pressure and possible bone cancer, because she had a high white blood cell count. She was also eight percent blind, possibly as a result of high blood pressure. That was also probably the cause of some bleeding in her gut that had shown up in her stool. While Bill had been in Birmingham with the cat, our local vet called me twice to see if he was back with Spotty yet and what the vets up there had said.

The weight of when to let go was heavy on our hearts. These decisions are very hard. We don't want animals to suffer when there is no hope of recovery. But we also do not want to deprive such highly sentient beings of any moments of pleasure in living that they might still have. Spotty was still responding to our pats and songs with her own series of happy, sharp *tweets* and *barks*, and head nudges against our hands.

I had lived in Alabama for thirty-five years by 2002 and I'd seen the weather patterns change. In earlier years warm tropical weather, my favorite, would linger long into the fall and early winter. I recall 75-degree temperatures on Halloween, Thanksgiving, and Christmas. I've listened to crickets sing on balmy evenings in January. There would be spells of really cold weather, below-freezing temperatures in the teens and twenties and even down below zero, but that would only last a few days and then we'd be borderline warm again. Spring warmup could start as early as February — I remember it being in the seventies on Valentine's Day once. But sometime in the '90s that seemed to change. I admit it may have crept up on me slowly.

Suddenly it seemed that every blast of cold air coming across the Great Plains swooped down on us, too. We were getting previously unheard-of sleet in November, and one January, our friend Davey, who travels as a musician, said that on a recent short tour it had been warmer in the Alps than it was here in central Alabama at the same time. (Years later I realized I should have come back with, "Colder in the Apps (Appalachians) than the Alps, eh?") Sustained frigid cold began lasting into March and April. The flowers and wisteria started to come out during warm spells in March, lasted a few weeks, and then got killed off prematurely by April cold snaps. Peach crops were lost due to this pattern of warm up and chill down. These things never used to happen in the earlier years. I do believe global warming is happening; the evidence as evaluated by scientists is just plainly there. All these weather shifts are part of the disruption. As Dr. Photon (Bill), says, putting increased energy, heat, into a closed system like the Earth's atmosphere, will result in differences in wind-flow directions and intensities, as well as turbulence. We were getting warm tropic air from the Gulf or cold Arctic air from the Great Plains, depending on which way the wind blew. There's always been a tussle between these upper atmosphere winds, but the Plains air was winning more often. I believe global warming is a true hazard to our planet, but what we were seeing in the Deep South in those years felt more like an "outhouse" rather than "greenhouse" effect: we were freezing our butts off here.

The December when Spotty began failing was one of the cold ones, with temperatures down into the teens every few nights, and the chill added to the dreary gloom that was descending over the house. Winter was always a bleak and difficult time for me, but this one was especially hard. Tough little cookie Spotty started eating again the next day, December 5; she was cheerful, purring and meowing, and responsive to talking, singing, and being snuggled on laps. If I even walked by her while doing something else, she reacted to my proximity by purring. December 6, 7, and 8, Spotty seemed to have rallied. She was more animated, engaged, and interactive, and she was eating even more. She was very affectionate, seeking comfort and attention. But on December 9, although she ate more in the evening, she staggered and seemed confused, hanging her head down, stepping in her water, and being less responsive at times. We thought she'd go that night, only to be surprised the next day by a perk-up.

At another visit with the local vet, she was friendly and responsive and purring. She always loved to show off and make friends with people. It wasn't time to let go yet, and we should continue supportive care to keep her comfortable, the vet indicated; it was just a matter of time. Back at home we both sat on the couch with the lights low. Spotty slept peacefully on one lap or the other, purring and occasionally moving from one of us to the other and back again. Brave little Spotty settled her frail self gingerly on us, while we sat quaking inside, trying to soothe her with a few words. We knew we were losing her. Bless her sweet heart, the vet called to ask about Spotty the next day.

On December 11, Spotty enjoyed purring in our laps, on this day and for the next several days. We opened all kinds of especially savory cat food to tempt her, but she would not eat much, although she did go for fish one morning but not again in the evening. She'd call to us, and she was sleepy in our laps, not as active. I sang to her as much as I could during the day, "By the Beautiful Sea" and all the other songs I knew.

On December 14, 2002, we lost Spotty. She could not stand up but still made her impossibly cute, musical sounds when I stroked her, calling meaningfully to me, purring. The vet delayed a trip out of town to check on her, and then to help us let her go. Worn out and running on fumes, I was unable to make the trip to the vet with Bill and Spotty. He sang "By the Beautiful Sea" to her all the way there. The vet found that she was going into congestive heart failure, and in a matter of hours, she would have ended up struggling for breath. Although I knew it was coming and I'd lost cats before, I felt like my heart was ripped out. Bill said she purred the whole time, and it was peaceful.

We buried her in the woods she had come out of, near Gray Cat and Orange Cat, and one of Mom's kitties who had passed a few years ago. A late fall meant the forest still had some bright speckles and spots in the trees, like the artful patterns of Spotty's tortoiseshell fur. Back in the house, life felt drab. She was "Little Bit," another of her nicknames; she had been the local colors of the house, now crossed into the spectral colors of the world beyond. She was the raconteur of the group, the noisebox who meowed more than all the others. Spotty had stayed sweet to us always although she was peevish with the other cats. I was reminded of how precious they all are, how they are all to be petted and cherished. It was a huge sadness. It would have been easy to sing the "By the Beautiful Sea" song to another cat, just plugging in a different name. But I never did. It was Spotty's song.

I had a Spotty meltdown several days later when Beethoven was played on the radio, revving up all my emotions even more. Both of us were really sad, missing Spotty terribly. There was a dank cold fog over me; Spotty haunted my thoughts. Under this sodden and stormy cloud of pain, I could not get into Christmas. The somber landscape matched my mood, and I had the Spotty blues bad. No more flashes of color, and streaks of piebald patchwork. No Christmas lights could illuminate the night the way Miss SpottaLee

Spot's entrance into the room could brighten up the place in daylight or night-dark. No more fussy little squawkbox. I even missed that voice.

Bill put Minx on my lap one night and she purred, and I dreaded the day I'd lose her, too. I'd had those two girls so long; they just went together. And after nearly twelve years of Minx, Spotty, Kudzu, and Minou, it felt like they were forever. Something about the combination just worked. Although in some ways it was a group whose sympathies clashed, they had settled and meshed into a sort of family. Each had a niche and any discord was brief and bemused, and I sensed they were all happy. Even if some pairs weren't wild about each other, they had become tolerant. Kudzu and Minou were pals, and Minx and Spotty would put up with each other despite Spotty's intense jealousies. Kudzu and Minou coped with the temperamental girls by simply dodging them. Kudzu still carried a torch for Minx but was worldly wise and capable of a certain amount of glee when his advances made her growl with anger. Minx avoided the boys; Spotty sassed them. Minou avoided the girls and usually slept alone, but sometimes he slept with Kudzu.

Yet even though they had their preferences, when I look back over photos of the four we had for twelve years, I see them snoozing in every combination. Although it was usually the boys snuggling in one place and the girls cozied up in another, it could at times be a boy with either girl. Both Bill and I were captured during this era with one or two or three cats aloft, all of them vying for space or snoozing on board. All we had to do was sit down, and we'd soon be catted. Or, all four would stretch across the couch: Kudzu, Minou, Spotty, Minx. Of all the sleeping duos, Spotty and Minx would form the tightest snuggles. Usually those were the result of Spotty, clever and determined little sweetheart that she was, winding herself further and further into Minx's space. (Pretty Girl was the one who never seemed to quite fit, didn't quite agree, and who seemed lonely, even while glad to be safe and fed and among us.)

Minx sailed through those years, perhaps feigning obliviousness, and stayed by me. It had been a kind of harmony, albeit a fretful one. Somehow everyone acknowledged in some catlike way that Minx was the alpha cat. No sense of mine, no instrument, could detect the particle or quantity of their agreements, friendships, stalemates, stand-offs, or resolved quarrels; nor could I spell it out if, by feline reasoning, they decided to put up with their dislikes of each other for the sake of food, location, and peace in a household that provided the company of other cats and of their two, mutually shared giants. I can only guess at what they thought of each other — and said to each other. Their inter-cat communications were mostly invisible and unheard, like a radiance at a distal and unseen end of a spectrum, or the perfect pitch of some un-meowed, cat-to-cat repartee outside the range of human hearing. Was there a low hum at the edge of my hearing? Or did this flow occur in the daily stretch and flick of cat movement?

There was nothing to do now but cherish all the remaining cats in this new configuration, whatever it would become, because who knew when they'd be ripped away, too?

A little lion and a scramble on The Gold House

In contrast to the subtleties of feline social life, their overtures toward us humans are much more demonstrative. They know we aren't as astute or canny as their own kind, and we require pointed looks, reassurance with blinks of their love, head nudges and bonks, a wide range of meows and *trills*, joyful rolls and stretches and contented sleeps, and any number of visual cues as to what they require and wish to express. Many times, they have to show us who's boss, too.

Days after Spotty left us, I was sitting between Pretty Girl and Minx when Pretty Girl walked across my lap and went and snuggled up to Minx. Minx groomed her briefly, then let her stay a moment, before getting up and moving away a short distance. I had petted both of them while they were together to encourage Minx to stay, but without success. Pretty Girl really wanted a cat friend but still wasn't having much luck.

On December 21, I had a dream about Spotty early in the morning. There she was, in all her color-splashed glory. She was using her claw to play an old phonograph record. Every now and then she'd lose contact with the record and have to start again. I could not recall what she played but I think it was music rather than words. This was part of a lengthy dreaming process that was not totally remembered, but the other parts I recall were not Spotty related. I'm making no comments on telepathy or the spirit world or precognition here but will leave that to the reader's particular flights, or not, of fancy. Dreams are the tumbling of the mind flexing itself while the waking consciousness rests. It would be comforting to think this was a message from Spotty in the beyond, and I've heard of people having such dreams after a loss and believing the lost pet or person is really visiting. I'm too practical and skeptical by nature to make a definite statement on this. But I've also had enough strange experiences not to rule it out, either. Intense Spotty longing followed over the next several days. I got the last photos of her back from the processor, but they weren't too good. The best one was out of focus, though her bright little spirit still came though. She'd been moving towards me, eyes gleaming, with "pet me" purpose.

An appalling convergence of "everything happens at once" still had its grip on us even as Spotty's harrowing downhill slide was happening. My mother had moved to here from Maryland back in 1990 and bought a house in a pleasant neighborhood in the city. We then bought the house next door, at a bargain price because it needed a lot of work. It was, however, structurally sound, and old enough to have been built with a wall sheathing of 1-by-6 lumber nailed at a 45-degree angle, forming a triangle — nature's strongest shape — that made it more likely to withstand tornadic winds than modern houses, which have foam board or particle board for sheathing. (This later proved to be correct when a tornado on April 27, 2011, leveled parts of town, including Mom's neighborhood. The walls of our house stood, while other houses nearby were smashed.) Bill's intention upon purchase was to fix it up for his parents when the time came for them to move closer to us, too. That time had come and several years later Bill's Mom, bless her, had passed on. Bill's dad and MochaBud the cat were living in the house, which still needed some work done on the outside. Bill was slowly replacing the exterior siding with lumber from pine trees on our land that had been killed by pine beetles or knocked down by storms. He obtained a building permit and nailed the big yellow sign to a front porch post, and he put some of the siding up. Bill worked on the house when he had the time and the money; admittedly, the trickle of both those commodities was slow.

One day a letter from the city came. Someone had complained about the house and it was scheduled for demolition despite our building permit, unless a long list of repairs were made in one week! I was so upset when I read it at the mailbox that, with my considerable fine-motor clumsiness due to the ailment, I accidentally hit my head on the iron gate in front of our drive as I ducked under it to get back to the house out in the forest.

We were on good terms with all the neighbors in town, who were homeowners and student renters alike in the immediate neighborhood. None of our neighbors had complained, and when Bill went around the block collecting signatures on a petition, they were all supportive and happy to sign statements that they had no problem with our house. Even people who lived blocks away and walked through our neighborhood were willing to sign. After all, we were quiet at night, which can't always be said for the students, and we were friendly and helpful to neighbors, and Bill had attended many meetings about neighborhood issues. Between my mother's efforts and ours we had rescued and placed in homes about thirty stray animals that were no longer reproducing on neighborhood streets.

Bill managed to get an initial extension of four months and later another three or four to complete the repairs, but we were financially unable to hire a crew, so he had to do all the work himself. Even then it was tough. We couldn't afford to lose that house, which was one of our last remaining re-sources, and we had nowhere else to house Bill's dad, Eddie, so Bill had to drop all efforts to develop his new business and work every day on the house repairs, buying materials with our dwindling bank account. I put off doctor's appointments because we couldn't afford the money or Bill's time away from the work to get me to the doctor.

That was a winter of unprecedented bitter cold; Bill worked out in the frigid air, in the rain, and in the dark with a light rigged up. Had friends not donated their labor to help Bill with some of the work, he would not have made the deadline and we would have lost the house. All this was going on when Spotty went into her decline.

Eventually, we got the demolition order lifted, but we never really recov-ered financially from the time taken away from business matters and the funds put into the house that should have gone elsewhere at that time. It's quite possible that my health is worse today because of doctors' visits I had to skip during the eight or nine months when all resources went into the house. We were all having a nervous meltdown every second until the house was safe, with not a micro-second to vent and express it.

In general, I disagree with furtive, anonymous complaints about one's neighbors and side-stepping neighbor-to-neighbor discussions. What hap-pened to the common courtesy of talking to someone face-to-face about grievances regarding cosmetic matters? That's the old, friendly neighborhood way. Usually if a house needs a little fixing up it's not because someone wants a state of disrepair, it's because they cannot afford to do otherwise. Our repairs were underway and a little patience would have resulted in the good-looking house that some unknown persons evidently required. Too of-ten these days we hear of someone reporting neighbors, who then get investi-gated by the authorities to ensure that pets are vaccinated or cars are licensed, as the victim of one such incident once wrote to the local newspaper. She objected to these tactics; I have to agree. I've been told that my true opinions of skulking complainers ain't fit for a decent cat book, so I'm mincing words here and leaving something to your imagination. But talking is the traditional — and proven way — to handle these matters. That way results in the con-genial, tight-knit communities of old that we all wish we could return to.

One little bit of whimsy brightened our spirits during this time. Down the street, Bill spotted a yard-sale item, a painted lion figurine standing about two feet high, built of plaster of Paris. He mentioned it to me and of course I sprang for it, at the nominal asking price of five bucks, and we took it home. Rarely were we ever so extravagant; those days we watched every dollar. We totally didn't need it, and we stored it on the side porch temporarily. Then the rain came in, unnoticed, and we left it forgotten in the crush of our difficult lives. We later found that as the paint was slowly pattered off by raindrops, the lion had become a snow leopard. Yet few occurrences from that time top that rare moment of gleeful and frivolous acquisition, of us riding home with that bargain, one-of-a-kind lion sitting tall in our back seat. It was totally worth it for the smile it put on Mom's face when I told her about it!

When the repairs on the house were completed, Bill stained the board and batten with a mustardy, antique-yellow color, because it was on sale for cheap. I thought I wouldn't like it, but it turned out to look really nice, especially with the magenta red-tips and fresh yellow-green leaves of early spring. We ended up calling the house in town "The Gold House"; Eddie said it was "the prettiest house on the block."

A sweetheart cat goes sugar-free

Bill made a gift for Minxie and me that Christmas, a wooden ramp with thin boards nailed on every few inches so that Minx could use it for easy access to the couch. He painted the word "Minxolator" on it, along with paw prints and "Here, kitty, kitty" at the top. It was a sweet and valiant effort, but Minx didn't seem interested in using it to ascend to the couch when I tried to show her how to move up the ramp. So I retained my duty of airlifting her when she wanted to get up to higher couch ground.

Minx had adapted very well to being airlifted when she began to need the assistance. Cats like to initiate and propel motion their own catselves. Airlift them and you usually get a squirming, scratching rendition of "Born Free." And that was Minx when younger, when there were many occasions when I had to transfer her away from mischief. You can't leave a cat on the counter with a muzzle sunk in your cake batter. But older Minx learned beautifully to employ my skills, training me precisely in the art of cat-moving once her need for the service became apparent to her.

During the weeks Spotty began to go down, I noticed a sweet Minx being especially affectionate towards me. Her eyes would look sad when I went off to bed without her, and she was even more diligent about getting on my lap. If she was on one couch and I sat on the other one, she'd look longingly my way. Sometimes she followed me around the room and parked herself wherever I was working or sitting. After we turned in on the night of December 7, she got through the loose cat lock by persistent door pulling, and I had to put her back in the living area three times. The fourth time I let her stay, lifting her onto the bed. She purred all night, sleeping at the foot of the bed. She remained an early riser, though, and I had to let her out of the back at 6:00

a.m. in the morning. She may have been comforting me because she sensed
my despair about Spotty being ill. Or she may have been seeking assurance
of our bond since Spotty was getting so much attention. She could also have
needed comfort, because Minx turned out to be not entirely well herself.

Minx was fourteen-and-a-half years old. Her hind legs were a little stiff,
so I obtained a glucosamine supplement made for cats and mixed a little in
her food. As December wore on, she began sleeping all the time, more than
cats' normal twenty hours out of every twenty-four. She drank more water,
urinated more, and wasn't acting quite right. She became constipated two
days before Christmas. On December 26, still puzzled and fearful about why
she was under the weather, I gave her a larger-than-usual meal of canned
food. Afterwards she fell asleep quickly and in a way that seemed uncom-
fortable, groaning and sluggish and just not normal cat sleep, which I'd had
abundant time to study. Then suddenly, from the patterns of when she ate,
got thirsty, was overcome in sleep, and considering the glucosamine supplement, I just knew: Minx was diabetic.

Bill thought there was no way I could be right about this, but agreed to
the series of tests. I discontinued the glucosamine, and I phoned the vet, who
said to get a diabetes dipstick at the pharmacy for a preliminary test of urine.
It was New Year's Eve before we finally got a good urine sample. The test
result was an off-the-charts, resounding positive for glucose. I was a little
stunned myself as I embarked on life with a Sugar Kitty.

We always walked to a neighborhood party on New Year's Eve at the
nearby gazebo called The Lodge, and this year there was a second party a
short way up the road that we planned to drop in on for a time, too. But getting confirmation of a diabetic Minx and overwhelming Spotty loss sadness,
along with feeling physically even worse than usual myself, kept me home
that night. The fireworks at midnight scared Minx, and I took her into the
back with me. She was perkier back there beside me, purring loudly. Then
she went into a restless sleep, groaning and jerking and snoring. I'd taken her
into the back to sleep a few nights before and gotten the same loud, humming
purr constantly. Late at night she rattled the door to get out into the front and
I let her, but in the morning she meowed and rattled to get back in, and again
later that day when I was in the back room taking a bath. From that time on,
she slept in the back with me. Whenever she woke she looked at me; she always did but now there was more urgency, more need for reassurance. She
was very insightful and considerate in sleeping at the foot of the bed to allow
me space; my most comfortable position by this time was with my knees
folded up. I woke frequently at night myself, and pushed gently against her
with my feet, and she purred and *chirped* in response. The next morning after

New Year's, I had to get up and let her out early; she came back and sat by the door to the back hallway, rattled it, and called to me for two or three hours while I slept late to recover from having been up to all hours due to excitement, fireworks, and party music drifting our way.

Minx began, at times, to seem too sluggish or confused to get to her water dish herself, and I'd hold the bowl up to her muzzle, and she'd drink, which would perk her up. Whenever she licked her lips repeatedly, I'd get her the water. On January 3, she went to a Birmingham clinic for more extensive testing. Her blood sugar was off the charts, but her kidneys were doing well. The Minx was officially diagnosed with diabetes mellitus and prescribed insulin.

It's reasonable to point to the high-carbohydrate content of dried cat foods as a major cause of the recent increase in feline diabetes. Indeed, as carnivores, cats don't need many carbs and some sources state that they don't even metabolize them very well. But the picture may also be much more complex. Alabama has a very high rate of human diabetes, and this might also be blamed solely on diet, a known factor in diabetes onset. My in-laws' table always contained, from early morning, four or five cakes waiting to be consumed after every meal, which continued throughout the day and night — not to mention all the iced tea sweet enough to gag a honeybee. Yet they never got Type 2 diabetes. Genetics, along with unknown environmental influences, can't be entirely ruled out. Some years later, I heard of a study that had identified a physical marker that, oddly enough, correlates with human cases of diabetes: a shorter-than-average leg, from hip to knee. As noted before, Minx was a relatively short-legged cat, whose equivalent hind leg areas were no doubt shorter than average, cat-wise. Food for thought. Minx also had a history of hyperthyroidism, which sometimes precedes feline diabetes; both are endocrine malfunctions.[2] The role of dry, high-carbohydrate cat food has become a source of heated debate, and no one can rule out diet as a possible cause, of course. In my Great State of Soaring Cascades of Blood Sugar After Every Meal, consumption of simple carbs certainly played a role in bringing on our high rate of Type 2 diabetes. Yet that doesn't explain everyone, and diet doesn't explain some of the non-diabetic folks you would expect to get diabetes when you look at their dietary sugar intake. Things are often more complicated than they seem.

The way Minx was acting was up and down; perky one minute, overcome the next, as we tried to learn what she needed at any particular moment during the next few weeks: food, water, or just pats. Bill started the insulin shots and she went back and forth to the local vet for weekly tests as we slowly titrated the dose upwards. When she was perky, she watched me. No matter where she and I were in the room, her keen gold eyes stayed on me and she wanted me to walk with her to her food, and even stay with her while she ate. She would keep turning to look back to make sure I was coming, and she would raise her head and look up from the food to make sure I was there. That wasn't totally new behavior, but she now also wanted me to go with her when she went to the litterbox. I can hear critics saying that this cat was too dependent on me. My response is that at this stage, the animal was old and not in peak shape, and why shouldn't she get some of her 'druthers? Then they'll say, "You are too dependent on the cat." And I'll say back, "My sphere of interactions is limited by far more than this cat." Ditto on the 'druthers.

Minx was remarkably good about the insulin shots and seemed oblivious to them on all but a few occasions. This contrasted with her usual sour viewpoint on needles and medical handling. We used very fine needles made for humans, and we had to be very careful to measure out the tiny insulin amounts permitted for felines, in contrast to the larger doses for humans. Body size is the factor here, and this is an important point when treating a diabetic cat: if you use human syringes, you must remember to use the small feline doses, not the human doses, which are massive and possibly fatal overdoses for a cat. At present, I have seen syringes made for pets advertised, but have no direct experience with them, so consult your veterinarian when designing treatment protocols for a diabetic pet.

Waves of raw Spotty grief still pulsed through my days. Spotty meltdowns and near tears kept on popping up. Minx's condition meant fear and dread of another loss, but at least diabetes was a treatable ailment, albeit a serious one. It would be six months or so later when I read an article by Karen Solomon in *Cat Fancy* on feline diabetes, indicating that it isn't exactly the same disease in cats as it is in humans. Cats, according to Solomon, did not live long enough to develop such complications as losing limbs or blindness, which may occur in diabetic humans.[3] Still, when Minx sometimes reacted to a meal with sluggishness, she was unresponsive and often took hard breaths. From my own medical reading I knew that lungs help blow off excess carbon dioxide, a function that helps control metabolic acids in the blood. But although her urine test strips never indicated any possible ketoacidosis, which is a serious diabetic complication, something appeared to be very hard on Minx's little body.

January 16, 2003, was the day Minx threw a famous hissy fit by turning into a raging tigress, rolling and screaming, after staying at the vet for two hours so they could attempt another blood draw at the optimum time. It was as though she was saying, *You are not draining one more drop of my blood.*

Fructosamine, my ass! You'll have to pardon the French but that's exactly how Minx put it. She could "cuss like a sailor," no offense meant to sailors, which makes sense as cats are seafarers from way back. (Cats dispersed around the world from their original desert homes by riding in ships, where they would have "picked up sailors' language.") The test had to be abandoned, and when Bill brought her home afterwards, she was still on a tear, growling for a considerable time. High sugar or not, she was still running the show.

Those who witnessed the fit would be incredulous to hear that at home, Minx was a really good patient about her twice-daily insulin shots. There was never a growl, a hiss, a swat, or a grumble regarding them. We used a very fine "comfort" needle, but there must have been at least a small sting with each shot. We ourselves were surprised. She didn't like the blood tests on her soft ears, dainty but large, but the insulin shots given in the loose skin above her shoulders were a breeze. After getting the glucose levels stabilized in relation to the insulin, we kept her ear blood tests to a minimum.

She had times when she seemed worse, having a hard time of it after eating, but when she perked up she was radiant, "bright-eyed and bushy-tailed," bobbing towards me with skirling *trills*, wanting food and pats. But she didn't seem to be able to walk much without stopping to lie down. The vets increased the insulin around the end of the month, and she became more active. Mouse scuffling sounds in the room always made her stiffen and rotate her ears towards the noise. Now that she was feeling better, she again went to the area of the room the mice frequented to try to catch them.

The mice were running rampant over us that winter. The cat-killing dog's demise had been right after Christmas, but the outdoor cats had not yet returned. The mice had benefitted from having had a few cat-free years to multiply in their exponential way; the humane trap was clanking every night, and we were catching at least two after dark every evening. So were neighbors in the area — all the best country houses have mice. And though our neighborhood had once been patrolled by a succession of feral and semi-feral cats, through our efforts, those cats now had cushy assignments in various homes instead.

Previously glued to my lap, Minx now evidently found it somehow unsuitable, no longer her comfortable snoozing substrate. But she stayed right by me on the couch I sat on by day. And by night she was always on my side of the bed. At first she'd get up at about 2 or 3 a.m. and want to go to the living room. She'd try to lead me there, stopping to look back to make sure I was coming, and I'd coax her back into the room if I could or just let her go on to the front. If I indeed had to let her out of our space in the wee hours, she'd rattle the door in the morning. Now that I was in the same room with her nightly, she became more active and vibrant, more like the natural bio-rhythm of a nocturnal hunter. Over the years and left alone out front while we slept, the cats had only adjusted to our schedule by a few degrees, sleeping more at night when we did, although they were still always up bright and early. Now that I was there with her I might well share in her adventurous night, she figured. My own bio-rhythms were off in those days anyway. I found it hard to fall asleep until late at night, 2 or 3 a.m., and in the mornings, I would sleep in the sun, like cats do.

Minx would purr for hours while we rested. She'd often sleep up against me a long time, but she eventually selected the foot of the bed as her sleeping place, probably to avoid my frequent turning throughout the night. I began to hear Banshee Cat outside late, from time to time. He had moved on from us to some other misty hollow in need of a good wail, but he was now back again after his walkabout.

There is a lot of theorizing on cat behavior these days. Are they simply instinctual wild animals who regard us merely as a feeding source, to be treated as a part of their territory? Is it anthropomorphic to believe that they love us? I don't think so. It's well-known that when cats know they are dying, they'll go off by themselves and hide. But less written about is the phe-nomenon I observed both with Spotty and Minx, and later with others. When cats are not dying, but perceive themselves to be less-well and vital than they previously were, they become more attached to their humans and stay with them on a much more constant basis, interacting more frequently, and giving absolute trust. I've seen non-lap cats become lap cats at these times. Clearly they derive comfort and love from the presence of their humans, recognizing that what they receive is affection and sympathy to their lesser state of health. It makes a difference to them to experience this in sickness. This goes far beyond the model of a cat as a solitary predator who only cares if he or she is fed and sheltered, and who will hide and withdraw completely when ill. With no human companions, they would likely behave this way. But with humans, they are both the initiators and participants in other scenarios.

Minx slowed down greatly but gradually. She'd breathe hard and groan as she slept after a meal, but later she'd spring up all aglow and ready for chow. She'd go on alert listening to the sound of the mice in the room, or in the walls or ceiling, and to the critters rustling outside. Bill started research-ing information about diabetic cats on the Internet. There was an information exchange group of people owned by diabetic cats, some of whom were kind enough to email us their experiences and knowledge. We learned a lot and I regret that due to my situation, I could not keep up an ongoing exchange with them as was customary on their list. Minx was getting every scrap of extra energy I had. We learned from them and other sources that dry cat foods are much higher in carbohydrates than canned. This is no doubt because they have corn, wheat, and rice, grains, with oil content that serves as a binder to keep the dry pellets together. I am no expert in feline nutrition, and I am sure many fine foods are made for cats this way. But nowadays there are those who think dry foods are not good for any cats, healthy or sick, while others say this isn't so; it's all controversial. In the case of diabetic cats, most subscribers on the list recommended high-quality canned foods or raw and home-cooked foods. Unfortunately, we were not in a position to prepare foods, which would have been best, but neither of us had the time. We did use the online list compiled by caregivers of diabetic cats, called the "Janet and Binky" charts, of protein/fats/and carbohydrate contents of a wide array of common cat food brands[4] as a guide to finding the best food plan for Minx.

I spent March and April of 2003 trying various combinations of foods, using more canned food than before. It just wasn't possible in our circumstances to entirely eliminate dry food from her diet. I used Minx's reactions as a guide. We read at least one article by a veterinarian stating that a cat's behavior was a good general indicator to go by with diabetes. The quick blood tests that could be done on a vein in a cat's ear were not always totally accurate. Some of the canned foods produced much better reactions than others — some crashed Minx hard and fast and kept her in deep, unresponsive slumber longer. Like most all cats, Minx was an epicure, and she enjoyed sampling different flavors; she'd especially favored the catfish. Our other cats liked it too. When Minx was up and sparkling she was voracious, and she ate with her same old gusto. Nevertheless, her seeming bad times were frequent enough that I remained concerned about her.

I recall having thoughts of Spotty while trying to adjust Minx's food. Chances were, if I'd been haunted by Spotty on a certain day, so had Bill.

There may be those who question spending money on treatments for the cats when our resources for our human needs were dwindling. I don't feel that way because to us, cats are family. When they need vet care and treatment for illnesses, they should get it. We've undertaken the responsibility to care for them and that also means in old age and sickness.

Springtime renewal in the forest

We had an early spring in 2003. Into the pastel forest where the pale light waited to slowly admix with stronger hues, the fresh, bright things came. The Judas tree began to leaf out not far into March. Redbuds flecked the woods and town with magenta, new leaves came out green and gold, and when the Judas tree reached full bloom several weeks later, the violets came out, too. Soon the tall blue wildflowers, called spiderwort, appeared; starting with a few out here, then by the yard-full in town. Birds conversed, seemingly trilling the same sentences again and again.

We missed Spotty; there was uncertainty about Minx. We talked about Kudzu's advancing age, too. The boys both hung out on the small couch now, with Pretty Girl on Kudzu's promontory spot. I'd sit with the boys and rub them both at the same time and feel them both murmuring. The light buzz was only lightly audible; both had the "stealth purr." Minx and Pretty Girl began to occasionally groom each other's heads, giving me some hope they might bond. I watched Minx as I wrote my journal; her expanse of dark fur was like looking into the soft, moist spring night. She regaled me.

At one of the vet visits during Minx's early days of diabetes discovery, we sat in the waiting area and a woman offered us a beautiful black rescue cat she had just had vetted. Sadly, I had to say no as we had our hands full with Minx and our others. But this was a smart way people used to rehome rescued animals: asking around the waiting room in their vet's office. The woman knew that the persons there with their pets were good pet parents who take their animals to the vet.

In the evenings we watched television. I couldn't go out much, and whereas I'd preferred reading books and going to concerts for most of my life, television shows did serve as a kind of modern storytelling, a literary form of sorts, like good films. Like some isolated foothills tribe, we listened to stories every night, told by the screen. It took the place of the old storytellers around the camp or home fires of the pre-television age. Bill checked out tapes of mystery movies from the library; we watched a Cher concert and a PBS special on Muddy Waters. With Minx by me on the couch, always in my peripheral vision, I'd frequently turn to her during the programs and stroke her, or we'd call and gesture to each other if she happened to be looking my way from another couch.

Every now and then my focus would drift back to the way life used to be, compared to this television-heavy existence. All too often I was having to let the TV people do my living for me. If I hadn't gotten sick, the conversations I would have had, the concerts I would have gone to, the visiting I would have done! Bill and I would have gone on deep-woods and deep-swamp walks around our land and around the state, with guides if needed. Always in the wilderness we would have watched for animals; maybe we would have seen cougar sign, or the actual panther in all its glory, and we'd have had more of our own stories to tell. I'd be churning out artwork and making paper

out of the kudzu down the road, and volunteering at animal rescues and foster care groups. I'd be in and out of the house, revved up from my adventures, and I'd be Minx-seeking, cat snuggling, upon every return. *Mighthave-
beens* will tear at my mind; there are times when I crave the real porch, with
the swing and the shimmering evening air and the friends there joking and
laughing, glances going back and forth, laughter contrapuntal, ascendant, the
cadenced storytellings accompanied by the strains of the insect musicians.
And at these somber moments I am discontent with the nightly sessions gathered around the television, the electronic raconteur. Some of these screen
stories are good, but they are not the natural refrains to the tales we had set
out to spin, the tunes we had started to unwind, so long ago.

By the end of March 2003, the wisteria was out and heavily sweet on the
wind for one warm glorious day. The brownish spidery spring woods felt
electric as twigs readied to catch a mist of green-gold leaves. It makes me
want to sprawl out in the woods, tell stories, camp out on natural verandas.
We stopped by the vet that day to discuss Minx, and we enjoyed seeing her
sleek, black clinic-dwelling cats. Days later, a cold snap came along and
killed off all the flowers. I began hearing the Banshee Cat again, but the
sound of him vanished yet again after several weeks.

At night Minx would meow to me for food, looking at me, bobbing her
head, and making a high-pitched, rumbling sort of bagpipe run as I shook
some kibble from a plastic bag into her bowl. She would meow and look up
at me as she ate, happy. Minx developed a pattern of wanting out of the bedroom after several hours, around 2 or 3 a.m. One morning at 6 a.m. a storm
woke me up; Minx was frantically rattling the door. I let her in and she slept
on top of my feet. I was glad I was still her go-to girl for safety.

By May everything was green and fresh; critters were yelling, *Spring!*
The Broad Leaf Magnolias, with two-foot-long and eight-inch-wide jungle
leaves, were starting to bloom. The Banshee Cat was back. Minx was walking shorter distances and continuing to do what I thought was, not too well
overall, but with perk-up intervals. Bill was researching a better insulin, a
beef product that was closer to actual cat insulin than the synthetics used for
human diabetics that we had started with, which were modeled after human
insulin. At night Minx raised her head every time I left the room and looked
at me like, *Where are you going?* Minx and I seemed perfectly attuned to
each other. One night, Minx groomed Pretty Girl's head and Pretty Girl
pushed it at her like Spotty used to do. Paroxysms of Spotty grief tangled
with hope that Pretty Girl would finally have a friend.

In late May I began to see evidence that the Banshee Cat may have been
doing more than just singing the blues; various smaller stray cats appeared in

the yard. They could have been girls drawn by his lamentations. Except for the Banshee Cat, it had taken a long time for the strays and ferals, as well as wandering owned cats, to feel safe here in our forest neighborhood again after the death of the cat-killer dog a few days after last Christmas. The cat appearances were in one sense an auspiciously good sign, as the nomadic cats would no doubt dine on indigenous rodents. But it could also become our problematic responsibility if one of them settled in the yard, especially a girl with kittens. But the Banshee Cat's fans disdained any contact with us and soon moved on.

As spring's swaths of frothy green, like lace trim, turned into the bumpy emerald velvet of summer, Minx was glorious. I was brimming with love for everyone. Minx was a joy, but she was breaking my heart when she seemed feeble. Spotty often parked in my mind, and I couldn't shake her off. Not that I wanted to. The saddest thing to me is when the lost loved ones fade from the mind as though they never existed. I wanted to be able to relive the glory that was Spotty, to recall in vivid detail all the stories, the look and feel of her fur, the rapid vibrato purr and the funny cascade of sounds that unfurled from my cupcake kitty. I was fine being Spotty-haunted.

Minx's expression would visibly brighten when I stroked her. When Bill passed by the bedroom and into view in the window we had made between the room and the hall, she'd always look up and around at him and speak, *mrrmrrr-row*. In late June he was ordering the new kind of insulin for her. We began hearing the katydids for the first time that season. These pale-green, grasshopper-lookalike insects that stay high up in the trees make a rhythmic noise in the forest at night, so loud you sometimes can't have a conversation without shouting if you're sitting outside. They are so-named because, supposedly, they sound like they are saying *Katy did, Katy didn't,* but all I know is the rhythm, clacking away high in the trees, makes me want to sway and dance. They made the cats want to move too, but in contrast to dance, our cats did the stalk-and-pounce whenever a katydid slipped into the house, as every insect out here in the leaves is prone to do. Katydid rescues while deflecting feline intentions, were regular events during summers and warm falls.

So I was poised to bask in summer's magical smells and greenness and steamy nights when suddenly Minx went into crisis illness. First she vomited her meals, then she ceased eating any food or drinking any water. She wasn't moving around much, mostly lying around listless and very sick. We went into frantic action, and the days that followed are hazy in my mind. I stopped my journal and its details. I thought we were going to lose her. Our local vet referred her to the big city clinic in Birmingham, where they diagnosed that it was either severe pancreatitis or gallstones. As sick as she was, Minx still exhibited the menacing side of her personality, and sedation would have been required to do further tests. But the clinic tests showed that her kidneys, heart, lungs, and liver were in good shape, and Bill brought her home.

We got injectable saline solution from the local vet to take care of her fluid needs right there in the house. Bill got on the Internet and found experts on feline pancreatitis and their phone numbers, and he e-mailed the group of owners of diabetic cats. Some replied that they had gotten their cats through episodes of pancreatitis with antibiotics. Bill called the experts who were kind enough to speak with him. One said it was probably part of a chronic, or ongoing, form of pancreatitis and that such cats had a poor prognosis. But as Bill walked into our vet's office to show her the lab report and to pick up the saline solution and syringes, he was on the phone with yet another expert. That vet asked for the data on the lab report, and it turned out that Minx's bloodwork indicated infection. Our vet was impressed that Bill had been able to get this guy's ear; he had authored veterinary textbooks. (Bill has a great knack for getting through red tape to people and knowing how to talk to them.) Our vet prescribed two antibiotics after consulting by phone with the specialist. She sent Bill home with pre-loaded syringes containing the anti-biotics, as well as the fluids. A whole lot of "sticks" for Minxie.

I held onto her by gently cupping the loose neck skin to control her head and loosely holding the front feet while Bill gave the first shot, but she barely reacted to the huge needle that delivered the fluids. That showed us that she was very sick, the vet said later. Her sugar was still high because of the infec-tion, although she was not consuming food, so she had two of the ear blood tests a day, two insulin shots, three or four hydration shots, and two different shots each with a different antibiotic, twice a day for a total of about twelve sticks a day. One night she walked to the door to the back, wanting to stay with me, but most of this time she spent parked in one spot or another in the living room. We did intensive care on her. I held onto her for each shot, and I cleaned up the urine when she peed indiscriminately. I changed out the "blankies" we placed about for her to rest on. I turned the television down low. Bill kept his trips to town brief. Sometimes when he was away, I ran to the back of the house, away from the cats, and screamed and cried. I didn't want to do this in front of the cats because they're so perceptive and can de-tect negative emotions instantly, in a thorough way. We thought she was gone. So did our local vet. But with her major organs still in good shape, we just couldn't let go without a fight.

In summer here, the blackness of nightfall spreads its way through the green, and lamps begin to make calico of the evening. We lived so deep in the woods and so far from neighbors that we didn't need to put curtains over our windows after the dark was complete. One night I was sitting on the couch next to a very sick, very unresponsive Minx. I heard a rapid tapping on the window, behind the couch. It was a large moth with a four-inch wingspan. The larger moths may be unknown to many except for the Luna Moth — we had those too, pale green and edged with purple and mauve, as well as an abundance of oversized moths that were not seen in town, and dozens of small moths in startling color combinations and patterns: pink and yellow, orange and black, black speckled with white, and one with inner wings that were red, while the outer wings were brown and black. The pink and yellow, I would later learn, is the Rosy Maple Moth, and the orange and black is the Ornate Tiger Moth. Sweetheart Underwing is the name of the moth with the colorful inner wings. I've seen the Painted Lichen Moth, too.

The huge moth that flapped at the window had dark earth tones with apple-green highlights, a thick body, and tiny gleaming eyes. The blackness of the night surrounding us, and my mind, feeling raw and skewed with the threat of Minx loss, unleashed fanciful thoughts. Minx had come to us after Bill's possibly prescient dream in which she began as a flying thing. Was this moth a flying thing, come to take her away from me to the spirit world? Like Poe's tapping raven, was it announcing its presence? Straight logic said it had come to the window for the light. I'm practical and no-nonsense. I like logic. But nonetheless, I felt a chill in the summer heat, and a shudder. This can happen to the most rational of us on a certain kind of night when a room in the forest feels like a haunted planetarium, wild with odd auroras refracted through the window-as-prism. I usually welcomed the large and strange moths, but this time it was a relief when the moth finally fluttered away into the black-green forest.

Fishing for solutions to Minx's ailments

Minx became sick on June 30 or July 1, right before the July 3 date that marked the fifteenth year since we'd found her. I thought fifteen years would be all I'd get. But remarkably, I recorded on July 9 that she was doing better. She was now reacting to the shots with some growls and spits, a sign of greater awareness and a return to being herself. The journal stopped again after that. I was too busy to bother with it. Gradually, though, she began to take a little food — she was on the mend! On July 13, I recorded that she was still inactive and could not move far, but she had recovered further. The next day we increased the insulin and she rallied even more. She was purring and sleek on the bed again, past the illness. She'd been sick for two weeks. I'd stayed home most of this time, from the 1st of July to the 14th. On the Fourth of July, we had gone over to Charlotte's house for a few brief hours, but hurried back. Everyone there was very sympathetic about Minx and wished her well. Friends called daily to find out how she was.

Minx was eating and drinking on her own, and her two-week course of antibiotics was over. Bill took the unused saline solution back to the vet, who was elated and amazed that The Minx had made such a complete turnaround. Everyone had thought this kitty would not make it. The vet said that maybe we could keep her another year or two. That sounded good to me, except that in two years, Minx would be only seventeen. I have so often heard from friends and acquaintances of cats that have lived twenty years or more, or at least eighteen or nineteen. This made me feel cheated when Gray Kitty died at fourteen and Spotty at fifteenish. But Minx came back roarin', turning my gloom to bliss. After I caught my breath a while later, I knew we really did pull her back from the brink; I felt both fear and joy.

The new insulin was in place. We turned our attention to re-vamping the diet. Minx would have small meals of canned food throughout the day and small, controlled nibbles of dry food at night, when she was in the back room with me. Many sources recommend small meals scattered throughout the day for diabetic cats. Smaller meals result in smaller blood glucose increases than do large meals. The smaller amounts are easier for the body to metabolize before the next meal comes along. Therefore, feeding decreased amounts over the entire day, instead of two or three large meals, helps to keep the blood sugar down. No more unrestricted chow-downs for Minx. I am not a veterinary or medical professional, and opinions on the feeding patterns differ. Some sources advocate feeding half the daily nutritional requirements with the first insulin shot and the other half with the second insulin shot. But every cat is different. We tried many things and we did what worked best for Minx, but may not work for all "sugar" kitties. The disease, the cats, and the treatments all vary and interface differently. There is no one best way that fits all. It would seem safe to assume that with smaller meals you would need to monitor the cat more closely for low glucose events, which are serious and potentially life-threatening. Because I was in the house most of the time, we were able to do this.

A *Cat Fancy* article by Karen Solomon about diabetes indicates that sometimes it's secondary to chronic pancreatitis.[5] If Minxie's severe attack was an increase of an ongoing subclinical and chronic pancreatitis, it would certainly seem possible that her diabetes was secondary to that, but we just didn't know for sure. Another article from *Cat Fancy*, this one on pancreatitis, mentions that fatty foods aggravate the pancreas during acute attacks. At the very least, fat digestion in humans is more complex than that of protein and carbohydrates and is the first to malfunction in a distressed gut, according to some of the research we'd done about my own illness. It seemed reasonable that this might be true in cats, also. So I selected a canned food from the list detailing cat food carb levels compiled by the owners of diabetic cats, one that had zero carbs and very low fat, the lowest I could find. And Minx did better on it. The food happened to be fish, a mixture of tuna and other ocean fish. I have come across some unproven and therefore possibly controversial research that suggests the oils in fish lower blood sugar so effectively that anyone on insulin should be cautious about eating it. This is not proven or generally accepted, so again, these are my experiences only and what works for one may not work for another. I can't speak definitively on these matters, but Minx did much better on a diet that included fish and on January 21, 2005, as I was writing the first draft of this book about a year and a half after the crisis, I noted that Minx was doing fairly well for a sixteen and a half year old, diabetic cat. She was living a cheerful life. We were living and working for these bright-eyed times. Bill handled the morning canned-fish feeding, and I schlepped her five small meals the rest of the day. My limited energy was maxed out by this, but it was what Minx needed so it's what I did. Many times I watched the television shows *Scrubs*[6] and *The West Wing*[7] from the kitchen while I scooped fish or fowl out of cans for Minxie.

To the fish-based food we added more of the high-protein, lower-fat and low-carb foods, (a nutrient profile that was not all that common in cat foods), using the "Janet and Binky" charts. We also chose the food lowest in phosphorus, which is always a concern in any ailment involving kidney function. Choosing low carb alone had not kept Minx from having the attack of pancreatitis. But adding low fat and high protein to the mix did the trick and would continue to do so. Eventually we found some research that suggests low fats alone do not help cats with pancreatitis, especially if the diet is high in carbs and low in protein. But I can only say that we had wondrous results with the low fats in a diet that was high in protein, low in fats and low in carbs. This is speculation, but perhaps carbs stress the sensitive pancreas, too, countering the beneficial effect of the low fats. There is some new information that also suggests a feeding tube is appropriate for a cat that will not eat, and that although fasting (which rests the pancreas) is recommended in pancreatitis, the lack of food has adverse effects on the liver. I don't dispute these findings, but although Minx did without food for some time, we saw a remarkable return to vibrant health in a cat that had not been expected to survive. We were perhaps fortunate in doing what was needed by instinct in the absence of today's expanded knowledge.

However, I would recommend extreme care in giving fish to any cat on insulin, or not feeding fish altogether. While we were still trying various food regimens, I fed Minx a can of fish that was a different mixture than the one we settled on eventually. The following day, about two hours after the insulin shot, Minx suddenly became anxious and moved towards the kitchen at a quicker trot than I had seen in a long time. She went for a bowl of the other cats' dry food and when I tried to stop her, she growled at me. She tipped it over, scattering kibble on the floor and began to eat voraciously. We tested her blood glucose and found it low. Blood sugar lows can result in death and thus are more critical in the short-term than high levels. We didn't have any Karo syrup, which can be rubbed on the gums of cats with low sugar, so we let her eat the dry food. Her sugar came back up, but I canceled a planned trip to town anyway and watched her like a hawk all day. We were trying to find foods that were least likely to aggravate her pancreas, and the new food may have been lower in carbs than the one we had been using. I don't believe this formula is still being made, and I can't recall exactly what it was. But it had to be higher in carbs than the fish food we eventually settled upon, since the carb content of that was near zero. We never used the particular blend of fish that triggered the low again, and we never had another low-glucose event. The idea that some of the omega-3 fatty acids found in fish can lower the body's need for insulin in humans is detailed in a book called *Fats That Heal, Fats That Kill* by Udo Erasmus, whose PhD is in biochemistry and genetics.[8] Dr. Photon hastens to add that our one anecdote does not prove this unproven idea, but most studies I was able to find have indicated fish-oil supplementation has some benefits but does not improve pre-existing insulin resistance. According to the Karen Solomon article in *Cat Fancy,* diabetes results from difficulty producing insulin, the blood becoming insulin-resistant, or a combination of both.[9] A few studies did show better glycemic control as a result of fish-oil supplementation, but I found these mostly on sites that sell supplements, and I couldn't trace the original studies. Dr. Erasmus does note that eating fish is better than using supplements, which must be produced using very strict procedures to remain effective until the time they reach the consumer.[10]

So, this remains a controversial matter. But what I saw after Minx ate from that one can of fish, a type I would never give her again, was dramatic enough to make me urge caution in giving fish to cats on insulin. We also remained mindful of the phosphorus factor and chose the fish flavors with the lowest levels.

We were latecomers to the computer age and at the time, I had not yet learned to do Internet research myself. Between elder care and working and my care and Minxie's extra care, Bill was stretched thin in those years and had limited time to look up information. I now find that fish is often not considered appropriate food for cats. There are opinions all over the map on this. It seems well-established that tuna canned for humans, especially when packed in oil, causes cats to lose Vitamin E, and commercial cat foods containing tuna now have added Vitamin E. According to some opinions this is sufficient, but others say it does not correct the problem, and even the supplemented Vitamin E is still lost due to this food. The food I used did indeed have added Vitamin E.

Another complaint is that fish does not contain taurine, a necessary amino acid that cats cannot live without. Commercial cat foods that contain fish now seem to all include added taurine, as the brand I used long-term with Minx did. Other complaints are that fish is high in mercury and in minerals that may cause feline urologic syndrome. Yet other researchers dispute the negative effects. Due to these many disparate opinions, I don't recommend a diet of fish alone for diabetic cats or others. But I can say that I saw no negative effects on Minx from her diet high in fish. My other cats have been mostly healthy at older ages, and I don't think the occasional fish-based cat food has harmed them either. The only times my cats ever got human tuna was when they had dashed out the door and needed coaxing back inside, but that was only in very minute amounts. I'm not a nutritionist and I can't speak to exact effects by fish upon the cats, but I have to recommend against a primarily fish-based diet as the preponderance of opinion seems to be against it.

Surely with so many negative reports there must be some reason for concern. Fish is high in phosphorus, which is good reason to eliminate it from the diet of a cat in chronic renal failure (CRF) or perhaps even in an older cat, although Minx never developed CRF. As for the idea that cats are descended from desert dwellers and therefore have no ancestral history of consuming fish, I must say that as seafaring world travelers and waterfront denizens, I daresay cats have historically gotten their chops on some fish, so maybe in moderation a little is okay. Among mid-sized wildcats there is a Fishing Cat species that wades, waits waterside to scoop up fish by its paws, dives and swims for fish, and even splashes the surface of water, making bug-like waves so fish will come check it out. They no doubt developed from other branches than the house cat, but still, you just can't say that no feline eats fish in the wild. Still today, several years after finding that Minxie did well on fish, I'd probably recommend zero to limited fish for the domestic feline diet. Naturally there's a difference of opinion about every aspect of feeding cats.

If the cats themselves were the researchers it would be a scrappy brawl rather than a gentlefolk's disagreement. Some say that no food at all between meals is the natural way to feed them. Others say twenty to thirty small nibbling meals a day is their natural choice and the authentic way of the wild. Many are totally against dry food; others advocate it as beneficial in helping to keep the teeth clean. There is complete agreement on the fact that cats are obligate carnivores and must consume meat; they cannot survive on vegetarian diets. Cats have no "salad days." Some advocate raw meat only, and others counsel against it. My own opinion is that this poses too great a risk of ingesting the rather nasty organisms that may contaminate meat. It's true that wild cats don't cook their food, and it's also true that they get parasites. However, to be comprehensive and open-minded, I have to note that many persons today are having great success feeding cats on raw food diets. I would have home-cooked for the cats had I been able to.

I see many more articles today about the study and knowledge regarding feline pancreatitis, as well as feline diabetes, than were available when my Sweet Baby Minx was sick. As in everything regarding the health of your cats, consult your veterinarians and do research if your kitty is ill. Diet is also something you need the advice of professionals to work out, as well as a careful perusal of the experiences of others. These are my experiences only and not intended as veterinary advice. Consult a veterinarian when you have a sick cat.

After Minx stabilized, she still had an occasional blood glucose high and every time it was a source of great anxiety and anguish. It was a challenge trying to control her blood sugar, trying to artificially manage a natural process that had failed. I gained a new respect and even awe for this amazingly intricate physiological system; when it works correctly, it's constantly making delicate adjustments and fine-tuning blood glucose levels. I had always known diabetics had it tough, and I gained an even greater appreciation for what they and their caregivers go through in trying to maintain correct blood-sugar levels. Many pet owners now try to manage this complex disease in their pets and after we struggled with it, I admire all those who do. One advantage we had was that I was in the house almost all the time and could watch Minxie's behavior for any signs of high or low sugar.

Wrapping my head around the intricate slosh of insulin and sugar through the bloodstream put me in a state of wonder regarding the complexity and finesse of this ever-watchful biological system and the way it keeps an organism going. I gained the same sort of astonished respect from reading about the autonomic nervous system, and later the enteric nervous system, which in my case are both out of whack. The enteric nervous system actually has more neurons than the central nervous system. If I were to wake up well one day, I think I'd go back to school in biology.

Despite the spotty episodes of high glucose, overall Minx was living a merry life with eyes gleaming and plenty of *meowsong*; cheerful behavior is, according to some veterinary literature, the best indicator of successful glucose management. With a big "whew" of relief we were again ready to chill out and more or less aestivate our way through the summer.

Kudzu's creeping illness

The night I wrote this, February 1, 2005, started with a good under-the chin rub and scratch of Minx. Right before Minx's big crisis, I was worried about Kudzu, Minx, and me. All during the 2000s I'd had some illness complications that were troublesome, both in terms of just getting through them and the possible implications for future deterioration. But, I was figuring, I'd lived with it for this long, so maybe I could keep on. Minx and I became even closer and she became a real refuge from the problems of illness and finances. I had frequent bathroom excursions at night, and every time I got up she raised her head as if saying, *where are you going*, and I'd whisper so as not to wake Bill, *I'll be back*, as I walked by the window between bedroom and hall, and she'd be looking up at me.

The Banshee Cat was hollering and the wanderers were strolling by; we were again firmly on the cat paths now that the cat-killing dog was long gone. There was an empty spot around the house, and we still missed SpottaLee, our Little Bit, terribly. She still occupied my mind; she haunted me. Minx would meow sharply to Bill when he appeared in the window from the hall at night. He would say "Good-night, girls," and she'd turn her head to look at him so that her side lips stretched out, taut and slightly open, showing a partial view of teeth, and then her lips would start to quiver as the loud *MaROW!* came. After Minx spoke her mind, then it was my turn to say good-night.

Kudzu had always been the healthiest of our kitties. His illness in the summer of 2003 crept up on us like a cold and fetid fog condensed from the effluents of unclean factory smokestacks. His vet check-up in February showed he was fine. His age was a mystery, but the vet said he could be as old as fifteen. All I knew was that come July 4th, 2003, we would have had him thirteen years.

By April I began to get lightly worried about him. He'd blown lots of hairballs. He seemed less active. In late April, we took him to the vet; nothing turned up in the exam. But not long after, it dawned on me that he'd quit playing stalk-and-pounce with shadows, and he had quit coming up behind me along the back of the couch to sniff my hair. He had even ceased rolling around in the path of his slinky Minx, though far down in the emerald depths of his eyes, I could still detect the glow when he turned towards her with his sideways manner of looking. He did, however, begin to sit on my lap now and then, which was unusual for him. He'd never been a lap cat. As the broadleaf magnolias started to bloom, Kudzu began to seem mopey at times and had some constipation. By the end of June, Kudzu seemed to slow down even further, more sleeping and less frisking around, but we expected some reduction of activity in an older cat.

About a week after Minx rallied mid-July, our joy at her recovery turned to apprehension concerning Big Zu. Kudzu was vomiting and I thought he was eating less. Bill was convinced it was okay and was just hairballs. But a few more days and his food and water consumption declined further, and he became more constipated. We were watching Hitchcock's *The 39 Steps*[11] the day this became evident, and I became frantic that we were losing him. He began staying in various "caves" he'd made for himself in the kitchen, in a grocery bag left down for the cats to use as a toy or under an antique chair with legs that were carved into angels.

Minou did some out-of-the-ordinary things during this time. Usually a lone sleeper, he'd begun to sleep beside Kudzu. He also groomed Kudzu's head a few times, and Minx's too. It was as if he knew that they were unwell. Kudzu began to act like his mouth was bothering him. He was only swallowing a few pellets of dry food and lapping small amounts of water. We did entice him to eat a fair amount of canned food with fish chunks. I wondered if he could have an abscessed tooth, so on July 24 he went to the vet for an overall exam, but she could find nothing wrong. His teeth were fine. He did eat better the next few days and got more active. But then he stopped eating again, and I thought I saw him staggering briefly. I admit I cried that day several times.

Bill was now very upset. Kudzu had begun to sit on Bill's lap more since Spotty had been gone and now he was seeking Bill out for a snooze with frequency. He was losing weight and moping, although he did eat well occasionally. Bill began giving him hi-cal, using the spoon to place it on the roof of Kudzu's mouth since he wouldn't take it on his own.

On August 4, Kudzu went to the vet and had an X-ray. It revealed a tumor in his underbelly the size of a lemon. He also had fluid in his chest, and his kidneys were shrunken and atrophied. There was no way to tell if this was cancer without surgery, which was risky considering his age and condition. Bill had taken Kudzu in to the clinic without me because my "go and do" strength was so limited. The vet discussed all the options with Bill, including letting him go before he got in too much discomfort. We were shocked, stunned, and heartbroken, even though we had known there had to be something very wrong with him. This explained it.

Kudzu nibbled, but not enough. Bill said there could be a spontaneous remission. It was raining a lot that August. The humidity made the dishtowels sopping; my cat duties multiplied as I tried various foods with Kudzu. He wanted to eat but just didn't; he showed interest but then didn't eat. On Mom's birthday, Minx's eyes were on me fixedly as I walked towards the door to go to town, like, *how can you leave me?* Mom sent me home with some chicken for Kudzu, and he ate some! But not much. At least it didn't rain that day.

Next day I watched the movie *Apocalypse Now*[12] with Bill. It was really a cool day for August, disconcerting because, despite the coolness of the air, the trees were still a hot, volcanic green. I was full of longing for all friends distant from me. I had that "awful autumn feeling" that you get when the sunlight starts to get a certain slant and dazzle, with sharper, more golden brights that render details in higher definition, and deeper darks, like what I always thought Faulkner's *Light in August* meant.[13] One August I had even seen a mulberry-pink, harvest-sized moon just at twilight. It only lasted a few moments before turning to the color of the usual gold moons that are more commonly seen in autumn. According to a quote whose origin I don't recall, the coming of autumn brings on a terrible, profound ancestral ennui. To the earliest humans, the hunter/gatherers, it meant migrate or die. In later farming cultures, it was a time to furiously grab, gather, preserve, and store everything needed for the coming winter, as well as to scrabble and strain to weatherproof the barn and house. Bill and I had both felt that seasonal angst many times. It showed up mostly as a peculiar kind of longing for who-knows-what, mostly undefined. It can be as late as November before the leaves fall down my way. Nevertheless, in August the light changes here. The bright areas become more golden, and details are more defined; the dark areas become deeper. It brings on something Bill and I call "that awful autumn feeling" — a profound and unspecified longing. We know we shouldn't complain; we could have two, even three more months of warm weather if all goes well. But that doesn't change the calendar, or the fact that all that golden light is going to one day smack us in the face, gathered, intensified, and thrown back at us by the harvest moon. Neither can we change the tilt and whirl of the planet, which changes the light and brings winter, eventually. It's a good thing actually, that we can't! But I'm not so fond of winter.

The following day, Kudzu wouldn't eat. He moped but he'd go look through the door panes at the woods like he always had. He may have had that awful autumn feeling and the wanderlust that comes with it, his ownself. He also wasn't drinking much water, so Bill began hydrating him with saline solution subcutaneously, as he had Minx the month before. I'd have to gently hold his feet as Kudzu tried to use his large claws, not liking this. After another eerily cold night for August, Kudzu began to wheeze, although it did soon stop. He showed interest in food but would not eat, and he laid around the entire day. I cried off and on that day. After Bill and I both had gone to bed, I went back out to the living room and stroked Kudzu. He purred a little and followed me to the back with his eyes when I left. I wished I could have had him in the back sleeping next to us, but with Minx there it would not have worked. I had to tend Minx at night, to regulate her food and make sure she had the right balance slowly doled out, to keep her blood sugar from soaring or crashing, a dangerous situation. The food could not be left out, and Kudzu needed a bowl available at all times for any nibbling he might want to do. We had to keep Kudzu and Minx separated at night due to their different food needs.

Kudzu kept going downhill. Bill kept him going with hi-cal and saline. He stayed out more instead of hiding, which meant we could pet him, as though he wanted comfort, purring when touched. Bill would call "Kudzu" and he'd come.

August 12, the Kudzu news was grim. Bill took him to the vet again to discuss issues of when to let go and whether surgery was survivable. On her exam table Kudzu rolled over, turned his head up, and purred — he always was such a flirt with all ladies. The vet wanted a second opinion and sent them on to another vet. The consensus was that he had a lack of lung sounds in some areas, indicating that the fluid seen on X-ray was in the lungs. And his tumor was in the intestines rather than merely pressing on them, making surgery far less survivable even if it wasn't cancer. However, the vets also felt it wasn't time to let go.

August 13, Bill drove Mom out to the house to see Kudzu, an ominous "last-time" visit; she sweet-talked him and praised him. He did get up on the sill of the open window that he liked so much, and he watched out the glass door for awhile. But he didn't eat or drink, and he was weak and subdued. Bill kept on hydrating him and placing hi-cal gel in his mouth. The vet had said Kudzu would let us know when it was time to move on, but I wished he'd just go gently on his own. He did still have the capacity to enjoy life, as he watched the outdoors. Bill clung to hope and said that nutrients and fluids might help him fight cancer. He showed a preference for hanging out in the area behind the wood stove, so Bill cleared it completely of stored items and made it into a cozy nook and placed a special Batman nightlight there for

Kudzu. Minx purred, ever beside me on the couch, and called to me when I left the room, charming me by extending her paw up to me when I was there.

August 14, Bill took Kudzu outside for a supervised outing. He had a big time; he walked around the yard and looked at everything, out of eyes the color of rained-on grass. Kudzu also started to walk steadily and purposefully fairly far up the road before Bill turned him back by heading him off. It was almost as if he knew where he was going as he passed the dogwoods, the vine tangles, the pines and hardwoods, and the road to the lakebed, as if he wanted to visit his old haunts, the places unknown to us where he'd come from. Or maybe, as when a cat with a urinary tract infection urinates outside the litter box, Kudzu just thought getting Away, a change of scene, doing differently, might end his ailment. I took photos and Bill took videos. For the rest of the day while Bill was gone, Kudzu wanted out; he came when he heard me open the door, almost at his old loping gait, or simply parked himself at the door. But it was just too risky for me to take him out alone; two people were needed in case of a raccoon or a dog event, even a friendly dog.

Clever Minx reached up onto the top of the trunk where we had placed the other cats' food and overturned a bowl of cat food that was too high-carb for her, scattering it on the floor so she could gobble a few kibbles before I got it all up. There was a carved duck motif on the front, and she had placed one paw on this, raised herself up, and used the other paw to pull the food bowl over. Smart kitty!

The next day Bill took Kudzu outside twice. I took more photos. He was weaker than the day before but perked up a bit outside. I cried. I was torn up at the thought he could be suffering, and torn up at the idea of letting go. He wanted out all the time now, showing us he had some *joie de vivre* left. These are hard decisions for me, because during my own illness I've had to endure a great deal of discomfort, but I was always still determined to live.

August 16, Bill took Kudzu to the vet for her to examine. She said his kidneys had just about quit. In forty-eight hours, he could be in crisis. Bill phoned me from her office to ask me if we should let him go, and I couldn't say. I just didn't know. Inwardly, I felt I couldn't endure without seeing him again. Bill hung up and said, "What should I do, Kudzu?" Zu raised his head and let out a big, loud *MEOW* — he had never meowed much — and Bill decided to bring him home. The vet said it was the right decision, that Kudzu was still alert. It was a joy to see Bill bring the carrier back in with the big black-and-white boy inside. He expanded his door-side entreaties to include nighttime, but he was depressed a lot, too. Then Minx had her low blood-sugar episode, and I stayed home from a planned town day. We got her glucose leveled back out several hours later.

August 17. Kudzu wheezed a bit while Bill was gone to town, but it stopped. I stroked him and he purred weakly, went to hide, and then was unresponsive for awhile. I feared we'd lose him soon. He walked around a bit when Bill returned and he took Kudzu outside, and he walked into the back of the house and looked about, meowing to Bill. But overall he got up less and hid more, and he was weaker. Holding him carefully, Bill carried him around outside and took him for a long walk that way, with his ears flicking at the sounds, his nose sniffing the air, and his eyes glancing around at things.

August 18. Kudzu did not go into crisis as expected. Instead, he wanted out all the time and seemed a shade more perked up. Bill was now on a twice-a-day outing schedule for Kudzu. Kudzu rolled over in a dusty spot in the road; he always loved to roll in dust, and as he swooped over, he meowed to Bill. He knew Bill was trying to make him feel better. He'd become Bill's lap cat. They sat together in the evening and I looked at Bill and saw beyond the façade of bravery, a deep fount of profound sorrow in his eyes. My heart was being wrenched around, waiting for Kudzu to leave us, taking bittersweet joy in his every slight outdoor pleasure. He meowed loudly and pulled on the door to the back last night after bedtime. Bill had stayed out in the living room with him late into the night.

August 19. Another day, and Kudzu tired more easily. His second outing of the day was in the evening, under waves and waves of thunderous cicada crescendo in the bewitching Southern twilight, like a humming roan sheen. It's the perfect time of day for outings, as cats are crepuscular animals, more active at dawn and dusk. Although he didn't like the momentary stick of the subcutaneous fluids or taking the hi-cal, when sitting on laps or purring or exploring the outdoors, Kudzu's eyes were still ablaze with enjoyment. Cats have enormous capacities to enjoy and attain pleasure, and as long as I can see that joyous light in their eyes, I don't think it's time to let go. I've never seen creatures so determined to bask in rhapsody and pleasure, even during serious decline, as cats.

Kudzu's days were stretching out. By August 21 his breathing was more difficult; I almost thought he was slipping away for awhile. But he was still scooting along cheerfully when Bill took him out, and then after each return, he would try to get Bill to take him out again. In the house, he sat on Bill's lap that night, and I snapped a picture. The three of us went out after dark and I took several more. Bill sat on the old metal glider in the yard with Kudzu beside him or on his lap, in fresh, late-summer night air smelling of warmth and earth. The cicadas had quit but the katydids were blasting out their rhythm to dance and sway to. Inside, we watched an old Hitchcock film, but I could scarcely concentrate. My mind was full of the sharp black-and-white patterned fur, the deep emerald eyes, the immensely curving top whiskers, like staircases festooning boldly into some huge and absent ballroom, above the lower jaw with its short, white whiskers; all that was Kudzu. Understated humorist, from some unknown funny place in the forest where leaves quipped and laughed; that, too, was Kudzu. When I saw Kudzu outside, the glimmers of his old self shimmering faintly through his feebleness, I felt joy for him, but also deep pangs for Spotty. She had gone down during a bitter cold winter, when going outside wasn't possible. And her failure to recognize us outdoors, outside of home context, would have made outings with her risky. Cats are both homebodies and wanderers, and I felt guilty about making ours live an all-indoor life. At the same time, I knew it was the only way to keep them safe and living to an old age.

The next day saw Kudzu far less active, although he improved in the evening. But he still couldn't walk as far up the road as before, and he couldn't roll over as he had a few days ago. After coming in, he meowed at the front door, wanting to get out again. Bill took him into the bedroom to stay the night, but soon let him back out at Kudzu's request. Kudzu had never responded much to my singing so I hadn't often sung to him directly, but I did in the days after he became sick. I would detect a faint flick of his ear, or a small flex of his paw, or a slight glance from eyes as green as a sprouting forest in spring light.

Kudzu continued to have ups and downs. He lived to go outdoors with Bill. I went whenever I could take a moment from the endless delivery of fish and chicken and turkey to a Minx. Some days Kudzu seemed to have an upturn — he'd be a bit stronger and he would even jump up to some favored spots. But he wouldn't eat or drink and was being kept alive by the hi-cal supplement and injected fluids. And wanderlust. The vet couldn't believe he was still alive. He tried to get outdoors all he could, and Bill took him three or four times a day, into the part-jungle of our yard where I watched him step carefully while gliding through the ferns and tall grasses, feeling his way with his grandly arcing whiskers.

Kudzu indeed had the most magnificent set of whiskers I've ever seen. Known as vibrissae, cat's whiskers are located on the lips and the sides of the face, over the eyes, on the chin, and on the back of the forelegs. On the cheeks, they are arranged in four rows, which I am unable to discern on most cats except for tabbies, who have dark dots at the base of their side whiskers. On Pretty Girl and my mother's tabbies, these dots were clearly in four rows. These sensors are thick, highly sensitive hairs, each deeply embedded in a base full of nerve endings that send information to the cat's brain. Whiskers detect by touching objects and feeling the air currents that flow around objects, enabling the cats to navigate in the dark and to know the width of spaces they wish to enter. A cat's whiskers also sense the exact position of prey caught with front paws or mouth. Whiskers are as important to the night-hunting cat as its keen visual acuity in low illumination.

August 28 found me videotaping the inseparable Bill and Kudzu. I wasn't in the room when Bill saw Kudzu notice a shadow, which he had not done for many months. He breathed hard for short spells but still trotted to the door when he thought he would be taken outside. He still got on his favorite perches like the arm of the old couch.

The next day Kudzu was not doing well. We both went out with him in the evening, into the shadowy light and the raspy song of the cicadas as Kudzu slowly poked around in the driveway, finding several places to his liking and stretching out for brief sits along the way. He had the sleekest, blackest fur of any of our cats. He was just glorious.

On August 31, he was weaker. I had that awful autumn feeling, bad. The next day he was again even weaker, and Bill and I sorrowfully talked about what to do. Minou didn't usually lick Kudzu's head but in the last few weeks he'd done that a few times. Even stranger, Pretty Girl, who usually ignored Kudzu, had groomed his head too. Cats just know things. Call it psychic if you will, or the result of senses unknown, like Roger Caras does in *A Cat is Watching*.[14] We let Kudzu come into the back for the night as he indicated that he wanted. He chose to park all night on the bathroom floor, the coolest spot in the back of the house. During each of my many nocturnal trips to the room, I greeted him with whispered words and pats on the head.

On September 2, we lost him. The signs were clear. It was time to help him move on. When we put him in the carrier, Minou came up and rubbed against it. Pretty Girl also walked up as if in sympathy. It was after hours, and we had to go to the 24-hour clinic near the larger city up the road. I rode in the back with Kudzu in the carrier and talked to him. He purred. It was a long drive, across an ocean of darkened forests and farms, but it was also too short.

The clinic was in an area of flat, open land that must have been farmland not long ago and was now being newly, slowly developed. There were a few businesses and a few houses around. It was no longer country; it wasn't city, and it wasn't neighborhood. It was amalgamous and anonymous, and it was the loneliest nondescript nowhere in the world that night. Then there was a long driveway and we pulled up slowly to the sudden island of artificial light against the dark. The old friend riding quietly beside me did not have long. The clinic reminded me somehow of the Edward Hopper painting, *Night-*

hawks. We were the only clients there except for a young couple picking up their dog. With the carrier open, we sat and waited. I placed my hand on Kudzu. He purred. When we were called in, the staff said his eyes were beautiful.

We buried him the next day in the woods near the others, among the same branches and leaves and shadows he had once walked straight out of and right up to us; now enhanced by thirteen more years of undisturbed growth. Bill said, "Kudzu has finally caught his own shadow." That evening I felt compelled to stand in the door and yell, "Kud—zu, here kitty kitty kitty," one last time, as I'd used to when he had first come up and lived outside. If he was there in spirit suddenly finding himself disembodied and alone, maybe calling signaled him that we were still there with him.

I cried off and on all the next day. Minx wailed at the louvered door the whole time I was taking a bath, but Kudzu stayed on my mind. As with Spotty, there was a huge empty gulf in the house and it seemed like Kudzu should be there. Our space felt wrong without him. Our vet, bless her, left a condolence message on our phone several days later. Early one morning I had a vivid dream set in the same room that I sleep in. I saw the table across from my side of the bed, normally cluttered with a jumble of papers, rolls of film, and whatever. But in the dream it was empty, except for Kudzu, stretched out all black-and-white, elegant, animated. It was so vivid and so real. There are those who would say that, like in the dream of Spotty playing the record, Kudzu was really there and Spotty had really been there, too. I'll leave it to others to puzzle over this. I don't know. As I've said, I don't believe in that spooky stuff, but events do make you sit up and take notice sometimes. Bill says, "Unusual can happen more than once."

Kudzu's big lion-face stayed in my mind. A few weeks later a storm came up as I was about to feed the cats their canned food. For a moment I actually thought, *I can't feed them now because Kudzu hides from storms and won't get his.* A storm had meant a feeding delay when Kudzu was alive, because otherwise he would have missed out on the canned chow; he wouldn't come out from under the couch until the rain and wind was over.

Late September and early October of that year were unusually cool. I looked at photos of Spotty and Kudzu, which revealed that there were not enough pictures! And none that captured them the way I really wanted to see them. I was feeling cold and alone. I lost an aunt in late September. We lived far from each other but our phone calls were a mainstay for me, and when I got the call and began to sob, Minx came running over to me. She was there for me as she always was. Every time I was about to leave the house she knew and would howl and howl at the door to the back where I'd gone to get ready to go, right before my leaving.

Given our experiences with Kudzu's shining joy at being in the yard, one might ask why we didn't immediately take the others outside to enjoy it. Changes in the neighborhood, an increase of both domestic dogs and wild canids (coyotes), would have made this increasingly perilous. Mushrooming work and elder-care responsibilities occupied more and more of Bill's free time, and he couldn't escort the cats or build that outdoor, enclosed catio we always wanted.

On September 11, 2003, we drove home from town at night, towards a huge full and rare moon, the brightest orange I'd ever seen in the sky. Bill called it a "bloody moon." In mid-October, more photos of Kudzu came back, but they weren't as good as I'd hoped.

Around this time another friend was losing a beloved old dog who was ailing. All he could do, he said, was to hold him and try not to cry too hard. An animal is a sentient and responsive being, and each one is an individual. Pets are family, and the pain of losing them is as deep and profound as it is with human friends and family. Each time it happens, the question arises, is it too much heartbreak? Would I rather not have any more animals, as I felt after losing our first three in the early years? In most cases, you will outlive a dog or a cat. (If it's possible that your pet might outlive you, arrangements should be made with a trusted friend, via a solid will, or with a no-kill shelter that will take your pet if you die or become incapacitated, in exchange for a donation. Needless to say you must check out these organizations carefully before committing.) But given that I feel that by definition, I live with cats, I have to say yes, living with them for their life spans and then losing them is worth it. This book of memories that I've dashed out to preserve against the future vagaries of age is one I plan to revisit fondly. Everyone who has shared life with an animal has such memories and stories. And considering that animals who need homes show up constantly, those of us who care about them should step up and provide homes whenever we can, whenever we have the means to live with more than one.

That said, how I miss my cats who have moved on! The best ending to these stories of cat loss, the best tribute to the lost ones, would be kitten or cat adoption from a shelter or rescue, after a mourning period. This is what I would have done after losing Spotty and Kudzu if my current circumstances had been different. We didn't know what would happen in the future, but for the moment our own circumstances and the three cats we still had required all of our available animal focus. But whenever circumstances permit, I'm in favor of sharing your heart with a new pet, when you are ready, rather than giving in to the feeling that you can't go through such sorrow again. Even sadder than the loss of old and beloved pets is the fate of those in shelters without a home and a person of their own, whose lives are ended prematurely. Or those wandering the streets with no one to nurture and tend them in their last days.

Increasingly I am reminded that none of us are forever. The arrangements regarding the pets or companion animals we might leave behind are often not as easy to arrange as they should be. In wills, pets are often considered property and therefore it is difficult to leave money and resources for their care. It's all too easy, legally, for heirs who may not be animal sympathetic to simply cart the pets to a nearby shelter. There needs to be some kind of special category or designation for pets left behind when we die, to protect them. This protection is also needed in cases of animal abuse, so that potential abusers will be deterred by the possibility of large civil penalties from causing the anguish of having one's pets deliberately injured or killed by an abusive miscreant. At the time I was writing this, damages were limited to the monetary value of the animal, which in the case of former strays and shelter-adopted non-purebred animals was considered to be zero or, at the most, equal to adoption fees. And whereas I'm not suggesting the same status as a child or a ward for companion animals, some expanded definition should be in place.

Changing the word "owner" to "guardian" would relinquish too many rights and safeguards against overreaching institutions, both public and private. But "owner" in itself doesn't embody enough protection against cruelty to the animal "property," nor does it provide enough recourse for injury by others. Certainly better enforcement of anti-cruelty laws would help enforce against mistreatment. Something is also needed that would address custody of pets in divorce cases and decide those cases on the best interests of the animal rather than on simple division of property. In early 2007, an event arose that underscored the need for greater legal recourse for the loss of or injury to companion animals: the large recalls of tainted pet food after many animals were sickened and/or killed. Definitions based on the idea of "sentient property" have been suggested.

Coping with our grief

I again felt cheated that my cats didn't get the twenty-year lifespan that some cats do. Minou now wailed mightily and mournfully at the door he used to guard side-by-side with Kudzu, the little Booper and the Big Bopper, ears attuned to the sounds, eyes scanning the woods outside for intruders.

The Whitefooted Gang, I used to call the two tuxies. We sensed depression and loneliness in Minou. He, too, missed Kudzu.

The Halloween after we lost Kudzu, there was a big reunion at the community bar that was soon to be closed, The Chukker. It had been a mainstay meeting place for some thirty or forty years, and many friends, good painters all, had left paintings on the walls and ceilings. Friends came into town for the event, some of whom were cat people who knew how hard it was for us to have lost Kudzu. The night of the event was tropically warm, the feel of the outside air, intoxicating. First we drove to our parents' houses in town. Mom's dim, somewhat dreary amber décor lighting seemed on this night atmospheric and suitable as she and her black cat, Good Old Boy, waited for trick-or-treaters. Then we went on to the bar.

After a fun but exhausting party I came home to my three cats. Although I was glad enough to see the others, it would have been a capital sort of night to see Kudzu sitting there among them, with his huge, black lion jaw and grand white whiskers. Instead, I had Halloween night with Minx, the most beautiful and clever black cat in the land. There were more shadows in her dark fur than any of us had ever written about or could ever capture. Sitting soft and regal, she always made me feel smug, satisfied. I felt it, but this year, lacking Kudzu, lacking Spotty, everything felt not quite … something, some elusive quality of indefinite misalignment.

During that brief time after Minx had rallied and Kudzu's ailment had not shown up, we had been designing an intense care program for Minx, and we soldiered on with it even during Kudzu's decline. Minx got her five or six meals of canned fish or turkey or chicken a day, while the other cats got two canned food meals a day. They adjusted to this unfairness, albeit unwillingly. We simply couldn't handle multiple canned food feedings for everyone. When we did feed them all canned food, they thought we could teleport it to them by magic. They didn't get that when your hands are at counter level with food, the chow can't instantly go to floor level without you stooping down and maneuvering the dish around and under the cats who are blocking the way in a furry mass, twirling around your feet between the food and the floor. But to the cats, a solid animal between the food and themselves should be no impediment to instantaneous delivery.

During summer in one of these years, Mom lost her little feral Winnie, who would not let anyone touch her and would not sit on a lap, although she had learned to sit close to us around Mom's house. She was such a pretty cat, the brightest orange and deepest black, and Mom loved her dearly, little wild thing that she was. After the vet released her, Bill brought her remains out to our woods for burial. I told her, "Goodbye little Wild Thing, you were a good cat." Bill repeated, with emphasis, "You were a good cat."

Minou, The Minx, and Pretty Girl all had their ways of keeping me grounded through the sad times. Everyday joys with them, along with hurt from the losses, impelled me to begin writing about our experiences with feline companions. I began this one book in two volumes in November of 2004. I worked at night as late as 3:30 a.m., slapping down the initial fresh narrative, with Minx the Muse beside me. Her ears would swivel, her tail would flick, she would reach for me with her paw, purring, her eyes oh so keen and gold, her fur so black and finely detailed. There was nothing like the company of a living animal, a consciousness so different from mine, so mysterious, but so integral to mine, too. I scrambled to record things about the cats.

Knowing cats is fascination; each has its own breathtaking, alluring captivations. We contemplate, and they perplex and tease and entertain endlessly. No words can explain them or describe these magnificent creatures. Not only their beauty and presence, but their quirky personalities defy capture and explanation. They are glorious. In a group, the idiosyncrasies of each individual, the clashing and/or meshing of personalities, is as intriguing as the dynamics of any group of humans together, a family, a circle of friends, co-workers, school-mates. It's as entertaining as any soap opera, drama, sit-com, porch-told story, or novel, if you watch carefully and learn how to notice. I want these books to be a celebration and a romp with cats that tells the depth that love with a pet can reach. *Minx, can we do that?* I asked her on a winter night. She answered with a blink.

The book project stretched through years and when MochaBud came to live with us, he displayed a flair for editing and became an Editing Cat.

"I been knowing all that," he chirped.

"Say again?"

"About how glorious I am. Tell me something I don't know, about Minou and Pretty Girl before I first smelled them."

I went on to tell Bud all about how Minou charmed us, and what a sleek, smart, clever smoothie the little guy was, even dancing in boxes. Bud hissed, and even though he'd asked, he said he wasn't studying Othercats. But I piqued his interest with some of my musings on Pretty Girl.

At one time I thought the seemingly subdued coloration of the brown tabby was plain. But it was in Pretty Girl's spots and stripes and patterns, her eyes edged in dark sepia, that I so often lost myself in looking, in the reverie and grasping for words to fit the ticked fur like a galaxy of star points, following the dark rivulets of pigmentation traveling from her back down her sides, and tracing the streaks that waver and trick like the oblique joinery and irregular latticework of tree branches in winter. She wore the wild. As she walked fluidly I saw the Original and Native Cat hidden and watchful amidst summer's aggregates, dense cover, all sun sparkled and shadow spliced with thousands of leaves. *What am I looking at, all lost in thought?* "Only the streaks and whorls and shadows on this tabby cat's head." Only a jillion light bits from the tips of her fur, like the sunstruck silt of a kicked creekbed. That wheatfield of tabby fur is rightfully called "glitter" in cat-fancy speak. Green-eyed brown mackerel tabby, phenotype, ancient pelage of *felis sylvestris catus*.

"I'll think on that and purr atcha later. Or hiss at ya," Bud said as he left my side and padded to the door. Looking out at the forest, he settled himself in a sunpuddle, then closed his eyes and went to sleep.

Author's Note

Over the course of fifty years, my husband William and I have lived with a total of fifteen cats. In all that time, we only ever answered one newspaper "free pets" ad (when we got our first kitty), and we have never adopted from a shelter. This was not because of any unwillingness to take in shelter cats, who are just as deserving and worthy of homes and love as other pets. Our kitties came to us as strays, and we have also rescued numerous other stray cats and a few dogs and helped to find homes for them. Our animal-rescue stories and experiences illuminate the massive nature of the stray population and the difficulties of finding homes for all who need them. Shelter animals had little chance when we were adopting, as the streets and woods were full of adoptable pets. Now, advances in home and veterinary care are extending the lives of cats, as well as other companion animals, keeping good cat homes occupied and out of the new adoptions loop for longer timeframes. For these reasons, I'm adding my voice to the chorus of advocates who say, spay and neuter your pets.

Since I began this book, advocates have questioned whether the pet population is actually greater than the demand for new pets, saying the "overflow" is simply the result of poor shelter management and a lack of efforts to find homes for the animals. I'm certainly open to that being the case, and I do not want pets to be killed in so-called shelters: I want the killing to stop NOW. I'm not making a definitive statement about the numbers either way as I simply do not know. I can only tell you my experiences and observations.

I began this book in November of 2004 and much of it was completed by the end of 2006. I have continued to find memories around the house since that time, to insert pertinent thoughts, and to write the continuing story of present-day kitties. Many of my thoughts about cats and their relation to various ecosystems (in Chapter 4) originated back in the earliest versions of the book. Since those days, there has been an explosion of dialogue online regarding animal issues, and many of my observations have been written about by others, which is why some readers might think, "Well, I've seen this idea before." The ideas were directly and freshly recorded when I wrote them, and I did search to try to find any other research in those areas that had been previously done. I have in most, but not all, cases elected not to go back and point out that new, ongoing research has taken place, since this book is the history of my thinking as it occurred. It's also worth noting: a substantial portion of the imagery in this book goes back to old notes written by me as far back as the 1970s and 1980s. On the Internet, I am "catwoods" on several websites and on my own "Catwoods Porch Party" Wordpress blog, so if someone points out that "catwoods" said it first, well, "catwoods" is me!

This book is mainly my personal observations, experiences, and opinions, and I present it both for entertainment and educational purposes. I offer observations and thoughts that I consider insightful, that I hope will add to cat science and knowledge, and to stimulate discussion and further study. However, as these are my thoughtful and carefully observed opinions only, they are not to be taken as hard science. I observe carefully, but I'm not an animal behaviorist, a zoologist, a veterinarian, or a natural history professional, and I do not guarantee that my content will be wholly scientific or accurate. Research widely and compare my experiences with other cat literature for educational purposes. If you have a cat behavioral problem, please consult a professional behaviorist and if you have a sick cat, take it to a veterinarian. Where facts about cats are described, gained through my observations, conversations, and the reading of many books, articles, and websites for context, additional facts, and comparison, I have tried to present the most accurate information available to the best of my knowledge, but I cannot guarantee it. The sources cited represent sound scholarship to the best of my knowledge, but I cannot endorse or guarantee the contents of sources written by myself or others. Citing a given expert's works does not mean I endorse all of their stances with regard to animals. Roger Caras wrote two excellent books about cats that I have read and will cite in this book. However, I need to point out that he and I have sharply parted ways, according to what I have read about his statements on several animal issues, notably feral cats, declawing cats, and the feasibility of no-kill animal sheltering. With regard to my own book, I am not responsible for the use or misuse of information recorded as both memoir and analysis of scientific studies.

Anyone planning to enter wilderness areas where encounters with wild animals are possible should seek the advice of local wildlife professionals, as well as those skilled in local woodcraft, prior to any actual excursions into the landscape. Learn the resident species of all spaces where you plan activities and how to handle encounters with each of them. Never approach a wild animal and never corner one. Never feed wild animals, as serious and sometimes fatal events have resulted from this. Learn to recognize plants that are toxic to the touch. Never eat or consume wild-gathered plants or game without a thorough knowledge of what is edible and what is not. Nature is grand but not easy. Nature and the wilderness require study. Be mindful of what microbes and other toxins have been found in specific bodies of water before engaging in water activities.

In addition, use caution and restraint when approaching, rescuing, and handling stray and feral domestic animals. Every year a few cases of rabies are found in the United States; sometimes these are in domestic dogs and cats. Observe potential rescue animals carefully. All rescued animals should be checked by a veterinarian immediately after capture or contact. Keep up with the news on rabies occurrences especially in your own area and especially if you rescue animals.

The information here is a record of my observations and thoughts. Do not use the anecdotes about the ailments that our various cats went through to help with diagnosis and treatment of any pet's illness. If you have a sick pet, consult a veterinarian.

This story is true, with only the slightest occasional embellishment of a few facts. The events of this book go back decades. Much has changed over the years regarding the care of companion animals and present opinions differ. To anyone who feels he or she will react with emotion and anger to narrated facts about issues such as spay/neuter, indoor/outdoor pets, and so on, I ask that you please read responsibly, as this is a history and not a conclusive discussion of present-day issues. Today's enlightened practices cannot always be a measure of the past.

Internet sources change rapidly. I've tried to find alternate sources for any that have disappeared. By the time this book is printed, some that are valid now may have changed again.

Things aren't perfect where I live, but few places are.

I am adventurous and experimental with words. I've used many regional ways of speaking from the southeastern United States in this book, such as "small little." Those may sound unfamiliar to some readers but are mostly actual usages, except in cases where I may have tweaked them playfully as I like to do with any expression, of any origin, that comes my way. In narration I often try for the cadence, structure, and expressions of humans actually talking. Sometimes I'm purposely eccentric with language. Events in our household are always nonlinear and with cats along for the ride, the book bounces around between blissful and giddy, somber, and scholarly. That's the way real life is, humans and animals, having moods and phases.

I sang songs and paraphrased songs to the cats, and I wanted to bring the music of the times we lived through into this book. However, in most instances I can't state exact wordings here because of the cost and paperwork of licensing song lyrics to quote or paraphrase. I encourage readers who are so inclined to look up and listen to the songs referenced.

NOTES

Chapter 1. The Naming of the Minx

1. Eliot, T. S. "The Naming of Cats." In *Old Possum's Book of Practical Cats.* San Diego, CA: Harcourt Brace Jovanovich, 1939. p. 1.
2. Engels, Donald. *Classical Cats, the Rise and Fall of the Sacred Cat.* New York: Routledge, 1999. pp. 13, 166.
3. Words@Random. "The Maven's Word of the Day, August 17, 1998." randomhouse.com.wotd/indes.pperl?date=19980817. Accessed 2005.
4. Breoghan, Siobhan. "Adventures in Etymology." *Early Period Quarterly.* www.housebarra.com/EP/ep04/13etymology.html. Accessed 2005.
5. "Minikin" defined as "beloved" is from the Encyclopedia Britannica Online, whereas Merriam Webster's Online Dictionary uses "a small or dainty creature." www.merriam-webster.com/minikin. Accessed April 2017.
6. *2001: A Space Odyssey.* Movie directed by Stanley Kubrick. Metro-Goldwyn-Mayer, 1968.
7. "Me and My Shadow," lyrics by Billy Rose, music by Al Jolson and Dave Dreyer.
8. "Am I Blue," lyrics by Grant Clarke, music by Harry Akst.
9. "Lady Sings the Blues," lyrics by Billie Holiday, music by Herbie Nichols.
10. "Mood Indigo," by Duke Ellington, Barney Bigard, and Irving Mills.
11. "Summertime," lyrics by DuBose Heyward and Ira Gershwin, music by George Gershwin, from the 1935 opera, *Porgy and Bess.*
12. "My Funny Valentine," lyrics by Lorenz Hart, music by Richard Rodgers, from the musical comedy, *Babes in Arms.*
13. "The Wild Mountain Thyme," traditional Scottish song first recorded by Andrew Scarhart in 1957. Scarhart possibly wrote the music, but Eric Winter is credited in the liner notes of the 1995 re-release of "The Corries: In Concert/Scottish Love Songs." Also said to be "an elegant variant of a Scottish song by Robert Tannahill (1774 – 1819), 'The Braes of Balquidder,'" to which son Francis McPeake added another verse. See http://cantaria.org/lyrics/wildmt.html and "Brobdingnagian Bands, A Band's Celtic Lyrics Directory" at https://www.thebards.net/music/lyrics/Wild_Mountain_Thyme.shtml. Accessed April 2017.
14. "Them There Eyes," by Maceo Pinkard, William Tracey, and Doris Tauber.

15. "My Girl," by Smokey Robinson and Ronald White. First released December 21, 1965, and performed by The Temptations.
16. "I Get A Kick Out Of You," words and music by Cole Porter, from the show, "Anything Goes," 1934.
17. "I Never Loved A Man (The Way I Love You)," words and music by Ronnie Shannon, performed by Aretha Franklin.
18. "It Had To Be You," lyrics by Gus Kahn, music by Isham Jones, 1924.
19. Hood, David. "Aretha to the Black Keys: The Muscle Shoals Story." *Song Facts.* www.songfacts.com/blog/writing/aretha_to_the_ black_keys_the_muscle_shoals_story/ Accessed 2007.
20. Thomas, Lewis. *The Lives of a Cell: Notes of a Biology Watcher.* New York: Lewis Thomas, Viking Penguin, 1974.
21. McCrum, Robert, Cran, William, and McNeil, Robert. *The Story of English.* New York: Penguin Group Inc., 1986. p. 12.

Chapter 2. Black and Beauty

1. Alford, William Edward Sr. *The Smoke Eater of Geneva County.* Authorhouse, 2007. p. 15.
2. Engels, pp. 142, 160 -162.
3. Malek, Jaromir. *The Cat in Ancient Egypt.* London: British Museum Press, Division of the British Museum Company, Ltd., 1993. pp. 133 - 134.
4. De Vinne, Pamela B. *American Heritage Illustrated Encyclopedic Dictionary.* Boston, MA: Houghton, Mifflin Company, 1982.
5. Sargent, Walter. *The Enjoyment and Use of Color, Charles Scribner's Sons.* New York: Dover Publications Inc., 1923. p. 51.
6. Sargent, p. 20.
7. Sargent, p. 65.
8. Sargent, p. 67.
9. Sargent, p. 67.
10. Sargent, p. 66.
11. Sargent, p. 140 (reflecting adjacents).
12. Sargent, p. 86 (surfaces).
13. Sargent, pp. 69 - 70 (neutrals).
14. "Glass Gem Corn." https://www.rareseeds.com/glass-gem-corn-/ Accessed 2018.
15. Sargent, p. 67.
16. Sargent, p. 72.
17. Sargent, p. 73.

18. Ball, Phillip. *Bright Earth: Art and the Invention of Color*. Chicago: The University of Chicago Press, 2001. p. 165.
19. "Color Theory for the Woodworker and Furniture Maker." www.shellac.net/color-theory-for-woodworkers.html Accessed 2005.
20. Dewberry, Pauline. "Origin of the Cat Flap." *The Daily Mews, 2001– 2006.* www.thedailymews.com/articles/originofcatflap.htm Accessed 2005.
21. Times, Johnny. "Issac Newton and His Cat, Spithead Made a Deal with a 'Cat Flap.'" www.johnnytimes.com/isaac-newton-spithead-cat-flap/ Accessed February 2018.
22. Lummus, Dominique. "Spitface; What's in a Name?" *Cat World UK*, no. 282. catworld.co.uk
23. Personal email correspondence.
24. Newton, Issac. "The Chronology of Ancient Kingdoms Amended, Front Matter." London, 1728. Published online through The Newton Project June 2006. www.newtonproject.ox.ac.uk/view/texts/diplomatic/THEM00184 Accessed May 2017.
25. Wright, J.F.M. *Alma Mater, or, Seven years at the University of Cambridge.* London: Black, Young, and Young, 1827. p.17. See also two biographies of Newton: *Sir Issac Newton* by S. Brodetsky (2007) and *Issac Newton: A Biography* by Lewis More (1927).
26. Wikipedia. "Pet Door." en.wikipedia.org/wiki/Pet_door Accessed 2014.
27. Finlay, Victoria. *Color: A Natural History of the Palette*. New York: The Random House Publishing Group, 2002. p. 135. Also mentioned in an endnote in *Turner's Painting Techniques* by Joyce Townsend (1999).
28. Hall, Marian. "The Manx Cat." *The Cat Fanciers' Association, 1995 – 2007.* cfa.org/Breeds/BreedsKthruR/Manx/ManxArticle.aspx Accessed May 2017. See also: "Tailless Cats" by Sarah Hartwell on Messybeast Cats, messybeast.com/bobtail-cats-manx.html Accessed May 2017.
29. Miller, Paul E. "Vision in Animals, What Do Cats and Dogs See?" Presented at the 25th Annual Waltham/OSU Symposium, October 27 – 28, 2001. www.vin.com/VINDBPub/SearchPB/Proceedings/PR05000/PR00515.pdf Accessed 2006.
30. Caras, Roger. *A Cat is Watching*. New York: Simon and Shuster, 1989. p. 36.
31. Caras, pp. 36 - 39.
32. Masson, Jeffrey. *The Nine Emotional Lives of Cats*. New York: Ballantine Books, The Random House Publishing Group, 2002. p. 184.
33. Caras, p. 37.

34. Masson, p.185.
35. Morris, Desmond. *Catwatching*. New York: Crown Publishers, 1986. p. 86.
36. Caras, p. 39.
37. Caras, p. 39.
38. Morris, p. 86.
39. Budiansky, Stephen. *The Character of Cats: The Origins, Intelligence, Behavior, and Stratagems of Felis Sylvestris Catus*. New York: Viking Penguin, 2002. pp. 119 - 120.
40. Budiansky, p. 119 - 120.
41. Budiansky, p. 8.
42. Budiansky, pp. 119 - 120.
43. Masson, pp. 185 - 186.
44. Masson, p. 186.
45. Drake, Nadia. "This is How Cats See the World." *Wired*, 2013. www.wired.com/2013/10/cats-eye-view/ Based on a project by Nickolay Lamm, in consultation with Kerry L. Retring DVM, DACVO of the All Animal Eye Clinic, Dr. D.J. Haeussler of The Animal Eye Institute, and the Opthamology Group at Penn Vet.
46. Christensen, Wendy. *Outwitting Cats: Tips, Tricks, and Techniques for Pursuading the Felines in Your Life That What You Want Is Also What They Want*. Guilford, CT: The Lyons Press, 2004. p. 141.
47. Holland, Barbara. *Secrets of the Cat*. New York: Ballantine Books, Random House, Inc., 1988. p. 103. Originally published by Dodd, Mead, and Co., as *The Name of the Cat*.
48. Holland, p. 103.
49. Holland, pp. 103 - 104.
50. Poe, Edgar Allan. "Ligeia." *The American Museum,* edited by N.C. Brooks and J.E. Snodgrass. September 18, 1838.
51. Campbell, Mike. "Behind the Name." www.behindthename.com/name/ligeia Accessed 2017.
52. Morris, Desmond. *Catlore*. New York: Crown Publishers, Inc., 1987. p. 111.
53. Originated by Robert Register.
54. "California Dreamin'," written by John Phillips and Michelle Phillips, performed by The Mamas and the Papas, 1965, 1966. Universal MCA Music Publishing, A Division of Universal Studios, Inc.
55. "Cullen" comes from the town of Cullen in Banffshire, Scotland. Also holly or holly trees. See "Cullen Family History" on Ancestry.com. www.ancestry.com/name-origin?surname=cullen Accessed May 6, 2017.

"Handsome young animal," is Celtic in origin. See "Cullen, Boy's Name, Meaning, and Popularity" at BabyCenter. www.babycenter.com/baby-names-cullen-1140.htm Accessed 2017.

Chapter 3. Neighborhood Cat Scan
No Notes

Chapter 4. *Aves* versus *Felis Sylvestris Catus*

1. Rue, Leonard Lee, III. *Complete Guide to Game Animals*. Los Angeles, CA: Times Mirror Magazines Books Division, 1968. p. 9.
2. Ehrlich, Paul R., David S. Dobkin, and Darryl Wheye. *The Birder's Handbook, A field Guide to the Natural History of North American Birds*. New York: Simon and Schuster/Fireside Books, 1988. pp. 495 - 501.
3. Ehrlich, et al., p. 129.
4. Morris, Desmond. *Catwatching*. New York: Crown Publishers, 1986. p. 65.
5. *Beep Beep, Merrie Melodies* (Wile E. Coyote and the Road Runner) series. Story by Michael Maltese. Warner Brothers, 1952.
6. Ehrlich, et al., pp. 349 - 353.
7. Engles, Donald. *Classical Cats, The Rise and Fall of the Sacred Cat*. New York: Routledge, Taylor and Francis Group, 1999. p. 7. See also "The Wisconsin Study: Bad Science Costs Cats' Lives, " *Alley Cat Allies*, https://www.alleycat.org/resources/the-wisconsin-study-bad-science-costs-cats-lives/. Accessed June 2018.
8. Kitchener, Andrew. *The Natural History of the Wild Cats*. Ithaca, NY: Helm Limited and Cornell University Press, 1991. pp. 114 - 119. See also: Arnold, Carrie, "Island's Feral Cats Kill Surprisingly Few Birds, Video Shows," *National Geographic*, September 1, 2015. https://news.nationalgeographic.com/2015/09/150901-feral-cats-birds-animals-science-nation/ Accessed July, 2018.
9. Rue III, p. 335, 617. See also *Rats, Lice, and History* by Hans Zinzer (1935).
10. Whitaker, John O. Jr., Robert Elman, and Carol Nehring. *The Audubon Society Field Guide to North American Mammals*. New York: Chanticleer Press, Inc., Alfred A. Knopf, Inc., 1980. p. 516. See also *Rats, Lice, and History* by Hans Zinsser (1935).
11. Whitaker, et al., p. 521.
12. Whitaker, et al., p.512.
13. Whitaker, et al., p.517.

14. Whitaker, et al., p 521.
15. Rue III, pp. 233, 333.
16. Rue III, pp. 331-332.
17. Spencer, Thomas. "Birmingham's East Lake Park Canada Geese captured, killed as threat to nearby airport's planes." Al.com, June 4, 2011. blog.al.com/spotnews/2011/06/birminghams_east_lake _park_can.html Accessed 2016. See also: "Cormorant, pelicans, ducks and gulls killed: 60 birds killed near Oakland airport." UPI, December 30, 2009. www.upi.com/60-birds-killed-near-Oakland airport/ 38341262212438/Accessed February 2018.
18. Stewart, Mary Margaret. "Invasive bushes in Decatur killing cedar waxwings." *Decaturish*, March 3, 2017. www.decaturish.com/2017/03/invasive-bushes-in-decatur-killing-cedar-waxwings/ Accessed March 2017.
19. Pomerantz, Leah. "West Nile Virus in Birds." Microbe Wiki, Spring 2014. microbewiki.kenyon.edu/index.php/West_Nile_Virus_in_Birds Accessed 2016.
20. Winkeler, Les. "The disappearing whippoorwill." *The Southern Illinoisan*, March 8, 2013. thesouthern.com/sports/outdoors/the-disappearing-whippoorwill/article_4cd065e0-879f-11e2-939a-001a4bcf887a.html Accessed June 2017.
21. Keim, Brandon. "Why are big, insect-eating birds disappearing? Maybe we're running low on bugs." *Anthropocene Magazine*, March 14, 2018.
22. Inglis-Arkel, Esther. "Field Cameras Catch Deer Eating Birds: Wait, Why Do Deer Eat Birds." *Gizmodo*, March 4, 2015. io9.gizmodo.com/field-cameras-catch-deer-eating-birds-wait-why-do-deer-1689440870 Accessed July 2016.
23. Dalzel, Stephanie. "Scrunchies saving wildlife from being killed by cats: study." ABC, March 20, 2015. www.abc.net.au/news/2015-03-20/scrunchies-prevent-wildlife-death-study-finds/6337222
24. Filardi, Christopher E. "Why I Collected a Moustached Kingfisher." *Audubon*, October 7, 2015. www.audubon.org/news/why-i-collected-moustached-kingfisher Accessed 2016.
25. Christensen, Jen. "Are cats the ultimate weapon in public health?" CNN, July 15, 2016. www.cnn.com/2016/07/15/health/cats-chicago-rat-patrol/ Accessed September 2016. anthropocenemagazine.org/2018/03/ running-out-of-bugs/
26. Bale, Rachael, and Tom Knudson. "Shot and gassed: Thousands of protected birds killed annually." *Reveal,* The Center for Investigative Re-

porting, May 13, 2015. www.revealnews.org/article/shot-and-gassed-thousands-of-protected-birds-killed-annually/. Accessed April 2018.

27. Schwägerl, Christian. "What's Causing the Sharp Decline in Insects, and Why It Matters." *Yale Environment 360*, July 6, 2016. e360.yale.edu/features/insect_numbers_declining_why_it_matters Accessed April 2018.

28. Alley Cat Allies. "The Wisconsin Study: Bad Science Costs Cats' Lives." 2018. https://www.alleycat.org/resources/the-wisconsin-study-bad-science-costs-cats-lives/

Chapter 5. Crazy About a Fox

1. A BBC performance of Shakespeare's *Macbeth* on November 5, 1983.

2. Nagelscheider, Mieshelle. *The Cat Whisperer*. New York: Bantam Books, The Random House Publishing Group, 2013, p. 101.

3. Nagelscheider, p. 101.

4. Behler, John L., and F. Wayne King. *The Audubon Society Field Guide to North American Reptiles and Amphibians*. New York: Alfred A. Knopf, Inc., 1979. p. 573.

5. "No evidence" as reported on Floridata at https://floridata.com/home/. Accessed 2006. "Anecdotal evidence" as reported by Gerald Hausman in "The War Between Cats and Skinks," in *Gulfshore Life,* August 2010. See http://www.gulfshorelife.com/August-2010/The-War-Between-Cats-and-Skinks/

6. Wikipedia. "Woody Woodpecker." en.wikipedia.org/wiki/WoodyWoodpecker. Accessed 2005.

7. Feldman, Paul. "Mel Blanc Dies; Gave Voice to Cartoon World." *Los Angeles Times,* July 11, 1989. www.latimes.com/local/obituaries/archives/la-me-mel-blanc-19890711-20160706-snap-story.html

8. Rue III, p. 113.

9. Whitaker, Jr., et al. (*Audubon mammals*), p. 550.

10. Rue III, p.119.

11. Whitaker, et al. (*Audubon mammals*), p. 546.

Chapter 6. The Scream

1. "The Scream," is the title of several works of art by Edvard Munch from around 1893.

2. Spoof of Stephen Spielberg's *Close Encounters of the Third Kind.*

3. Alford, William Sr. *The Smoke Eater of Geneva County*. Authorhouse, 2007. p. 24.

4. Bragg, Rick. *All Over But the Shoutin.'* New York: Vintage Books, 1997. p. 3.
5. Whitaker, et al. (*Audubon Mammal Guide*), p. 598.
6. Rue III, p. 174 (map). The scream description is attributed to N. Hollister (p. 180) and the black cougar (p. 172).
7. Caras, Roger A. *A Cat is Watching.* New York: Simon and Shuster, 1989. pp. 182 - 183.
8. Faulkner, William. *The Reivers.* New York: Vintage Books, 1962. p. 20.
9. Faulkner (*The Reivers*), p. 66.
10. Dylas, Cheryl Lyn. "Phantom of the Forest: Could the Cougar Again Haunt Eastern U.S. Woodlands?" *National Geographic,* November 4, 2015. voices.nationalgeographic.com/2015/11/04/phantom-of-the-forest-could-the-cougar-again-haunt-eastern-u-s-woodlands/ Accessed 2017.
11. Smith, Michael Peter. "Panther in Michigan." 1986. michaelpeter-smith.com/lyrics/panther.shtml Accessed February 2018.
12. Earth Touch News. "Back in Black: Another melanistic serval spotted in East Africa." February 8, 2017. www.earthtouchnews.com/discoveries/discoveries/back-in-black-another-melanistic-serval-spotted-in-east-africa Accessed 2017.
13. Florida Fish and Wildlife Conservation Commission. "Florida Panther." http://myfwc.com/panther Accessed 2018.
14. Whitaker, et al. (*Audubon Mammals*), p. 601.
15. 1994 Florida Panther Conference by Florida Panther Society.
16. Thomas, Elizabeth Marshall. *The Tribe of Tiger.* New York: Simon and Schuster, 1994. pp. 36 - 39.
17. Causey, M. Keith, and Mark Bailey. "Cougar: Alabama's Native Lion." *Alabama Wildlife Magazine*, Winter 1999. www.alabamawildlife.org/alabama-wildlife-magazine/
18. Alford, William, Sr. *The Smoke Eater of Geneva County.* Authorhouse, 2007. p. 80.
19. Causey, M. Keith, and Mark Bailey. "Cougar: Alabama's Native Lion." *Alabama Wildlife Magazine*, Winter 1999. www.alabamawildlife.org/alabama-wildlife-magazine/
20. Bailey, Mark. "The Myth of the Black Panther." *Alabama Wildlife Magazine*, Summer 2003.
21. Ibid.
22. Hartwell, Sarah. The Messybeast Cat Resource Archive www.messybeast.com Accessed 2005. For extensive information on color variations, see:

"Hybrid and Mutant Animals" at messybeast.com/genetics/hybrid-cats.htm
"Mutant Pumas" messybeast.com/genetics/mutant-pumas.html;
"Mutant Leopards" at messybeast.com/genetics/mutant-leopards.html;
and "Mutant Big Cats — Terms" at messybeast.com/genetics/mutant-bigcats-terms.html All sites accessed July 2017.

23. Wikipedia. "Eastern Cougar." en.wikipedia.org/wiki/Eastern_Cougar Accessed 2007.

24. Wikipedia. "The Pink Panther." en.wikipedia.org/wiki/The_Pink_Panther Accessed 2014. The Pink Panther character was designed by Hawley Pratt and Friz Freleng. The opening sequence of the film of the same name was done by DePatio-Freleng Enterprises, with music by Henry Mancini.

25. Shuker, Karl. "The Truth About Black Pumas — Separating Fact From Fiction Regarding Melanistic Cougars." *ShukkerNature*, August 16, 2012. karlshuker.blogspot.co.uk/2012/08/the-truth-about-black-pumas-separating.html Accessed September 2013.

26. Edgemon, Erin. "Cougars possibly living in Alabama, says state wildlife biologist." Al.com, December 31, 2015. www.al.com/news/index.ssf/2015/12/cougars_possibly_living_in_ala.html#incart_river_index Accessed 2016.

Chapter 7. A Midsummer Cat's Gleam

1. Rue III, p. 116.

2. Rue III, p. 116 - 117; and Whitaker, et al. (*Audubon mammals*), p. 550.

3. Whitaker, et al. (*Audubon mammals*), p. 276.

4. Rue III, p. 5.

5. These figures are available online from the Centers for Disease Control at https://www.cdc.gov/rabiesandkids/ Accessed 2018.

6. Morris, Desmond. *Catlore*. New York: Crown Publishers, Inc., 1987. pp. 63 - 66.

7. Busch, Heather, and Burton Silver. *Why Cats Paint: A Theory of Feline Aesthetics*. Berkeley, CA: Ten Speed Press, 1994.

8. "A Little Night Music," musical composition by Wolfgang Amadeus Mozart; also a musical with lyrics by Stephen Sondheim and a book by Hugh Wheeler.

9. Segelken, Roger. "It's the cat's meow: Not language, strictly speaking, but close enough to skillfully manage humans, communication study shows." *Cornell Chronicle*, May 20, 2002.

www.news.cornell.edu/stories/2002/05/meow-isnt-language-enough-manage-humans Accessed 2016.

10. Morris (*Catlore*), p. 122.
11. "Heartworm in Cats" by Pam Johnson-Bennett is reprinted on: www.catbehaviorassociates.com/heartworm-in-cats/ The original article is from The American Heartworm Society: www.heartwormsociety.org/

Chapter 8. The Ascent Into The Meow-Storm

1. Dickey, James. "Kudzu." *Genius*. genius.com/James-dickey-kudzu-annotated. Accessed May 2017.
2. Cox, Tom. "A walk on Dartmoor: face to face with a homemade grim reaper." *The Guardian,* December 16, 2014. www.theguardian.com/lifeandstyle/2014/dec/16/walk-dartmoor-homemade-grim-reaper Accessed 2017.
3. Cobham, Alan. "Calamanco: A Glossary of Lancashire Words as Spoken in Mawdesley." www.mawdesley-village.org.uk/dialect.php Accessed 2009. See also: *Dictionary of Phrase and Fable* by E. Cobham Brewer (1898), available at www.bartleby.com/81/2817.html; the *London Encyclopedia* at www.archive.org/stream/londonencyclopae05londiala /londonencyclopae05londiala_djvu.txt; and the Itchmo Forums For Cats And Dogs at itchmoforums.com/miscother-pet-discussions/of-torties-calicos-calamancs-t9143.0.html
4. Paraphrased from T.S. Eliot's *The Naming of Cats*.
5. "The Blue Dog" paintings by George Rodrigue are really special: georgerodrigue.com/art/paintings/blue-dogs/ Accessed 2015.
6. Ball, p. 233.
7. Burgress, Gelet. "Purple Cow." *The Lark,* May 1895. www.poets.org/poetsorg/poem/purple-cow Accessed March 2017.
8. Hartwell, Sarah. "Genetics of Colour and Conformation." Messybeast Cats. messybeast.com/cat-genetics-basics.htm Accessed July 2006.
9. Starbuck, Orca, and David Thomas. "Cat Color FAQ: Cat Color Genetics." *Fanciers*. fanciers.com/other-faqs/color-genetics.html Accessed 2006.
10. Hartwell; also, Starbuck and Thomas.
11. Hartwell; also, Starbucks and Thomas.
12. See Hartwell; also, Heather E. Lorimer's "Solid Colors and Dilutes" from *Cat Fancier's Newsletter* September 1994 and re-posted to Synergy Cats at http://helorimer.people.ysu.edu/BasicCol.html
13. Starbuck and Thomas.
14. Lorimer.

15. Starbuck and Thomas; also, Lorimer.
16. Lorimer.
17. Starbuck and Thomas.
18. Hartwell.
19. Lorimer.
20. Hartwell.
21. Tortie Tom. "Tortie Toms, Calico or Tortoiseshell Tomcats." tortietom.nidoba.nl/tortiete.html Accessed 2006.
22. Bradshaw, John, and Charlotte Cameron-Beaumont Kingdom. "The signalling repertoire of the domestic cat and its undomesticated relatives." In *The Domestic Cat: The Biology of Its Behavior*, ed. by Dennis C. Turner and Patrick Bateson. Cambridge, UK: Cambridge University Press, 1998. p. 72.
23. "By the Beautiful Sea," music by Harry Carroll, lyrics by Harold R. Atteridge in 1914.

Chapter 9. Paper Boy

1. Thomas, Elizabeth Marshall, pp. 95 - 96.
2. Eliot, T.S. "The Wasteland." 1922.
3. Herriot, James. "Buster, The Feline Retriever." *James Herriot's Cat Stories.* New York: St. Martin's Press. 1994. p. 149.
4. Randolph, Elizabeth. *How To Be Your Cat's Best Friend.* New York: Ballantine Books, A Division of Random House, Inc., 1981. p. 71.

Chapter 10. Snuggling Through the Rain

1. Rue III, p. 207.
2. Rue III, p 211.
3. Rue III, p. 203.
4. Garman, Andrew. "Bobcat." Big Cats Online. web.archive.org/web/20130411010458/http://dialspace.dial.pipex.com:80/agarman/bco/ver4.htmAccessed June 2017.
5. Hartwell, Sarah. "Small Wildcat Species." Messybeast Cat. messybeast.com/small-wildcats.htm Accessed June 2006 and May 2017.
6. Garman, "Bobcat."
7. Rue III, p. 208; and Whitaker and Elman (*Audubon mammals*), p. 605.
8. Whitaker and Elman, p. 604; and Rue III, p. 208.
9. Ciszek, Deborah. "Lynx Rufus." Animal Diversity Web. animaldiversity.org/accounts/Lynx_rufus/ Accessed May 2017.

10. International Society for Endangered Cats Canada. "Bobcat."
    www.wildcatconservation.org/wild-cats/north-america/bobcat/Accessed
    May 2017.

11. Convention on International Trade in Endangered Species of Wild Fauna
    and Flora. www.cites.org. Accessed June 2006.

12. "Puttin' on the Ritz," by Irving Berlin, 1946.

13. "Grand Texas." Its lyrics, sung in Cajun French, are said to have been
    composed by Jules "Papa Cairo" Lamperez to a melody from a tradition-
    al tune which originally had a different title. In 1952 Hank Williams,
    probably with Moon Mullican, wrote new lyrics and re-made the song in-
    to "Jambalaya." Mullican was uncredited but would have received royal-
    ties. The melody was based on an old song sung in Cajun French, called
    "Grand Texas." Lyrics may have been co-written by Williams and Moon
    Mullican, who would have been uncredited but would have received roy-
    alties. See "Big Texas" on Early Cajun Music by WF at earlycajunmu-
    sic.blogspot.com/2015/07/big-texas-julius-papa-cairo-lamperez.html.
    Accessed August 2017.

14. From the diary of Churchill's private secretary, John Colville, on July 27,
    1940. See also "Leaders; cat types vs. dog types" at leisureguy.
    wordpress.com/2008/06/13/leaders-cat-types-vs-dog-types/; and "10 pets
    that ruled the world" atyourcommunity.tescobank.com/t5/
    Blogs-and-Articles/10-pets-that-ruled-the-world/ba-p/10407.
    Accessed May 2017. There are also several books written by John Col-
    ville relevant to this topic.

15. Holland, p. 104.

16. Budiansky, p. 29.

17. Alger, Steven M., and Janet M. Alger. *Cat Culture: The Social World of
    a Cat Shelter.* Philadelphia, PA: Temple University Press, 2003. cat-
    human interaction pp. 17 - 18; cats convey preferences, pp. 24; p. 35, 38
    - 39, 69 - 70; buddy groups, pp. 58 - 59, 85 - 86, 95 - 96, 100 - 101, 104 -
    105, 108, 110; supported newcomers pp. 86 - 87, 107, 131; aggressive
    cats from single cat households p. 84; ferals will live in groups, p. 103,
    130, 139; adaptable animals p. 155.

18. Colette, Sidonie-Gabrielle. "The Long Cat." 1933.

19. Jerrard, Rob. "Royal Navy and Maritime Reviews, a review of *Ship's
    Cats in War and Peace*, by Val Lewis." August 2002.
    www.rjerrard.co.uk/royalnavy/rnbooks/rncats.htm Accessed May 2017.

20. Lillian Goldman Law Library. "President Roosevelt's Message to Con-
    gress on the Atlantic Charter." avalon.law.yale.edu/wwii/atcmess.asp
    Accessed May 2017.

21. Caras, pp. 90, 178 - 180.
22. Morris (*Catwatching*), pp. 19 - 20.
23. Amory, Cleveland. *The Cat Who Came for Christmas*. New York: Viking Penguin Group, 1987, pp. 59 - 60.
24. Morris, p. 77.
25. London, Jack. *Call of the Wild*. New York: Macmillan Publishers,1903.
26. A statement attributed to Billy Carter.
27. Plotnick, Arnold. "Polydactylism (Extra Toes)." Manhattan Cat Specialists. www.manhattancats.com/article-archive/genetics/polydactylism-extra-toes/ Accessed June 2006.
28. Hartwell, Sarah. :Polydactyl Cats, Part 1." Messybeast Cats. messybeast.com/poly-cats.html Accessed June, 2006. See also "Colours, Lhttp://messybeast.com/colours-conformation-index.htm Accessed 2017.
29. Hartwell, "Polydactyl Cats, Part 1."
30. Hartwell, Sarah. "Radial Hypoplasia and Femoral Hypoplasia." Messybeast Cat. messybeast.com/hypoplasia.htm Accessed June 2006.
31. Budiansky, p. 53.
32. Murray, Bill. "The January 24, 1997 Tuscaloosa Tornado." Alabama Wx Weather Blog, January 24, 2010. www.alabamawx.com/?p=26248 Accessed May 2017.

Chapter 11. Answering The Call of The Wily
1. Kitchener, p. 2.
2. "Wild Thing," by New York-born songwriter Chip Taylor. Originally recorded by The Wild Ones in 1965. It was recorded by the British band The Troggs in 1966 and became no. 1.
3. Halls, Vicky. *Cat Confidential*. New York: Penguin Group Inc., 2004. p. 16.
4. "Sea of Love," written by John Phillip Baptiste (as Phil Phillips) and George Khoury in 1959. Recorded by Phillips in 1959 and became no. 1 on U.S. Billboard R&B Chart and no. 2 on the Billboard Hot 100. Recorded by many, including the Honeydrippers and Del Shannon.
5. Coleridge, Samuel. "The Rime of the Ancient Mariner." 1797 – 1798.
6. Blake, William. "The Marriage of Heaven and Hell" in *Songs of Innocense and Experience*. 1790–1793. "If the doors of perception were cleansed, everything would appear to man as it is, infinite. For man has closed himself up, till he sees things through narrow chinks of his cavern."
7. Blake, William. "Auguries of Innocence." 1800 – 1803.

8. Gethers, Peter. *A Cat Abroad*. New York: The Random House Publishing Group, 1993. p. 142. "Sur le Pont, D'Avignon" is a traditional French song from the 15th Century.

Chapter 12. Splendor In The Grass
1. "[That] though the radiance which was once so bright/Be now forever taken from my sight, /Though nothing can bring back the hour/ Of splendor in the grass, of glory in the flower." From William Wordsworth's "Ode: Intimations of Immortality from Recollections of Early Childhood," 1802 − 1804.
2. Solomon, Karen. "Living with Diabetes." *Cat Fancy,* June 2003. p. 43 - 44.
3. Ibid.
4. "Janet & Binky's Canned Cat Food Nutritional Information." http://binkyspage.tripod.com/CanFoodNew.html Accessed May 2017.
5. Solomon, p. 43 - 44.
6. *Scrubs*, created by Bill Lawrence.
7. *West Wing*, created by Aaron Sorkin.
8. Erasmus, Udo. *Fats That Heal, Fats That Kill*. British Columbia: Alive Books, 1986, 1993. pp. 259, 342.
9. Solomon, p. 43.
10. Erasmus, p. 264.
11. *The 39 Steps*. Movie directed by Alfred Hitchcock. London, Gaumont British Distributors, 1935.
12. *Apocalypse Now*. Movie directed by Francis Ford Coppola. Zoetrope, 1979.
13. Gwynn, Frederick L. and Joseph L. Blotner. *Faulkner in the University*. New York: The University of Virginia Press/Random House, 1959. p. 199.
14. Caras, p. 29.

Don't miss Volume 2 of *Catwoods*, featuring:

- Stories of Minou, Minx, MochaBud, Good Ole Boy/Little Buddy, Pretty Girl, Anna, Tiger, Ultraviolet, and Franklin.
- Minx and the author in the night.
- Minou's box dance.
- On-the-spot studies of changing dynamics in multi-cat households.
- Domestic cat history.
- Sensible notions about rabies, heavily researched.
- Sensible notions about toxoplasmosis, also heavily researched.
- Ferals becoming snugglers.
- Dynamics of cats finding their places in homes with other cats.
- Animal welfare issues, my take.
- Bud the crusty Editing Cat.
- Kellas Cats.
- Our friend's cat, Shelley.
- Ferals roaming our yard after the Tuscaloosa tornado of April 27, 2011.

CPSIA information can be obtained
at www.ICGtesting.com
Printed in the USA
FSHW021719180920
73440FS

9 781733 916523